Teaching in the secondary school

HARPER & ROW, PUBLISHERS   New York, Evanston, London

Exploration Series in Education under the Advisory Editorship of

JOHN GUY FOWLKES

Teaching in the secondary school

THIRD EDITION

Nathan S. Blount / Herbert J. Klausmeier

THE UNIVERSITY OF WISCONSIN

Illustrations and cover by Arvis Stewart

Contents

Editor's Introduction

The first edition of this book appeared in 1953 under the title *Principles and Practices of Secondary School Teaching*. In recognition of the inseparability of principles and practices of teaching, the new volume is appropriately titled *Teaching in the Secondary School*. It will be noted that this is the work of two men rather than one. Dr. Nathan S. Blount, a distinguished specialist in the field of English education, has joined Dr. Klausmeier in organizing and writing the third edition.

Today there is widespread recognition of the fact that effective teaching stimulates learning. Teachers are no longer associated with hickory sticks or monotonous drill sessions, but with patient understanding, encouragement, and genuine regard for the strengths and weaknesses of the student. It is therefore essential that the teacher become familiar with the physiological, psychological, and sociological characteristics of the student as well as the functions and objectives of the school system.

This book is an interesting, informative contribution to educational study covering a wide range of basic material for secondary school teaching. By means of pragmatic discussion, it covers the aims and objectives essential for effective teaching. The volume concludes with a realistic examination of the ethics and responsibilities of the secondary school teacher. Not only those who are preparing for their first full-time assignment, but the experienced as well, will find this work a valuable handbook of philosophical matters and concrete suggestions for use in everyday contact with high school students.

John Guy Fowlkes

April, 1967

Preface

This third edition of *Teaching in the Secondary School* incorporates the results of research and decision-making on teaching and learning in a highly productive decade, a decade in which large sums of money and vast amounts of the time of professionals have been invested to insure excellence in secondary education in America. In the years since the second edition of this book was published, the federal government, learned societies, philanthropic organizations, and business have entered educational activities on new history-making bases.

This volume is addressed both to experienced teachers and to college students preparing to enter the teaching profession. Without the genuine commitment and sincere effort of these individuals, any recent knowledge of learning or of adolescent development, any innovation such as team teaching or nongrading, any devices for autoinstruction or for the use of instructional technology, any values obtained from recent teaching materials, any improved techniques for measuring student progress, and so on, can have little or no impact on education.

The first section of this book, Part I, "Foundations of Creative Learning," consists of five chapters. In Chapter 1 attention is given to the goals of education—goals determined by the needs of society and of the learner and by subject-matter content—and to quite contemporary patterns for organizing instruction, team teaching and nongrading. Chapter 2 treats adolescent development and the teacher's responsibility toward helping youth to make progress in economic independence, to achieve intellectual maturity, to develop well-integrated personalities. In Chapter 3 some of the conditions of learning—motivation, cognitive learning, skill learning, attitudinal learning, and retention and transfer—

are focused upon. In Chapter 4 attention is given to recent developments in subject-matter content and sequence; to attempts to define, or delimit, subject areas; and to efforts by national groups to develop new instructional materials that incorporate recent scholarship. After some attention to curriculum in an historical perspective, Chapter 5 treats recent patterns in the vertical and horizontal organization of curriculum and recent patterns in grouping students—again, team teaching, nongrading, and so on.

Part II, "Creative Teaching-Learning Activities," consists of eight chapters. In Chapters 6, 7, and 8 various decisions are considered that affect planning for learning: organizing meaningful units, planning modes of instruction, planning the size of groups for instruction. References to Chapters 9 and 10 will assist the reader in selecting the best in instructional materials and in using autoinstruction; and in making the most effective uses of audio-visual aids as adjuncts in teaching and learning, respectively. In Chapter 11 suggestions for helping learners improve work and study methods are included. And Chapters 12 and 13 treat measuring, evaluating, and reporting pupil progress.

The theme that controls Part III is "Expanding Responsibilities and Challenges." In Chapter 14 provisions for gifted and talented students, slow learners, educationally deprived students, and social deviants are discussed. Chapter 15 presents some conditions for promoting mental health and self-discipline for all youth. Chapter 16 has as its emphasis the leadership role of the classroom teacher in guiding and counseling young people. In Chapter 17 the teacher's valuable work with adolescents in cocurricular activities is discussed. In the final chapter of the book, Chapter 18, some of the responsibilities of a member of the teaching profession, to maintain continuous educational growth and to utilize all resources for improving teaching, are presented.

The approaches to teaching and learning in this book are sometimes heuristic. Although tentative generalizations and related practices accompany each question raised, the authors hope that their readers will keep in mind that some generalizations are tentative only. The authors hope that their readers will themselves participate in research, development, innovation, and in the dissemination of knowledge in order to improve learning in the setting of individual schools.

The authors are indebted to many people for their help in completing this volume. We wish to thank Mrs. Shelby Johnson for her part in the work that went into Chapters 4 and 7. Our thanks also go to Mrs. Maryann Petraitis and to Mrs. Jan Rabidou for typing the manuscript. And, finally, we are especially grateful to Professor John Guy Fowlkes, our colleague, advisory editor, and good friend, for his helpful advice and for his constant encouragement.

Nathan S. Blount
Herbert J. Klausmeier

Madison, Wisconsin
April, 1967

part I

FOUNDATIONS OF CREATIVE LEARNING

1 Objectives of secondary education

𝓕rom the birth of Christ to 1750, knowledge doubled. It doubled again in 1900, again in 1950, and then again in 1960. It promises to expand even faster in the future. Laymen and legislators ask for more education for more young people, and the number of students outgrows the number of well-qualified teachers and the space available in school buildings. The juvenile crime rate rises; slum schools develop in the cities; the number of culturally disadvantaged children multiplies. The issue of racial desegregation continues to be a subject for controversy. Among adults, there is more mental illness, more divorce. The use of automation increases; therefore, there is more leisure for adults, whose life-expectancy increases. Society discerns the need for adolescents to study new curricula—to learn inquiry, discovery, and creative thinking, as well as new content. Forward-thinking educationists challenge the existence of the self-contained classroom of 30 students and speak of the promise of team teaching and of multiage classes. In experimental computer-based areas in selected schools, automated teaching equipment guides adolescents through learning sequences.

These randomly chosen, seemingly unrelated generalizations and facts become related when considered as challenges to education. Somehow, the school, as the institution organized and supported to promote efficient learning of knowledge, skills, and attitudes must help children acquire the important concepts from the rapidly changing content of various disciplines. The school must help the student achieve a reasonable degree of self-realization if he is to be a useful citizen in a democracy and in a rapidly changing world. The school must utilize new technology, new learning principles. And, although adolescents have the biological characteristics for learning, what they ultimately make of these characteristics depends in part on the efficiency with which the schools meet the objectives dictated by the needs of society, by the needs of the learner, and by the structure of the various areas of knowledge.

In recent years, it would seem that in some schools in America there has been a trend toward emphasizing content goals as teachers stress intellectual achievement and mastery of subject matter in the classroom. *Enrichment, rigor, excellence,* and *stress on fundamentals* have been key words. And in some schools, at least, the pendulum would seem to have swung back to the late 1800s to that period's emphasis on knowledge of the prescriptive and conservative listings of subject matter and requirements framed by colleges and universities.

And yet certain leaders in education, noting the ever-changing nature of concepts and "truth," urge teachers to prepare students to go beyond content that is of temporary significance only to such process goals as will help attain new knowledge when the need arises. *Discovery, creativity,* and *inquiry* have been key words for educators concerned with process.

Concomitantly, other leaders and thinkers remind us of the school's obligations to society: To produce students with vocational competence, with well-integrated personalities, and with a genuine commitment to democracy.

The needs arising from the nature of the learner, from society, and from the structure of knowledge are all valid objectives in the secondary school curriculum. Problems have arisen only as the educational objectives of a school or a school system have tended to stress any one category at the expense of the other two categories. Problems have arisen only as the history teacher is so bent on lecturing on Washington's role in our country's early history that he provides no opportunity for students to sift facts for themselves. Or as the English teacher is so preoccupied with attempting to cover sentence modifiers that he allows students no chance to interact in small groups. Or as the mathematics teacher is so eager to explain aspects of set theory that he fails to consider the students' readiness for learning or their upper limits of learning.

The point of view controlling this book is that judicious balance should be given objectives according to the dictates of (1) the learner, (2) organized knowledge, or content, and (3) society.

Formulation of educational objectives and goals in the light of what is known of learners will be a continuing concern for the remainder of this book. However, detailed consideration of cognitive abilities will be found in Chapter 2, "Adolescent Development," and its subsection on the work of Guilford, and in Chapter 3, "Conditions of Learning." In Chapter 12, "Measuring and Evaluating," other objectives in the cognitive domain will be discussed, especially the work of Bloom. In Chapter 14, objectives for adolescents will be indicated, objectives classified according to various special categories, such as gifted and educationally deprived students.

Objectives arising from the nature of organized knowledge are treated at length in Chapter 4, "Subject-Matter Content and Sequence." Attempts to define, or to delimit, the scope of various subjects; to state the structure of a discipline, together with methods of inquiry and styles of thinking unique to the area; to provide for sequence and articulation; and to develop and use varied instructional materials will all be considered.

In the remainder of this chapter, we will examine how various aspects of secondary education, including general objectives, change continuously to meet the needs of youth and society and to reflect current knowledge in a given area. The ensuing discussions are intended to give a quick, but balanced, historical view of objectives. Knowledge of the historical evolution of educational objectives should help avoid having to rediscover certain long-held tenets. We will consider the National Education Association's (NEA) *Schools for the Sixties* in some detail. It is a contemporary and yet forward-looking statement for schools in the second half of the twentieth century, a statement that considers learner, organized knowledge, and society in its recommendations.

EMERGING PATTERNS OF
SECONDARY EDUCATION

The increase in the amount and quality of secondary education is one of the fascinating stories in our history and in the history of mankind. At present, instruction is the greatest service provided our youth by organized government. When we look at the high schools of 1900 and compare their enrollment, instructional methods, and organization with those of the present, we discover that the progress achieved in the past half-century represents an outstanding contribution toward democratic life in America.

Enrollment

The increasing enrollment in high school during the first half of the present century is one of the truly significant stories of the century, clear testimony of the faith of people in progress through education.[1] In the school year of 1889–1890, about 7 percent of the total population 14 to 17 years of age were enrolled in public schools. By 1899–1900, eleven percent of the total population 14–17 years of age were enrolled in public and private high schools. The percents increased to 15 in 1909–1910, 32 in 1919–1920, 51 in 1929–1930, and 73 in 1939–1940. Enrollments decreased during World War II. Part of this decrease resulted from the fact that young people were engaged in military service and related activities during the war and part from the lower birth rate during the 1930s. Although the total enrollment in 1949–1950 was below that of the previous decade, the percent of young people in the age group 14 to 17 enrolled in school had increased slightly to about 77 percent. By 1959–1960, about 86 percent of the young people in the age group were enrolled.

The increase in the number of students who have graduated from high school has tended to parallel the growth in enrollments, although

---

[1] For a concise and complete account of the history of secondary education, 1880–1920, see Edward A. Krug, *The Shaping of the American High School* (New York: Harper & Row, 1964); relevant annual bulletins of the Research Division of the NEA and statistical bulletins of the U.S. Office of Education contain more recent statistical information of the type included in this chapter.

not to the same degree. In 1889–1900 about 3.5 percent of 17-year-olds were graduated from high school. In 1959–1960, the number of graduates in that age group had risen to about 65 percent.[2]

From the preceding facts, we can draw several conclusions. First, schooling has made highly significant progress since 1900. However, we still have a large number of young people who do not graduate from high school. Because about 90 percent of the eligible students are enrolled in high school for at least a part of the program, we can assume that they represent a whole range of abilities and interests. Attention must be given to this fact in planning high school programs. Finally, high school enrollments will continue to increase rapidly through 1980, and perhaps beyond, if the birth rate continues its upward trend. This calls for an ever-increasing number of capable teachers and other educational workers.

Curriculum and instruction

In the latter part of the nineteenth century, a primary objective of the school was to develop the mental faculties of students. Classical languages, modern foreign languages, and mathematics were emphasized as subjects well suited to developing reasoning and other so-called faculties. Lectures, reading and recitation lessons, and long assignments to be completed outside of class were commonly used. Those who advocated these subjects and approaches believed in the theory of formal discipline based on mental faculties. These educators thought that the faculties could be strengthened much as muscles are through tough (mental) exercises. Even those educators who did not specifically subscribe to the mental faculty theory thought that subjects should be taught well and thoroughly in order to develop the students' reasoning powers. However, as early as 1890, some educators felt that the more "modern" subjects such as English, history, and the sciences could be used for this purpose just as well as the classical languages and mathematics. This position had the effect of making the more modern subjects more respectable, and thus broadened the curriculum to a degree.

The nature of the learner, rather than just the subject, began to be stressed in the period immediately before and after the turn of the

[2] *Ibid.*

century, especially by John Dewey.[3] Dewey insisted that learning is an active, not a passive, process; that the learner should be actively engaged in learning; and that human beings are constitutionally active and want to participate in problem-solving. Furthermore, Dewey believed that public school education should be a fundamental method of social progress and reform; therefore, instructional procedures in the classroom should be focused on helping the learner develop so that his expressive and creative abilities would be directed toward socially significant goals.

There were other developments that influenced attitudes toward curriculum and instruction. Theories of learning espoused by such men as Thorndike, James, and Judd, in the early part of this century, presented different ideas about the manner in which students learn.[4]

The theory of identical elements focused the attention of curriculum workers on the skills and knowledge needed in adult life; and during the 1920s more attention began to be paid to those classes that best appeared to provide such skills. The generalization theory caused the schools to attempt to identify major principles, generalizations, and processes that could be applied to many different situations and problems.

Social forces were also having their effects. Vast numbers of immigrants had tended to settle in the urban areas, and the schools were urged to "Americanize" these people and their children as rapidly as possible, to make them useful, good citizens and contributing members of society. The doctrine of social efficiency was advocated, and high school subjects began to be evaluated in terms of their ability to make their students socially efficient. Demands for vocational education, industrial education, homemaking, and vocational guidance were all heard by the schools and, in most cases, were eagerly accepted.

World War I and the Great Depression of 1929 and the early 1930s only increased the concern about the importance of the social goals to be achieved through high school education and the need to build a

---

[3] For an account of the influence of various learning theories on education, see Frederick J. McDonald, "The Influence of Learning Theories on Education (1900–1950)," and Ernest R. Hilgard, "The Place of Gestalt Psychology and Field Theories in Contemporary Learning Theory," *Theories of Learning and Instruction,* Sixty-third Yearbook of the National Society for the Study of Education, Chicago: University of Chicago Press, 1964).

[4] *Ibid.*

unified democratic society. The question of the extent to which instructional procedures should be directed toward individual development as compared to developing the individual for more effective participation in group life became—and remains—a central issue. Interest in such concepts as developmental tasks and group dynamics has been reflected in the school's program. Group projects involving cooperative effort, group discussions centering on the solution of social problems, and such activities as student government and field trips illustrate the emphasis on social objectives.

Events following World War II have focused interest on the study of international relations, as well as on the challenges of the "isms" and the problems of emerging underdeveloped nations. Technological advances in the production and widespread distribution of printed materials and of audio-visual aids to instruction have made it possible to improve classroom instruction. Paperback books, magazines, and other materials can be published quickly and inexpensively, allowing the teacher to have more current and authoritative data. Developments in the race for space have also affected the instructional program. Much greater emphasis has been given to certain subjects such as science, mathematics, and foreign languages; and attempts have been made to improve the teaching of these and other subjects through the increased use of technology and different patterns of instruction, such as team teaching.

The Elementary and Secondary Education Act of 1965, generated in part by the civil rights movement and by the race into outer space, is further recognition of the role of the secondary school, and of education generally, in strengthening the fiber of American democracy. Here is an expression by the people through their federal government that education is so essential that its financing cannot be left solely to the local governments and states. The poor in our cities and rural areas must receive a better quality of education; the dropout rate must be reduced; educational attainment must be improved. More attention is given to this in connection with the discussion of providing for the educationally disadvantaged in Chapter 14.

Vertical and horizontal organization

During the first half of this century, the vertical organization of secondary schools shifted markedly. In 1900, the typical pattern of organization was 8–4, an eight-year elementary school and a four-year high school. Numerous objections were raised concerning the long period of elementary schooling, and various recommendations were made for a new institution, the junior high school, as an intermediate school between the elementary grades and high school. Proponents of the junior high school reasoned that it would allow for better transition between elementary and high school; that more practical subjects could be introduced; that differentiated courses of study could be offered students earlier; and that more stress could be given to studies common to all students. By 1910, a number of communities opened junior high schools, consisting of grades seven, eight, and nine. Thus the 6–3–3 vertical organization came into existence. Other current plans of vertical organization include the 6–6; the 6–2–4; the 6–4–2, and the 6–4–4. In the latter plan, the junior college is considered part of the pattern.

Controversy about the effectiveness of the junior high school continues, there being many enthusiastic proponents and equally emphatic detractors. Since 1945, many new junior high schools have been constructed. This was not due solely to proven effectiveness. Rather, with increasing child populations, starting first with kindergarten, it was more convenient to erect junior high schools that would take students from several elementary schools and also ninth-graders from one or two high schools.

Shortly after the turn of the century, another new institution, the junior college, was organized. Some educators had suggested this kind of division earlier; in 1896 the University of Chicago used the terms *junior college* and *senior college* to describe the freshman-sophomore years and the junior-senior years, respectively. But the Joliet Junior College of Joliet, Illinois, founded in about 1902, is usually credited with being the first public junior college, in the sense of being an upward extension of the secondary school program. Exact figures on the number of junior colleges are difficult to ascertain because of the way in which they are defined. However, the increase in the number of junior colleges has been phenomenal and is still continuing. Also, vocational schools, both public and private, have experienced remarkable expansion. Although not junior colleges, they are a form of post-high-school education that will undoubtedly continue to expand very rapidly.

In reviewing the growth of junior and senior high schools and of the junior colleges just described, we recognize that the need for competent teachers at all levels is also growing. Both the junior high school and the junior college are frequently staffed with teachers who are certificated or licensed as high school or secondary school teachers. Especially critical is the lack of teachers in grades seven and eight to teach basic skills in the language arts and mathematics.

Horizontal organization, that is, the arrangement of curriculum and instruction within the junior and senior high school and the junior college, is in a state of fluidity. For example, it is not uncommon in the same school building to find class periods of unequal length, students of different grade levels attending the same class, class size ranging from 8 to 200 or more students, independent study in specially designed areas, individual tutoring, team teaching instead of single-teacher classes, and seminars. A brief description of two high schools in Florida that have received much publicity indicates the extent of change from the typical organization. The principal of the Melbourne High School dismisses the idea of grades (freshman, sophomore, and so on) in this manner:

> The durable attractiveness of the grade lies in its administrative convenience. It serves as a comfortable holding pool in which school administrators can and do throw youngsters for custodial purposes and forget them for a year. By comparison, nongrading is an administrative prickly pear constantly needling for attention to the learning needs of youngsters.[5]

Instead of grades, Melbourne uses *ad hoc* learning arrangements called *phases*. Students are assigned to these phases on the basis of their scores on standardized achievement tests, rather than on IQ or age. A fuller description of Melbourne's phases will be given in Chapter 5, "Curriculum Organization."

Other characteristics of Melbourne High School are also unusual. There are no study halls or standard texts and typing classes average 125 students with a single teacher.

Another attempt to break away from "the graded lockstep" and, indeed, from a multiplicity of traditional educational practices is seen at Nova High School. The director of the school spent three years visiting outstanding schools throughout the country to incorporate

---

[5] B. Frank Brown, "The Non-Graded High School," *Phi Delta Kappan*, XLIV (February, 1963), 206.

into the plans for the Nova High School all the best modern educational methods for improving instruction. The advocates of the school believe that all the equipment, teaching aids, and instructional methods have been tested and proved in other school systems. The curriculum of the school is described thus:

> Nova is a space age school. Its philosophy is based on a concept best described as scientific learning for a scientific age. Interestingly, to achieve the goals of such a philosophy, there has been a return to a "hard-core" curriculum. Each Nova student pursues a schedule of studies which includes mathematics, foreign language, English, science, social studies, technical science, special studies, and physical education. A student may choose a foreign language from among Latin, Spanish, French, Russian, and German. His choice of a technical science or special studies course comes from electronics, mechanical and scale drawing, music, home economics, art, personal typing, mechanical technology, safety and driver education, physiology, and home nursing.[6]

Recall that, with the nongraded approach, what might seem a rather rigid-sounding curriculum loosens up considerably. Thus, seventh-year students may be studying mathematics on what is traditionally thought of as a tenth-grade level. Nova does not assign letter grades of A, B, C, D, or F. The school uses numerous short achievement levels called *units* in each subject area. Capable students finish a unit in about a month; below-average pupils take up to six weeks. To pass from one unit to the next, the student must pass a final unit test. The trimester plan is used with a single month's vacation; only near the end of the trimester preceding the vacation is there any pressure on students to complete all the units in progress.

The techniques, media, and facilities used at Nova include team teaching, closed-circuit television, overhead projection in every room, a reading laboratory, science and language laboratories, and varying numbers of students in group instruction. Unusual facilities include wall-to-wall carpeting, resource centers, teaching machines, microfilm readers, and complete air conditioning. Supposedly, these innovations were made possible by excluding a large auditorium and a cafeteria kitchen from the building plans.

---

[6] Burt Kaufman and Paul Bethune, "Nova High, Space Age School," *Phi Delta Kappan*, XLVI (September, 1964), 9.

CHANGING OBJECTIVES

Formulating objectives of secondary education that have general applicability to all parts of the country has been the problem of a number of individuals and groups. While different statements have been formulated during the past 70 years, only a few of them will be discussed here. Cremin presents the details of the transformation of education during the first half of this century.[7] We shall present selected statements of groups affiliated with the NEA, and of other groups interested in secondary education, in the following order:

1. The Committee of Ten, 1894
2. The Commission on the Reorganization of Secondary Education, 1918
3. The American Youth Commission, 1935
4. The American High School Today, 1959
5. Schools for Slums and Suburbs, 1961
6. Schools for the Sixties, 1963
7. National Curriculum Studies

The committee of ten, 1894

In 1892, the NEA appointed a Committee of Ten on Secondary School Studies, that in turn appointed nine subcommittees. In 1894, this committee submitted a report on secondary education in which it stated that the main purpose of secondary schools was to prepare for the duties of life the small proportion of all the nation's children who could profit from education up to the eighteenth year and whose parents were able to support them in school.[8] The committee intended that the colleges should accept all high school graduates, as long as they had taken one of the four courses or "programmes" recommended by the committee, or any other good secondary school course. The effect of the report was to make modern academic subjects equivalent to the classics; they became more respectable. The report also endorsed the principle of electives.

---

[7] Lawrence A. Cremin, *The Transformation of the School: Progressivism in American Education* (New York: Knopf, 1961).

[8] NEA *Report of the Committee of Ten on Secondary School Studies* (Washington, D.C.: NEA, 1894).

The commission on the reorganization of secondary education, 1918

The rapid increase in high school enrollment during each decade from 1900–1930 was accompanied by drastic changes in other fields. There was a rapid shift toward greater centralization of wealth after 1890, the hours of work per week in factories were generally decreased, labor organizations became stronger, and the United States entered World War I. The need for more secondary schools to accommodate more young people and the need to make secondary education more valuable for students who did not intend to go to college became apparent. These changes and needs led to the formation of the Commission on the Reorganization of Secondary Education in 1913.

Recognizing these and many other factors that were operating in the American economy, and realizing the future role of public secondary schools in democratic life, the commission, in its statement of goals issued in 1918,[9] proposed (1) that every normal boy and girl be encouraged to stay in school until age 18, (2) that the second six years of school be specifically designed to meet the needs of pupils in the age group 12 to 18, (3) that free education be extended to the junior college level, and (4) that education in a democracy be such as would develop in each individual the knowledge, interests, ideals, habits, and powers to find his place in society and to shape both himself and society toward nobler ends. The committee proposed, as the "main objectives of education," the following cardinal principles:

1. Health
2. Command of fundamental processes
3. Worthy home membership
4. Vocation
5. Citizenship
6. Worthy use of leisure
7. Ethical character

Vocation, family life, citizenship, constructive use of leisure, and character development, in particular, are learning outcomes that are related to the role of education in an urban society. The commission's

---

[9] Commission on Reorganization of Secondary Education, *Cardinal Principles of Secondary Education*, Bulletin No. 35 (Washington, D.C.: Government Printing Office, 1918).

statement in 1918 thus indicated that many functions previously performed by the home, and to some extent by the elementary school,
should now be performed by the secondary school. Also, this statement
suggested that a career in a profession, entered through the college and
university, was simply one of many useful vocations.

The report really presented no startlingly new ideas; rather, it summarized and made explicit many of the ideas of the period. The opening sentence of the report stated that ". . . secondary education should
be determined by the needs of the society to be served, the character
of the individuals to be educated, and the knowledge of educational
theory and practice available." And the committee felt that changes
in these areas had been sufficient to "call for extensive modifications
of secondary education."

Further, the report advocated the comprehensive high school, rather
than specialized or differentiated high schools, partially because the
form. The report felt that the elements of the culture "essential to
school was one agency that could help make American life more uni-
American democracy" could not be taught solely in the elementary
school; the secondary school was also necessary to teach these common
elements to young people of diverse backgrounds.

The Great Depression of the 1930s brought increasing attention to
the role of secondary education in the life of our young people. More
parents and other adults became concerned about what could be done
for unemployed youth not in school and also for youth in school to
prepare them to meet more efficiently the problem of earning a living
in periods of nation-wide economic distress.

The American youth commission, 1935

In 1935, the American Council on Education organized the American
Youth Commission. This commission, which functioned until World
War II, devoted its attention to studying the problems of youth in
modern society. The information it brought together clearly demonstrated the necessity for giving more young people the opportunity to
attend school and also for tailoring secondary education to better fit
the needs of those already in school. After examining the needs of
representative school-age groups, identifying the facilities available to
youth in their communities, and helping some communities to experiment with improving their services, the commission published its most

important findings in a series of books—*How Fare American Youth,
Youth Tell Their Story, Matching Youth and Jobs,* and *Equal Educational Opportunity for All Youth.* These publications, perhaps as much
as any others during that period, acquainted teachers with the undesirable effect that quitting school prior to graduation had on youth. To
some extent, the commission made its audience conscious of what good
secondary schools might do for our young people, as well as of the
serious consequences inherent in allowing young adolescents to quit
school and, after squandering their time and abilities on unproductive
activities outside the school, to drift finally into a life of wastefulness
and unhappiness.

The outbreak of World War II in 1939 and Japan's attack on Pearl
Harbor in 1941 created a sudden demand for youth to enter the armed
forces. As a result, attention shifted from the demoralizing effect of
the Depression on young people to preparing them quickly to enter
military service.

From this period until after World War II and into the 1950s, a
number of groups revised and extended the ideas embodied in the
cardinal principles, including the idea of education for all youth and
education to achieve social goals.[10] However, many criticisms were made
of secondary education. Conant's statements reflect some of the demands for improving education; and the objectives formulated in *Schools
for the Sixties,* all of which are reproduced in this chapter, reflect the
great change in education from the first to last half of the twentieth
century.

The American high school today, 1959

A grant from the Carnegie Corporation to study the American high
school resulted in James B. Conant's report, *The American High School
Today.* The study had been begun before the launching of the first Rus-

---

[10] Among the more significant statements are these: North Central Association of
Colleges and Secondary Schools, *General Education in the American High School*
(Chicago: Scott, Foresman, 1942); Educational Policies Commission, *Education
for All American Youth* (Washington, D.C.: National Education Association
and American Association of School Administrators, 1944); Educational Policies
Commission, *Policies for Education in American Democracy* (Washington, D.C.:
NEA, 1946), pp. 192, 212, 226, 240; "The Imperative Needs of Youth of Sec-
ondary School Age," *The Bulletin of the National Association of Secondary
School Principals,* XXXI (March, 1947).

sian satellite provoked panic and confusion among many Americans and set off a chain reaction of criticism of the public schools. Conant's report, although greeted with somewhat mixed feelings by educators, was helpful to the extent that it suggested no drastic alteration of the school system.

In the first place, Dr. Conant recognized fairly clearly the forces in American life that had produced our unique school system, and the comprehensive high school in particular; he felt that there should be no change in this fundamental pattern. He saw the major objectives of the comprehensive high school to be

> . . . first, to provide a general education for all the future citizens; second, to provide good elective programs for those who wish to use their acquired skills immediately on graduation; third, to provide satisfactory programs for those whose vocations will depend on their subsequent education in a college or university.[11]

Conant made 21 recommendations for improving public secondary education. All should be studied, although not necessarily accepted, by anyone interested in education from kindergarten through graduate school. Few besides Conant would agree with all 21 recommendations. He has been criticized properly for stating the objectives of general education simply as the number of years or semesters in various subjects required of all students for graduation. He did not state what students of varying intellectual abilities were to achieve through taking the subjects, and he did not give his value system, which led to this and other recommendations. These criticisms are more apparent after studying the following two recommendations:

Recommendation 7: Diversified programs for the development of marketable skills

Programs should be available for girls interested in developing skills in typing, stenography, the use of clerical machines, home economics, or a specialized branch of home economics which through further work in college might lead to the profession of dietitian. Distributive education should be available if the retail shops in the community can be persuaded to

---

[11] James B. Conant, *The American High School Today* (New York: McGraw-Hill, 1959), p. 17. By permission.

provide suitable openings. If the community is rural, vocational agriculture should be included. For boys, depending on the community, trade and industrial programs should be available. Half a day is required in the eleventh and twelfth grades for this vocational work. In each specialized trade, there should be an advisory committee composed of representatives of management and labor. Federal money is available for these programs.

The school administration should constantly assess the employment situation in those trades included in the vocational programs. When opportunities for employment in a given trade no longer exist within the community, the training program in that field should be dropped. The administration should be ready to introduce new vocational programs as opportunities open in the community or area. In some communities, advanced programs of a technical nature should be developed; these programs often involve more mathematics than is usually required for the building trades or auto mechanics programs.

. . . the students enrolled in programs which develop marketable skills should also be enrolled in English, social studies, and other courses required for graduation. Furthermore, efforts should be made to prevent isolation from the other students. Homerooms may be effective means to this end . . .[12]

Recommendation 9: *The programs of the academically talented*

A policy in regard to the elective programs of academically talented boys and girls should be adopted by the school to serve as a guide to the counselors. In the type of school I am discussing the following program should be strongly recommended as a minimum:

Four years of mathematics, four years of one foreign language, three years of science, in addition to the required four years of English and three years of social studies; a total of eighteen courses with homework to be taken in four years. This program will require at least fifteen hours of homework each week.

Many academically talented pupils may wish to study a second foreign language or an additional course in social studies. Since such students are capable of handling twenty or more courses with homework, these additional academic courses may be added to the recommended minimum program. If the school is organized on a seven- or eight-period day (Recommendation 12), at least one additional course without homework (for example, art or music) may also be scheduled each year.

If as school policy a minimum academic program including both mathematics and a foreign language is recommended to the academically talented pupils and their parents, the counselors will have the problem of identifying as early as possible the members of the group. It may well be that, in the

---

[12] *Ibid.,* p. 52.

next lower 10 or 20 percent of the boys and girls in terms of scholastic aptitude on a national basis, there are a number who ought to be guided into similar but less rigorous programs.[13]

Although recommendation 9 is dogmatic, another recommendation provides for individualized programs for each pupil, including the opportunity for academically talented students to take some work in the fine arts. Conant would not classify pupils according to various curricula or tracks, such as college preparatory, vocational, or commercial. In addition, if a talented girl had no interest in mathematics and disliked it strongly, she would not be required to take four years of mathematics. Likewise, Conant would not require an uninterested girl or boy to take the third year of science.

Schools for slums and suburbs, 1961

Conant recognized that both the suburbs and slums were enrolling students who were quite different from one another in home background, socio-economic status, and other characteristics, such as interest in schooling and level of educational attainment. He summarized part of the problem this way:

> The task with which the school people in the slum must struggle is, on the one hand, to prepare a student for getting and keeping a job as soon as he leaves school, and, on the other hand, to encourage those who have academic talent to aim at a profession through higher education. . . . In the suburban high school from which 80 percent or more of the graduates enter some sort of college, the most important problem from the parents' point of view is to ensure the admission of their children to prestige colleges. . . . From the educator's point of view, however, the most vexing problem is to adjust the family's ambitions to the boy's or girl's abilities.[14]

According to Conant, neither the suburban nor the slum school is comprehensive, although a far greater problem exists in the latter; in the slum school we are allowing "social dynamite" to accumulate.

---

[13] *Ibid.*, p. 57.
[14] James B. Conant, *Slums and Suburbs* (New York: McGraw-Hill, 1961), pp. 1–2. By permission.

Schools for the sixties, 1963

In 1959, the NEA authorized the Project on the Instructional Program of the Public Schools, with a 14-member national committee and a headquarters staff. In 1963, a far-reaching set of recommendations was presented. Whether this set of recommendations was the forerunner of much of the improvement activity that has followed and is currently being planned, or whether the committee faithfully reported major trends already under way, is yet debated by some. Nevertheless, we are including the entire set of recommendations and invite you to consider seriously how many of them have now taken tangible form in the more advanced high schools of the second half of the twentieth century. Engage others in discussion regarding the implications of the recommendations, because many of the principal ends and issues facing us for the next decades are represented here.

RECOMMENDATIONS OF THE NATIONAL COMMITTEE OF THE NEA PROJECT ON INSTRUCTION (A SUMMARY LIST)

Decision-making

Who should make what decisions about education?

Recommendation 1

Local school boards. Local school boards are the legal instruments through which the state fulfills its responsibility for education. The distinction between lay control of school policies determined by the board of education and implementation of these policies by the professional staff, with the leadership of the local superintendent, should be delineated, understood, and respected.

Recommendation 2

Federal government. The federal government should provide the types of assistance needed to improve local and state systems of education. Two types of federal assistance should be stressed: (a) the federal government should provide general financial assistance for the improvement of public education, (b) the U.S. Office of Education should have an expanded role in stimulating experimentation and innovation in the schools, in providing statistical analyses of importance, and in disseminating information about educational problems and promising practices.

Recommendation 3

Local school faculties. Local school faculties should have the freedom and the authority to make decisions about what to teach—within state and local requirements—and how to teach. Final instructional decisions should be made by the teacher, taking into consideration recommendations from appropriate local, state, and national groups representing the teaching profession, academic scholars, and the public.

Recommendation 4

State educational authorities. State educational authorities should establish standards for public school instruction, provide adequate resources for their achievement, and give dynamic leadership to curriculum development, experimentation, and innovation in local schools.

Recommendation 5

State legislatures. State legislatures should set forth general goals for the schools, provide adequate financial support, and delegate broad powers of implementation to the state and local educational authorities. The state legislature should not prescribe curriculum content or legislate specific courses.

Research, experimentation, and innovation

How can an extensive program of educational research, experimentation, and innovation be developed?

Recommendation 6

Money, time, and personnel. School systems should allocate an appropriate proportion of their annual operating budgets—not less than 1 percent—for the support of research, experimentation, and innovation.

Adequate time should be provided for each staff member to participate in curriculum-planning, research, evaluation, and other activities designed to improve the instructional program.

Recommendation 7

Regional curriculum and instruction centers. Adequately staffed and supported regional curriculum and instruction centers should be encouraged. These centers, located mainly in universities, should work in partnership with local schools to initiate innovation and conduct experimentation and research to improve the instructional program of the public schools.

Recommendation 8

Nongovernmental groups. Efforts of nationally oriented, nongovernmental groups to stimulate curricular and instructional experimentation and innovation should be encouraged. Scholars in the academic fields and the teaching profession should be involved in such efforts.

Educating all children and youth

How can the instructional program of the school be designed to develop the individual potentialities of all members of the school population within the framework of a society that values both unity and diversity?

Recommendation 9

The individual and the nation. The instructional program should provide: (a) opportunities for developing the individual potentialities represented in the wide range of differences among people; (b) a common fund of knowledge, values, and skills vital to the welfare of the individual and the nation.

To achieve these objectives, the instructional program cannot be the same for all. Provision for individual differences should be made by qualified teaching personnel through diagnosis of learning needs and through appropriate variety of content, resources for learning, and instructional methods.

Establishing priorities for the school

What are the distinctive responsibilities of the school in contrast to those that are distinctive to the family, the church, industry, and various youth-serving agencies?

What responsibilities should the school share with other institutions and with other youth-serving agencies?

What, then, should be included in the school program?

What should be excluded from it?

Recommendation 10

Distinctive and shared responsibilities. Priorities for the school are the teaching of skills in reading, composition, listening, speaking (both native and foreign languages), and computation . . . ways of creative and disciplined thinking, including methods of inquiry and application of knowledge . . . competence in self-instruction and independent learning . . . fundamental understanding of the humanities and the arts, the social sciences and natural sciences, and mathematics . . . appreciation of and discriminating taste in literature, music, and the visual arts . . . instruction in health education and physical education.

Responsibilities best met by joint efforts of the school and other social agencies include: development of values and ideals . . . social and civic competence . . . vocational preparation.

The decision to include or exclude particular school subjects or outside-of-class activities should be based on: (a) the priorities assigned to the school and to other agencies; (b) data about learners and society, and developments in the academic disciplines; (c) the human and material resources available in the school and community.

The school's role in dealing with national problems related to youth

What is the school's role in dealing with serious national problems such as youth unemployment and juvenile delinquency?

Recommendation 11

Youth unemployment and juvenile delinquency. The schools can help to combat such serious national problems as youth unemployment and juvenile delinquency by: (a) evaluating the intellectual and creative potential of all children and youth in the schools; (b) identifying early the potential dropout and delinquent; (c) developing positive programs to challenge these young people to educational endeavor; (d) participating in cooperative programs with parents and with community groups and organizations—business and industry, labor service groups, government agencies, and the many youth-serving agencies.

Teaching about controversial issues and about communism

What is the school's role in teaching about controversial issues and about communism and other ideologies?

Recommendation 12

Controversial issues. Rational discussion of controversial issues should be an important part of the school program. The teacher should help students identify relevant information, learn the techniques of critical analysis, make independent judgments, and be prepared to present and support them. The teacher should also help students become sensitive to the continuing need for objective re-examination of issues in the light of new information and changing conditions in society.

Recommendation 13

Current social forces and trends. To help the student think critically about current issues, the curriculum should provide opportunities for adequate instruction concerning social forces and trends. Attention commensurate with their significance in modern society should be given to issues such as international relations, economic growth, urbanization, population growth, science and technology, and mass media.

Recommendation 14

Teaching about Communism. The school curriculum should include a study of political and social ideologies focusing upon Communism.

The methods of rational inquiry should be stressed. The study should be set in the perspective of the modern world and be incorporated into the instructional program at appropriate points. If a special unit on Communism is deemed desirable in the secondary school, it should supplement and complement earlier study of these topics.

As with other areas of the curriculum, decisions about what to teach and how to teach about these topics should be based upon policies developed by school administrators and teachers of the local school system. In the formulation and implementation of such policies, school personnel should utilize the resources of scholarship and be supported in their decisions by the school board and by an informed community opinion.

A balanced program

How can the school provide a balanced program for the individual and maintain it amidst various pressures for specialization?

Recommendation 15

Ways of achieving balance. The school can provide and maintain a curriculum appropriately balanced for each student by offering a comprehensive program of studies, making early and continuous assessment of individual potentialities and achievements, and providing individualized programs based on careful counseling.

To avoid the imbalance that can result from limiting financial support to certain selected subjects and services, general financial support should be provided for the total program. This applies to local, state, and federal support.

Selecting content

How can schools make wise selections of content from the ever-growing body of available knowledge?

Recommendation 16

Bases for selecting content. The objectives of the school, with a clear statement of priorities, should give direction to all curriculum-planning.

This applies to adding content, eliminating content, or changing the emphases on various topics and fields of study.

Recommendation 17

Keeping content up-to-date. Each curriculum area should be under continuous study and evaluation and should be reviewed periodically. One purpose of such reviews is to determine whether recent findings in the academic disciplines are, or should be, reflected in the instructional program. These reviews should utilize the knowledge and skills of the teacher, the school administrator, the scholar in the academic disciplines, the scholar in the profession of teaching, and the lay citizen, each contributing his special competence to the total task.

Recommendation 18

National curriculum projects. In making selections of content, school staffs should study the results and recommendations of curriculum projects sponsored by nationally oriented groups with a view to applying promising findings.

There should be a systematic procedure for studying the results of these curriculum projects. The procedure should recognize the importance of balance and continuity in the total school experience of students and include the steps prerequisite to curriculum changes.

Organizing content

How should the content of the curriculum be organized?

Recommendation 19

Bases for organizing content. The content of the curriculum should be organized in such ways that students may progress, from early to later school years, toward an increasingly mature utilization and organization of their knowledge. Helping learners see interrelationships and achieve unity from the diversity of knowledge is basic to any organization of content.

School staffs should experiment with a variety of ways of organizing content. The nature, meaning, and structure of the discipline and differences in the ways students learn should be taken into account in selecting a particular plan of organization and evaluating its effectiveness.

Organizing the curriculum

How should the curriculum of the school be organized to give appropriate direction to the instructional process?

Recommendation 20

Educational objectives. The aims of education should serve as a guide for making decisions about curriculum organization as well as about all other aspects of the instructional program.

The public, through the local school board, is responsible for determining the broad aims of education. The professional staff is responsible for translating the broad aims into specific objectives that indicate priorities and define clearly the behaviors intended for the learners. The local board of education has responsibility for seeing that an acceptable statement of objectives and priorities is prepared and for endorsing such a statement.

Recommendation 21

Curricular sequence. In each curricular area, the vertical organization of subject matter should take account of: (a) the logical structure of the subject; (b) the difficulty of material as related to the student's intellectual maturity; (c) the relation of the field to other fields.

Procedures and instruments for evaluating pupil progress must be specifically geared to the school's educational goals and to the curricular sequence in use in the school.

Recommendation 22

When to teach what. The fact that very young children can learn relatively difficult aspects of science, mathematics, and other subjects is at best an incomplete answer to the question of whether they should learn them at this particular stage of their development. Decisions about when to teach what should be based on both the learner's ability to understand and the relative importance of alternative ways of using the learner's time at any given point in his school experience.

Organizing the school and the classroom

How should the school and the classroom be organized to make the most effective use of the time and talents of students and teachers?

Recommendation 23

Nongrading, multigrading, grading. The vertical organization of the school should provide for the continuous, unbroken, upward progression of all learners, with due recognition of the wide variability among learners in every aspect of their development. The school organization should, therefore, provide for differentiated rates and means of progression toward achievement of educational goals.

Nongrading and multigrading are promising alternatives to the traditional graded school and should be given careful consideration in seeking to provide flexible progress plans geared to human variability.

Recommendation 24

Bases for ability grouping. The assignment of pupils to classroom groups should be based on knowledge about students and teachers and on understanding of goals to be achieved.

Efforts to set up groups in terms of ability and/or achievement do little to reduce the over-all range of pupil variability with which teachers must deal. However, selective grouping and regrouping by achievement sometimes is useful, particularly at the secondary school level.

Recommendation 25

Team teaching. In order to provide individually planned programs for learners, taking into account the specific objectives to be achieved, the horizontal organization of the school should permit flexibility in assigning pupils to instructional groups that may range in size from one pupil to as many as a hundred or more. Well-planned cooperative efforts among teachers—efforts such as team teaching, for example—should be encouraged and tested.

Recommendation 26

Self-contained classroom. The school should be organized in such a way that it provides opportunity for each student to (a) experience continuity and relatedness in his learning, and (b) have a close counseling relationship with competent teachers who know him well. Various forms of organization should be explored to determine their effectiveness for these purposes.

The contributions of specialized personnel should be used as students progress through the elementary and secondary school. At whatever point specialized personnel are brought into the instructional program, their work should be coordinated with and related to the total program.

Recommendation 27

Classroom grouping. In schools where the classroom is the unit of organization, teachers should organize learners frequently into smaller groups of varying types and sizes. Decisions as to size and membership of such groups should be based on knowledge about learners and on the specific educational purposes to be served at a given time for each learner.

Instructional materials, technology, space

How can the quality of instructional materials be improved? How can the products of modern technology be used effectively? How can space be designed and used to support the instructional program?

Recommendation 28

Instructional materials centers. In each school system, there should be one or more well-planned instructional materials and resources centers, consisting of at least a library and an audio-visual center. In each school building, there should also be an instructional resources facility.

These centers should be staffed by persons who are adequately prepared in curriculum and instruction, in library service, and in audio-visual education.

Recommendation 29

ETV and radio. The use of educational television (ETV) and radio to broaden and deepen learning should be encouraged. Such use should be accompanied by a vigorous program of research and experimentation.

Recommendation 30

Programed instruction. Schools should make use, with proper supervision, of self-instructional materials and devices (programed instruction) that facilitate varied learning opportunities and continuous progress for learners of widely divergent abilities. The use of programed instruction should be accompanied by a vigorous program of research and experimentation.

Recommendation 31

Instructional media. A comprehensive study and action program is needed to improve the quality and use of printed teaching materials and other instructional media. Such a study and action program requires the participation of both the producers and the consumers of these instructional materials and media.

Recommendation 32

Automation. School authorities should examine the potentialities of automation for storage and retrieval of pupil personnel data and instructional materials.

Recommendation 33

Space utilization. New concepts of space should permit and encourage (a) varying sized groups ranging from small seminars to multiple class; (b) independent study with visual and/or acoustic privacy as required; (c) access to a variety of instructional media; (d) multiple use.

Key considerations in planning for better utilization of space are (a) flexibility, and (b) environment, which respects the learner and his need for a sense of amenity if his learning is to be most efficient.[15]

National curriculum studies

The preceding statements deal with the development of objectives that in turn should result in new and different educational materials and activities in the schools. Always, however, textbooks and related educational materials have influenced objectives and activities to the extent that the content of the textbook has often determined what the teachers have taught and what the students have learned. Since the 1950s, one of the main emphases in secondary education has been the production of textbooks and related materials by representatives of learned societies and professional groups who have a primary interest in one subject field.[16]

The first of the large-scale efforts for producing textbooks and related material was in mathematics and science, funded with millions of dollars by the National Science Foundation (NSF). Later, many English and social studies projects were funded by the U. S. Office of Education. Starting in 1965, the humanities were given special attention. New laws with appropriations in the millions are continuously being enacted by the federal government to improve education.

Perhaps the most pervasive of all the efforts thus far connected with textbooks and related materials has been the Biological Sciences Curriculum Study.[17] Several different versions of biology textbooks have been prepared, including one for the educationally disadvantaged. Each version presents somewhat similar biology information in a different manner. The materials are used widely throughout the United States and have been translated for use in many foreign countries.

Our purpose in mentioning this approach to changing the objectives and curriculum of the secondary schools is to emphasize the fact that a new group of people with a different strategy has appeared on a large

---

[15] NEA, *Schools for the Sixties*, A Report of the Project on Instruction (New York: McGraw-Hill, 1963), pp. 123–135. By permission.

[16] Robert W. Heath, ed., *New Curricula* (New York: Harper & Row, 1965).

[17] Biological Sciences Curriculum Study, *Biology Teachers' Handbook* (New York: John Wiley, 1963).

scale, supported mainly by the federal government. Experts in a subject matter field, behavioral scientists, and engineers with a strong interest in the schools, but who are not concerned with the total educational program, are now producing much of the new instructional materials and equipment.

SUMMARY

Equally valid objectives for the secondary school curriculum arise from the nature of the learner, from the needs of society, and from the structure of knowledge. From the recommendations of the Committee of Ten, 1894, to the recommendations of various national curriculum study groups in the 1950s and in the 1960s, general objectives have changed continuously to meet the needs of youth and society and to reflect current knowledge in a given area. Some of the sharp differences in objectives from 1894 to the present date can be explained in part by rapidly increasing enrollments, changing patterns for curriculum and instruction, and new approaches to the vertical and horizontal organization of the school.

Schools for the Sixties is one of the best statements of a balanced set of objectives for schools now well into the second half of the twentieth century.

QUESTIONS AND ACTIVITIES

1 Discuss the growth of knowledge in your own field during the last several decades. Contrast the rate of growth of knowledge in your area with the rate of growth of knowledge in another area of study in the secondary school.
2 List some of the skills, attitudes, and knowledge that must be considered as goals of education as the secondary school serves its obligations to society.
3 List some of the objectives of education in the junior and senior high school that arise from the needs of the learner.
4 Consulting U.S. Office of Education publications, write a brief report on the changing patterns of enrollment in the secondary school in our century. In your report, include what you think to be the implications of the changing patterns for secondary school teachers.

5 Do further reading on programs in schools characterized by innovation, such as Melbourne High School and Nova High School. Discuss which features of these programs you would like to try out during your own career as a teacher.

6 Compare and contrast objectives from the Committee of Ten, 1894, to the national curriculum-studies projects on the basis of the emphases given to objectives arising from the needs of the learner, the needs of society, and the structure of knowledge.

7 To what extent do you think secondary schools should assist students in developing marketable skills? To what extent are secondary schools justified in designating courses to be of humanistic rather than pragmatic value?

8 Compare the home backgrounds, socio-economic status, and other characteristics of students enrolled in schools in the suburbs with those of students enrolled in schools of the slums. How must the institutional objectives differ between schools for slums and schools for suburbs?

9 *Schools for the Sixties* calls for federal support for research, development, and dissemination dealing with the various ways of improving secondary education. To what extent has the federal government financed research, innovation, and general improvement in secondary education since the publication of *Schools for the Sixties?*

10 Since the early 1950s, experts have played an important role in developing new teaching materials for use in the secondary schools. Examine two different series of very recent teaching materials in your own field, materials that scholars have helped prepare. Compare them on the basis of recency of scholarship, of provision for differing ability and achievement, and for the qualifications of the authors as experts in their field.

SUGGESTIONS FOR FURTHER READING

BLOOM, BENJAMIN S., ED., *Taxonomy of Educational Objectives; Handbook I: Cognitive Domain*, New York: McKay, 1956.

BROUDY, HARRY S., B. OTHANEL SMITH, AND JOE R. BURNETT, *Democracy and Excellence in American Secondary Education*, Chicago: Rand McNally, 1964.

CONANT, JAMES B., *The American High School Today*, New York: McGraw-Hill, 1959.

CONANT, JAMES B., *Slums and Suburbs*, New York: McGraw-Hill, 1961.

CREMIN, LAWRENCE A., *The Transformation of the School*, New York: Knopf, 1962.

EHLERS, HENRY, AND GORDON C. LEE, EDS., *Crucial Issues in Education*, New York: Holt, Rinehart and Winston, 1963.

GROSS, RONALD, AND JUDITH MURPHY, EDS., *The Revolution in the Schools*, New York: Harcourt, Brace, & World, 1964.

KRATHWOHL, DAVID R., BENJAMIN S. BLOOM, AND BERTRAM B. MASIA, *Taxonomy of Educational Objectives; Handbook II: Affective Domain*, New York: McKay, 1964.

KRUG, EDWARD A., *The Shaping of the American High School*, New York: Harper & Row, 1964.

Project on Instruction of the National Education Association, *Schools for the Sixties*, New York: McGraw-Hill, 1963.

2 *Adolescent development*

A recent phenomenon in American society is the possible crystallization of a youth culture. The youth culture is a set of attitudes and behavior patterns, along with artifacts peculiar to the present generation of youth. It stems from the attempts to fill in the ever-lengthening transitional period from childhood into independent adulthood. It sets youth apart from physically immature children and from independent adults who hold jobs, are married, or both. Some youth from junior high school age through college age are in fact forming into groups that are impenetrable by parents, teachers, and other adults. Although unemployed teenagers of minority groups comprise a large part of the rebellious group, college students most clearly manifest the effects of prolonged dependence and provide the leadership of the youth culture.

Although physically mature, they are still preparing for the "real" life that comes after college. The extent to which a definite youth culture exists and the proportion of youth who are involved have not yet been fully ascertained, according to Smith and Kleine.[1] They point out that decision-making by many youths is still influenced by adults, including teachers, on many matters.

---

[1] Louis M. Smith and Paul F. Kleine, "The Adolescent and His Society," *Review of Educational Research*, XXXVI (October, 1966).

Wise teachers accept the fact that adolescence is a period during which the young person is finding himself, trying earnestly to be independent in many matters and yet recognizing his dependence as long as he remains in school. Committed teachers realize that the majority of adolescents are worthy youth, that they are desirable young people in all regards, that they come to school not only to learn subject matter, but also to learn about themselves and others, to make their way in an imperfect social world and a rapidly changing physical environment. Thus, the modern high school must be far more than a storehouse of subject matter to be dispensed to clients of various abilities and interests. High school education must be concerned with making youth a constructive force in the total society. The mature, enthusiastic high school teacher, whether in a self-contained classroom or a team, is concerned with boys and girls as total maturing human beings. Even though priorities may vary among teachers, a total high school program should contribute toward aiding the adolescent to develop in:

1. Understanding and accepting one's own physique
2. Establishing satisfactory relations with agemates
3. Establishing more mature relations with adults
4. Achieving emotional maturity
5. Making progress toward economic independence
6. Achieving intellectual maturity
7. Achieving a well-integrated personality

UNDERSTANDING AND ACCEPTING ONE'S OWN PHYSIQUE

With the onset of the rapid development of the ovaries in the female and the testes in the male, secondary sex characteristics appear. The most pronounced of these in a girl are the growth of pubic hair, development of the breasts, and widening of the hips. In the boy, pubic hair appears, the voice deepens, the chest broadens, and the beard grows. In early adolescence there is usually a sharp increase in height, weight, and strength in both sexes. Understanding these changes and accepting them as part of the growing-up process is a major need of adolescents because adjustment problems may arise in those areas concerned with physical maturation: change in size, in proportion, and in function.

Actual size is important in determining attitudes toward oneself and others. To have had one's height and weight increase very slowly for many years and then attain adult stature in from one to three years presents many problems. Not to grow when one's classmates do leads to greater difficulties. Adolescents may be grouped into four categories on the basis of severity of problems related to size: (1) early developers, for example, the 10-year-old girl in the fifth grade who begins to menstruate; (2) late developers, the high school senior who has not yet begun to shave; (3) boys who at maturity are considerably below the average in height and strength; and (4) girls who at maturity are considerably taller or heavier than the average. The problems of the last two groups are peculiar to our culture, mainly because so much prestige is given to tall, strong athletes in competitive events and to slim but shapely girls of medium height in popularity and beauty contests.

Change in proportion is closely related to size as far as the developmental sequence is concerned. During early adolescence the arms and legs of both boys and girls grow longer quite rapidly. The boys' shoulders widen and their hips become proportionately slender. The girls' breasts enlarge and their hips widen. The ideals of masculinity and femininity that adolescents have set for themselves are important, for they constitute possible sources of adjustment problems. The girl whose heritage runs to a tall, heavy, flat-chested figure may isolate herself from the group after dieting, exercise, and medicine have failed to alter her growth pattern. The short, fat, narrow-shouldered boy and the extremely tall, skinny boy face equally difficult adjustments. Nicknames—"Skinny," "Shorty," "Fatty," "Flabby"—are often bestowed in the shower rooms of both junior and senior high schools. They indicate roughly the extent to which adolescents are made aware of their variations from the ideal.

Changes in the functioning of organs is another accompaniment of maturation. Sweat glands begin to secrete profusely. The sex organs, heretofore dormant, begin to secrete hormones. The processes accounting for the first menstrual period and the first nocturnal emission are hard to understand in themselves. It is difficult for adults to understand the reproductive process, and even more difficult for a youngster fifteen years old. Comprehension of the entire process is important for adolescents. Help in understanding and undergoing these changes in function can be provided in both the home and the school. To neglect this vital need constitutes a serious weakness in helping adolescents develop into normal adults.

An interesting investigation, conducted by Stolz and Stolz,[2] yielded useful information for teachers. Of 93 adolescent boys and 83 girls, they found that 31 percent of the boys and 41 percent of the girls had suffered anxieties concerning their physical development. The six factors that the boys found most often disturbing were small size (particularly height), fatness, poor physique, lack of muscular strength, facial features, and overdevelopment around the nipples. For the girls the factors were tallness, fatness, facial features, general physical appearance; tallness and heaviness; and shortness and heaviness.

Understanding and accepting their physique are important to adolescents, if for no other reason than because physical development is the basis for other development. Hence, to be dissatisfied with one's own physique constitutes a serious adjustment problem and affects that person's development in all other fields.

DEVELOPING SATISFACTORY RELATIONSHIPS WITH AGEMATES

Closely related to the acceptance of one's physique is the need to develop social skills so that one can establish good relationships with the opposite sex. Prior to puberty, boys typically associate with other boys, and girls with other girls, in informal groups called "gangs." Frequently the two groups delight in antagonizing each other. Thus, when boys and girls mature and the sex need appears, both have had few previous success experiences in relationships with the opposite sex. They must learn new skills and attitudes if they are to get along with each other in a mixed group, the "crowd." In learning these new skills, adolescents behave somewhat as adults do, except that they have fewer experiences upon which to draw. We shall use John to illustrate the sequence of learning a new social skill.

John engaged actively in games with other boys throughout the seventh and eighth grades. He was a leader in football games and in rough-and-tumble activities of all kinds. The other boys admired him for his strength and skill; they accepted him as their leader on the playground and in the neighborhood gang.

---

[2] Herbert R. Stolz and Lois M. Stolz, "Adolescent Problems Related to Somatic Variations," *Adolescence, Forty-third Yearbook of the National Society for the Study of Education* (Chicago: University of Chicago Press, 1944), pp. 86–88.

Toward spring in the eighth grade, pubic hair started to grow; and that summer his height increased more than two inches. When he came to school in the fall, he found that the girls, whom he had scarcely noticed before and whom he thought were silly, were very different.

Now, for some vaguely understood reason, John wants to know these girls better. What does he do? First he tries the things that worked with the gang of boys; he relies upon previously established patterns of behavior. But these do not work. Obviously he must try something else. He may scuffle with the girls, pull their hair, or pick wool from the sweater of the girl who sits next to him in the classroom. He may even —blushing and perspiring profusely—ask her to meet him after school for a soda.

If he persists in this experimenting and finds that certain tactics lead to getting better acquainted, they become part of his behavior pattern until he finds better ones. If he meets with no success, he is likely to do one of two things: He will become aggressive and take it out on the girls, the teacher, and his other classmates; or he will withdraw from activities, devoting himself to daydreaming or reading pulp literature.

And what have his teachers been doing to help John? When teachers recognize that making a satisfactory adjustment to the opposite sex is a basic problem for adolescents and that young people must solve this problem if they are to derive maximum profit from the academic program, they will provide many opportunities for boys and girls to associate with one another on a friendly basis in the classroom. To rule out this classroom association contributes to maladjustment. The teacher who does not encourage young people to develop social skills in the classroom is placing a social block in the path of adolescent need-satisfaction.

Typically, the development of good relations with the opposite sex goes through these steps: (1) Adolescents become interested in the opposite sex, particularly the physical characteristics. (2) They have their first date; this is often a bewildering experience that is accompanied with great anxiety. (3) They have dates with several young people and fall in and out of love frequently. (4) The number of individuals dated decreases and "going steady" is the common pattern. (5) In some cases, a marriage partner is finally selected. All of these are important learnings. The high school teacher who helps adolescents with these problems is contributing greatly toward the maintenance of better school relations and, ultimately, the development of a healthy home life.

ESTABLISHING MORE MATURE RELATIONSHIPS WITH ADULTS

As boys and girls mature, they seek greater independence of parents and other adults. The adolescent boy, now taller and stronger than his mother and perhaps also his father, wants psychological freedom from the restraints so long imposed upon him by virtue of his parents' physical superiority. All through childhood his parents have been saying, "You can't drive the car; you can't drink or smoke; these are things you must not do until you grow up."

Now the adolescent boy has reached that age—or thinks he has. Many boys have not, because their parents have not paralleled their sons' growth by changing their attitudes. Loving and wanting to continue protecting their child, the parents attempt to hold him for a few more years—at least until graduation from high school. To avoid physical violence, parents frequently resort to economic measures to keep the adolescent psychologically dependent. Young people whose parents have not given them increasing opportunities to develop independence and self-control frequently react to their teachers as they do toward their parents simply because the teachers also symbolize adult domination. The boy who has been severely rebuked by his father at the breakfast table for reckless driving responds negatively when his teacher criticizes him for not having prepared an assignment. The girl whose mother has reprimanded her for buying a form-fitting sweater responds negatively to her English teacher's remark that Lady Olivia concealed her beauty with ruffles.

Teaching requires that crises be avoided between teacher and pupil. As in developing new social skills, adolescents need to work out ways to get along better with teachers, parents, and other adults. They themselves feel that they are adults and should be treated as adults; but they do not have the requisite skills, nor do adults give them many opportunities for behaving in a grown-up manner. Adolescents need to establish a new relationship with parents—one that involves mutual affection and respect plus increasing independence in making decisions. One way in which the teacher can help here is to organize activities that call for adolescents to assume responsibility for their behavior and to exert less and less control. A very effective way for him to interfere here is to dominate the adolescents and give them no opportunity to establish adult associations with him or with their agemates.

The common sequence in achieving independence of parents is marked by these stages: (1) As the child approaches puberty, he obeys parental commands without much rebellion. (2) Early in adolescence, he seeks independence in choosing clothing, friends, and activities. (3) Agemates of the opposite sex replace the parent as the primary objects of affection. (4) This greater freedom and association with agemates make him feel less need for parental affection. (5) Plans and decisions are made in discussions with parents but are not dominated by them. (6) Economic independence is the final step in gaining full freedom from parental control.

ACHIEVING EMOTIONAL MATURITY

It is often said that a person's behavior in a particular situation is determined more by how he feels than by his knowledge of what to do. The fact that this idea is generally accepted indicates the great need to help adolescents learn how to control their emotions.

Two factors operate during emotion; there is a physiological and a psychological reaction. When a person becomes angry, scared, or highly excited, certain physiological changes occur in his body without voluntary or conscious action on his part. Thus the heart beats faster, the digestive juices, including saliva, cease to flow, blood leaves the visceral organs and goes to the muscles, blood sugar is released from the liver, and the rate of respiration increases. The body uses more energy and eliminates waste at a faster rate. The perspiring palms and forehead, flushed face, greater strength, dry mouth, and trembling limbs that result from these physiological changes are usually called the overt or outward expression of emotion. To a limited degree, this observable expression can be controlled; the inner physiological expression cannot.

The psychological aspect of emotion is described as fear, anger, love, or shame, terms that denote the feeling accompanying the physiological reaction. Psychologically, emotion ranges in intensity from mild to disruptive. Mild emotion tends to stimulate wholesome activity. Frequent outbursts or prolonged spells of intense emotion are harmful to health as well as to efficiency in learning. One does not learn to solve arithmetic problems while extremely angry; one does not do his school work well when very upset by his fear of failing. When an intense emotion like shame or anger is accompanied by a feeling of disorganization or unpleasantness, one usually learns to fear the situation in which it occurred. When there is a feeling of pleasantness and exhilaration, one experiences enjoyment and tends to try to reproduce the situations in which this feeling occurred. Thus, emotions are motivational forces, serving to direct activity.

Maturing boys and girls, facing problems for which as yet their responses are inadequate, frequently find themselves in situations that involve disruptive emotions. But adolescents are expected not to hit or yell when angry, run when afraid, or cry when ashamed. Attaining emotional maturity demands that they increasingly refrain from relieving emotional tension by outward expression. This in turn means that adolescents must be able to handle situations involving disruptive emotions, for unrelieved tensions that build up and are not expressed outwardly may produce serious maladjustment.

The teacher has an important role in this kind of learning. In the first place, he must avoid situations that could produce emotional crises. A flushed face, quavering speech, and trembling knees are warning signals that an adolescent is suffering and should be pushed no further. Belligerent words and gestures directed at the teacher or classmates mean "Stop." Nosebleeds and headaches during examinations indicate acute emotional distress. Teachers are responsible for controlling the emotional atmosphere of the classroom and they should maintain a healthy one.

Classroom activity directed toward assisting boys and girls to develop the following competences will facilitate the attaining of emotional maturity: (1) Understanding socially approved methods for relieving emotional tensions and substituting these for childish or otherwise disapproved methods; (2) analyzing emotional situations objectively; (3) obtaining a broader understanding of situations in which disruptive emotions are produced; (4) acquiring many social skills to meet new situations; and (5) eliminating fears and emotionalized patterns of response that are already firmly established.

MAKING PROGRESS TOWARD
ECONOMIC INDEPENDENCE

Unemployment and the lack of ability by adults to earn a livelihood are acute problems of the modern era. Although achieving economic independence is included in most statements of objectives of secondary education, educational programs to achieve the objectives are inadequate. In fact, after Sputnik the push toward a more rigorous high school education resulted in students studying mainly five subject fields —English, foreign languages, mathematics, the sciences, and social studies. Interest in vocational subjects declined markedly until very recently. Despite this, James B. Conant, as early as 1959, vigorously defended strengthening the comprehensive high school, including its role in vocational education.[3] Although he proposed that the academically talented students should take 20 units in the five "academic" subjects prior to any electives in vocational subjects or the fine arts, he also insisted that the majority of high school students should learn a marketable skill through a program of vocational education. For girls, he suggested courses such as home economics, typing, stenography, and the use of clerical machines; for boys, auto mechanics, machine shop, and others.

Obviously, there is need to reappraise the whole field of vocational education today, to identify relationships between work and personality development, and to find balance in the high school curriculum among general education, concentration in the five "academic" subjects, and work in vocational education and the fine arts. The importance of students' being aided by the school in achieving economic independence merits further discussion of the preceding points regarding vocational education.

Reappraisal of vocational education

Since 1960, several conditions have resulted in a further study of vocational education in the high school. Unemployment among young people of ages 18 to 24 is alarmingly high, despite the demands of military

---

[3] James B. Conant, *The American High School Today* (New York: McGraw-Hill, 1959).

service. Many college students are quitting prior to graduation for lack of money. The home is increasingly unable to provide vocational education. Chase has recently stated the case for vocational education.

> Unless interest in vocational education is awakened on a massive national scale, the United States will lose a crucial lap in "the race between education and catastrophe"—in H. G. Wells' annually more apt definition of history.
>
> Today rational education must include training for the 80 percent of all young Americans who enter the labor market without college degrees. To ignore their vocational training is a reverse twist on the Eskimos' fabled custom of pushing their unproductive senior citizens onto the ice pack. That practice at least has a certain economic logic. Our system is managing to be at once inhumane and economically suicidal.[4]

The need for vocational education is indicated by recent information about our population and jobs. Out of every ten youngsters now in grade school, three will not finish high school. Seven will be graduated from high school. Three will go to work, some as wives and mothers. Four will continue into higher education, but only two will finish college. Twenty-six million young workers will have started work between 1960 and 1970. The most rapidly expanding occupations for the decade are, in this order: professional and technical, clerical and sales, service, skilled workers and proprietors, managers about equally, and semiskilled last.[5]

The changing picture of both jobs and the labor force suggests a need for a reappraisal of the entire field of vocational education, similar to what is occurring in the academic subject areas. Although this is the case, the comprehensive high school should now have a strong program in business education and in distributive education. Technicians, machine operators, mechanics, and others in jobs related to the production, operation, and maintenance of machines will be needed in increasing numbers. Schools should be equipped immediately to teach general shop skills, psychomotor skills, knowledge, and attitudes that have transfer value for the jobs enumerated. The future of home economics and agriculture is uncertain, inasmuch as life in the home and on the farm

---

[4] Edward T. Chase, "Learning to Be Unemployable," *Harper's Magazine,* CCXXVI (April, 1963), p. 40. By permission.
[5] P. G. Haines, "A Time for Professional Statesmanship," *Delta Pi Epsilon Journal,* V (February, 1963), 33.

is changing so rapidly. Fewer persons will work on the farms; more women will work outside the home. There is clearly a greater need for other types of vocational education.

In spite of the need for appraisal, we cannot afford to eliminate vocational education from the comprehensive high school. On the contrary, it should be possible for any student, including the academically talented, to pursue a major of three units in a vocational field. The larger high school might profitably have at least four general vocational programs, two particularly appropriate for girls and two for boys. Not every student should be required to take even one semester in a vocational subject, but a major of three units should not be denied to any student who desires to elect it. It is possible, of course, that many academically talented students will elect courses in the nonverbal fine arts rather than in a vocational field.

Vocational education is not solely for students who do not attend college. Many college students require vocational education because their families cannot support them. Further, they do not receive vocational education in their homes. The urban family, especially, experiences difficulty in providing household chores, much less providing work experience and vocational education, for children. Parents find it impossible to locate work activities, in or outside the home, with or without pay, that are suited to the interests and abilities of adolescent boys, ages 13 to 18. High school girls who baby sit, clean house, and prepare meals get little or no satisfaction from these activities, when repeated year after year. Manual labor tasks, distasteful to adults or for which the hourly rate is low, are about the only ones available to high school students, and also to college students. Even these jobs for youth are disappearing as the chronic unemployment of unskilled and semiskilled adults increases.

Education about work and careers also is meager in the modern home. The son usually does not see his father at work, much less learn the job from him. The same is true of the girl whose mother works. Most parents are only semiliterate about economic affairs, apparently preferring to permit others to manipulate much of their economic life. So poor is the total program of vocational education in the home and school that many unmarried female college graduates with majors in one of the liberal arts or sciences subsequently enroll in a business college in order to prepare themselves for a job. Also many industries employ some of the liberal arts graduates for less money than they pay equally young skilled workers—high school graduates with four years of work experience.

Work and personality

Work is closely related to individual personality and to culture. Man has progressed from prehistoric times to his present state only as he has been able, through work, to change the environment so that his many abilities might emerge and develop. His evolution is not so much a process of adjusting to the environment as adjusting the environment to suit his needs and emergent abilities.

Smith points out that most capitalist and socialist writers have treated work behavior narrowly—either as a means of production, as a source of wealth, or as a limited aspect of technology—and not as a critical aspect of human behavior and adjustment. He then develops a comprehensive theory to explain work as the primary determinant of the human condition. In this comprehensive theory, he relates how work in man has contributed to his evolution, how its feedback effects define the personality of each individual, how it has provided the dynamic human motivation toward social and economic development, and how its behavior mechanisms are regulated.

From a bio-social account of work, Smith theorizes how the feedback effects of occupation determine the specific properties of individual adjustment, mental health, motivation, social integration, aging, and individual behavior resources. In referring to work and personality, he says,

> Throughout the ages of man's civilized existence, the events of work have borne an interacting relation to what is called personality. This relation at times has been decisive not only in structuring the human condition of existence and aspiration, but in specifically determining the social circumstances of individuality. In ancient periods, occupation determined class, caste, and the dominant personality association of each. . . . As the structure of institutional organization in industry has become more complex, the pattern of individual social behavior within the organized work systems has become more stylized and group-structured, leading to greater emphasis than heretofore on both the assessment and control of the over-all pattern of social-emotional behavior.[6]

---

[6] Karl U. Smith, *Behavior Organization and Work* (Madison, Wis.: College Printing and Typing Co., 1962), pp. 5-1, 5-2. By permission.

This approach to work behavior bears analysis, not only in America, but throughout the world. Until recently, a minority in most nations of the Western world has argued successfully for the liberal education of a wealthy elite ruling class, educated to accrue wealth, to rule, to lead, and, on the other hand, low-cost technical education or no education for the masses of working people. Until recently, America has successfully pursued a different course through its comprehensive high school, which has included vocational education as a primary objective.

Balance in the curriculum

Although changes should be made in secondary schooling in the next decades, let us assume that the majority of high school students will spend from three to five years completing what are now normally grades 9 through 12 in a comprehensive high school. The balance to be achieved in high school is among the three main objectives: general education, incorporated in the required program for all students; vocational education, including the acquisition of a marketable skill or the beginning of it; and education to prepare for college attendance. Klausmeier has outlined a program that is intended to achieve this balance. Its main elements are expressed here.[7]

The general education requirement for all students might be nine years or units: three in English; two in social studies; one each in mathematics, science, and fine arts; and one additional unit in one of the first four subject fields. The student who does not plan to go to college might take the remaining seven of 16 units in any combination of subjects but should probably take at least three in a vocational area.

Unless there is some threat to national security of which the authors are unaware, the taking of twenty units of work in the five academic subjects prior to any work in the fine arts or vocational subjects cannot be justified. On the contrary, every student, including the academically talented, should be permitted to take a full major of three units or years of work in a vocational area. If college-bound students are permitted to acquire a saleable skill at a beginning level or to pursue a nonverbal art, there is some hope that vocational education and the

---

[7] A complete set of recommendations is given in Herbert J. Klausmeier, "Balance in High School Education," *Teacher's College Record*, LXVII (October, 1965), 18–25.

nonverbal arts will survive in the comprehensive high school for the noncollege-bound students. We should not expect any vocational subject to survive when the many students who think they will go to college, the high school counselors, principals, and teachers in the academic subjects shun these courses as unworthy of serious study, unworthy of credit toward graduation. Unless a larger percent of our youths become economically independent in young adulthood, the rest of us shall carry a heavy tax load to support them in the future.

ACHIEVING INTELLECTUAL MATURITY

We have indicated that secondary education must give attention to the development of the adolescent as a total individual. Although this is the case, the primary function of the school is to aid students to acquire subject matter knowledge and develop related intellectual abilities or skills. In this connection, recent knowledge concerning general intellectual ability, specific intellectual abilities, and cognitive development during childhood and adolescence bears careful study.[8] In general, we are much more enthusiastic about what can be accomplished through education than we were even a decade ago.

General intellectual ability

General intellectual ability, also referred to as mental ability or intelligence, is a composite of many abilities that are useful in performing a large number of tasks. High intelligence is associated, most closely, but far from perfectly, with high attainment in English, mathematics, science, and social studies—any activity where ideas are incorporated in symbols. General ability is not closely associated with any kind of motor activity or with any set of attitudes or beliefs.

Two assumptions about intelligence have prevailed from the early part of the twentieth century through World War II and are still adopted by some people. One is that intelligence is fixed and unchangeable; the other is that the individual's potentiality for all types of activity

---

[8] For a more complete discussion of these topics, consult Herbert J. Klausmeier and William Goodwin, *Learning and Human Abilities: Educational Psychology*, 2nd ed. (New York: Harper & Row, 1966).

is determined by heredity. According to the first assumption, the individual's IQ remains constant from birth throughout life. The second assumption implies that the individual has inherited the potentiality for all his behavior and that the environment merely provides triggering mechanisms for the potentialities to unfold. Evidence from physiology and psychology may be interpreted to support or refute both assumptions. Evidence tending to refute the assumptions has been disregarded in the United States until recently; but the tendency now is to place greater emphasis upon environmental influences, especially during the early years of life. Hunt concluded that ". . . it might be feasible to discover ways to govern the environments, especially during the early years of their development, to achieve a substantially faster rate of intellectual development and a substantially higher adult level of intellectual capacity."[9] According to Bloom, an impoverished environment in childhood might so retard the development of the individual that he could not subsequently make it up, and an enriched environment might accelerate his development.[10] Bloom estimated that 50 percent of mature intelligence is achieved by age 4 and that a deprived and an abundant environment can result in differences in intelligence scores of at least 10 points until age 4. Similarly, with 80 percent of mature intelligence being achieved at age 8, the difference resulting from environment can be at least 16 points; and at age 17 the difference can amount to 20 IQ points.

In interpreting the change in IQ due to environment, we assume an average IQ of 100 with about two thirds of all individuals having IQs between 84 and 116. Thus, a change of 20 IQ points is considerable. For example, two individuals at age 17 might have IQs of 120 and 100, the difference being due to an enriched or an impoverished environment. The indivdual with the IQ of 100 would not be expected to complete the baccalaureate whereas the one with a 120 IQ would be expected to complete the baccalaureate and also to do graduate work in some field. We think a difference in excess of 20 IQ points may be attributable to environmental influences.

Age 17 was used by Bloom for convenience as the age for full intellectual maturity. However, intellectual growth continues well after age

[9] J. McV. Hunt, *Intelligence and Experience* (New York: Ronald, 1961), p. 363.

[10] Benjamin S. Bloom, *Stability and Change in Human Characteristics* (New York: Wiley, 1964).

17 as indicated in a number of representative longitudinal studies.[11] For example, Bayley found an increase in some intellectual abilities until age 50.[12] The authors accept the idea of continuous improvement in some intellectual abilities long after age 16 and also that good education, an enriched environment, is related to intellectual development. We are much more cautious now than we were even ten years ago in predicting adult achievement on the basis of IQ scores of children.

Specific intellectual abilities

Specific or specialized abilities may be contrasted with general intellectual ability in that a specific ability underlies performance of a narrow range of tasks rather than a broad range. Specific abilities, like general intellectual ability, are usually inferred from test results. Specific abilities are not as well understood as is general intellectual ability. Less longitudinal research has been done regarding specific abilities, and the relationships of the many specific abilities to achievement in the various school subjects are not established clearly. Tests of specific abilities have not yet proved more effective than general intellectual ability in predicting the efficiency of learning in different tasks in school, including secretarial work, handwriting, English, mathematics, and others. Nevertheless, the concept of specific abilities is well established and is particularly relevant to the development of creative abilities.

Figure 1, based on Guilford and Hoepfner, indicates 120 possible human abilities in the cognitive domain. An ability is a combination of an operation or process, a content, and a product. Each of the five operations, in combination with one of the four contents and with one of six products, constitutes an ability. Guilford calls each of these an intellectual factor. Specifically, each of the operations, contents, and products is[13]

OPERATIONS   Major kinds of intellectual activities or processes; things that the organism does with the raw materials of information.

[11] *Ibid.*

[12] Nancy Bayley, "On the Growth of Intelligence," *American Psychologist,* X (December, 1955), 805–818.

[13] John P. Guilford and R. Hoepfner, "Current Summary of Structure-of-Intellect Factors and Suggested Tests," *Report of Psychological Laboratory,* No. 30 (Los Angeles: University of Southern California, 1963). By permission.

OPERATIONS

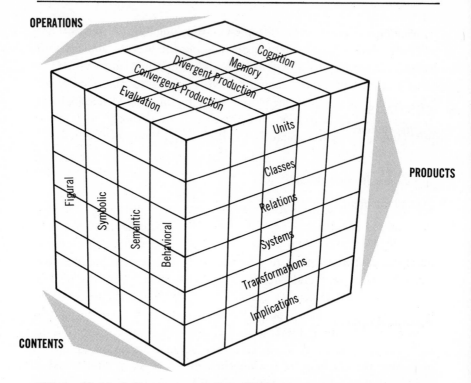

PRODUCTS

CONTENTS

FIG. 1   *Model of the structure of the intellect. (J. P. Guilford and R. Hoepfner,* "Current Summary of Structure-of-Intellect Factors and Suggested Tests," Reports from the Psychological Laboratory, No. 30, Los Angeles: University of Southern California, 1963, p. 2.) By permission.

Cognition	Immediate discovery, awareness, rediscovery, or recognition of information in various forms; comprehension or understanding.
Memory	Retention or storage, with some degree of availability, of information in the same form in which it was committed to storage and in response to the same cues in connection with which it was learned.
Divergent production	Generation of information from given information, where the emphasis is upon variety and quantity of output from the same source. Likely to involve what has been called transfer.
Convergent production	Generation of information from given information, where the emphasis is upon achieving unique or conventionally accepted best outcomes. It is likely that the given (cue) information fully determines the response.

Evaluation   Reaching decisions or making judgments concerning the goodness (correctness, suitability, adequacy, desirability, etc.) of information in terms of criteria of identity, consistency, and goal satisfaction.

CONTENTS   Broad classes of information.

Figural content   Information in concrete form, as perceived or as recalled in the form of images. The term *figural* implies some degree of organization or structuring. Different sense modalities may be involved, e.g., visual, auditory, kinesthetic.

Symbolic content   Information in the form of signs, having no significance in and of themselves, such as letters, numbers, musical notations, and other "code" elements.

Semantic content   Information in the form of meanings to which words commonly become attached, hence most notable in verbal thinking and in verbal communication.

Behavioral content   Information, essentially nonverbal, involved in human interactions, where awareness of the attitudes, needs, desires, moods, intentions, perceptions, thoughts, etc., of other persons and of ourselves is important.

PRODUCTS   Forms that information takes in the organism's processing of it.

Units   Relatively segregated or circumscribed items of information having "thing" character. May be close to Gestalt psychology's "figure on a ground."

Classes   Recognized sets of items of information grouped by virtue of their common properties.

Relations   Recognized connections between units of information based upon variables or points of contact that apply to them.

Systems   Organized or structured aggregates of items of information; complexes of interrelated or interacting parts.

Transformations   Changes of various kinds of existing or known information or in its use.

Implications   Extrapolations of information, in the form of expectancies, predictions, known or suspected antecedents, concomitants, or consequences.[14]

---

[14] *Information* is defined as "that which the organism discriminates."

A few examples and definitions clarify the preceding contents and processes. You will find it profitable to slow your reading and think of examples other than those given.

Figural content is information in concrete form as experienced directly through seeing, touching, hearing, and so on. The information does not represent anything but itself (information refers to anything that is sensed and discriminated). Imagine yourself in a forest. Everything you see, hear, feel, or smell that is not embodied in signs or words is figural content. *Symbolic content* is information in the form of signs that have no significance in and of themselves. Such information includes the letters of the alphabet, numerals, musical notations, and any other elements used in coding systems. Observe these letters—*a, x, s*— and these numerals—2, 7, 5. You are observing symbolic content. *Semantic content* takes the form of meanings attached to words and is thus most important in verbal communication and thinking. Reread and think about the last sentence. You are dealing with semantic content. *Behavioral content* is nonverbal information related to interactions with human beings. Awareness of the attitudes, moods, desires, intentions, and perceptions of others and of oneself is important. The identification of abilities involving this type of content has not proceeded to an appreciable degree up to the present, and the precise nature of the abilities is problematic.

The six products by which information in each of the four content areas can be classified require clarification. A *unit* is an entity, a relatively segregated or circumscribed item of information. For example, 3 is a symbolic unit, and *democracy* is a semantic unit. *Classes* are sets of items of information grouped by virtue of their common properties. Some concepts embody classes; for example, *birds* and *mammals* embody a large number of units, classified according to their common properties. *Relations* involve recognized connections or associations between units of information. For example, we state that round objects roll down hill and that the number set represented by 6 is larger than that represented by 5. Relations between semantic units are expressed in the first part of the sentence and between symbolic units in the second part. The category, *systems*, is the most inclusive of the four— units, classes, relations, and systems—and implies organized aggregates of information. The laws regarding the arabic numbers comprise a symbolic system. The laws or rules regarding the transmission of information in sentences—rules of syntax—clarify our language system, in this case a semantic system. Now consider an example of units, classes, relations, and systems in symbolic content: 3 and 8 are *units*; uneven numbers and even numbers represent *classes*; "3 is to 6 as 5 is to 10" indicates a *relationship*; and the associative and commutative laws are parts of a *system*.

Transformations and implications are not a continuation of the hierarchy from units through systems. *Transformations* involve making changes of various kinds in existing or known information or in usages of this information. For example, changing 65 in base 10 to 145 in base 6 involves *transformation*. Changing "the man hit the boy" to "the boy was hit by a man" also requires transformation. Writing a plot for a story requires transformation of the given information into something else. *Implications* take the form of predictions, statements of expectancy, known or suspected antecedents of events, consequences of certain actions, and other extrapolations of the given information. For example, identifying questions, the answers to which should help reach a decision in a conflict situation, requires implications from known information. Adding the detailed operations needed to make a briefly outlined plan succeed also illustrates implications with semantic content.

The last set of the triad is processes. *Cognition* refers to immediate discovery, awareness, rediscovery, or recognition of information that has been discriminated. Comprehension and understanding are synonyms for cognition. If one could not distinguish figural, symbolic, semantic, or behavioral information, one could not cognize it. *Memory* refers to the retention or storage of information in the same form in which it was initially learned, and also the capacity for recalling or reproducing it. Tests of memory are such that if the individual cannot recognize, recall, or reproduce what he has learned, we assume that he no longer has the information in storage; he has forgotten it. *Divergent production* refers to the generation of new information from given information, where the emphasis is upon variety and quantity of output. Divergent thinking leads in different directions to responses that cannot be scored as correct or incorrect. For example, giving clever titles to a story plot leads to responses that cannot be scored as right or wrong. The solutions or ideas produced through divergent thinking are novel to the producer, not necessarily to others. *Convergent thinking* implies the generation of

TABLE 2.1. *Illustrative Tasks, Processes, Contents, Products, and Abilities.*

Task	Process	Content	Product	Ability
Finding correct synonym for word	Cognition	Semantic	Unit	Verbal comprehension
Selecting word in a set that does not belong to the class	Cognition	Semantic	Class	Conceptual classification
Selecting word to complete meaningful relationship	Cognition	Semantic	Relation	Semantic relations
Solving problems with minimal arithmetic computation, maximum reasoning	Cognition	Semantic	System	General reasoning
Writing words containing a specified letter; e.g., *r*	Divergent production	Symbolic	Unit	Word fluency
Listing classes of uses for an object	Divergent production	Semantic	Class	Spontaneous semantic flexibility
Listing steps in appropriate order for completing a project (e.g., building a birdhouse)	Convergent production	Semantic	System	Semantic ordering
Naming an object that could be made by combining two given objects; e.g., a coil spring and a beach ball to make a punching bag	Convergent production	Semantic	Transformation	Semantic redefinition
Indicating each digit in a row of 30 digits that is like the first one in the row	Evaluation	Symbolic	Unit	Symbolic identification
Judging whether symbolic conclusions are true or false based upon given premises	Evaluation	Symbolic	Relation	Symbolic manipulation

SOURCE: Based on John P. Guilford and R. Hoepfner, "Current Summary of Structure-of-Intellect Factors and Suggested Tests," *Report of Psychological Laboratory, No. 30* (Los Angeles: University of Southern California, 1963). By permission.

new information from given information, where the emphasis is upon achieving correct or conventionally accepted best outcomes. For example, $2-2=?$ requires convergent thinking. *Evaluation* requires reaching decisions or making judgments concerning the goodness, correctness, suitability, adequacy, or desirability of information in terms of criteria. The criteria might be consistency and goal satisfactions. Processes, contents, and products have now been dealt with separately. Table 2.1 shows certain tasks; the combination of process, content, and product involved; and the names of the factors. Examples are given of each task that is thought to be difficult. Study the material carefully and think of other examples.

Guilford indicates three possible types of intelligence associated with the various contents. *Concrete intelligence* involves the abilities connected with figural content. Mechanics, operators of machines, artists, and musicians depend heavily on these abilities. *Abstract intelligence* pertains to abilities concerned with symbolic and semantic content. Learning to recognize words, to spell, and to operate with numbers involves abilities with symbolic content. Abilities with semantic content are required for understanding verbal concepts and ideas of all types. Present-day intelligence tests are heavily loaded with test items requiring the use of abstract abilities. *Social intelligence* is concerned with behavioral content, with understanding the behavior of others and oneself. Teachers, lawyers, social workers, politicians, and leaders are hypothesized to be high in social intelligence.

Substantial evidence is accumulating which indicates that specific abilities can be identified in children, youth, and adults. However, the chronological age at which the separate abilities become differentiated is not clear. Apparently the specific abilities that are manifested with increasing maturity and experience evolve from earlier general intellectual ability. A further clarification of change with age is provided in the next section of this chapter.

Perhaps the most significant results of Guilford's pioneering work are the renewed interest in nurturing the creative abilities, or divergent production abilities, and the relationship of general intellectual ability to creative abilities. The relationship between general intellectual ability and divergent thinking abilities may be summarized briefly from the results of two of many studies. Klausmeier and Wiersma found only modest positive relationships between IQ scores and scores on creative-thinking tests.[15] And although low IQ students are consistently lower than those of average and high IQ in divergent thinking, they are considerably lower than the average and high IQ in educational achievement. IQ tests are not useful in identifying students of varying creative abilities, according to Getzels and Jackson.[16]

The implication from the work thus far in relating creative abilities to other cognitive abilities is reasonably clear. We should not expect children of low and average IQ to be as creative as children of high IQ. At the same time, we must not confuse IQ and creativity. There is wide variation among the children of the same IQ level in creativity. The same implications hold for grades made in the various school subjects and creativity.

Turning to the renewed emphasis on nurturing creative abilities in the school program, we find that many professional journals and books recommend it. Even though creativity is encouraged verbally, considerable sentiment also is expressed that teachers should concentrate on securing high subject-matter achievements rather than creativity. Getzels and Jackson call for more emphasis on creativity and indicate that there is discrimination by teachers against creative students in the schools generally.[17] Social studies teachers are thought by Torrance to avoid the elicitation and encouragement of most types of creative thought in their classes.[18] In our studies of creativity in Wisconsin schools, the majority of teachers at all school levels did their best to encourage creativity. They were eager to discuss practical suggestions as well as general principles and theory regarding creativity. A small minority expressed negative points of view: The primary aim of the school is to encourage mental discipline; students cannot be creative until they have mastered a vast amount of the subject matter; therefore, any attempt to encourage creativity before Ph.D. study is ineffective. We believe, however, that creative abilities should be nurtured throughout the school years. There are not any final guidelines for nurturing

---

[15] Herbert J. Klausmeier and William Wiersma, "The Effects of IQ Level and Sex on Divergent Thinking of Seventh Grade Pupils of Low, Average, and High IQ," *Journal of Educational Research*, LVIII (March, 1965), 300-302.

[16] Jacob W. Getzels and Philip W. Jackson, *Creativity and Intelligence: Explorations with Gifted Students* (New York: Wiley, 1962).

[17] *Ibid.*

[18] E. Paul Torrance, "Explorations in Creative Thinking," *Education*, LXXXI (December, 1960), 216-220.

the creative abilities of high school students. However, a few "Do's" and "Don'ts" may be accepted tentatively:

Do	Don't
Encourage students to express their ideas in many forms: art, music, drama, dance	Confine student expression to the verbal—nothing but words and other symbols
Emphasize divergent abilities such as fluency, originality, flexibility	Enforce conformity to only one way of proceeding or only to activities where one correct answer is accepted
Encourage expression of emotional sensitivity; independence; self-confidence with the new; and questioning traditions	Do not try to mold every student into the same "middle-class" personality
Encourage student production of novel methods and ideas	Require and reward only the reproduction of the known and tried

Change in thought processes

Piaget's ideas about cognitive development were ignored for many years in America, in part because of his methods of research and in part because the climate of opinion here was unfavorable toward the ideas. At the present time, Piaget's work, and the related research of many others in America and England, is given serious attention by individuals and groups preparing curriculum materials and instructional programs. Recently, Flavell summarized many of the publications of Jean Piaget.[19] The ideas that follow are drawn largely from Flavell.

Among many other ideas, Piaget proposed five stages in intellectual development: sensorimotor, birth to 2 years of age; preconceptual thought, 2 to 4 years; intuitive thought, 4 to 7 years; concrete operations, 7 to 11 years; and formal operations, 11 to 15 years. The year indications are only rough approximations and vary among individuals and cultures. Our interest in this book is not in the first three stages, but we must consider the relationship of concrete and formal operations.

Some of the most salient ideas about concrete and formal operations are summarized here:

[19] John H. Flavell, *The Developmental Psychology of Jean Piaget* (New York: Van Nostrand, 1963).

Designation	Age Level	Characteristics
Concrete operations	7–11	Actions can be carried out in thought but are still closely tied to concrete objects and actual situations, to the perceivable world of things and events
		Class concepts, such as of relation, weight, time, animal, and so on, are formed; further, two classes can be put together to form a superordinate class; classes can be broken down; equivalent classes can be recognized
		Relationships among perceivable things and events are formed; sequences of action forward and reversed are thought out; things can be classified according to size, amount, weight; events can be ordered according to time
		Information presented with concrete objects can be retained for considerable periods of time
Formal operations	12–15	Abstract thinking about ideas is done in the absence of things and events; ideas, second-order relationships, are manipulated
		A complete range of possibilities or hypotheses can be considered
		Application, synthesis, and evaluation of ideas not concretely presented are carried out
		Thinking of relationships among relationships is done
		Concepts are formed that are completely removed from concrete contexts; concepts such as of proportion, energy, heat, and atom occur

From the preceding it may be seen that one of the main differences between the two stages involves the ability to manipulate ideas. During the early phase of concrete operations, ideas can be manipulated only in the presence of the actual things and events and when based on immediate experiences. Later, the child can manipulate concepts, based on the concrete and immediate, but concepts that are not in the immediate context. In formal operations, ideas about ideas, second-order relationships, are manipulated in the absence of the concrete. Note that the child in the early stage of concrete operations engages in intuitive and logical thinking in connection with the concrete and immediate. Although the adolescent engages in these also, he has acquired the higher intellectual capability of manipulating abstract relationships directly, which the child in concrete operations cannot perform.

We should not think of these stages as differentiated sharply by chronological age or unrelated to the experience and capabilities of the child. According to Ausubel and Ausubel, the stage concept suggests nothing more than that identifiable, qualitative differences in intellectual functioning are characteristic of the two broad age levels.[20] We should expect differences in age levels among children and youth of the various nations of the world and also among groups within our country. Furthermore, there are differences within the same individual among the various subject fields. It is entirely possible that if science instruction is emphasized with attention on learning scientific concepts, and if social studies concepts are not taught, the student will function at the concrete level in social studies and at the abstract level in science. Although this is true, we cannot teach young children abstract concepts in any subject at any age. The youngest age at which a child can deal with the abstractions of various subjects has not been finally determined. We may be certain, however, that the younger child needs more concrete experiences in order to acquire concepts than does the adolescent.

Although as a general rule children of elementary school years need more concrete experiences, junior and senior high school students also profit from concrete experiences with concepts with which they are yet unfamiliar. They also profit from problem-solving activities and inductive discovery. However, already having developed a storehouse of concepts, they can also profit from instruction that does not use so many concrete experiences. In other words, as children grow older the need for direct experiences and concrete objects should lessen rather than increase. Older students should profit increasingly from the study of printed material.

Ausubel interprets the work of Piaget, and of many American researchers, to mean that high school students will profit markedly from a verbal expository type of teaching that uses concrete and firsthand experiences mainly to clarify abstract ideas, rather than to generate concepts intuitively. He would eliminate laboratory exercises that require the student to manipulate materials to arrive at concepts already specified by someone else. He summarizes thus: "There is a good reason for believing, therefore, that much of the time spent in cookbook laboratory exercises in the sciences could be much more advantageously employed in formulating precise definitions, making explicit verbal distinctions between concepts, generalizing from hypothetical situations, etc."[21] Ausubel ap-

---

[20] David Ausubel and Pearl Ausubel, "Cognitive Development in Adolescence," *Review of Educational Research*, Vol XXXVI, No. 4 (October, 1966), 410.

[21] *Ibid.* By permission.

parently assumes that much prior concept learning has occurred in connection with concrete experiences, that prior education was not exclusively verbal or symbolic.

The preceding discussions regarding abilities and thought processes indicate that adolescence is a period during which much subject matter can be learned efficiently. Many students are making tremendous gains in knowledge and are developing a variety of intellectual abilities. A continuing challenge to the conscientious teacher is to find adequate materials and to use methods that will be effective with a larger proportion of our youth.

DEVELOPING A WELL-INTEGRATED PERSONALITY

Manifestations of an integrated personality in young adulthood include behaviors implied in the preceding discussions of the six main topics. Physical, social, emotional, economic, and intellectual maturity are indicated as the goals that adolescents seek and toward which education should be directed. Normal development in all these areas lays the basis for a well-integrated personality. Normal, however, is not a fixed modal behavior because individual patterns of development vary markedly. Different patterns of development, which result in different adjustments, are indicated in the lives of Vera, Lena, and Bernice:

Vera

Vera had a twinkle in her eyes and a smile that radiated enthusiasm for life and living. Nothing, it seemed, would bother her for long, and everything seemed to interest her. Immaculate in her grooming, confident, poised, and mature, Vera was pleasant to meet. "A sweet girl," one teacher said. "There seems little more to say."

Life was wonderful to Vera, and school was one of the wonderful things about life. She liked every subject she took, and only once did she indicate even a least-liked course. . . .

At the time Vera was completing the senior year in high school, she became engaged to her friend of some years' standing who was being graduated from the university as a teacher of music. Because it appeared that he would soon be drafted into the armed forces, they decided that while he was in the service it would be better for both if Vera took a job instead of going to college. With his savings and her earnings, they thought that they could save enough to start a home when he returned.

Lena

Lena was a neat, well-scrubbed little girl from a farm who was exceptionally enthusiastic about things agricultural. Nothing in Lena's behavior was put on for effect. . . . Her two greatest disappointments were that she had not done as well in high school as she had in a rural school ("because I spent too much time reading") and that the study of veterinary medicine seemed impossible for her. She was the youngest student in her class, but the adjustments which that situation required were made easily. . . .

A change in family fortunes, attributed to increases in cattle prices, and an opinion by an educator that Lena was not too young for college caused the family to change its plans, and Lena registered in the course in home economics at the state university. She reported that "so far" she liked it very much.

Bernice

Bernice is living with her mother-in-law. I scaled a fifteen-foot muddy embankment up to this little run-down house. Apparently there is a more accessible route from the rear. Bernice required very little explanation. I asked her how long she had been out of school.

"I quit two weeks before the end of school a year ago. I was only fifteen at the time but I talked to Mr. McCoy (principal). He said that they wouldn't come get me because I would be sixteen before fall. I just didn't take the exams. I knew I wouldn't pass anyway because I didn't do any work except in typing. I really loved typing. It seems I didn't like all of my teachers. I got kicked out of English six times. Me and the teacher couldn't get along. I don't think half the kids liked her. She talked about the same thing for about a week and you didn't learn anything. Then she would spend the whole period with one kid. I took a dislike to her the first two days. I guess I could have gotten along with her but after that I didn't try. And then I just didn't understand general math I suppose because I don't understand arithmetic. I love it but I don't get it. I just love fractions, but those reading problems, I could never get those all the way through school. I was really going to go all the way through Home Ec because I liked it, but then my schedule was changed so I could be in a different gym class. They said they wanted to break up a gang of us girls because we were beating all the other teams and smarting off a lot. Then I got changed to a gym class with a lot of these high class girls, as we call them. They think they are better than everyone else. They got a lot of money. They don't like us and we don't like them. When my class was changed, I didn't even dress for gym. So I failed that too."

"Bernice, what seems to be the rub with those high class kids?"

"Well, they seem to look down on us kids in this neighborhood. You know, they think we are scabs. You know, those kids always hung out on the east side of the building and us kids were always on the west side. Then in class, the rich kids always had their lessons. They never came without their lessons. Then if us kids didn't have ours, and we usually didn't, they would look at us. There were only two girls, Sally Clancy and Georgia Lane, that I could get along with out of that bunch. I guess it's a good thing I quit school because whenever there was any trouble, I was in the middle of it, street fights or anything else. It seems like it has been that way all my life. My temper gets me into trouble. I slap and ask questions later. That's the way my Mother and Dad were and I guess that's the way I am."[22]

More details of the change in behavior with age are obtainable from the study of individuals from infancy into young adulthood. In the first case that follows, you will note that the girl was aggressive and destructive as a child but that these behaviors dropped out during adolescence. As a young adult, she did not manifest hostility and aggressiveness because doing so would violate ideals she had formulated. In the second case, the boy changed markedly in early childhood but was more consistent from elementary into high school years:

At 2 years of age S's nursery-school behavior was often punctuated with aggressive outbursts.

"S seldom talks or shows any outward sign of emotion. She is by far the most physically bold child, doing much jumping and climbing. She often reacts to other children destructively, pushing them down, pulling out hair, and absconding with toys. . . ."

Two years later, at 4 years of age, S's nursery-school behavior was clearly competitive and aggressive.

"S was habitually aggressive, but she was not a successful leader. She was very competitive and seized every opportunity to equal or excel the feats of the other children. She liked to tease, and she had great sport with Mary and Peter, both of whom would yell or whine when she plagued them. Occasion-

---

[22] The cases of Vera and Lena are reprinted from John W. M. Rothney, *The High School Student: A Book of Cases*, copyright 1953 by Holt, Rinehart and Winston, Inc. More information about the girls is found on pp. 123–127 and 138–143 of the Rothney volume. The case of Bernice is drawn from Robert J. Havighurst, *Growing Up in River City* (New York: Wiley, 1962). By permission. More information about Bernice is found on p. 13 ff.

ally she played cooperatively with others, but more often she put herself in the role of a rival. S complied with adult requests at times, but at other times resisted with all her might. She needed to be reminded to take turns and to respect property rights. It was not because she did not know about these nursery-school principles, but rather because she could get such a rise out of other children by pushing in front of them or by snatching at their toys."

When S visited day camp at 6½, the predisposition toward unprovoked aggression was still clearly present.

"S was somewhat shy and wary in social situations and made few social advances. She was almost eager in her response when others made advances to her. She seemed to expect that she might not be accepted and was surprised and pleased when other children were nice to her. S was very easy to have around when she was busy. Sometimes in free moments she went a little wild. The other children complained that she pushed them, knocked their sand constructions down, or poked her finger in their clay work. These outbursts were over in a flash. She needed no provocation other than idleness to start her off. She never made excuses for her behavior or even admitted anything about it. S was out for her own advancement and was sort of a lone wolf. She seemed to feel no deep identification with the group or with any of its members."

During the early school years S was independent, and verbally rebellious and attacking. She was competitive with peers and began to gain some peer respect because of her daring, verbal skills and athletic prowess. By age 10 a dramatic shift occurred in her behavior. She became interested in her attractiveness to boys, and this new motive was accompanied by a sharp decrease in overt aggression. At age 10 the day-camp observer wrote:

"There has been a good deal of change in S's appearance: straightened posture, hair washed clean with French braids, and frilly, nice clothes. The big thing seems to be the big shift in S herself. She no longer needs to express her hostility and alienation toward the world. She has the possibilities of becoming a very attractive little girl. Socially S has loosened up a great deal. Though no one in this group was congenial with her, she was much more outgoing than in previous years. At the races she got to the tomboy state, loudly boasting and jeering at one girl for being so awkward. *Most of the time she had a quiet, almost demure, air about her, listening to what others had to say and smiling in a friendly fashion. . . .*"

By 12½ years this girl had adopted more completely the traditional feminine-role behaviors. The home visitor wrote:

"S has passed conspicuously into adolescence. Since the last time I saw her, her breasts have developed noticeably, and she has a very pretty figure and is becoming quite attractive. The mother told me privately that S had bought a new bathing suit, a one-piece affair, and when she tried it on for the family, her older brother gave a long, low whistle, which embarrassed her terribly. Mother shows considerable interest in S's appearance and in helping her to become attractive. She mentioned today that before school starts, she plans to take S to a hair stylist for a special cut. She also remarked that S says she wants to grow up and marry and have children, 'so that's what we're getting ready for.' "

S did very well academically in high school and college and decided to go to graduate school. On first impression S appeared quiet, reserved, and neither competitive nor aggressive. She became conflicted over an intellectual career because the required competition in graduate school threatened the self-image she was trying so hard to retain. She was sufficiently insecure about her conception of herself as a woman that intense involvement in an intellectually aggressive atmosphere made her uncomfortable. During the adult interview she tried to explain why she withdrew from graduate school.

. . .

S was a highly motivated and excellent student in elementary and high school. He received a scholarship to college, graduated valedictorian of his college class, and won a competitive fellowship to graduate school. When interviewed as an adult, he expressed a strong motivation for achievement and recognition, and he looked forward with confidence to an intellectually creative career.

However, at age 2½ S was distractible and gave no clue to his future achievements.

"S spent an unhappy first week at nursery school. He cried a great deal and looked ready to cry even when he was not actually doing it. He drew away when other children approached him as if he were afraid of them. He required much adult attention to get him to do anything. He stood around, did nothing, and looked rather lost. After the first week, he became happier and played primitively in the sand out-of-doors. He did some climbing on ladders and slid alone. *In the room, his activity was not constructive. He did a lot of wandering from room to room, and he liked to throw things: balls, colored cubes, or tin dishes.* He watched the other children a great deal, identifying himself with the play of others by laughing when they did. Despite S's lively coloring he was not a lively, dramatic child. In fact, the teachers remarked that when they were tallying up the children to see who was there, they were always most likely to forget S's presence."

Let us contrast this summary at 2½ with a nursery-school report three years later, at 5½ years of age.

"S was one of the most adult-centered children in the group. The particular quality of his relationship is hard to describe. It was on a very verbal level. He came to tell you things, show you things, act things out, and explain things. S has a very active play life. There was a constant stream of verbal descriptions, and an observer would know every minute of the time what S was doing, what technique he was using, and why he was doing it. *S seemed to have a very strong calvinist sense of needing to get things done and not wasting time.* He would say, 'In a few minutes I will be through with this.' Although he was still ineffectual in holding on to things, he had really become more skilled."

"By choosing the less coveted objects and getting into an obscure corner in which to work, he had a chance of carrying his projects through. *S seemed really happy just to be making things.* There was a great emphasis on the detail without an over-all pattern. The Christmas tree gave him a very good goal to work toward, and he did more than his share of hanging materials. At the end of the session S was one of the most jubilant in wrapping up his booty to take home."

"In his scrutiny of the books and the retelling of the stories there was an emphasis on every tiny detail; every part coming in its sequence. S often asked questions to find out where parts fit in; how this different world of nursery school was supposed to run; what peoples' ideas about things were. Once told, he would store the knowledge away for the future. S was a great storyteller; long lectures on how things worked and on events at home. S's exceedingly high standards and an inability to relate to the world are his most salient features."

At 16½ years of age he was interviewed at the Institute.

E: "Would you tell me some of the things you are interested in?"

S: "Oh—my grade standards, various forms of amateur scientific research—I like to play around with. Like down at school, every once in a while I read about something interesting that someone has done, and if facilities permit, I like to try it out."

E: "Anything else you are interested in?"

S: "Well—I read a good bit—my main format of reading is in the science fiction class. I kind of enjoy learning. Of course, I may be rather conceited, but I don't think, except in a few classes, I actually learn anything. However, it excites my interest toward discovering things for myself."

E: "Are your grades important to you?"

S: "Oh, I like to have them—I figure I should get along with a B just as well as an A, but then I don't have to work much harder to get an A, so I might a well have it."[23]

The preceding cases suggest caution in predicting behavior from one developmental level to the next and also hopefulness concerning the modifiability of human behavior, especially during adolescence. Most adolescents respond desirably to interest and helpfulness on the part of the teachers. Few are unalterably committed to lives of crime, hopelessness, or mental illness if sufficient knowledge and resources can be brought to bear upon helping them individually and if undesirable condi-

---

[23] These two cases are reprinted from Jerome Kagan and Howard A. Moss, *Birth to Maturity: A Study in Psychological Development* (New York: Wiley, 1962), pp. 112–115, 126–127. By permission.

tions in the home, neighborhood, and school can be ameliorated. A few "Do's" and "Dont's' regarding nurturing healthy personalities are worth considering:

Do	Don't
Develop an emotionally secure environment in the classroom and school, characterized by student orderliness, student respect for authority, student interest in subject matter, and high teacher interest in the students	Foster student insecurity and high stress through lack of standards of conduct and achievement, or through arbitrary and rigid rules and standards
Encourage students' self-acceptance and acceptance of others. Make sure that each student has at least one good friend in each class and that he perceives teachers and other students as helpful	Encourage chronic guilt feelings or lack of satisfaction with self through continuous high demands. Never encourage ridicule of or discrimination against one or more students by other students
Help students to attain realistic goals and to experience success. Make sure that each student learns something that you and he regard as worthwhile each day and each week	Set unattainable standards that result in repeated failures
Use class time in any subject field to find resolution of interpersonal conflicts	Initiate or condone unresolved personal conflicts between you and the students or among the students
Recognize that one or two poor teachers can cause more "problem" students than any number of guidance counselors or psychologists can "cure." Specialists should work with teachers in order to resolve problems brought to the school, not to resolve problems created by the school and teachers	Attempt to circumvent the teacher's role in personality development through referring problem cases to others for solution; (it is possible that most high school dropouts are pushed out by the teaching staff and inadequate curricula)

We do not imply here that all difficulties encountered in school by students result from inadequate curricula, including poor teaching. Many do, however. Furthermore, as long as many teachers accept as inevitable many student failures and dropouts, we shall not secure improvement. It is possible that special schools are needed and that many new educational methods and procedures must be invented in order to meet the challenges of modern times. Teachers and others in secondary education should provide the leadership for refining traditional procedures and for inventing better procedures and material that will enhance adolescent development.

SUMMARY

In recent decades, American society has witnessed the possible crystallization of a youth culture. Although some youth groups are rebellious, most adolescents are worthy young people who see the value in secondary education not only for learning subject matter but also for its role in helping them learn about themselves and others and in helping them make their way in a rapidly changing social and physical environment.

It is a complex task for the teacher to provide for the developmental needs of adolescents. In addition to helping the adolescent achieve intellectual maturity, the teacher has a responsibility for aiding the adolescent to develop in understanding and accepting his own physique, in developing satisfactory relations with agemates, in establishing more mature relations with adults, in making progress toward economic independence, and in developing a well-integrated personality.

Progress is being made as teachers and others learn how to help adolescents achieve intellectual maturity. We realize more than ever that a deprived or an abundant environment can affect our measures of general intellectual ability. The work of Guilford has shown us some of the possible abilities in the cognitive domain and has renewed interest in nurturing creative, or divergent production, abilities. Too, Piaget's ideas about cognitive development are being given serious attention by individuals and groups preparing curriculum materials and instructional programs. Thus, our conceptions of readiness for learning and of the upper limits of learning have changed markedly in recent years. And abilities in the cognitive domain are being identified and subsequently nurtured through instruction.

Although the school may not explicitly try to shape personality through an organized program of instruction, adolescents in our schools learn knowledge, skills, abilities, attitudes, motives, values, and interests that are at the very heart of personality. Because he exercises a strong, positive force in building healthy, zestful personalities, the teacher should develop an emotionally secure classroom environment, encourage the student's self-acceptance and acceptance of others, help students attain realistic goals and experience success, and help resolve interpersonal conflicts.

QUESTIONS AND ACTIVITIES

1 Why is it important that adolescents understand and accept their physique?
2 List some ways in which the classroom teacher can help the student in developing satisfactory relationships with agemates.
3 List classroom activities in your subject field that can facilitate students' attaining emotional maturity.
4 Discuss your own position on the values of the comprehensive high school.
5 What characteristics of the decades in which we live necessitate the reappraisal of vocational education?
6 To what extent do you agree with Karl Smith that the feedback effects of occupation determine the specific properties of mental health, motivation, social integration, aging, and individual behavior resources?
7 Define and give examples of each of the four contents, the six products, and the five intellectual processes specified by Guilford.
8 For the age level in which you are most interested, write a brief summary of developmental trends as indicated by Piaget. Secure further information as necessary from Flavell or from other sources.
9 Figure 15, Chapter 15, presents six bases of personality integration.
   a Rate yourself on the six bases, using an A to mean that you are particularly strong in relation to it, B to indicate moderately strong, C to indicate moderately weak, and D to indicate particularly weak.
   b Discuss the role of the teacher in each of the six, as applied to students at any level in the secondary school.

SUGGESTIONS FOR FURTHER READING

BLOOM, BENJAMIN S., *Stability and Change in Human Characteristics*, New York: Wiley, 1964.

CONANT, JAMES B., *The American High School Today*, New York: McGraw-Hill, 1959.

"Educational Programs; Adolescence," *Review of Educational Research*, XXXVI, No. 4, 1966.

FLAVELL, JOHN H., *The Developmental Psychology of Jean Piaget*, New York: Van Nostrand, 1963.

GRINDER, ROBERT E., *Studies in Adolescence*, New York: Macmillan, 1963.

MUSSEN, PAUL H., JOHN J. CONGER, AND JEROME KAGAN, *Child Development and Personality*, New York: Harper & Row, 1963.

3 Conditions of learning

$\mathcal{W}$hy does one student want to learn well whereas another does not? Why does one student remember historical events or chemistry formulas, whereas another forgets quickly? How can we get more students to want to learn, to learn well, and to remember what they learn? These are some of the concerns of critical importance to teaching and are considered in the discussions of:

1. Purposeful learning
2. Motivation
3. Cognitive learning
4. Skill learning
5. Attitudinal learning
6. Retention and transfer

In this chapter, relevant information from learning theories, research studies, and observations in school settings is presented regarding each of the categories listed.[1] The information is then summarized in the form of generalizations. Based on these generalizations, principles of teaching are stated. These generalizations and principles are intended to have wide applicability. Therefore, you should try to find applications to your own field of teaching or to your personal learning situations.

---

[1] For more comprehensive information about each of these topics, see relevant chapters in Herbert J. Klausmeier and William Goodwin, *Learning and Human Abilities: Educational Psychology*, 2nd ed. (New York: Harper & Row, 1966).

PURPOSEFUL LEARNING

The sequence in purposeful learning is shown in Figure 2. At a given stage in maturation, an individual is motivated to reach a goal. As will be shown in the later section on motivation, a student's motives arise in connection with many phenomena, including activities of the teacher.

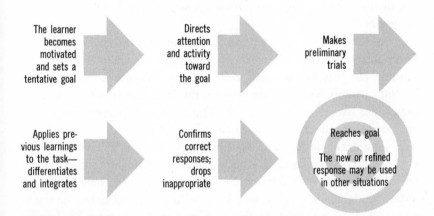

FIG. 2 *General sequence in purposeful learning.*

Once a goal is set, attention and activity are directed toward it. Preliminary trials involving overt actions and thought are made. The adolescent applies previous experiences to the task, differentiating various elements of the present situation and integrating responses into a new or higher-level response. In this process of differentiation and integration, he discards inappropriate methods, confirms the correct one, and incorporates it into a learned behavior pattern that is available for use in other situations. Mental activity is involved from beginning to end. If the student had been able to attain the goal immediately by using responses he had already acquired, he would not have learned, and his behavior pattern would have remained unchanged.

Learning shorthand provides a good illustration of these five steps:

1. The teacher gives each member of the class a shorthand pad and suggests that each student write his initials on it in shorthand so that he will know which pad is his. Although John cannot write his initials in

shorthand, his book shows the letters and the corresponding symbols. John wants to perform as well as the other students. In other words, he wants to master the situation; and the goal—writing his initials in shorthand—leads to action.

2. Now that he is motivated, John gives close attention to the task and is ready to expend energy in guiding his pencil in the proper patterns. The teacher suggests that the students open their pads and practice writing their initials on the first page. John may continue this for five or ten minutes. He learns from his attempts as long as motivation continues.

3. As John works, he resorts to intelligent trial-and-error activities to find a new way to use his pencil in writing the shorthand symbols or to improve the way he has been writing them. Because he is intelligent, he compares his symbols with those in the book and tries to make them look more like those in the book. The teacher, of course, helps John and the other students whenever they need assistance.

4. John draws on his previous learning experiences. The straight lines, circles, and arcs he has used in regular cursive writing are utilized in the present situation. As he differentiates characters and sees how the various letters can be made quickly, he learns. As he gains proficiency in writing one symbol, he moves on to the next, and soon integrates his learning of the symbols for his initials into a higher-level response. The ability to differentiate and integrate enables him to use previous learnings and to analyze the present situation more adequately. Through this process, he develops a new or improved pattern of action for writing his initials in shorthand. If he has learned efficiently, this new learning enables him to write his initials more quickly than he could in longhand.

5. In the process of differentiation and integration (this process will be used again later when he learns to join letters into syllables and into words quickly and with fewer symbols), he discards inappropriate methods. John and the other students will learn shorthand as long as they are motivated; the skill acquired in the shorthand class can be used in other situations. When he no longer wants to improve, has no further motivation, he will cease to learn. Similarly, without motivation, many college students fail to improve their handwriting, although they write more each year in college than they did during all of elementary school.

Table 3.1 shows the sequence in purposeful learning and indicates appropriate teacher actions related to each component of the sequence. The actions, stated as principles, serve as an overview of the conditions of learning that will be treated throughout the chapter. Study each of the next ten points carefully by relating the sequence in learning to something personal in your school life, such as typing or playing in an orchestra. Also, think about what the teacher did for you and your classmates to facilitate the purposeful learning sequence.

TABLE 3.1. *Teacher Actions and the Sequence in Purposeful Learning.*

Sequence in purposeful learning	Teacher actions
1. Student becomes motivated; sets goal	1. Motivates students
2. Directs attention and activity toward goal	2. Clarifies objectives; supplies models
3. Makes preliminary trials— productive thinking and physical activity	3–4. Sequences instruction; guides initial trials; manages practice; provides for individual differences
4. Applies previous learning to task	
5. Reaches goal; confirms correct response; experiences success or Does not reach goal; experiences frustration	5. Evaluates performances, corrects, counsels; provides for recall; aids in applying to new situations

1. *Motivating students* is essential for securing consistent effort. Four broad categories of behaviors may be undertaken by the teacher to motivate adolescents: (1) manipulating materials and activities to arouse curiosity and interest; (2) engaging in goal-setting procedures with the students; (3) manipulating rewards, punishments, and similar extrinsic conditions; (4) and providing knowledge of progress.

2. *Clarifying objectives of instruction* facilitates goal-setting and efficient learning by the student. Because society indicates through the school and the teacher what students should learn, realistic goal-setting by students is possible only insofar as instructional objectives are clear to them. This clarification of objectives should specify the type of performance expected of the student so that he has sufficient knowledge to appraise the situation, including means-goals relationships.

3. *Supplying a model*—actual persons, verbal descriptions of procedures, and representations by audio-visual means—facilitates the learn-

ing of responses that are new to the learner, responses he has not yet made. For example, the adolescent who has never spoken Spanish profits from hearing new vocabulary pronounced by the teacher. He may also learn from observing the teacher's movements and expressions. By observing a model, many of the student's incorrect preliminary trials are eliminated.

4. *Guiding initial trials* aids in the establishment of correct responses and the avoidance of habitual errors. Words, physical contact, or demonstration may be used. Early guidance directs the learner's attention to more adequate skills or knowledge, aids him in understanding the nature of a successful performance, provides encouragement to continue, and relieves the possible anxiety that may appear if he is uncertain about his ability to perform the task.

5. *Sequencing of the subject matter* enables the student to cognize information initially, think productively about it, remember it, and use it in new situations. Logical organization of the subject matter results in a hierarchical, topical sequence. Psychological organization is based upon conditions under which material is learned efficiently. These two types of organization may be identical; however, the sequencing of subject matter has not been studied intensively until very recently. Lack of knowledge about sequence and organization makes the student's appraisal of means-goals relationships and initial trials difficult.

6. *Managing practice effectively* is essential to goal attainment in both the psychomotor and cognitive domains and to improved performance in most subject fields. Most practice usually requires both productive thinking and physical activity. A teacher can manipulate whole-part relationships, the length and spacing of practice sessions, reinforcements, knowledge of progress, and other conditions to make practice effective.

7. *Providing for individual differences* is necessary so that each student reaches his goal and learns efficiently in the process. Two practices that facilitate individualization are becoming increasingly common in the schools: Grouping students to secure greater homogeneity in relation to learning tasks, and improving materials and physical arrangements for independent study. In some schools, adolescents are being arranged into instructional groups that do not depend on age and grade level, such instructional groupings as have been used for many years in music and athletic activities. Also, individual study booths are provided

wherein each student has available a variety of instructional materials suited to his rate of learning.

8. *Evaluating student performance* can help in reinforcing desirable learning. Informing students of their progress and aiding them to overcome errors facilitates learning because it provides encouragement to continue and eliminates inadequate or incorrect responses. Lack of progress and a simultaneous failure in reading goals are principal contributors to a student's losing his zest for learning and his interest in subject matter and schooling.

9. *Providing for recall and long-term retention through systematic verbal material and the spaced practice of skills* is essential. One way of providing review and practice is to elicit from students the necessary information and skills that are needed to perform a novel task. The novel tasks may be arranged on a daily basis so that there is cumulative improvement. The procedure that utilizes cumulative tasks produces more permanent learning than does holding one review or practice session immediately prior to a monthly or semester examination.

10. *Helping students apply knowledge and skills in new situations* facilitates both long-term retention and use. A verbal description of applications is less effective than actual situations in which new knowledge and skills can be put to use. The great loss in learning from one year to the next and the inability to cross from one subject to another or from a school situation to an out-of-school situation often results from the lack of opportunities to apply new knowledge and skills.

The teacher's actions, as well as the sequence in purposeful learning, will become clearer to you as you read the next sections. You may find it effective to study one section at a time and then review each section in relation to Table 3.1. It is good practice to try to recall the main points after reading each section.

MOTIVATION

Many students want to learn what the school and the teacher desire, and they also have the ability to perform the desired tasks efficiently. But some students are forced to go to school when they do not desire to go; some do not want to learn what the schools want them to learn, at least not when and as the teacher desires; and some students cannot perform the required learning tasks. Furthermore, in some classrooms, motivation for learning is exceedingly low among most adolescents, whereas in other classes of the same school, it is high. In this section, the point of view is that the school and the teacher should organize and manipulate the physical and social environment so that most students want to learn, are confident that they can learn what the teacher desires, and believe that what they learn is worthwhile for them.

We are properly concerned with what the teacher can do to increase the motivation of students. Discussions can be held with the class, printed material and various audio-visual material can be used, and activities in addition to discussion can be engaged in so that students determine in part what is to be learned. The situation can be organized so that the students' biological and social needs are satisfied. In turn, the satisfaction of higher-level needs, such as the needs to know and understand and to achieve mastery over things, including subject matter, takes precedence. Rewards and punishments, cooperation and competition, and other external incentives can be manipulated. The learning activities can be made more meaningful to the students. Prestigeful exemplary models can be provided for imitation. This brief overview of what is meant by organizing and manipulating the physical and social environment to enhance motivation will be clarified in the subsequent discussion.

Sears and Hilgard indicate that the teacher has a number of choices in connection with motivation:

> The significance of motivation for learning is usually assumed without question. On the one hand, the promise of reward or the threat of punishment provides means by which the teacher can keep the pupil at work; on the other hand, interest, curiosity, and self-selected goals keep the learner at work without pressure from the teacher. The teacher has a choice between using specific goals or enlisting self-activating motives or perhaps employing some combination of these.[2]

This point of view is similar to ours except that we would add that the teacher must be prepared to apply different principles with different

---

[2] Pauline S. Sears and Ernest R. Hilgard, "The Teacher's Role in the Motivation of the Learner," *Theories of Learning and Instruction*, Ernest R. Hilgard, ed., Yearbook for the National Society for the Study of Education, LXIII, Part I (Chicago: University of Chicago Press, 1964), p. 182. By permission.

children. The principles that follow are not exhaustive; rather, only the more important ones are listed opposite the generalization.

Generalization	Principle
Because certain objectives are to be achieved, the students' attention must be directed toward those objectives	Focus student attention on desired objectives
Positive motives—curiosity, interest, and achievement—can be aroused	Encourage the development of positive motives
Setting and attaining goals encourage consistent effort, thereby permitting knowledge of progress and feelings of success to operate effectively	Help students to set and attain realistic goals
Continued effort and favorable attitudes toward learning are promoted by a warm, business-like environment	Create a warm, orderly atmosphere
Rewards are effective with some students in initiating and directing behavior; punishment may suppress undesirable behavior	Provide incentives; and punish, if necessary

Focus attention on desired goals

Many elements of the physical environment of the classroom can be manipulated to direct student attention toward the objectives. Here is how the teacher of an eighth-grade general science class began a unit on electrical current, the second unit on electricity:

> On this table we have three objects: a bar magnet, a coil made from insulated wire, and a galvanometer that measures electric current. I'm going to connect the ends of the coil to the galvanometer. Now watch the needle of the galvanometer as I pass the magnet through the coil and then back again. What is happening that makes the galvanometer react?

In geography, a beginning teacher described attempts to focus attention on a study of Japan:

> The first day of the unit the students walked into an environment that contained many Japanese objects. In the front of the room was a wall map of Japan and a travel poster. Bulletin boards were filled with pictures of Japan. Some of the many products made in Japan were on the table in the front of the room. Few students were in their seats when the bell rang. Students were raising questions; but instead of answering, I asked more questions. Every student was interested in trying to identify and name the products made in Japan.

These examples show that pupil attention can be focused through the use of materials and activities that involve a number of sensory perceptions. To focus class attention toward the desired outcomes, it is essential to appeal to more than one sense, because the usual class always has some students who respond better to visual material than to spoken words. The teacher takes a positive role in order to make certain that the necessary materials are arranged and available; in addition, he decides whether or not, once their attention has been generally directed toward a learning outcome, the students will begin studying from books directly or will engage with him in planning activities.

Encourage the development of positive motives

The needs to know, to understand, and to achieve are powerful motives because they direct activity toward some end. One does not have to deprive the individual of his biological, safety, love and belonging, or esteem needs in order for these other needs to take over in guiding and directing behavior. In fact, the biological needs must be satisfied before these higher level needs—to know, to understand, and to achieve—related to learning can operate.

Representative of positive motives are curiosity and interest. Human beings are curious about many objects and phenomena in the environment. However, curiosity is generally expressed toward new and novel objects, ideas, and events rather than toward familiar ones. The arousal of curiosity is not dependent on any form of reward or punishment, nor is it attached to any specific drive situation, such as hunger or thirst. Also, after an object, idea, or material is no longer novel, it loses its curiosity value. Novel ideas and material can be used purposefully to arouse curiosity. Any other activity or goal-setting connected with the unit of work is then designed to capitalize upon the curiosity aroused.

Interests in activities serve as positive motives. To find out about students' interests, one may ask them which of several classroom activities they prefer most. Even though they might not be highly interested in any activity, giving students a choice may itself encourage interest. When students feel that subsequent instructional arrangements will be based upon their own stated interests, they express themselves freely and reliably. In high school and college, expressed interests are frequently used as a basis for dividing classes into smaller groups. When four or five different activities are to be undertaken, the entire class is invited to express interest in the activities; and then subgroups are arranged accordingly. Underlying interest-grouping is the idea that motivation is higher when the students are working on activities that attract and hold their attention.

When a person sets a goal, he tries to attain it. The attainment of goals is accompanied by feelings of success. Nothing encourages continued effort and further realistic goal-setting more effectively than a backlog of goals successfully attained.

Individual goal-setting proceeds like this in a beginning typewriting class. All students start at the same point—not being able to type—and engage in the usual instruction and demonstration procedures, including distributed practices to increase speed and accuracy. Six or more weeks might be needed to attain any competence. Once a beginning is made and the students know their speed and accuracy, each sets the goal he expects to attain one week hence in terms of number of words per minute and number of errors on a timed test. At the end of the week, the timed tests are used to ascertain the extent to which the goal is achieved. After this first experience, the student should set a more realistic goal for the following week. After several experiences in goal-setting at weekly intervals, more distant goals of two or more weeks in the future are appropriate. Along the way, the teacher continuously acquires better estimates of the students' abilities and helps them raise or lower goals as the situation demands. At the end of the year, we might properly anticipate that some students would set and achieve goals in terms of a speed two or three times higher than others.

In a seminar for talented high school seniors, each student set goals for the semester; no one set the same goal. One girl set a goal of writing children's literature. After identifying a vast amount of children's literature during the first weeks, she started to read and study it and to try out some selections with neighborhood children with guidance from her teacher. Upon becoming better acquainted with the literature, she had to readjust her goal in the early part of the semester to complete more of the reading. After spending much time in these activities, she then started her first writing. Here the teacher helped her both to state her goal clearly and to make progress toward achieving it. In the same seminar, another student set the goal of getting a better understanding of "beatnik" literature. After reading several novels, she found difficulty in understanding and evaluating them. The teacher then helped her develop criteria and locate critical reviews on the "beatnik" movement and on the specific novels.

These two examples show that class activities and discussions led by the teacher, smaller-group discussion led by the teacher or by designated pupil chairmen, and individual conferences between the teacher and pupil are essential for implementing purposeful and efficient learning based upon goal-setting.

Create a warm, orderly atmosphere

Warm, businesslike, imaginative teacher behavior is associated with high and consistent pupil achievement and high emotional security. Inconsistent student achievement and low achievement for insecure children are associated with sentimental and unplanned teacher behavior. Low achievement in rebellious students and low emotional security in most children is associated with aloof and routine teacher behavior. The association of lower and higher achievement with certain kinds of teacher behavior involves motivation. A few examples will clarify this point.

In classes led by punitive and nonpunitive teachers, children were asked about pupil misconduct. Those who had the punitive teachers were less concerned about learning and school values than were the children whose teachers were nonpunitive. Also, children under punitive teachers manifested more aggression in their misconduct and were more unsettled about misconduct.[3] In a study by Reed, the personal warmth of the teacher and student interest in science were also highly related.[4]

A warm, nuturing environment without teacher-domination fosters creativity better than does a nonsupportive environment with teacher-domination. Formal group instruction in which shame was used as

---

[3] Jacob S. Kounin and Paul V. Gump, "The Comparative Influence of Punitive and Non-Punitive Teachers Upon Children's Concepts of School Misconduct," *Journal of Educational Psychology*, LII (February, 1961), 44–49.

[4] Horace B. Reed, "Implications for Science Education of a Teacher Competence Research," *Science Education*, XLVI (December, 1962), 473–486.

punishment had a negative relation with creativity.[5] On the other hand, Sears reported that the teacher's manifesting interest in the student's ideas and listening to the student was positively correlated with creativity.[6]

Provide incentives and punish if necessary

Adults as well as children seek concrete and symbolic rewards. Promised rewards serve the purpose of getting people to perform inherently unpleasant tasks. If the tasks were pleasant or undertaken to achieve important goals, no rewards would be necessary. Rewards used in the schools are of two main types: concrete and symbolic. Concrete rewards take the form of money, prizes, special privileges, and the like. Symbolic rewards include letter grades, favorable comments, nonmonetary awards, and others.

Keeping rewards small and giving them early in the learning situation gets initial effort started on inherently meaningful learning tasks, and the learner associates the pleasantness of receiving the reward with the task. Furthermore, as progress in the task is made, the accompanying experiences of success and knowledge of progress may make continuing rewards unnecessary. Students cannot always evaluate their own responses without help and need confirmation of correct or appropriate responses. For example, one group of students received its test papers back corrected and was given five minutes to go over them. The second group did not have its papers returned. One week later, the test was again administered to the students. The results were clear-cut and decisive. Students who were given the opportunity to inspect their papers scored considerably higher, one week later, than did those who did not inspect their papers.[7]

[5] Robert L. Spaulding, *Achievement, Creativity, and Self-Concept Correlates of Teacher-Pupil Transactions in Elementary Schools,* U.S. Office of Education Cooperative Research Project No. 1352 (Urbana: University of Illinois Press, 1963).

[6] Pauline S. Sears, *The Effect of Classroom Conditions on Strength of Achievement Motive and Work Output of Elementary-School Children,* U.S. Office of Education Cooperative Research Project No. 873 (Stanford, Calif.: Stanford University Press, 1963).

[7] Letha Plowman and James B. Stroud, "Effect of Informing Pupils of the Correctness of Their Responses to Objective Test Questions," *Journal of Educational Research,* XXXVI (September, 1942), 16–20.

Similarly, 74 teachers administered whatever test would next occur in the usual course of instruction. The students, unaware of any experimentation, were randomly assigned to one of three experimental treatments: one third had their tests returned with no teacher comments; another third, with free teacher comments (that is, with comments that were natural and appropriate for the particular students concerned); and the final third of the pupils had their tests returned with specified, but generally encouraging, teacher comments. In their next objective exam, the free-comment group scored significantly high and the no-comment group significantly low. Thus, appropriate and natural teacher comments had a facilitating effect on student motivation.[8]

The teacher must be alert in using rewards, for pupils are indeed different. Differential effects of material and nonmaterial rewards have been noted on children of lower and middle social class.[9] Nonmaterial rewards were quite effective with pupils of middle social class, but ineffective with pupils of lower social class.

Rewards can be used more reliably than punishments. Punishments may, however, be used at times in connection with suppressing misbehavior and eliciting desired behavior. If punishments are used, certain procedures are apparently more effective than others. For example, the punishment should be continued until the misbehavior ceases and the desired behavior is manifested. Thus, if a student misbehaves, a privilege may be withdrawn or an unpleasant stimulus may be administered until the misbehavior ceases and the desired behavior is manifested. Also, punishment that comes early in the sequence of misbehavior is more effective than one following long after the misbehavior has ceased. Finally, the type of behavior, as well as the form of punishment, bears careful analysis.

Students distinguish between two types of disapproval by teachers: Disapproval of inadequate performance and disapproval when the student has done his best.[10] The former has a favorable effect on

---

[8] Ellis B. Page, "Teacher Comments and Student Performance: A Seventy-four Classroom Experiment in School Motivation," *Journal of Educational Psychology*, XLIX (August, 1958), 173–181.

[9] Glenn Terrell, Jr., Kathryn Durkin, and Melvin Wiesley, "Social Class and the Nature of the Incentive in Discrimination Learning," *Journal of Abnormal and Social Psychology*, LIX (September, 1959), 270–272.

[10] Howard Rosenfeld and Alvin Zander, "The Influence of Teachers on Aspirations of Students," *Journal of Educational Psychology*, LII (February, 1961), 1–11.

motivation, whereas the latter has a detrimental effect. Similarly, an indiscriminate bestowal of rewards by the teacher minimizes the teacher's influence, whereas rewards given only for adequate performances increase the teacher's influence.

In summary, the widespread use of concrete and symbolic rewards as motivational devices is questionable. However, when a teacher cannot get pupils to perform worthwhile learning tasks by other means, it is better to use rewards than to use punishments. We cannot simply allow students to sit day after day in the classroom without making any effort to learn. Thus, it is essential to develop a system of rewards and punishments that will work effectively. We cannot permit adolescents to control us. We have enough knowledge to control them but must put it to use judiciously.

COGNITIVE LEARNING

Most subject matter is comprised of factual information and concepts. When organized systematically, the concepts and information constitute the knowledge of a discipline. In addition to content, there are also abilities to be nurtured in the cognitive domain. These abilities can be classified in many ways; but two of the more important groups can be designated as problem-solving and creative abilities.

Generalization	Principle
Relating the new material to be learned to an already existing cognitive structure (what is already known) facilitates acquisition and retention of the new material	Use advance organizers
Concepts are extended through active searching, including their application to new situations	Encourage and guide student discovery
Problem-solving is enhanced through perceiving relationships among the elements of a total situation	Organize problem situations that encourage insight
The nurture of creative abilities requires both cognitive and personality development	Foster divergent production; foster a creative personality

The subsequent outline of generalizations and principles pinpoints some of the most reliable information regarding cognitive learning. You will observe that the direction of the learning outcomes—factual information, concepts, problem-solving, and creativity—moves from the simple to the complex. The generalizations and principles also move in the same direction; and, thus, they can all be considered as primarily applicable to cognitive, rather than psychomotor or attitudinal, learning.

Use advance organizers and sequence material properly

Let us designate as factual that information presented to students in books, lectures, motion pictures, and the like that teachers accept as correct and want the student to accept as correct. With these modes of presentation, the student does not secure an answer independently as when solving a problem. The answer is provided. For example, dictionaries give the correct spelling, pronunciation, and definition of words; atlases give locations and directions; textbooks give historical information; motion pictures present actual sequences as they occurred, and so on.

Suppose that one has little knowledge about a field and is to learn new material. What can be done to facilitate the learning? According to Ausubel, studying material of higher generality and inclusiveness than the new material provides an organizational framework for the new material and facilitates learning.[11] In one experiment, two specially prepared, sequentially related passages dealing with the endocrinology of pubescence were to be learned by college students who did not know this subject matter.[12] A control group was given a 500-word introductory passage dealing with uniformity and variability among different cultures in the behavioral aspects of pubescence. This material supposedly would not serve as an advance organizer. The experimental group was given an expository organizer (advance organizer) of 500 words that provided an organizational framework for the first passage in terms of the different kinds of uniformity and variability prevailing

[11] David P. Ausubel, *The Psychology of Meaningful Verbal Learning* (New York: Grune & Stratton, 1963).

[12] David P. Ausubel and Donald Fitzgerald, "Organizer, General Background, and Antecedent Learning Variables in Sequential Verbal Learning," *Journal of Educational Psychology*, LIII (December, 1962), 243–249.

among the primary and secondary sex characteristics. This organizing material was pitched at a higher level of abstraction, generality, and inclusiveness than the subsequent new material. As was predicted, the experimental group receiving the appropriate advance organizer learned the new material better. Thus, an advance organizer works when the learner has little previous knowledge about the new material.

The advance organizer can also function as transitional material to relate new material to old.[13] A comparative type of organizer was used that delineated clearly and precisely the main similarities and differences between material to be learned for the first time (about Buddhism) and knowledge already acquired (about Christianity). The students who studied the comparative material, couched in a high level of abstractness and generality, learned and remembered the new material on Buddhism better than did students who studied a historical introduction to Buddhism. The learning and retention of the unfamiliar verbal material was facilitated when the unfamiliar material was discriminated from previously learned material.

Preparing an advance organizer requires considerable practice. The substantive content is selected on the basis of its suitability for interrelating the material it precedes with what has already been learned. The content of the organizer is also more abstract and more general than that which it precedes or follows. In this way, the advance organizer provides the learner with a general overview of the more detailed material that follows. It also provides more inclusive organizing elements that take into account the particular content of the material to be learned. There is no final answer as to how frequently advance organizers of this type should be used. However, if one thinks of a body of material for a semester or year as being organized into a series of related units, one would probably start the instruction with an organizer for the total material and would also start each unit with a comparative organizer that would enable the student to differentiate and compare ideas between the unit just completed and the one to be studied.[14]

---

13 David P. Ausubel and Donald Fitzgerald, "The Role of Discriminability in Meaningful Verbal Learning and Retention," *Journal of Educational Psychology*, LII (October, 1961), 266–274.

14 David P. Ausubel, "A Transfer of the Training Approach to Improving the Functional Retention of Medical Knowledge," *Journal of Medical Education*, XXXVII (July, 1962), Part II, 647–655.

Encourage and guide student discovery

A trend away from rote learning in favor of so-called *discovery learning* is under way. The University of Illinois Committee on School Mathematics,[15] the School Mathematics Study Group,[16] and the Chemical Education Material Study[17] emphasize a type of textbook, film, and other instructional material from which students are to discover generalizations and concepts. Millions of dollars are going into the preparation of these materials that supposedly assist students in discovery. These programs, however, in no sense intend for the student to proceed without instruction. At least three features are usually incorporated into these and other programs:

1. Bringing to the students a problem that is real and meaningful
2. Encouraging and guiding students in gathering information
3. Providing a responsive environment in which students get accurate feedback promptly so that they can ascertain the adequacy of their responses[18]

Also, the attempt is made to sequence the printed instructional material so that students are guided into arriving at only the correct concept or generalization, not an incorrect one discovered independently.

When these procedures are carried out, the instructional environment is highly controlled, and the objective is to get the student to learn what mankind already knows about a given discipline. The main difference between discovery method and other methods is that other methods often give the answer before the student has had an opportunity to find it himself. Features of the discovery method that encourage the student to raise questions and to find his own answers increase temporary motivation for learning; facilitate initial learning, retention, and subse-

---

[15] Max Beberman, "An Emerging Program of Secondary School Mathematics," in Robert W. Heath, ed. *New Curricula* (New York: Harper & Row, 1964), pp. 9–34.

[16] William Wooton, "The History and Status of the School Mathematics Study Group," in Robert W. Heath, *ibid.*, pp. 35–53.

[17] J. A. Campbell, "CHEM Study—An Approach to Chemistry Based on Experiments," in Robert W. Heath, *ibid.*, pp. 82–93.

[18] Joseph R. Suchman, "The Child and the Inquiry Process," in A. Harry Passow, ed., *Intellectual Development: Another Look* (Washington, D.C.: Association for Supervision and Curriculum Development, 1964), pp. 59–77.

quent use of concepts; and may also result in a permanent attitude of inquiry toward learning.

What is really meant by guiding independent activity, or the discovery process? Does giving students some information about the structure of the subject matter, about a strategy or a principle to use in securing information facilitate concept learning? The answer to these questions is *"yes."*[19] Giving students information about a principle for arriving at answers to problems and for understanding material has had a uniform history of securing better initial learning than having the students proceed completely independently.[20]

The varying degrees of direction result in more efficient initial learning, retention, and subsequent use under certain conditions; but these conditions require more study. Previous knowledge of the student, his previous strategies or methods of learning, his attitudes toward independent learning, the subject-matter field, the general climate for learning in the school, and the methods of the teacher are all related to the extent to which freedom for independent discovery operates effectively.[21] Balance is required between giving too much information and direction and giving too much freedom and responsibility. How much to help, when to help, and in what way to help require decision-making by the teacher in the immediate situation.

Organize problem situations that encourage insight

The developmental sequence in purposeful learning outlined previously in this chapter is essentially a model for building problem-solving abilities. Insightful solutions can be attained by following the model. Insight is the mental process by which a person perceives a relationship between the parts of a problem; it enables him to solve a problem that

---

[19] Herbert J. Klausmeier, Chester W. Harris, and William Wiersma, *Strategies of Learning and Efficiency of Concept Attainment by Individuals and Groups,* U.S. Office of Education Cooperative Research Project No. 1442 (Madison: University of Wisconsin Press, 1964).

[20] Bert Y. Kersh and Merlin C. Wittrock, "Learning by Discovery: An Interpretation of Recent Research," *Journal of Teacher Education,* XIII (December, 1962), 461–468.

[21] Merlin C. Wittrock, "The Learning by Discovery Hypothesis," a paper read at the Conference on Learning by Discovery, New York, January, 1965.

previously was not solvable. Once insight is attained, the learning can be applied in new situations without additional practice.

Constructing one triangle identical to another provides a good illustration of the role of insight in problem-solving. The student has a protractor, a ruler, a pencil, and the given triangle. He is to construct another triangle identical to the one he has. After some experimentation, he perceives that measuring the base and the two adjacent angles of the given triangle and constructing another triangle having the same base and adjacent angles produces an identical triangle. He has perceived all the elements in the problem—materials, methods, solution, and the relationships of all the elements. When he perceives these relationships, he gains insight into the solution of the problem; and he can thereafter construct identical triangles with little or no practice.

Insight in problem-solving challenges "blind" trial-and-error learning and meaningless repetition. Trial-and-error learning, as often interpreted, implies searching for an answer and coming upon it accidentally. In the classroom, trial-and-error learning occurs when students work on problems, first one way and then another, until a chance activity leads to the solution. Insight means that the pupil purposefully directs his activities toward solving the problem, applies his previous learnings, experiments with the most reasonable hypotheses that might lead to a solution, and discovers a solution that works. In this case, the solution is the product not of chance factors or of blind searching, but of intelligent activity directed toward perceiving relations and toward organizing them in a unified response.

Insight poses a challenge for drill that is based on one of two assumptions: That formal drill should precede perceiving solutions, or that drill provides a means of acquiring understandings. In the example involving the identical triangles, suppose the teacher drilled the pupil in the separate steps required in constructing identical triangles before the student gained insight into the whole procedure. It is entirely possible that the student might go through all of the steps—measuring the base and the adjacent angles and plotting the triangle step by step—without grasping the procedure as a whole. Many students who can prove the Pythagorean theorem perfectly, step by step, cannot use this knowledge to compute the length of a brace for a stairway.

The degree to which insight operates in problem-solving depends on such factors as mental maturity, previous related learning, and the way the problem is presented. Teachers can do a great deal to organize learning activities so that relationships are readily perceived.

Foster divergent production

As indicated previously in Chapter 2, creative abilities, such as fluency, originality, and flexibility, do not imply lawlessness or lack of values. But they do indicate a readiness to make changes in behavior to meet circumstances that have not been met satisfactorily previously or an ability to cope with completely new circumstances. In connection with increasing knowledge, we are constantly meeting situations for which we have no known means of responding productively. We must foster divergent production, rather than teach only one strategy of learning or method of proceeding as the correct one.

Teaching only one method as correct has done much to block divergent production. For example, many athletic records stood for years simply because coaches generally agreed that there was only one proper or correct form for such things as putting the shot, shooting a basketball, running the mile, running the 100-yard dash, and the like. Fairly static top limits were expected for decades. Then, a coach permitted a young man to follow his own method in putting the shot, and very soon the record went up markedly. Basketball players were encouraged to start shooting one-handed, and a much higher percent of accuracy emerged. The forward pass greatly changed the character of football. To give examples from another area of learning, over many years a given content and methodology of oil painting was observed. Eventually, some nonconforming individuals broke away from this tradition, and soon we had different forms and content in art. American composers required many years to depart from the style and general form of the composers of Western Europe. Once a break was made, new forms of uniquely American music emerged.

Foster a creative personality

Cognitive abilities have been emphasized in the previous discussion. These abilities do not develop, however, unrelated to the personality of the individuals, as was indicated before in Chapter 2.

Adjectives such as *conforming, conventional,* and *dependent* do not appear in the research as traits of creative individuals. *Impulsive, sensitive, self-confident, independent,* and *unconventional* do. We need to examine our own attitudes to decide which of these characteristics in students are associated with warm and accepting behavior on our part. It is clear, too, that creative individuals are not lawbreakers, seeking to destroy values and mores that have been decades and centuries in building. Creative individuals are, however, more questioning of traditions, less inclined to consider all the possible outcomes before acting, and less concerned about how others regard them. We must encourage a wider range of approved behavior patterns than we do at the present time in order for the creative student to feel relatively comfortable in the school.

SKILL LEARNING

A skill refers to a combination of actions by which a task is performed. For example, writing cursively, hitting a golf ball, typing, and playing the piano are psychomotor skills. Performing arithmetic operations correctly, spelling accurately, and reading rapidly are also skills. However, the latter involve only a low level of motor activity and are often referred to as verbal skills. The generalizations and principles that follow are applicable to all kinds of skills. Inasmuch as we have already indicated principles for cognitive learning, we shall focus this discussion on the noncognitive aspects of skill-learning. As may be inferred from the following generalizations and principles, practice is of high concern in skill learning.

Generalization	Principles
Strategies to guide the learning of skills can be formulated and communicated to students	Guide initial responses
Properly executed practice facilitates skill learning through eliminating errors and strengthening correct responses	Arrange for appropriate practice
Feedback facilitates skill learning by providing knowledge of results	Provide knowledge of results and help correct errors

Guide initial responses

Oral or written instructions to the student can be used to describe the final performance desired, to indicate the abilities necessary to perform the task, to outline a strategy or method of attack for developing the skill, and to clarify previous achievements related to the task. In skill learning, the attempt is often made to incorporate a strategy for learning the skill into a set of instructions.[22] Instructions are effective with both motor and verbal skills.

Davies used verbal instructions with a psychomotor skill, and the instructions proved helpful to the students.[23] An experimental group was taught an accepted technique of shooting a bow and arrow and was referred to as the tuition group. The experimenter gave the tuition group the verbal instructions, describing the nature of the skill and strategies for improving performance. The subjects in the control group were given only the necessary equipment and minimum safety instructions, and thereafter they proceeded on their own. At the end of the semester, the tuition group performed better than the control group. Differences favoring the tuition group were apparent early in the semester and became greater as practice progressed. The control group acquired an inefficient method and stayed with it during successive class periods even though progress was poor. In at least three ways, the instructions aided the students: By directing the learners' attention to more adequate techniques than those they had acquired and had been employing; by promoting intellectual insight into the factors related to success; and by providing a feeling of security and confidence in relinquishing a familiar mode of behavior and seeking a more effective one. These three conclusions indicate the main purposes for providing guidance of the learner's activities while he is developing a skill.

Arrange for appropriate practice

That practice is essential to the improvement of skills is a truism. However, the conscientious teacher raises many questions concerning

---

[22] George A. Miller, Eugene Galanter, and Karl H. Pribram, *Plans and the Structure of Behavior* (New York: Holt, Rinehart and Winston, 1960).

[23] Dorothy R. Davies, "The Effect of Tuition upon the Process of Learning A Complex Motor Skill," *Journal of Educational Psychology*, XXXVI (September, 1945), 352–365.

desirable conditions of practice. Whole-part arrangements, the context in which the skills are practiced, variety of methods, and distributing practice sessions are the more important conditions, other than motivation, associated with effective practice. These require brief clarification.

The whole-part nature of skills can be examined from the standpoint of the organization of the skill itself. Some skills are closely knit; others are loosely organized. Baseball is an aggregation of skills, each part of which must receive concentrated practice. Diving is a closely knit skill and must be practiced as a continuous series of actions. Should complex skills consisting of aggregate skills and closely knit skills be taught in entirety during each practice session?

Experiments completed from 1890 to 1952 in connection with learning to receive the Morse code are most encouraging and are typical of those that favor teaching as much of the whole skill as early as possible.[24] There was much opportunity to try out efficient methods of teaching Morse code during World War II. From several features that were finally incorporated into the military teaching procedures, four are appropriate to the present discussion of skill learning. The whole method of teaching, prompt reinforcement of the correct response, a standard-speed presentation of signals, and distributed practice. In the whole method, all 36 symbols of the code—26 letters and 10 digits— were introduced to the learners in the first practice session. This method contrasted sharply with previous ones wherein early instruction was devoted to lengthy practice on separate symbols with the intent of eventually teaching all the symbols. The results of applying the four procedures resulted in vastly superior learning.

Practice of a skill should not be too far removed from the conditions under which it is actually carried out. Two methods have been used in order to overcome this difficulty in business education. First, an office-practice class is offered. Here students carry out duties similar to those they will perform after graduation. The room for the office-practice class resembles general offices, with the usual filing cabinets, desks, typewriters, and other office equipment. The students perform the secretarial work of the school. In a second arrangement, the high school student goes into office work in a local business or other establishment

---

[24] Robert S. Woodworth and Harold Schlosberg, *Experimental Psychology*, rev. ed. (New York: Holt, Rinehart and Winston, 1954).

for part of his instruction, thus getting experience in the situational context in which the skills are actually used. Generally, these two procedures result in better performances after high school graduation, especially in the first weeks on the job.

The proper context for practice may also be illustrated in the internship in teacher education, an internship similar to that in medical education. Leaving the college to perform the duties of the regular teacher is a form of internship different from and better than verbal classroom instruction about student-teaching. Internship in teaching is as useful as internship in the medical profession. The more similar the practice of complex skills is to the situations in which the skills are actually to be used, the more efficient the results. The medical intern, the teaching intern, and the student secretary in high school practice more realistically than do most students in a regular classroom setting.

A teacher who encourages a variety of methods with large groups of students secures good results. Conversely, a teacher who adheres to a particular method or to a specific use of material interferes with skill learning. Even though the teacher thinks he knows the one best method, he should re-examine his method if his students do not make progress after repeated efforts. After working with students over a period of several weeks, only to find that they are no better than when they started, the teacher should rightfully conclude that something is wrong with his method.

The dramatic results in learning Morse code, achieved in part through distributing practice, were discussed previously. Equally significant results have been obtained with other skills. For example, learning to juggle is more efficient when 5 minutes per day are used in practice than when 15 minutes per day are used on alternative days.[25] In fact, the distributed practice was almost twice as effective. Similar results have been attained with high-speed perceptual motor tasks.[26] In many studies, superior performance has resulted from distributing rather than mass-

---

[25] Clyde G. Knapp and William R. Dixon, "Learning to Juggle: I. A Study to Determine the Effect of Two Different Distributions of Practice on Learning Efficiency," *The Research Quarterly of the American Association for Health, Physical Education, and Recreation*, XXI (October, 1950), 331–336.

[26] Jane Mackworth, "Performance Decrement in Vigilance, Threshold, and High-Speed Perceptual Motor Tasks," *Canadian Journal of Psychology*, XVIII (September, 1964), 209–223.

ing practice. The conclusion is clear that shorter practice sessions with an interval of time between sessions produce excellent results in any skill provided two conditions are met: The practice session is sufficiently long to bring about improvement and the space between sessions is not so long that forgetting occurs.

High school teachers usually have no control over the length of class periods. They often work in schools where class periods are of the same length, usually from 45 to 75 minutes. In any subject where skills are part of the desired outcome, the teacher should raise questions such as these: Within a class period of this length what is the best arrangement of active practice and rest? for a beginning class? for an advanced class? Will the students acquire skill more rapidly through active practice each day of the week or through active practice on alternate days?

Provide knowledge of results and correct errors

Knowledge of results is a powerful variable in skill learning. There is no improvement without knowledge of results, progressive improvement with it, and deterioration after its withdrawal, according to Bilodeau and Bilodeau.[27]

When the student can observe the results of his actions immediately, for example in writing, driving a car, or typing, he guides his next tries on the basis of feedback from the previous ones. In performing many verbal skills, the student cannot interpret his previous performances to determine their adequacy or inadequacy, correctness or incorrectness. The teacher, however, should provide arrangements so that knowledge of results is readily available.

The teacher can readily provide the learner with knowledge of his progress if time is available and used for this purpose. Information can be given by saying "correct" or "incorrect"; a verbal analysis can be given of any object that the student has produced; and the results of performance tests of all sorts can be incorporated in charts or given to the student directly. Verbal presentations are limited in that some

---

[27] Edward A. Bilodeau and Ina M. Bilodeau, "Motor-Skills Learning," *Annual Review of Psychology* (Stanford, Calif.: Stanford University Press, 1961), pp. 243–280.

actions cannot be explained, nor can accuracy or speed always be measured. In this case, the teacher can demonstrate; and the student, by observing, can compare his performance with that of the teacher.

ATTITUDINAL LEARNING

Attitudes and values toward self, others, school, home, and the like are important learning outcomes in their own right. In addition, the attitudes of the student markedly affect his learning of all subject matter. For these reasons, the school cannot leave attitudinal learning solely to the home, to the neighborhood, or to chance factors. Proper attention must be given to attitudes in school, preferably by all teachers. Therefore, make a special effort to understand the next four generalizations and principles and to find applications of them.

Generalization	Principle
A receptive observer incorporates a model's behavior into his own pattern through imitation	Provide exemplary models
Positive reinforcers strengthen attitudes by linking pleasantness with the manifestation of the attitude	Provide pleasant emotional experiences with attitude objects
Acquiring new information modifies attitudes differentially	Extend informative experiences about attitude objects
Testing of attitudes and commitment to them requires group interaction	Use group techniques to facilitate commitment

Provide exemplary models

People serve as real models for each other. Verbal descriptions can be classed as symbolic models. Television provides in between representational models, incorporating both people and verbal descriptions. Much social behavior is acquired through imitating models. Ways of expressing emotions, aggressive behavior, dependency behavior, self-control, and the like are heavily dependent upon learning through observation and imitation. Therefore, exemplary models are of critical importance in all social learning, including attitudes.

One interpretation of the motivation to imitate is that the observer identifies with the model.[28] When identifying with a model, the observer behaves, feels, and thinks as if the attributes and behavior of the model belong to him. This may occur without the person's actually being aware that he is identifying with or imitating the model. Thus, a child does not always deliberately set out to behave like a model in the same manner that he tries to read or to write. Two conditions are necessary for identification to occur: One, the child must want to possess some of the model's characteristics; two, he must have some basis for feeling that he and the model are similar. Associated with wanting to possess some of the characteristics of the model is a warm relationship between the observer and model. A parent as a model controls goals that the child desires, including power over the child and other people, mastery over the environment, and love. Identification with the parent is fostered through the child's desire to possess what the goals imply.[29]

When one feels like the model, he thinks he is similar to the model. The feeling emerges in two ways: As already stated, an observer adopts his model's attributes and behavior. Or, others may tell a maturing youth that he is similar to whomever he models. As the adolescent perceives similarity of behavior with the model and is told that in mastery over the environment, power over other people, and so on, he is like the model, identification with the model is strengthened.

Modern television advertising illustrates the importance of identifying figures, who are intended to serve as exemplary models. One mass media technique is to have the heroine or hero endorse the product. Other techniques are embodied in statements that attempt to associate prestige with the product: "Scientists have found . . . ," "Four out of five doctors recommend . . . ," "The thinking man. . . . " So personal is this advertising that by buying the product the user feels better, because he is like whoever does the endorsing or recommending. The schools have much to learn about models. Teachers must themselves be better identifying figures for students. Also, reading materials must be selected

---

[28] Jerome Kagan, "The Concept of Identification," *Psychological Review*, LXV (September, 1958), 296–305.

[29] Paul H. Mussen, John J. Conger, and Jerome Kagan, *Child Development and Personality* (New York: Harper & Row, 1963).

to present a wider range of exemplary models, especially for the non-college bound students and for the culturally disadvantaged students.

Provide pleasant emotional experiences with attitude objects

As shown in the preceding section, some social behaviors indicative of attitudes are acquired through imitating a model. They are strengthened through rewards and other reinforcers. Positive reinforcers strengthen attitudes in that a feeling of pleasantness becomes associated with the attitude. This is accomplished best when there is close temporal contiguity of the reinforcer with the behavior indicative of the attitude. Furthermore, after an attitude becomes internalized, behavior not in accordance with it produces anxiety. In this manner, reinforcements are eventually not needed for the continuation of behavior that is in line with an internalized attitudinal system.

Positive reinforcers more reliably strengthen desired responses than do the withholding of a positive reinforcer and the administration of punishment. The hedonistic principle carries strong weight in attitudinal learning. If a teacher wishes to have students develop favorable attitudes toward school, he will make the classroom attractive and comfortable, present a good personal appearance and dress attractively, show warmth to the students, demonstrate enthusiasm in the subject matter, and make it possible for each student to experience success on some school learning tasks. Most students will develop unfavorable attitudes toward both the classroom and the school if the opposite things are done.

Extend informative experiences about attitude objects

The learning of an attitude initially is facilitated through acquiring information about the relevant objects and situations. Information is acquired by direct experiences with persons, ideas, and objects; by reading books and other material; by listening to radio or watching television; by seeing motion pictures with sound tracks; and the like. The effects of various types of information on influencing attitudes will now be considered.

Students underwent three information-giving procedures in order to ascertain which procedure might be most effective in changing attitudes toward persons of different nationality backgrounds.[30] In one group, the student members of the various majority and minority groups were classed together on the basis of expressed interests in particular work and play activities. In a second group, factual information about ethnic groups was presented to the students in lectures, discussions, and reading assignments. In a third group, the students in classroom groups were provided a minimum amount of factual information but were given a variety of short stories, novels, and plays to read. Some informal dramatizing also was done by the third group. The last method achieved the best result. In the two schools in which it was used, there was a greater increase in acceptance between majority and minority groups than in the schools using the first two approaches.

New information does not always direct opinions in the desired direction. For example, when the distance is small between the individual's own attitude and that presented to him, he judges the information as fair and factual. However, with an increasing distance between the individual's attitude and that presented in the information, the favorable judgment is sharply reduced, and the information is perceived as propagandistic and unfair. In addition, individuals whose attitudes or whose opinions are greatly different from the attitudes and opinions advocated in the information do not change.[31] Thus, both informative and emotional experiences, as discussed previously, are critical in attitudinal learning.

Use group techniques to facilitate commitment

The formation of attitudes is influenced by the groups to which the maturing individual belongs. Informal groups are highly important sources of information, reinforcement, and emotional release for adolescents. Parents and teachers become relatively less influential in the life of the child as he grows older and as he identifies with his generation.

---

[30] Margaret L. Hayes and Mary E. Conklin, "Intergroup Attitudes and Experimental Change," *Journal of Experimental Education*, XXII (September, 1953), 19–36.
[31] Carl I. Hovland, O. J. Harvey, and Muzafer Sherif, "Assimilation and Contrast Effects in Reactions to Communication and Attitude Change," *Journal of Abnormal Social Psychology*, LV (September, 1957), 244–252.

Desiring to be like other members of an age group is a powerful motivating force. In the informal groups of adolescence, many attitudes are tested out; and eventually the individual commits himself to standards implied by the attitudes of his peer group, regardless of how adults may feel about the standards or lack of them. Teachers can influence attitude development through working with student groups within and outside regular classroom hours. Sound films, discussions, and group decision-making deserve special consideration in this regard.

In sound motion pictures and television, identifying figures are shown, and pleasant emotions are experienced by the observer. Discussion both before and after the presentation is needed in order to profit most from the viewing, as shown in an experiment carried out with high school students.[32] Students who scored high, middle, and low in ethnocentrism were identified and were then assigned randomly to one of three groups. One group saw a film unfavorable to ethnocentrism but did not discuss it; another group saw and discussed the film; the control group neither saw nor discussed the film. Five important results were obtained: (1) A significant reduction in ethnocentric attitudes occurred in the group who had seen the film and followed the viewing with discussion. However, those students who did not take part in the discussion actively after seeing the film did not change attitudes. (2) The permanence of the attitude change after one month was higher for the discussion groups than for the film-alone group. The film-alone group had regressed significantly toward their original attitudes. (3) The amount of information learned from the film and discussion was related to the degree of ethnocentrism held by the individual: The higher the degree of ethnocentrism, the less he learned. (4) Active participants in the film-plus-discussion group learned more from the film than did students who were passive during the discussion. (5) No significant relationship was found between intelligence and attitude.

Being presented information about appropriate and inappropriate conduct is vastly different from arriving at the conclusions through group decision. An individual who shares in making a decision abides by that decision to a greater extent than does a listener or observer. For example, in an attempt to get housewives to use meats that they were

[32] Leonard L. Mitnick and Elliott McGinnies, "Influencing Ethnocentrism in Small Discussion Groups through a Film Communication," *Journal of Abnormal Social Psychology*, LVI (January, 1958), 82–90.

not using—beef hearts, sweetbreads, and kidneys—researchers presented information in attractively arranged lectures to one group; another group, led by a trained leader, discussed the possibility of using these meats until a decision was reached. Subsequently, it was found that only 3 percent of those who listened to the lecture were using the recommended meats, whereas 32 percent of those who shared in the group decision were using them. In another experiment, some groups of housewives were presented lectures for the purpose of increasing their home consumption of milk. Other groups were led in discussion and arrived at a group decision. The same information about milk consumption was presented to both the lecture and decision-making groups. In this experiment, about 45 percent of those who had shared in decision-making and about 15 percent of those who heard the lectures were using more whole milk two and four weeks later.[33]

More frequently than at present, the schools should arrange situations whereby a large majority of the student body, organized into small groups, would agree to display behaviors implied in the attitudes listed earlier in this chapter. They could keep the corridors relatively clean and quiet, get to class on time, start work promptly when getting to class, and respect the ideas and property of others. The result would be less need for policing and rule-pronouncing than is now required in many schools. Commitment to socially approved attitudes is sorely needed.

RETENTION AND TRANSFER

School people desire that what students learn today will be remembered at a later time. Furthermore, it is anticipated that what is learned and remembered will help in meeting new situations in and out of school. Concepts, skills, attitudes, methods of learning, and ways of relating to others—all these may be learned in school, remembered, and used in other situations. But much is also forgotten and is not applied to any situation other than that in which is is learned.

In the previous sections, we have already indicated that motivation

---

[33] Kurt Lewin, "Group Decision and Social Change," in Eleanor E. Maccoby, Theodore M. Newcomb, and Eugene L. Hartley, eds., *Readings in Social Psychology*, 3rd ed. (New York: Holt, Rinehart, & Winston, 1958), pp. 197–211.

and other conditions are essential for learning various outcomes. We shall not repeat any of these principles, although they are applicable for improving retention because better initial learning facilitates retention. You may wish to review them before considering the three generalizations and related principles that are particularly applicable to retention and transfer.

Generalization	Principle
Practice increases the stability of knowledge and thus reduces forgetting	Distribute practice and review, thus arranging for sequential, cumulative learning
Concepts, generalized attitudes, and skills transfer readily to new situations	Emphasize general concepts and abilities
The inclusiveness and generality of one's knowledge, attitudes, and skills are extended through use in a variety of situations	Provide for application

Distribute practice and review

Earlier in this chapter, the desirability of distributing practice was shown. Overlearning through practice and review facilitates permanent retention by increasing the stability and clarity of the individual's knowledge and abilities.[34] To illustrate, a situation was arranged whereby testing and reviewing were accomplished simultaneously with prearranged groups at intervals of one day, 14 days, 28 days, and 63 days.[35] Retention improved significantly with systematic review. Best results were secured when the review tests were administered one day after initial instruction rather than later. Also, if not corrected, incorrect or erroneous concepts persisted; if the errors were not corrected, students tended to accept and retain the errors as correct.

Critics of programed instruction state that repetition of the same items in one sitting makes the instructional situation monotonous. It may have this effect for it does not improve immediate or long-term retention.[36] However, interspersing short reviews of the preceding ma-

---

[34] Ausubel, *The Psychology of Meaningful Verbal Learning.*

[35] Herman R. Tiedeman, "A Study of Retention in Classroom Learning," *Journal of Educational Research,* XLII (March, 1948), 516–531.

[36] James H. Reynolds and Robert Glaser, "Effects of Repetition and Spaced Review upon Retention of a Complex Learning Task," *Journal of Educational Psychology,* LV (October, 1964), 297–308.

terial in subsequent instructional sequences greatly improves retention. Thus, in programed instruction, as in regular instruction, spaced review proves effective in encouraging retention.

Of course, complex skills, concepts, attitudes, and abilities are not fully acquired in one day, week, or year but are acquired cumulatively through distributed effort over a period of time. The various disciplines require many years of study in order for one to become moderately literate. Thus, careful attention must be given when outlining a sequence of instruction from kindergarten through grade 12 in order to encourage continuity in learning. At the same time the teacher is faced daily with the problem of deciding how large or comprehensive a unit of learning to attempt in order for the student to acquire something that can be carried through to the next day or week. Obviously if nothing is learned today, it cannot be retained or used tomorrow. In spelling, for example, it is better to learn three words well each day of the week than to be given 15 words at one time and end up at the end of the week not knowing any of them. In foreign language instruction, it is better to emphasize a smaller dialogue than to assign a long one that is neither learned nor remembered.

Emphasize general concepts and abilities

In order to facilitate transfer, the teacher must identify the outcomes and abilities to be learned well, retained, and transferred by the students. Most students studying Latin do not independently select Latin words on which many English words are based. Geometry students do not find the many possible applications of facts and principles to their daily activities or to subsequent careers in engineering or architecture. Besides identifying outcomes and abilities, the teacher also has a responsibility to emphasize those outcomes with the greatest possibility for transfer. General information, concepts, and principles, methods of learning, generalized attitudes, and methods of adjustment have greater possibility of transfer to many situations than do specific facts, attitudes, and technical information.

Provide for application

Shakespearean plays may be studied for the inherent satisfaction derived. If, however, the purpose of such a study is to assist in a better interpretation of English history or to relate the play to the present scene in England or America, most students will need help in applying the pertinent ideas from the plays to the contemporary world. Comparing Shakespeare's style of writing and modern writing, comparing the characters in Shakespeare's plays with those in modern plays, or relating the themes of Shakespeare's plays to themes that exist in modern life are means of finding applications.

Suppose that a teacher intends to secure transfer from one problem to similar problems. Practice on a variety of problems resembling the initial one, rather than on exactly the same ones, facilitates transfer.[37] Does the same conclusion hold when the attempt is made to secure transfer from one class to other classes of problems of the same class? Teachers who know the subject matter well and its applications are more effective in securing transfer than are those who know the subject matter but are weak on its application.

SUMMARY

Knowledge is increasing at a rapid rate in the content fields. The same is true in the behavioral sciences, particularly in connection with human learning. Knowledge about the conditions that are essential for efficient learning has been extended markedly in the last decade, and new materials and procedures are being developed that make the goals of the school more attainable. Much optimism is prevalent, and warranted, concerning the enforcement of efficiency of learning in school settings. This is true not only of the usual subject matter but also of creative abilities, attitudes and values, and personality integration.

From the vast accumulation of information, only that pertinent to the following areas has been synthesized and evaluated in this chapter: A sequence in purposeful learning, motivation, cognitive learning, skill learning, and attitudinal learning. Generalizations drawn from research and theoretical positions form the basis for deriving instructional principles. In turn, the instructional principles require application to the many subject fields and settings of the local schools. Each teacher must

---

[37] Merlin C. Wittrock and P. A. Twelker, "Verbal Cues and Variety of Classes of Problems in Transfer of Training," *Psychological Report*, XIV (June, 1964), 827–830.

eventually identify and try out the application in his particular situation. Sufficient research and experience underlie each principle included in the present chapter to warrant a serious attempt at application.

QUESTIONS AND ACTIVITIES

1 Ten teacher actions are related to a five-step sequence in purposeful learning. Arrange the actions in order of least to most difficult for you personally to execute in a teaching situation. Very briefly indicate why the first action in your list is least difficult and why the last is most difficult.

2 Five principles of motivation are given. Which two were least well implemented in your high school classes and which were best implemented? Give concrete examples.

3 Based on your personal experiences, cite concrete examples of excellent motivational procedures used by teachers with students who did not go to college, or with students currently in high school who do not plan to go to college.

4 Indicate the types of rewards and punishments that some parents seem to use effectively but which teachers cannot or do not use effectively.

5 Write an advance organizer of about 1500 words for this chapter.

6 Give your criteria of discovery learning, including how much guidance of the student's activities is accomplished by the teacher and by instructional materials.

7 Compare what the teacher should do to foster creativity and to foster conformity in students.

8 Only three principles of skill learning are outlined. In connection with a skill that you have developed such as reading, playing a piano, or swimming, give concrete examples of the violation or implementation of each principle by your teacher.

9 How is providing knowledge of results and correction of errors different from using rewards and punishments? How similar?

10 Indicate five attitudes that students should acquire or strengthen while attending a class that you teach.

11 In connection with the attitudes you listed for question 10, describe how you would implement each of the four principles of attitudinal learning.

12 Which of these three do you think is most difficult and which is the least difficult to provide: exemplary models, pleasant emotional experiences with the attitude object, or informative experiences with the attitude object? Discuss briefly.

SUGGESTIONS FOR FURTHER READING

ASSOCIATION FOR SUPERVISION AND CURRICULUM DEVELOPMENT, *Learning and Mental Health in the Schools*, Washington, D.C.: National Education Association, 1966.

HILGARD, ERNEST R., ED., *Theories of Learning and Instruction*, Sixty-Third Yearbook, National Society for the Study of Education, Chicago: University of Chicago Press, 1964, chs. 8, 10, 17.

KLAUSMEIER, HERBERT J., AND WILLIAM GOODWIN, *Learning and Human Abilities*, 2nd ed., New York: Harper & Row, 1966, chs. 3, 7, 8, 9, 10, 11.

Subject-matter content and sequence

$\mathcal{I}$n the past decade, there has been widespread concern with the subject-matter content of school curricula. Increasingly, scholars and curriculum specialists are emphasizing the need for precise definitions of the disciplines and for the establishment of a structure, or organization, of the knowledge within the disciplines. In the early decades of the twentieth century, with the rise of educators influenced by the work of John Dewey, educational objectives were oriented toward the needs of society and of the learner. The content areas, or disciplines, so important in the curricula of the nineteenth century, were given secondary emphasis. The late 1950s saw the completion of a full swing of the pendulum when interest and attention were again turned toward the disciplines. But this time, scholars and teachers began to realize that rote learning of facts and details is only a small portion of the possible learning outcomes that each discipline has to offer. With this recent emphasis on the disciplines came a renewed investigation of educational objectives, of the content areas relevant to those objectives, and of the structure of knowledge within the content areas.

In 1948, at a convention of the American Psychological Association, a group of college examiners conceived an idea for a classification of educational objectives that would be specific enough to be useful, yet sufficiently general to have application in most areas of education. After eight years of individual and group work, the committee published the *Taxonomy of Educational Objectives,* cognitive domain, edited by Benjamin S. Bloom. The *Taxonomy,* which considers educational objectives from the more simple to the complex, includes six main classes: knowledge, comprehension, application, analysis, synthesis, and evaluation. This ordering of objectives is based on the idea that each successive process increases in difficulty over the previous one. For example, problems that require our knowing specific facts (knowledge) are answered correctly more frequently than problems that require our understanding of some principles based on the facts (comprehension). Each of the six classes of the syntax is divided into subcategories that define more specifically the kinds of knowledge, the kinds of comprehension, and so on.[1] Because of its general yet precise character, the *Taxonomy* can be applied to nearly every discipline and can serve as a guide for many scholars and curriculum specialists.

Simultaneously with the attempt to formulate more comprehensive educational objectives came an awareness of the need to update and to revise subject-matter content and sequence. Scientists and scholars, who had secluded themselves for too long in the archives of the graduate library or the labyrinths of the research lab, felt the need to organize the most recent discoveries and trends of their discipline and to filter them into the classrooms of elementary and secondary schools. Subject-matter content as taught in kindergarten through grade 12 seemed appallingly obsolete; the organization and sequence of concepts appeared now unnecessarily redundant, now weak and loosely connected. The recognition of a need for nationwide revision of subject-matter content would not have been enough to spark any sweeping reforms had it not been for the availability of large-scale financial support. Both government and private funds are making it possible for scientists, content experts, curriculum specialists, administrators, and teachers to cooperate in planning curricula and in constructing and trying out modern instructional materials.

Mathematicians and scientists were the first to investigate the structure of their disciplines and to study the existing curricula in depth. In 1959, the National Academy of Sciences called together a group of 35 scholars, educators, and scientists at Woods Hole in Cape Cod,

---

[1] Benjamin S. Bloom, ed., *Taxonomy of Educational Objectives* (New York: McKay, 1956).

Massachusetts, to discuss the improvement of science education. One of the outcomes of the Woods Hole Conference was Jerome S. Bruner's *The Process of Education*,[2] which, along with Bloom's *Taxonomy*, provided some of the impetus for the nationwide explosion of interest in curriculum innovation. Scholars and teachers began to re-evaluate the educational objectives of each discipline, to define the area of the discipline, to search for an underlying structure of the knowledge included in this area, and to adjust, sometimes radically to change, the curriculum. In 1963, five years after the first science and math conference, the Ford Foundation awarded a grant to the Music Educators National Conference for a six-year study; that same year a Commission on Humanities was established to investigate ways of improving education in that area; and health education is undergoing a four-year School Health Education Study, supported by a private fund.[3]

This sudden interest in modernizing the disciplines resulted in the realization that the first step toward educational improvement is a comprehensive investigation of the structure of knowledge that each discipline encompasses. Accepting Bruner's idea, we speak of the *structure of knowledge* as that body of fundamental underlying principles that permits us to relate phenomena. To illustrate briefly the types of principles forming the basis for a structure of knowledge, let us consider one of the processes involved in a child's learning to speak English. In imitating adult speech patterns, a child unconsciously grasps the principle of word order and in time is able to produce simple two- or three-word utterances. In one study of the growth of speech patterns, a child conversing about trucks said, "Put truck window."[4] Quite obviously, this is not a direct imitation of the adult model, which would have been "Put *the* truck *in the* window." Yet the utterance does follow a standard pattern of syntax. The child did not say, "Put window truck," or "Truck window put." He had formed a generalization from which he could generate utterances entirely new to his repertoire.

---

[2] Jerome S. Bruner, *The Process of Education* (Cambridge: Harvard University Press, 1960).

[3] NEA, *Schools for the Sixties*, A Report of the Project on Instruction (New York: McGraw-Hill, 1963), p. 48.

[4] Roger Brown and Ursula Bellugi, "Three Processes in the Child's Acquisition of Syntax," *Harvard Educational Review*, XXXIV (Spring, 1964), 133–151.

One of the important underlying principles in science is the kinetic, or particle, theory of matter, which states that all matter—solids, liquids, and gasses—is composed of molecules in constant motion. A firm understanding of this theory supplies for us the means with which to explain innumerable phenomena, such as the evaporation of a bottle of perfume, the miniature explosion of a popcorn kernel, or the breathing mechanism of a goldfish. Clearly, the kinetic theory allows us to see the relatedness of diverse, seemingly disparate, happenings. We are very likely to find this theory among those principles considered as basic to the structure of scientific knowledge.

Recent efforts at subject-matter revision are based on the idea that the curriculum is determined by the principles in the structure of knowledge and by a well-planned sequencing of those principles. In order to allay any doubts as to the importance of teaching the structure of knowledge, Bruner gives four very reasonable justifications.[5] The first is that, by teaching the fundamental principles, we make our subject more comprehensible to the student. For instance, the generalization that men strive to satisfy unlimited wants sheds light on the secondary economic principles of barter and exchange, or production and consumption.

The second point in support of teaching the structure of knowledge is that one tends to forget details and facts that are not placed within some general framework of theories or principles. Also, by understanding principles, one can always reconstruct the specifics supporting those principles. Instead of memorizing a list of Centigrade temperatures equivalent to certain Fahrenheit degrees, we simply remember one formula: $F = 9/5\,C + 32$. From this, given C, we can calculate F; or vice versa if, in addition, we understand the theory of equivalent equations and the associative laws of addition and multiplication. Realizing how the content we are learning relates to the overall structure of a specific body of knowledge permits us to store this new learning within the supporting framework and to recall it more easily.

Bruner's third claim rests on the belief that transfer of learning, one of the objectives of most curricula, occurs more readily when we understand the relatedness of things. The basic theories we learn serve as models for the understanding of phenomena never before encountered

[5] Bruner, *op. cit.*, pp. 23–26.

or investigated. One who is familiar with the concept of capillary action would have little difficulty understanding why a kerosene road marker can burn all night or how flower pots absorb water from the bottom.

Finally, in order to teach the structure of knowledge, it is imperative to reappraise periodically the nature of subject-matter content. The result of this reappraisal would be a decrease in the time lapse between the development of new knowledge and its appearance in curriculum content.

Believing that teaching the structure of a discipline contributes to more efficient learning, and realizing that in many curricula the content of disciplines overlaps, nearly all curriculum committees are faced with the problem of defining their discipline and of structuring, or organizing, the knowledge within the discipline. Does a study of the Victorian period belong in a history course or an English course? Who teaches the relationship between the acceleration of a body at rest and the distance it travels, the geometry teacher or the physics teacher? Although it appears fairly simple, the problem of stating the scope of a discipline precisely is not easily solved. Innumerable meetings are held and many long hours are spent formulating and revising, debating and compromising, before a committee of experts is able to issue a definition of their discipline that may be accepted by a majority of teachers, scholars, and curriculum specialists. Periodically, the definition of a discipline, a definition that at one time was satisfactory, must be updated, expanded, or further delimited. According to the NEA Project on Instruction, the need for continuous educational reappraisal arises from three factors:[6] One factor involves the fundamental changes in contemporary American society. These changes occur so rapidly that we feel an increased need for schools to provide us with the training and knowledge necessary to cope with and to understand social changes.

The second factor is the nearly overwhelming growth of bodies of knowledge per se. Man's knowledge grew very slowly at first, not doubling itself until approximately 1750. A second doubling is estimated to have occurred in 1900; a third occurred in 1950; and the fourth, in 1960, a mere decade later. This astounding growth demands that the content and structure of each discipline be scrutinized carefully and

---

[6] NEA, *op. cit.*, pp. v–vi.

that decisions be made concerning the inclusion of certain segments of knowledge in the classroom curriculum.

A third factor that increases the need for constant re-evaluation of the curriculum is the recent knowledge derived from research concerning the teaching-learning process. We not only know more than we ever did about our subject matter, but we are also more knowledgeable in the "how's" and "why's" of teaching.

For the remainder of this chapter, we are going to summarize some of the more recent efforts being made in the major disciplines to define the subject area, to structure knowledge, and to reorganize school curricula in the light of the results of modern research. Although research, development, and innovation are being conducted in each field in secondary education, space limitation permits discussion of only five areas: mathematics, English, science, social studies, and foreign languages. Arbitrarily, mathematics and English are treated more fully than the remaining three subjects in an effort to give you some idea of recent trends in examining subject-matter content and sequence. Omission of your area of interest is not intended to suggest that changes in the teaching of your subject are not as dramatic or as clearly worthwhile as the reforms in any of the areas treated in this chapter.

SUBJECT-MATTER CONTENT AND SEQUENCE IN MATHEMATICS

Because the curricula of the early American schools were based quite understandably on the existing European school curricula, emphasis in the first Latin grammar schools of New England was on classical knowledge—Latin, Greek, theology, and so on. Very minimal attention was given to the importance and role of mathematics until Benjamin Franklin's plea for the utilitarian or practical disciplines placed mathematics training in a relatively prominent position in the curricula. The rudimentary skills needed for commerce, finance, surveying, and small business operations were taught to enterprising young men. With the establishment of public high schools in the nineteenth century, mathematics became more specialized; but, in accordance with the educational theory of mental discipline, the fundamental principles of mathematics that are so important today were neglected in favor of grueling mechanical exercises intended to "train the mind."

In 1916, the Mathematical Association of America (MAA) appointed the National Committee on Mathematics Requirements which recommended that the three aims for mathematics instruction be (1) the practical or utilitarian aspect, (2) the disciplinary training of analytical skills, and (3) the cultural or personal satisfaction gained from mastery of mathematical skills.[7] Until 1950, the utilitarian viewpoint again prevailed, with the content remaining basically the same.[8]

Although individuals had previously proposed a reorganization of the mathematics curriculum, not until 1940 was there any organized effort to specify the structure of mathematics. In that year, a Joint Commission of the MAA and the National Council of Teachers of Mathematics (NCTM) proposed a structure of mathematics organized according to seven major content areas: number and computation, geometric form and space perception, graphic representation, elementary analysis, logical thinking, relational thinking, and symbolic representation. Each area was to be subdivided into the basic principles and skills embodied in it. The Committee on the Function of Mathematics in General Education, in its 1940 report, also recommended seven major areas, but these areas consisted of the underlying fundamental principles of mathematics and not the specific content employing the principles. The seven proposed areas were: formulation and solution, data, approximation, function, operation, proof, and symbolism. The idea that structure of mathematical knowledge could be organized according to principles and not according to the traditional subject fields still continues to influence mathematicians and curriculum specialists today.[9]

By the 1950s, the increase in mathematical knowledge and the deep concern for a curriculum more appropriate for modern American youth prompted several reports of recommendations for curriculum revision. In a position paper published in 1958, the National Association of Secondary-School Principals emphasized the need to provide mathematics study suited to individual abilities, interests, and future plans. Recognizing that mathematics instruction had been primarily for the

---

[7] Kenneth B. Henderson, "Research on Teaching Secondary School Mathematics," in N. L. Gage, ed., *Handbook of Research on Teaching* (Chicago: Rand McNally, 1963), p. 1009.

[8] For one account of historical background in the teaching of mathematics, see Donald E. Shipp and Sam Adams, *Developing Arithmetic Concepts and Skills* (Englewood Cliffs, N.J.: Prentice-Hall, 1964).

[9] Henderson, *op. cit.*, p. 1010.

college-bound in the past, the Association recommended that all students, grades 7 through 9, have a minimum of three hours of mathematics per week, and that in grades 10 through 12 all should have one year, with those of high ability encouraged to progress more rapidly.[10] As a result of a three-year study, the Commission on Mathematics, appointed by the College Entrance Examination Board (CEEB), reported that much of the traditional mathematics curriculum is necessary for modern youth but that some is quite useless. Also, the manner of teaching of mathematics lacks what is needed for deep understanding and favorable attitudes.[11] In 1959, the Secondary School Curriculum Committee of NCTM also stated that mathematics consists of "selected traditional topics" but suggested they be extended and presented with a new viewpoint. More important, the committee included in the scope of a mathematics curriculum new topics such as statistics and probability, analytic geometry, and calculus. The committee urged that four years of mathematics be available to students and that two years be required for graduation. This attitude is quite different from that of earlier days which placed mathematics instruction among the "incidentals" of the curriculum.[12]

The result of the efforts of these groups and others was a nationwide movement to revise and update mathematics content and curriculum. Federal and private funds are providing the support for research and for production of new instructional materials. In 1966, the National Science Foundation alone is funding at least nine major mathematics projects, some on the elementary level, some on the secondary level, and others covering the entire range from Kindergarten through grade 12.

Content and process in mathematics

The increase in the amount of modern mathematical knowledge available to college students has demanded revisions in the secondary school curricula, which, in turn, requires certain changes in mathematics instruction at the elementary level. In addition to receiving updated,

---

[10] Dorothy M. Fraser, *Current Curriculum Studies in Academic Subjects,* a report prepared for the Project on Instruction, NEA (Washington D.C.: Government Printing Office, 1962), pp. 35–36.

[11] William Wooton, SMSG: *The Making of a Curriculum* (New Haven: Yale University Press, 1965), pp. 7–8.

[12] Fraser, *op. cit.,* 29–30.

modernized knowledge, children are being introduced to this knowledge at an earlier age than ever before, and they are learning the underlying structure of mathematical knowledge, a structure that was just beginning to be defined when their parents attended school. According to the Secondary School Curriculum Committee of NCTM, the most significant difference between old and new mathematics lies not as much in the content as in the modern approaches which teach students to see the interrelations of mathematical areas and to grasp the unity of the entire field.[13] Modern mathematics instruction stresses the structure of mathematics together with a deep understanding of the principles and processes involved. Most knowledge selected for inclusion in a curriculum is chosen on the basis of its mathematical significance, not on its potential utilitarian values.

In the elementary school, most modern mathematics programs have as objectives development of an understanding of the number system, of the fundamental operations (addition, subtraction, and so on), of measurement, and of the problems encountered in social situations. Shipp and Adams, in *Developing Arithmetic Concepts and Skills*, mention several specific revisions in content. Among these are a heavy stress on the *structure of numbers*, that is, a thorough understanding of numbers in the base 10, using the concepts of *place value* and place *holder*; an increase in the importance of decimal fractions and a corresponding decrease in emphasis on common fractions; a limitation of the number of measurement units to only the most useful; the introduction of simple geometry in early grades. As an example of two of these content changes, study Figures 3 and 4, which are sections of an arithmetic program developed for grade 1. Figure 3 illustrates one kind of exercise designed to give first-graders practice in counting sets that contain more than ten objects. The counting process is not merely a mechanical recitation of a series of memorized numbers; it is the grouping of objects into sets of ten and accounting for the remaining objects. Later, the children will learn to write 16 instead of *one 10 and 6*. One type of geometry training included in grade 1 is shown as Figure 4. Before working through this exercise, the children are familiarized with open and closed curves and with the four concepts of square, rectangle, triangle, and segment.

---

[13] *Ibid.*, 29.

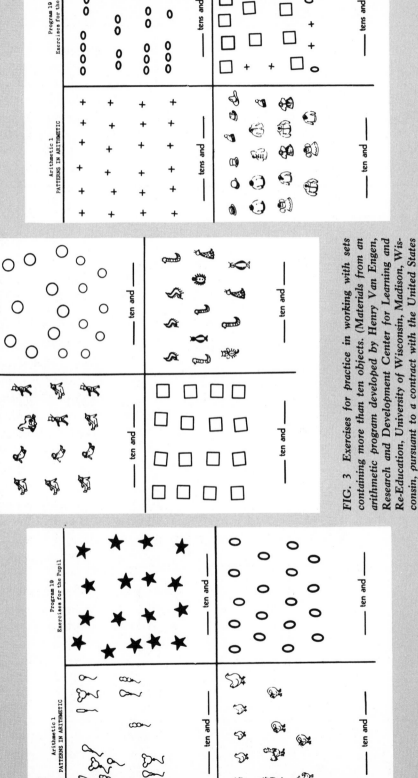

FIG. 3 Exercises for practice in working with sets containing more than ten objects. (Materials from an arithmetic program developed by Henry Van Engen, Research and Development Center for Learning and Re-Education, University of Wisconsin, Madison, Wisconsin, pursuant to a contract with the United States Office of Education, Department of Health, Education, and Welfare, under the provisions of the Cooperative Research Program; Center No. C-03/Contract OE 5.10-154.)

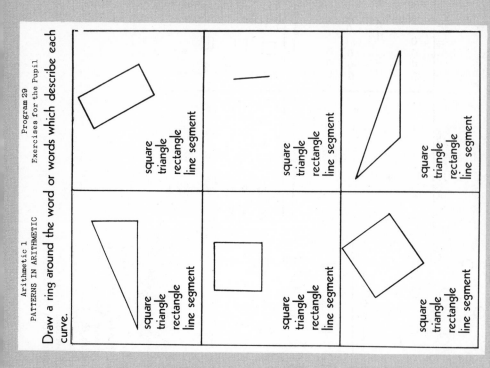

FIG. 4 *Introductory materials in geometry. (Materials from an arithmetic program developed by Henry Van Engen, Re-* to a contract with the United States Office of Education, Department of Health, Education, and Welfare, under the provisions

We also find that, in mathematics as well as in other disciplines, the teaching-learning process is being modified by research on human learning. Historically, the methods of teaching mathematics have had three major stages. During the nineteenth and early twentieth century, the drill theory, or *mental discipline* theory, prevailed. Believing that rigorous mental exercise develops the ability to think, educators confronted children with problems similar to this one. "A lady, being asked the hour of the day, replied that two thirds of the time past noon equaled four fifths of the time to midnight, minus four fifths of an hour; what was the time?"[14] Around 1920, when classroom teaching reflected the theories of the "progressive" movement, many mathematics classes emphasized the social aspects of mathematics. The incidental, or activity, theory resulted in a nearly unstructured curriculum. By 1935, educators began to advocate meaningful learning theory, the idea that learning is more effective when it has meaning and relevance. This approach accounts for many of the changes in content and process that subject fields are experiencing today.

The great emphasis on teaching the structure of mathematics, in order to develop in children a thorough understanding of the principles and processes, influences instructional materials and teaching practices in several ways. One of the foremost concerns of mathematicians and teachers is the establishment of a set of meaningful terms and a consistent use of precise language. Differentiating *number* from *numeral*, or the symbol from its referent, is one of the first skills children must develop. To clarify vividly the concepts involved, concrete, manipulable objects—pencils, marbles, pennies—are presented for children to count, to arrange into sets, and so on. At the appropriate stage when processes are well understood on the concrete level, the actual objects are laid aside and pictures, semi-concrete objects, are used (Figure 3). The next operation is at a still more abstract level. Teaching of this type decreases the emphasis on rote memorization of addition or multiplication tables, with drill exercises employed only after the complete process involved is fully comprehended. At all times, in textbooks and classroom procedures, an effort is made to incorporate meaningful situations into a teaching activity. Nonsense problems like the too familiar "If a

---

[14] Shipp and Adams, *op. cit.*, p. 6. Reprinted by permission of Prentice-Hall, Inc., Englewood Cliffs, New Jersey.

chicken-and-a-half lays an egg-and-a-half . . ." are replaced by problems involving more relevant up-to-date experiences. In a lesson for grade 3, one might find a problem such as this:

> At a stop, a school bus with some children on it picked up 12 more children. Then there were 35 children on the bus. How many were on the bus before this stop?
>
> $$12+35= x$$
> $$12+ x=35$$
> $$x+12=35$$
> $$35- x=12$$

Another recent innovation in mathematics instruction is the increasing use of the discovery approach, which is considered as effective as the expository method. Recognizing the value of discovery, the University of Illinois Commission on School Mathematics (UICSM) has prepared, tested, and revised instructional materials for grades 9 through 12 that stress discovery learning by leading the student through a series of steps by which he can formulate, test, and refine his own generalizations. This inductive approach is considered by many mathematicians to be valuable in teaching the principles and the applications of principles to varied processes.

Sequence and articulation in mathematics

The sequencing of content does not seem to pose as great a problem for the mathematics curricula as it does for some other disciplines. This may be because the scope of mathematics is fairly well defined and because certain skills exist that are obviously required for the understanding of higher-level processes. An expansion of knowledge and a greater understanding of human learning, the two most powerful factors in modern curriculum innovation, exert their strongest influence over different areas of the mathematics curricula. On the secondary level, the greatest change during the 1950s and 1960s has been the introduction of courses dealing with the new areas of mathematics—statistics, probability, calculus, and so on. Although revisions in secondary curricula push some content areas down to lower levels, at the elementary level materials and methods seem to be more influenced by an enlarged understanding of the development of cognitive processes in children.

A child in the early grades is no longer faced with the task of memorizing at one time the tables or rules for the fundamental operations of addition, subtraction, multiplication, and division. Instead, he learns these facts in groups that are spread over a period of years to lighten the burden and to provide time for understanding the processes in depth. Figure 5 presents part of a lesson designed for the early weeks of grade 3. Here a child uses what he has learned about sets to understand the simple multiplication facts. At a later time when he is ready, he will learn more about multiplication and will work on a higher, more abstract level. The desirability of reteaching content is being realized, and what is taught in one grade is reviewed in the next before new material is introduced.

Although concern on the secondary level is also with the methods of effective teaching, perhaps the most obvious change in mathematics sequence involves the number of modern courses introduced into the curriculum. In its 1959 report, the Commission on Mathematics of the CEEB recommended the following sequence for college-bound students grades 9 through 12.

Grade 9: Elementary Mathematics I. Theme: The nature and use of variables, with elementary ideas and notions of sets employed to simplify, clarify, and unify the introduction to algebra

Grade 10: Elementary Mathematics II. Theme: Geometry and deductive reasoning; a "somewhat curtailed" treatment of plane geometry, some coordinate geometry, and the essentials of solid geometry and space perception to be included

Grade 11: Intermediate Mathematics. Theme: Real and complex numbers; study of algebra and elementary trigonometry to be centered around coordinates, vectors, and complex numbers

Grade 12: Three alternative programs: (a) Elementary functions, introductory probability; (b) elementary functions, introduction to modern algebra; (c) elementary functions expanded to two semesters of work[15]

Because beginning ninth-graders often have a background in algebra, they are ready at this year and each succeeding year for higher-level training. Consequently, the type of mathematics offered to twelfth-grade students is usually most controversial and most varied from one school to another. A survey, conducted in 1962-1963 by the U.S. Department of Health, Education, and Welfare, studied the types of grade 12 mathe-

---

[15] Fraser, *op. cit.*, 28–29. By permission.

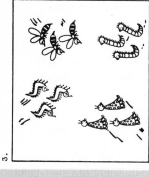

Arithmetic 3
PATTERNS IN ARITHMETIC

Program 17
Exercises for the Pupil

A. In each picture think of the sets coming together. Then circle
    each name below the picture that tells how many there are in all.
    The name should also tell what is happening in the picture.

1.
2 sets of 3
3 times 2
3 + 3
3 twos

2.
4 fives
5 × 4
4 times 5
5 sets of 4

3.
4 × 3
3 × 4
4 sets of 3
3 + 3 + 3 + 3

4.
2 fours
4 times 2
4 + 4
4 × 2

5.
7 sets of 3
3 × 7
3 times 7
7 + 7 + 7

6.
4 × 2
2 sets of 4
4 twos
4 times 2

FIG. 5 Materials for teaching multiplication. (Materials from an arithmetic program developed by Henry Van Engen, Research and Development Center for Learning and Re-Education, University of Wisconsin,
under the provisions of the Cooperative Research Program; Center No. C-03/
Contract OE 5-10-154.)

matics courses offered by 66 selected schools in 20 states, schools that were considered by state supervisors to be leaders in the development of a firm program in mathematics. One conclusion of the survey was that in the titles of fourth-year courses (those assuming three years of previous mathematics training), trigonometry and algebra were the most frequently mentioned topics. In fifth-year courses, the most frequent topics were analytic geometry and calculus. The acceleration needed for advanced courses was most frequently effected by lowering algebra to grade 8. Some schools offered two courses in the same year; others provided an honors program, or a three-year sequence covered in two years.[16]

One of the largest nationwide movements for mathematics reform is the School Mathematics Study Group (SMSG), established in 1958 at Yale and later moved to Stanford. SMSG, supported by National Science Foundation (NSF) funds, had as its main objectives an improved mathematics curriculum, more enticing mathematics courses that would attract capable students, and preparation for teachers who would handle the new courses. To meet these goals, SMSG had to devise new textbooks. Each summer a writing session was held to plan and execute or to revise sample textbooks grades 7 through 12 for tryout the following year. The first books were used by more than 400 teachers and 42,000 high-ability students.[17] Here is a brief survey of the content of the materials.

Grade 7: Numeration; number systems; plane geometry (intuitive); and applications of these
Grade 8: Graphs; plane, solid, and nonmetric geometry (intuitive); probability, additional work with number systems; and applications
Grade 9: Elementary algebra
Grade 10: Euclidean plane and solid geometry
Grade 11: Algebra and trigonometry
Grade 12: Elementary functions and matrix algebra[18]

---

[16] Lauren G. Woodby, *Emerging Twelfth-Grade Mathematics Programs,* Report of the U.S. Department of Health, Education, and Welfare (Washington, D.C.: Government Printing Office, 1965), pp. 1–6.

[17] Benjamin DeMott, "The Math Wars," in Robert W. Heath, ed., *New Curricula* (New York: Harper & Row, 1964), p. 57.

[18] William Wooton, "The History and Status of the School Mathematics Study Group," in Heath, *ibid.,* p. 42. By permission.

In 1962, SMSG issued for average ability students a similar series of texts containing the knowledge most widely applicable and offering the most insight into a variety of situations. The method is less formal, with more concrete examples. Later projects of the SMSG include a five-year longitudinal study of the effects of various curricula, a study of the students' and parents' attitudes toward mathematics, the preparation of movies, monographs, and autoinstructional materials, and the translation into Spanish of grades 7 through 9 texts. New bylaws of SMSG now state that its purpose is to foster research and development in the teaching of mathematics. Accordingly, new groups have been formed to investigate testing and programed learning.[19]

Development and use of instructional materials

Nearly all of the funded mathematics curriculum projects have been developing and testing a variety of instructional materials. In their initial stages, projects usually focus on writing textbooks and teacher materials and later extend their efforts to supplementary materials such as films and packaged lessons.

One major effort in the revision and distribution of new mathematics materials is sponsored by the state of New York in cooperation with the federal government. The New York State Mathematics Curriculum Activities Group works continuously to revise mathematics instruction at all levels in that state. Its statewide dissemination of up-to-date materials seems quite effective, with an estimated 76,000 teachers using the complete program in 1964-1965.[20]

The University of Illinois Committee on School Mathematics (UICSM) represents an ideal working relationship between university scholars and high school teachers. Established in 1952, UICSM has as its goal the development of materials that will produce students who are enthusiastic and who understand mathematics. By 1958, the group had courses for four years of high school being used by 1700 students in 12 pilot schools. To produce students who truly understand, the

---

[19] *Ibid.*, pp. 35–53.

[20] *Third Report of the Information Clearinghouse on New Science and Mathematics Curricula* (College Park, Md.: Information Clearinghouse, 1965), p. 92.

program follows two guiding principles. The first is to use precise, consistent language; the second is to enable students to make discoveries on their own. Both exercises and exposition are written so that a student can discover and state generalizations and rules. Drill work is employed for proficiency, but only after the processes are understood. After much testing and revision, UICSM now has 11 units available for grades 9 through 12. UICSM is also producing programed texts, mainly incorporating the content of the first four units.[21]

SUBJECT-MATTER CONTENT AND SEQUENCE IN ENGLISH

English is a relative newcomer to the curriculum. During the last quarter of the nineteenth century, for example, English literature served as a model for composition and was studied by means of rhetorical analysis. Thus, literature was often subordinated to composition and to grammatical analysis. College entrance requirements were such that the public schools concentrated on a narrow list of classics, emphasizing a detailed knowledge of the production of the classics and of their authors.

In 1917, a group known as the National Joint Committee on Reorganization of English in Secondary Schools made recommendations that were to broaden the scope and function of English extensively. Among the Committee's recommendations were (1) that English not be viewed primarily as a body of facts to be memorized, but rather as a complex of skills to be achieved; and (2) that English not be viewed as composition, grammar, and literature, but rather as the communication arts of reading, writing, speaking, and listening.

In 1956, *The English Language Arts in the Secondary School,* a report of the Commission on the English Curriculum of the National Council of Teachers of English (NCTE), still formulated the goals of the English classroom and described preferred teaching practices in terms of four language arts, or communications arts, skills: reading, speaking, listening, and writing. One generalization that controlled the

---

[21] Max Beberman, "An Emerging Program of Secondary School Mathematics," in Heath, *op. cit.,* pp. 9–34.

volume was ". . . the problems of communication, both intimately personal and set in the framework of social conflict, are a major concern in language arts today."[22]

Yet it seemed to many critics that the English classroom was being used to achieve ends and needs not being met elsewhere to such an extent that its aims were very diffuse and often peripheral to the discipline of English. Some English curricula were designed as humanities courses, presenting the history of art, the history of music, the literature of Western civilization in translation, the dance, philosophy, and so on. In other curricula, English was the handmaiden of social studies, supplying the skills by which the student could communicate the content of social studies. Still other curricula might call for a unit in etiquette or a unit in the choice of a vocation. Critics said that the time devoted to these learnings and activities was time that might be better spent in teaching semantics, history of the English language, lexicography, rhetoric, and so on. And all too frequently, there were English programs that lacked any sequence or articulation and that failed to utilize the scholarship then current.

In 1958, the Ford Foundation supported a series of conferences of representatives of the College English Association, the Modern Language Association, and the National Council of Teachers of English to set forth some of the basic issues in the teaching of English. The Basic Issues Conferences listed 35 issues requiring study and experimentation; the first issue was, "What is English?"

One effort to define English, to clarify responsibilities, and to set priorities in English, was made by the Commission on English of the CEEB, which held summer institutes on 20 university campuses in 1962, and, in 1965, published the results of five years of study in its *Freedom and Discipline in English. Freedom and Discipline* reaffirmed the commission's early position that instruction in English encompasses a tripod of language, literature, and composition. In reply then to the question "What is English?" the commission members said,

The answer rests on the unstartling assumption that language, primarily the English language, constitutes the core of the subject; and on the

---

[22] National Council of Teachers of English, *The English Language Arts in the Secondary School,* prepared by the Commission on the English Curriculum (New York: Appleton-Century-Crofts, 1956), p. 11.

further and equally unstartling assumption that the study and use of the English language is the proper content of the English curriculum.[23]

Such a definition seeks to avoid the diffusion of the content of English often found in previous decades, the earlier uses of the English class-room to meet all needs not met elsewhere; it seeks to reassert the existence of a unique body of knowledge having humanistic, as well as pragmatic, values. The commission's delimitation of English was ac-cepted in many quarters. For instance, the concept of English as a tripod of language, literature, and composition underlay the organization of the general English institutes funded under the National Defense Education Act in the summer of 1965.

However, a new NCTE Commission on the English Curriculum in its first publication, *Ends and Issues: 1965–1966*, establishes several ad-ditional categories. As well as the tripod of language, composition, and literature, the commission discusses the categories speaking and listen-ing and popular culture. The commission raises unresolved, often con-flicting, issues in the areas of major interest in the English curriculum, saying that any call for complete unanimity in a definition of English would be premature, if not impossible, and that any boundaries pro-posed would be disputed as too confining or too elastic.[24]

At present, an effort continues to define the knowledge, skills, atti-tudes, and concepts that are uniquely the responsibility of the teacher of English; the knowledge, skills, attitudes, and concepts that, although the responsibility of the teacher of English, are also the responsibility of the teacher of social studies, of science, of modern foreign languages, and so on; and the knowledge, skills, attitudes, and concepts that are the common, shared concern of all teachers of general education courses.

Content and process in English

The "explosion of knowledge" has been dramatic in English. Structural and transformational grammars have come to vie with traditional gram-mar in the English curriculum. New critical approaches have altered the literature program. Syntheses of the results of many years of research

---

[23] *Freedom and Discipline in English*, report of the Commission on English (New York: CEEB, 1965), p. 2.

[24] NCTE Commission on the English Curriculum, *Ends and Issues: 1965–1966*, Alexander Frazier, ed. (Champaign, Ill.: NCTE, 1966), pp. 1–2.

in the teaching of composition and research on rhetoric have led to the questioning of previously held tenets as to how a student comes to write well.

The traditional school grammar, which has often been criticized for relying on the apparatus of Latin grammar and on models of eighteenth-century grammars of English, for being unduly prescriptive, for relying more on word meaning than on form, and so on, has been challenged by structural and transformational grammars. Arising in part from the work of C. C. Fries, structural grammars examine, more or less inductively, a body of spoken English to create four form classes and a varying number of function classes of English words. Structural grammar shows how given a sentence such as, "Several sperksy turfees rimmeled aflout," a native speaker of English can categorize the form words by using such attributes as word order, function words, inflection, and affixes, rather than by meaning. It notes the role of pitch, stress, and juncture in producing significant contrasts in utterance. It calls attention to a limited number of basic sentence patterns such as "Hondas roar," "The sky is grey," or "The noise breaks the silence," out of which more complex sentences are made. Transformational grammars seek to set forth a list of rules by which English words can be combined to produce every English sentence. Transformational, or generative, grammars present rules that enable a native speaker to produce from a kernel sentence such as "Bob broke the window" the transformations, "Did Bob break the window," "Bob did not break the window," "The window was broken by Bob," "that Bob broke," and "who broke the window." Both structural and transformational grammars, whether taught for humanistic or for pragmatic ends, seem more realistic descriptions of the syntax of English than do the classifications and systems of traditional and school grammars.

The change in the literature program is attributable, in part, to the need to include very recent authors, such as Saul Bellow, Iris Murdoch, or James Baldwin, and, in part, to the need to utilize new critical techniques, new processes. More traditional critical approaches stressed the study of the background of the work, of the author's life and works, of sources of the work, and so on. Modern criticism, however, has often preferred text-centered literary study, techniques that divert the reader directly to the structure and texture of a given work. Other approaches such as the generic, the archetypal, the psychological, and the thematic have contributed to the shaping of the literature program and to teaching the skills needed to read literature in depth.

The curriculum in composition, too, has received fresh attention. The work of Braddock in reviewing research on writing called attention to the inadequacy of most of the existent studies that have examined the environmental factors, the instructional factors, and the subject-matter factors in the act of writing.[25] Very recent research has been directed toward establishing the uses of the new grammars in editing, in studying style, in perceiving alternative structures and in acquiring new structural patterns. Scholars continue to work to attain a new theory of rhetoric that will better describe English prose. Experimentation continues in the use of lay readers, in finding better devices to evaluate writing, in using models for writing, and so on.

As new information, new content, is acquired in English, educational leaders attempt to help students gain ways to deal with, to verify, to use, and to attain knowledge. For example, the process of learning inductively has been built into some of the recently developed materials in English. The Carnegie Curriculum Study Center in English (Co-operative Research Project No. H-015) has produced materials in which an inductive method of teaching and learning is used with literature, composition, and language. Here is a lesson plan for the first day of a tenth-grade unit on "Structure Signal Words":

Objectives

> *In New Terms*–to enable the students to recognize and understand function of structure signal words
>
> *In Traditional Terms*–to recall to students certain functions of parts of speech, especially the preposition, the article, the demonstrative adjective, and the adverb

DAY 1

> *Previous Assignment:* Distribute L5. Ask the students to list the number for each blank in the proper column on the lower half of the page. To do this, the students will have to determine the part of speech of each blank.
>
> *New Material:* L5 (The teacher's version contains answers.)

---

[25] Richard Braddock, Richard Lloyd-Jones, and Lowell Schoer, *Research in Written Composition* (Champaign, Ill.: NCTE, 1963), pp. 29–53.

Directions

Determine the part of speech of each numbered blank, and list the number under the proper heading below.

The ___1___ thought it was very ___2___ for us to ___3___ without ___4___ . She ___5___ the ___6___ more ___7___ . On some ___8___ the students ___9___ her by moving very ___10___ through the ___11___ . On other ___12___ the ___13___ were quite ___14___ . We ___15___ the work easily when we studied at ___16___ . Most of the ___17___ each student ___18___ his own ___19___ very ___20___ . Those ___21___ who made ___22___ grades ___23___ much ___24___ .

Nouns (Class I) Verbs (Class II) Adjectives (Class III) Adverbs (Class IV)

Procedure

1. Write the following headings on the board: *Nouns* (Class I), *Verbs* (Class II), *Adjectives* (Class III), *Adverbs* (Class IV). Drawing from the students' homework, list under each heading the numbers which the students have about classification.
2. a. Have students name the word or words before each blank which signals the word class to which each blank belongs. (Such a word is called a "structure signal word.")
   b. Have the students tell how this word indicates the class that the blank belongs to (*i.e.*, what part of speech it is).
   Examples from L5:
   > *without*=preposition which signals that a noun follows
   > *a, the*=articles signaling nouns
   >> *this*=demonstrative adjective signaling nouns
   >> *very*=intensifying adverb signaling adjectives and adverbs
   > *through the*=Teacher, please note: *both* words are structure signal words. Such a situation is quite frequent in English. Other examples might be *to the, in a* (or any preposition and article situation).
3. Ask students to give the part of speech of each signal word. Be sure to point out to the students that such words as *a, the, this, that, these,* and *those,* often function in the sentence as structure signal words. The adverbs

very, quite, and *too,* also frequently serve to signal adjectives or adverbs. Also emphasize that a noun used as the subject or the direct object will signal a verb. In like manner, a verb will signal the presence of a noun used as the subject of the sentence, or as the direct object; it signals also a predicate word (predicate noun, adjective, or pronoun).

Assignment

Fill in the blanks of L5 with plain-sense words. Note to teacher: Many of the numbered blanks have more than one signal word. Though most people will think of blank 7 as an adverb ("She worked the machine more *easily*"), please note that it can be a noun ("She asked the boy more *questions*"). Blank 22 *precedes* the word which indicates what part of speech it is.[26]

The Nebraska Curriculum Development Center (CRP # H-003), too, is developing materials that provide for inductive learning.

The Curriculum Study Center at Florida State University (CRP # H-026) is developing materials for junior high school students that utilize some of the cognitive processes involved in skills basic both to the study of language and of literature: Perception of meaning, recognition of form, relation of particulars to universals, and the process of generalization.

Sequence and articulation in English

The English program has long suffered from a lack of articulation. A student might well study traditional English grammar in grades 4 through 13, starting anew each time. He might read *The Rime of the Ancient Mariner* in grades 7 through 12; he might be asked to memorize the facts of Shakespeare's life in each grade in the secondary school, as well as to construct a model of the Globe theatre, to draw Elizabethan costumes, and so on. He might go through several grades doing very little writing or almost no reading in the novel. Too often, the English teacher has not known what was taught in earlier grades or what would be taught in later grades. Under these conditions, all too little consideration has been given either to a logical hierarchy of content in English or to a consideration of the changes in cognitive abilities that might occur with age.

---

[26] Erwin R. Steinberg, *et. al.*, "The Inductive Teaching of English," *English Journal,* LV (February, 1966), 147–148. By permission.

However, in keeping with the philosophy of the time, experts in English and in English education have now begun to reconsider the vertical organization of subject matter, especially the aspects of organization of the curriculum that take into account the logical structure of English and the relationship of the difficulty of given concepts to the student's cognitive abilities. A great deal of attention has been devoted to a consideration of the teaching of English in the elementary schools where the teachers often lack knowledge of literature, composition, or language, although a large portion of each child's day may be spent in language-arts study.

A number of curriculum centers supported by the U.S. Office of Education have shown concern for sequential materials. Two centers are working on kindergarten through grade 12 curriculum materials; seven centers are working on materials for grades 1 through 12.

The effort for more effective articulation can be seen, to choose but one example, in the work of the Wisconsin English-Language-Arts Curriculum Project (CRP # H-029). Sponsored by the University of Wisconsin and the Department of Public Instruction of the State of Wisconsin under a grant from the U.S. Office of Education, participants from secondary schools and from universities have prepared sequential growth curricula kindergarten through grade 12 in literature and in speaking and writing. The materials present various types of organization, bibliographies for both teacher and student, suggestions for teaching methods, methods of evaluating, and so on.

The proposed language program of the Wisconsin English-Language-Arts Curriculum Center begins with a listing of principles such as: Study of language should be spiraling and sequential from kindergarten through grade 12; the grammar taught should be eclectic; experience with language should be acquired empirically; and so on. In kindergarten through grade 6, it is envisioned that children should become aware of language processes through games and song, through observing word order in written and in oral discourse, from practicing verb forms in sentence patterns, and so on. In grades 7 through 9, various concepts in the structure of English are taught to the end that students learn to generate varied sentences, in addition to acquiring the ability to classify words as parts of speech. In grades 10 through 12, various concepts of transformational grammar and of rhetoric are to be taught; emphasis is on building sentences for a more effective expression of ideas.[27] The concepts taught in the various areas of English are sequenced in both a logical hierarchy and a hierarchy based on what is known of a child's abilities at a given age.

Development and use of varied instructional materials in english

Another trend in the 1960s has been concern for producing materials that provide for intraindividual variability and that help avoid using a single textbook as the course of study for all students. The development of varied instructional materials in English can be seen in curricula developed in USOE Curriculum Centers and in the recent work of the NCTE.

Gateway English, the Project English Curriculum Center (CRP # H-022) at Hunter College, has investigated materials and methods for culturally disadvantaged students in the junior high school. The investigators have produced units of high interest to the underprivileged, using materials centering around individuals who are themselves members of minority groups, who live in urban settings, and so on. The materials stress problem-solving as a means of learning.

In 1965, concerned with the lack of dissemination of information and of materials on teaching English to the disadvantaged, the NCTE appointed the Task Force on Teaching English to the Disadvantaged. Professors of English, of education, of linguistics, of sociology, directors of projects for the disadvantaged, supervisors and administrators from large cities, and representatives of state departments of education surveyed programs for teaching English to the culturally disadvantaged— in preschool, elementary school, secondary school, and adult basic education settings. The Task Force's report, *Language Programs for the Disadvantaged,* makes a number of recommendations on the study of dialect, on sequencing of instruction in usage, on the values of oral language practice and of imaginative literature for the disadvantaged. The

---

[27] Robert C. Pooley, "A Brief Digest of the Proposed Program in English Grammar for the State of Wisconsin," *Wisconsin English Journal,* VIII (January, 1966), 3–8.

report cites numerous recent materials on educating the disadvantaged, especially on language-learning.

The program of the Carnegie Curriculum Study Center (CRP # H-015) is for able college-bound students in grades 10 through 12. The program of the Indiana University English Curriculum Study Center (CRP # HE-080) is for academically talented, average, and slow-learning students. These are only a few examples of the wide range of projects producing materials for students of various abilities.

SCIENCE

Science instruction was introduced into the school curriculum under the name of natural philosophy in about 1750, at the same time that mathematics instruction first began. Natural philosophy at first included a smattering of physics, chemistry, and astronomy; and later, by the early nineteenth century, botany, zoology, and geology. Biology did not appear until the beginning of the twentieth century. Gradually, these areas of science began to be specialized courses, strong enough to merit a separate and permanent position in the curriculum. As the movement for the establishment of junior high schools gained momentum, general science courses were established. These nonspecialized courses were introduced to give students experience in a variety of scientific areas and, therefore, to help them decide which specialized courses to pursue in high school. Another general course that is relatively new to the secondary curriculum is the physical science course, designed to provide nonscience majors with some knowledge of chemistry and physics.[28]

Early methods of teaching science stressed the memorization of small, unconnected bits of information. For a long time, teaching was strictly on the verbal level, until teachers began to use crude demonstrations with physical objects to illustrate principles and relationships. Active student participation in science courses gained impetus with the introduction of biology and the desirability of analyzing and naming the physical components of plants and animals. Gradually, laboratory work was introduced in other courses, especially chemistry, which until the

---

[28] For one account of historical background in science education, see Nathan S. Washton, *Science Teaching in the Secondary School* (New York: Harper & Row, 1961), pp. 49–62.

1860s had been taught as a book course. Today nearly every science course has some integrated lab work to involve students actively in the learning process.

In a position paper published in 1964, the National Science Teachers Association (NSTA) defined *science* as ". . . the activity through which best explanations are sought for the observed facts of nature." According to NSTA, every science curriculum should include three aspects of the scientific enterprise: natural history (observation and factual description of nature), science (comprehension of the observed phenomena), and technology (use and control of phenomena). The purpose of science education is not only to teach the observed facts but also to get students intellectually involved in exploration, in discovery, and in examining and using their interests and abilities.[29]

The major problems facing science specialists and teachers today are essentially the same as those encountered by the other disciplines: How to assimilate new knowledge into the curriculum; how to utilize the recent findings on human learning and the devolpment of cognitive abilities; how to structure knowledge around basic principles and processes; and so on. Science curricula have long been plagued by the lack of articulation in kindergarten through grade 12. Elementary teachers are not aware of what knowledge in science they should be teaching to prepare the foundations for junior high study; and, in turn, junior high teachers have little idea of what goes on in elementary schools. Attitudes toward science are also of great concern to scientists and teachers who would like to promote the belief that science courses are not just for students who intend to pursue scientific careers. These two areas—improved articulation and the development of courses suitable to every student—are major concerns of most present science curriculum projects.

The NSTA in 1958 and 1959 issued policy statements to guide science improvement programs. Emphasized in both statements is the necessity for continuity in the development of fundamental principles and concepts underlying the structures of the various scientific fields. Principles taught at each level of instruction should be dependent on previous knowledge. The National Association of Secondary School Principals also issued a position paper in 1958, stating that content should be selected for inclusion in a curriculum on the basis of its im-

---

[29] "Theory into Action," a position paper on Curriculum Development in Science, a service report of the NSTA (Washington, D.C.: NSTA, 1964), Appendix.

pact on the lives of students. A conceptual rather than descriptive approach was recommended.[30]

Most curriculum projects focus on a single subject within the science field. To present a general picture of what is being done, a few of the major curriculum projects will be summarized.

The Physical Science Study Committee (PSSC), the first major curriculum project, was established in 1956 at the Massachusetts Institute of Technology (MIT). This joint effort of teachers, professors, and scientists resulted in the publication in 1960 of a secondary physics textbook, accompanied by laboratory guides, lab apparatus, and teachers' manuals. More than 40 films are now available for use with the course, which is organized into four sections: the Universe, Optics and Waves, Mechanics, and Electricity and Modern Physics. During its first three years of operation, PSSC conducted science institutes supported by NSF grants for more than 1300 teachers.

One widely known project is the Biological Science Curriculum Study (BSCS), begun in 1959 by the American Institute of Biological Sciences. Working on the high school level, one group of BSCS has produced three alternative textbooks, each approaching similar material from a different viewpoint. One textbook takes the ecological and evolutionary approach; another, the genetic and developmental approach; and the third, a biochemical and physiological approach. A second committee concentrated on the development of *laboratory block programs* in which students participate in scientific inquiry by carrying out extensive experiments. The task of a third committee was to prepare materials for the gifted student. These materials concern problems considered by research biologists as still unsolved. During the first year of nationwide testing, approximately 14,000 students received BSCS courses. After revision and further writing sessions, BSCS has provided high school biology teachers with a variety of materials from which to choose programs especially suited to their locale and student population. In addition to the three texts (blue, yellow, and green versions) and their accompanying teacher's manuals, there are now at least 12 complete lab programs, which promise to be one of the major innovations in teaching science.[31]

---

[30] Fraser, *op. cit.*, 15–19.
[31] Bentley Glass, "Renascent Biology: A Report on the AIBS Biological Sciences Curriculum Study," in Heath, ed., *op. cit.*, pp. 94–119.

A chemistry course, comparable in many ways to the BSCS programs, has been produced by the Chemical Education Materials Study (CHEM Study) for the first year of chemistry in high school. Materials include a text, lab manual, teacher's manual, and supplementary aids such as 16 mm films, charts, tests, and equipment. The emphasis of the course is on discovery through lab work and on the importance of a knowledge of the structure of concepts.

The Science Manpower Project, perhaps the largest single group to study the improvement of science articulation in kindergarten through grade 12, was organized in 1956 at Columbia University. The main effort of the project has been to propose a well-sequenced curriculum for the use of administrators and teachers in planning a science curriculum through the publication of a series of monographs for the teaching of physics, chemistry, and biology at the elementary and secondary levels.

The NSF has sponsored a number of summer and academic year institutes; and most projects, especially BSCS, provide traveling consultants who are available for help with the innumerable problems that must occur in any experimental program.

SOCIAL STUDIES

Because the area of social studies involves varied and complex problems, curriculum-revision in social studies is just beginning to gain momentum. Defining the scope of the discipline is especially a problem because social studies is, in fact, an aggregation of at least seven separate disciplines: history, political science, geography, economics, sociology, anthropology, and social psychology. Quite obviously, if a school curriculum allowed one year for each area, there would not be time for all. Until just recently, innovations in social studies content have been hindered by specialists debating what content should be given priority.

A second related problem is the fact that many areas of social studies deal with sensitive, controversial topics that local administrators and lay people are hesitant to put into a curriculum. A study of these topics—race relations, world population, and origin of man, Communism, politics, and so on—could easily take the form of propaganda if not handled objectively. Another barrier to the updating of social studies programs is the lack of funds needed to put ideas into practice. Even today, most projects are supported by private foundations.

In spite of these difficulties, several projects, smaller in scope than projects in science or mathematics, have been organized. There is general agreement among specialists and teachers that a background of basic concepts is necessary to any curriculum whether its objective is to train responsible citizens or to teach basic content.

In 1963, Project Social Studies under the U.S. Office of Education, established Curriculum Study Centers at the Carnegie Institute of Technology, Harvard, and the University of Minnesota. The Carnegie Center is developing a sequential program in history and social studies, grades 9 through 12. Materials emphasize the inductive approach, the methods of scientific inquiry, and the structure of knowledge. The materials produced at Harvard for grades 8 through 10 concentrate on five problem areas of society:

1. The problem of keeping individual and societal conflict within tolerable and reasonable limits
2. The problem of maintaining a reasonable balance between individual liberty and community cohesion
3. The problem of maintaining or developing a just priority of privileges among men within society and among nations
4. The problem of providing a standard of living for all men sufficient to maintain a "civilized" existence
5. The problem of determining the range of behavior necessary for men to express reasonable dissent in their efforts to effect social change[32]

Created as a "spiral" curriculum, the program calls for a reintroduction and expansion of the five areas at higher levels of complexity. The outline presented subsequently illustrates one treatment of the first problem.

Problem: The control of violence

In order to introduce the problem and to dramatize the fact that violence control can be thought of as a problem, a brief emotional impact lesson might be staged. This could consist of descriptions of atomic explosions, perhaps pictures of Hiroshima after the blast; photographs, films, or descriptions of a lynch crowd or other similar mob action; perhaps a description of the breakdown of social controls during great natural disasters.

---

[32] Frances A. J. Ianni and Lois S. Josephs, "The Curriculum Research and Development Program of the U.S. Office of Education: Project English, Project Social Studies and Beyond," in Heath, *op. cit.*, pp. 202–203. By permission.

FIRST ROUND

Topic A: The Family

This topic would present a fairly simple introduction to the problem. By what means is violence controlled within the family? Probably, we would draw on personal statements, hypothetical cases, and some clinical documents. The Cain and Abel story might be good.

The basic concept would be *restraint*: external restraint of parental authority; internal restraint of conscience; love, fear, and regret as motivations.

Topic B: The Peer Group

What are the limits on violence within the students' peer groups? We would start by focusing on personal experience as above. In order to broaden the context, assuming that the students with whom we worked were by and large nonviolent middle class, we may use situations in which there is more tolerance for intragroup violence. This could include the use of violence as a ritual means of acceptance and of settling disputes—violence as a part of the rules of the game. Excerpts from *Lord of the Flies* might provide good material.

Concepts. The inadequacy, in this context, of the restraints of internal regret or external superior authority which are operative in the family. Introduce *rules of the game*—small-group laws and sanctions. This might lead to questions of how rules are arrived at, when they are applied, and who directs each of these forces. The discussion might then move to *social role, function,* and *structure;* also the question of why does one go along with rules, i.e., *motive. Shared values* would also be important. It must be remembered that these concepts will be presented in very simple form to begin with. In each following topic, for this and other problems, concepts introduced earlier will be repeated and developed.

Topic C: Primitive Cultures

What kinds of different norm systems exist in a variety of primitive societies in order to control violence? Cases could be based on the "Ways of Mankind" recordings which present a wide range of primitive conceptions of law.

Concepts. Law as rules of the game in a larger society than the peer group; *culture; institution; rights; power; authority; legitimacy; control; adjudication.* Definitional concepts of *vagueness,* and *ambiguity:* What constitutes violence?

Topic D: American Communities

What kinds of value-systems and legal-social controls exist to control violence in American communities? This topic would aim to develop the relationship between law and social order in specific situations relatively familiar to the students. Cases might be: a typical middle-class community, with minimum violence-control problems; Clinton, Tennessee, in 1957; Oxford, Mississippi, in 1962; labor violence in a Northern one-company town; Kentucky or West Virginia coal towns; Vigilantes in 19th century California or Southwest.

Concepts. Rule of law, consent; elaboration of prior sociological categories.

SECOND ROUND

The second round of the problem of violence control might be a study of the development of Western legal and political systems. The study would not be a detailed examination of political movements, theorists, and systems so much as a schematic history of the development of such concepts as the *social contract, rule of law, constitutionalism, personal freedoms* (speech, religion, association, press), *federalism, due process, social justice,* and the like.

THIRD ROUND

The third round would focus on the question of what happens when there is a breakdown of law and social order within societies leading to redefinition of law and the terms of social order. Possible cases here would be, in order of ascending complexity: the American Revolution or Civil War; the French Revolution; the Russian Revolution.[33]

The structure of knowledge and an identification of basic concepts are the main concerns of the University of Minnesota Center, which will define the structure of each discipline according to its range, methodology, and concepts. The Center's ultimate goal is to establish a curriculum that will guide the development of teaching materials for kindergarten through junior college.

An extensive study of social studies curricula is being conducted by the American Council of Learned Societies in conjunction with Educational Services Incorporated. Teams of curriculum specialists and scholars are working on both elementary and secondary content sequencing. Programs are designed with two objectives in mind: (1) To integrate the related concepts of the disciplines and (2) to train students to choose relevant facts and to discard the irrelevant in thinking about the problems of a society in flux.

These groups and several others are working effectively toward planning and developing an integrated, well-sequenced social studies curric-

---

[33] *Ibid.,* pp. 203–205.

ulum. In the future we may anticipate more widespread concern by scholars and curriculum-planners in reorganizing the content and sequence of the social studies disciplines.

FOREIGN LANGUAGE

Only since the early 1950s have foreign language courses been regarded as a necessity in a school curriculum. Before that time, in the nineteenth and early twentieth century, modern foreign language received very minor consideration. Secondary students were taught with the "grammar-translation" approach and most likely completed the maximum two-year course with no instruction in the techniques of pronunciation or conversation.

During World War II, the need for trained speakers of foreign languages became increasingly apparent to the government and to educators; and "crash" language programs were set up by the Armed Forces. Through books, films, recordings, and conversational drill, the personnel received intensive, nearly totally oral, training for nine months to one year, with the total time equaling some six years of high school language courses. The continued need for trained people was stated strongly by the U.S. Commissioner of Education whose statement that foreign language be included in school curricula at all levels gave much impetus to foreign language movements.

In 1952-1953, with the support of the Carnegie Foundation and the USOE, the Modern Language Association (MLA) began an extensive study of language instruction, a study that was the prime influence for modern languages being included as vital to the country in the NDEA of 1958. A policy statement in 1956 of the MLA proposed three major objectives for foreign language study. The student should (1) acquire the skills that would give him mastery of the language; (2) gain understanding of language in general, his own as well as the second language; and (3) develop at a basic level the idea of differences between cultures through experiences and training.

Within the past 10 or 15 years, the most obvious foreign language curriculum revision is the increasing number of schools that provide modern language instruction in the elementary school. Although elementary schools gave instruction before 1950, it was as enrichment for gifted students. Today many communities include in the elementary curriculum foreign language instruction not only for the gifted but also for those whose abilities and work habits afford time for some kind of enrichment. A nationwide plan for this kind of instruction, however, is yet to be adopted.

Although many specialists are advocating a longer sequence of training, the modern innovations in foreign languages are perhaps not as much concerned with curriculum revision as with instructional methods. The trend has been away from emphasis on reading and translating toward comprehending and using the spoken language, the audiolingual approach. John B. Carroll of Harvard University lists four prominent characteristics of the relatively contemporary methods being used in the schools today:[34] One is that any training in the written language is usually preceded by instruction in listening and speaking. Advocates of this system believe that learning in the spoken language will facilitate reading skills, although there is no research to indicate that this is absolutely true. Studies do show, however, that the audiolingual approach does not hinder the development of reading skills but is equally as effective as more traditional methods.[35]

The second characteristic of modern methods involves a consideration of the results of scientific analysis of the differences between the student's native language and the new language. Possible difficulties in pronunciation can be predicted in advance quite accurately.

The third characteristic, conversational drill, the overlearning of language patterns, is given much more emphasis today than previously. *Pattern practice* usually involves repetition and drill with similar sentence patterns but different elements. For example, the sentences "Je ne sais pas" and "Ils ne savent pas" have the same basic sentence pattern but dissimilar elements. Although the amount of time available for this kind of drill may be limited, many schools are making efficient use of language labs and autoinstructional materials and devices to provide drill practice for 30 or more students simultaneously.

The fourth characteristic of modern language teaching is the attempt to eliminate the use of the student's native language in instructional situations. Pictures, maps, films, and so on are used to avoid the inter-

---

[34] John B. Carroll, "Research on Teaching Foreign Languages," in N. L. Gage, ed., *Handbook of Research on Teaching* (Chicago: Rand McNally, 1963), pp. 1063–1064.
[35] *Ibid.*, p. 1078.

vention of the native language and to de-emphasize the tendency to translate from one language to another.

With the change in emphasis from the ability of students to read and translate to the ability to listen and speak came the need for a revision of instructional materials and media. In 1959, through the Language Development Program, authorized by the NDEA, government funds made possible the establishment of over 165 projects for research, surveys, and materials development.[36] Several of the more important projects are the Modern Language Materials Development Center and the Audio-Lingual Materials Project, which is preparing a complete set of materials for a six-year secondary sequence in French, German, Italian, Russian, and Spanish. Other programs are producing testing and evaluation devices, instructional materials in less common languages such as the Asian and African languages, and well-sequenced programs for the elementary level.

Modern technology has given the study of modern foreign languages a flexibility which was virtually impossible 15 years ago. Through language labs, each student can receive intensive, individual practice in speaking the language, and in understanding a variety of foreign language speakers. All of the students' time may be devoted to participating actively in the learning process with little time spent in passive absorption. Because the teacher may monitor at random any student's performance, more individual instruction may be given, and better bases for evaluation are provided than in the traditional classroom. In the future, improved programs and more sophisticated technical advances, perhaps synchronized visual materials, promise to relieve the monotony characteristic of some of the present language lab programs.

SUMMARY

The last several years have brought dramatic changes in the teaching of various subjects—mathematics, English, science, social studies, modern foreign languages, fine arts, applied arts, reading, physical education, and so on. (Limitations of space in this book permit discussion of only the first five of these.) Although at the level of research and theory

---

[36] Fraser, *op. cit.*, 69.

there has long been concern for sequential curricula in various areas, curricula reflecting the current state of knowledge and current psychology of learning, it is only recently that large-scale financial support has been available. Any real experimental, developmental programs have awaited the massive support of grants from foundations, professional organizations, and the U.S. Office of Education.

The many recent curriculum projects have involved professors in academic areas, specialists in education, learning specialists, teachers, supervisors, and so on. Such projects have frequently been national in scope. The projects have often concerned themselves with defining subject areas, with content and process, with sequence and articulation, with the development and use of instructional materials, with bringing materials up to date, and with providing for learners of different levels of ability and achievement.

The existing curriculum projects seem to be only a first step in a large, long-range effort. Scholars and teachers of the future will continue to ask what knowledge to teach, how to structure knowledge, the age level at which students can learn selected concepts, the most effective materials and methods, and so on. Such continuing reforms place a great responsibility on the teacher to keep abreast of current curriculum developments and of new knowledge in his particular area.

QUESTIONS AND ACTIVITIES

1 Turn to the literature in your area of interest and read on the efforts of various national groups to define, or to delimit, its area. Write a brief paper in which you compare and contrast various positions on definitions.

2 Discuss the implications of the *Taxonomy of Educational Objectives* for teaching and for building curriculum.

3 Report on some groups that have been working on up-dating curriculum in your area.

4 In the light of what you know of the structure of knowledge in your field, list some basic principles and concepts in a well-planned sequence that might make the principles and concepts more comprehensible to a student.

5 Discuss the extent to which knowledge is growing rapidly in your field of study.

6 Study further in the historical backgrounds of teaching in your own subject-matter field.
7 When might the discovery method be especially appropriate in your own teaching? In your own learning?
8 Justify the need for articulation in your area by recalling the effects on you of those courses you have taken that lacked articulation.
9 Examine, evaluate, and report on some of the most recent instructional materials in your field. Comment on their best uses.
10 List some of the reasons why, as a professional, you should participate in inservice education after you begin teaching.

SUGGESTIONS FOR FURTHER READING

BROWN, SANBORN C., NORMAN CLARKE, AND JAYME TIOMNO, ED., *Why Teach Physics?* Cambridge, Mass.: M.I.T., 1964.

DARROW, HELEN FISHER, *Social Studies for Understanding,* New York: Bureau of Publications, Teachers College, Columbia University, 1964.

Education and the Structure of Knowledge: Fifth Annual Phi Delta Kappa Symposium on Educational Research, Chicago: Rand McNally, 1964.

FINOCCHIARO, MARY, *Teaching Children Foreign Language,* New York: McGraw-Hill, 1964.

Focus on the Social Studies, A Report from the 1965 Department of Elementary School Principals, Washington, D.C.: National Education Association, 1965.

FORD, G. W., AND LAWRENCE PUGNO, ED., *The Structure of Knowledge and the Curriculum,* Chicago: Rand McNally, 1964.

KEPES, GYORGY, ED., *Structure in Art and in Science,* New York: Braziller, 1965.

KRUG, EDWARD A., *The Secondary School Curriculum,* New York: Harper & Row, 1960.

LIBBISH, B., ED., *Advances in the Teaching of Modern Languages,* New York, Macmillan, 1964.

NATIONAL SCIENCE TEACHERS ASSOCIATION, *New Developments in High School Science Teaching,* Washington, D.C.: National Education Association, 1960.

RITCHIE, ROBERT W., ED., *New Directions in Mathematics,* Englewood Cliffs, N.J.: Prentice-Hall, 1963.

Using Current Curriculum Developments, Washington, D.C.: Association for Supervision and Curriculum Development, 1963.

5 Curriculum organization

*W*hat educative experiences should a student have during a year? What should he learn each day? The objectives listed here cover instruction in various courses for an eleventh-grade girl during a single day. As the teachers wrote the plans, each objective is equally applicable to each student in the class.

CHEMISTRY

1. Continues to develop an appreciation of the significance of chemistry
2. Improves in the ability to distinguish fact from inference
3. Learns of the work of Becquerel and Curie as historical background for a study of natural radioactivity
4. Considers radioactivity as it helps determine the age of the earth
5. Learns the resemblance of alpha particles to helium nuclei

ENGLISH

1. Increases ability to make an intellectual as well as an emotional response to poetry
2. Gains in ability to recognize terms related to tone in poetry: irony, paradox, understatement
3. Discusses such biographical facts on Poe as shed light on the meaning of *The Haunted Palace*

4. Discusses what *The Haunted Palace* implies about a human mind
5. Examines figurative language in several of Poe's poems

FRENCH

1. Learns pronunciation of new words by imitating the teacher in a short drill
2. Learns general rules for syllabication
3. Learns general pattern for intonation in French
4. Continues working on the use of negatives in sentences
5. Reviews previously learned vocabulary

HOME ECONOMICS

1. Obtains an overview of making a garment
2. Develops appreciation of skilled workmanship
3. Understand symbols important to efficient use of a pattern
4. Understands how to follow pattern instructions for layout, cutting, and marking
5. Learns steps in preparing fabric: Identifying the right side, locating the grain and nap, making allowance for plaids and stripes, and so on

TYPEWRITING

1. Improves in stroking rate
2. Improves in developing word-level responses
3. Develops in appreciation for neatness and correctness
4. Learns how to make neat erasures
5. Learns how to change a typewriter ribbon

It is immediately apparent that the objectives listed imply the content and method of instruction in this high school and that instruction is organized into separate subject areas in the junior year. Do these subject-matter outlines constitute the curriculum of this student? Not completely, although a good portion of the curriculum is implied in the course objectives. The curriculum of a school is more than the subjects taught.

Krug has defined *curriculum* as ". . . the means of instruction used by the school to provide opportunities for student learning experiences leading to desired learning outcomes."[1] Among means of instruction,

---

[1] Edward A. Krug, *Curriculum Planning*, rev. ed. (New York: Harper & Row, 1957), p. 3. By permission.

he lists classroom studies; guidance or counseling programs; school and community service projects; school-related work experience; school health services, camps, library; and extracurricular activities.[2]

In this sense, the all-school curriculum consists of all the experiences that students have under the guidance of the school. In a like manner, a given student's curriculum is the complex of educational experiences —the classes, guidance activities, and so on—guided by the school.

In today's comprehensive high school, nevertheless, there is considerable separation of "the means of instruction" for administrative purposes. This separation is indicated by the titles and duties of the various personnel: (1) The curriculum coordinator, consultant, or director assumes leadership in formulating the school's objectives, coordinating the pattern of school subjects and extracurricular activities, planning curriculum guides, and providing for various aids to classroom instruction. (2) The subject supervisor or general supervisor works with teachers to improve instruction in a particular subject-matter field or to help work out general problems that the teacher encounters. (3) The guidance director or coordinator coordinates the special guidance and counseling program. (4) The health officer is in charge of health services in the school—immunization and vaccination, physical examinations, and so on. As these titles and descriptions suggest, the tendency is to differentiate according to content of instruction, methods of instruction, and special services.

But although these differentiations are useful for administrative purposes, present-day curriculum theory recognizes that the curriculum consists of all the means used to guide students' behavior in desirable directions. Theory also recognizes that the means of instruction must be carefully organized and executed because students must perceive the meaning and relationship of all their learnings if education is to be most profitable.

Provision for learning experiences requires careful planning of whatever is to be done in the classroom. Krug has defined *curriculum-planning* as ". . . the process of orderly study and improvement of schooling in the light of objectives."[3] Then, for purposes of discussion, he lists five aspects of curriculum-planning, activities that occur con-

---

[2] *Ibid.*
[3] *Ibid.*, p. 17.

currently and continuously, in this fashion: "(1) Identifying and stating educational objectives; (2) developing the all-school program; (3) teaching and learning; (4) providing curriculum guides; (5) providing instructional aids and materials."[4] These activities are the theme of many of the chapters of this book.

Such educational planning is done in light of the knowledge of the needs of society or the culture, the needs of the learner, and the unique content of the various subject-matter areas. Such planning is done at its best by teams of both professional and nonprofessional people: subject-matter consultants, classroom teachers, psychometricians, representatives of the general public, building principals, guidance counselors, learners, and so on.

CURRICULUM IN AN HISTORICAL PERSPECTIVE

In the present decade, there are many different patterns for organizing courses in the secondary school. As a rule, a certain number of specified courses are often required of all students for graduation. In addition, each student selects a particular track or course—college-preparatory, business education, vocational—in which he must take certain courses. However, he can also take certain electives—machine operation or office practice, for example, if he is pursuing business education—and free electives, often enrichment courses, not directly connected with his graduation requirements. The student can receive credit toward graduation for participating in music or athletic programs, student government, school-community projects, work in a community business enterprise, and so on. In the discussion that follows, we will see that this kind of flexibility has not always been found in secondary schools.

The Latin grammar school, 1635

The traditional European secondary school, in the form of the Latin Grammar School, was introduced into the American colonies in 1635. The school had as its major purpose the preparation of a small number of young people for college. Its curriculum consisted primarily of in-

---

[4] *Ibid.*, p. 4.

struction in Latin to be used by ministers, magistrates, and teachers of Latin, among others. It also taught small amounts of Greek and religion.

Harvard College, founded in 1636, set a pattern for college domination of the secondary school curriculum. Its admission requirements in 1642 included reading Cicero at sight, reciting Latin poetry and prose, and conjugating Greek verbs. Other colleges established after 1636 had similar entrance requirements. Thus, the curricula of Latin grammar schools established after 1635 also laid heavy emphasis on Latin and Greek, the two inescapable requirements for admission to colonial colleges.

Franklin's academy, 1753

The Latin grammar schools continued to dominate secondary education until 1753, when Franklin's academy was chartered in Pennsylvania. Benjamin Franklin, its founder, proposed that curricula be more practical for young people and that such useful education be available to more students. The subjects he proposed—many of them were not adopted—included writing, drawing, English grammar, composition, literature, arithmetic, geometry, astronomy, history, science, agriculture, gardening, and mechanics. No religious instruction was provided.

Other academies were founded after 1753, some endowed by private sources, some supported by religious groups, some supported by the public. They continued to spread in New England and in the Middle Atlantic States until about 1850. At this time, college and university entrance requirements had come to dominate the curricula for the academies, too, because academy students often came from relatively well-to-do homes and usually attended college after graduating.

The academy is chiefly responsible for freeing the curriculum of religious subjects, for opening secondary education to girls, and for providing practical courses for young people.

The English high school, 1821

The Latin school and the academy did not meet the needs of those who could not afford to pay the tuition and boarding expenses required for such education. Free elementary school education was provided for children of the middle class, but this economic group wanted public-supported secondary education as well. The English High School, established in Boston in 1821, was the first attempt to meet this need. It was a three-year high school designed for boys twelve years or older who did not intend to go to college. The curriculum featured English literature and composition, geography, arithmetic, algebra, geometry, surveying, navigation, United States history, and natural and political philosophy. It included no foreign language or religion.

In 1827, Massachusetts passed a law saying that each town having five hundred or more families must establish such a school. Thus, in the New England States, Latin schools and academies, which usually required fees, and English high schools, which usually required no fees but had comparatively few pupils, both served as secondary schools. It remained for the frontier section—the region now called the North Central States—to establish the free public high school open to everyone of school age.

The free public high school

The idea of creating one public-supported secondary school for all youth was implemented in Michigan in the Kalamazoo decision in 1872 when the supreme court of that state ruled that school boards could levy and collect taxes for the support of secondary schools. This precedent was followed in the neighboring states—Wisconsin, Illinois, and Indiana. States admitted to the Union after the Kalamazoo decision also provided for free secondary schools. This decision brought to an end the establishing of new Latin schools and academies. And by 1900 the free public high school was universally accepted as a continuation of the elementary school.

The new high schools drew upon established institutions for curricular patterns. Colleges and universities continued to specify credit requirements in Latin, mathematics, and other subjects.

Proposals of national committees, 1895–1911

The Committee on College Entrance Requirements began its work in 1895 and issued its first report in 1899. The committee approved the inclusion of Latin, Greek, French, German, English, history, civics, economics, geography, biology, chemistry, and mathematics in high school curricula. In general, it confirmed the report made by the Committee of Ten in 1893, which recommended four types of secondary school courses as college preparatory: the Classical, which included two ancient and one modern foreign language; the English classical, which included one ancient and one modern foreign language; the modern language, which included two modern languages; and the scientific, which included one foreign language. Many members of both committees were on the staff of various colleges and universities, a fact that probably accounts for the emphasis on the college-preparatory function of secondary education at the expense of the obligation of secondary education to make high school education appropriate for students who did not go to college.

To clarify the role of the high school in preparing for college entrance, the Committee on College Entrance Requirements recommended that each student's high school record show that he had completed four units in a foreign language, two units in English, two units in mathematics, one unit in history, and one unit in science. The committee also recommended that four hours of class attendance per week throughout the school year constitute a unit.

In 1906, the Carnegie Foundation for the Advancement of Teaching proposed that five periods of class work per week throughout the school year constitute a unit. This stipulation became known as a *Carnegie unit*, a unit of measurement for admission to college.

The recommendations of the Committee on Entrance Requirements were upheld by the Committee of Nine on the Articulation of High School and College, when, in 1911, the Committee on Articulation proposed that the high school program include 15 units, of which three should be in English, one in social science, and one in natural science. Furthermore, it proposed that all high schools offer three units each in two majors other than English and two units in one minor. The two majors were to be selected from Latin or a modern language, mathematics, social science, or natural science. The requirements for graduation were not to specify more than two units of mathematics or two units of a foreign language. Thus, 11 of the 15 units would be drawn from the five subject fields specified for majors, and the other four units might be taken in mechanical arts, household science, commercial work, or any other field that best met the interest of the student. Physical education was also required but without credit toward graduation.

Generally, the recommendations of these committees were widely adopted in the secondary schools of the period. They continued to exert a strong influence throughout the 1920s and are still in force in some high schools today. Here, for example, is a transcript of credits issued in 1931 from a four year high school:

English	4 units
Latin	3 units
European history	1 unit
American history	1 unit
Economics	½ unit
Civics	½ unit
Commercial arithmetic	1 unit
Algebra	1½ units
Plane geometry	1 unit
Geography	1½ units
Biology	1 unit
Physical education	½ unit
Health	½ unit
Art	½ unit
Music	½ unit

Note that the four completed majors—English, foreign language, social studies, and mathematics—and the minor—science—were proposed as majors in 1911. Note also that all except the last four subjects were included in the 1899 proposals of the Committee on College Entrance Requirements.

The school discussed here was a small consolidated school in a rural area of southern Indiana. Every ninth-grade student in it was required to take Latin and algebra. Every student had to complete at least 16 units, of which not more than four could be elected. Less than one third of the students who entered the school graduated. Considerably less than half of those who finished the eighth grade started the ninth. From 1927 to 1931, there were no classes in agriculture, business, industrial arts, physics, chemistry, dramatics, speech, orchestra, or band.

The eight-year study

The cardinal principles of secondary education stated by the Commission on the Reorganization of Secondary Education in 1918 did much to focus educators' attention on the problem of designing a curriculum that would achieve the objectives of health, command of fundamental processes, good home relations, vocation, citizenship, profitable use of leisure, and good character. Since that time, both junior and senior high schools have experimented with curriculum design and practice.

One comprehensive study that gave great impetus to this experimentation was the Eight-Year Study, sponsored by the Progressive Education Association and directed by Wilford Aikin, which began in 1933. A broad range of schools was represented by the 30 secondary schools that participated in the study—private and public, large and small, traditional and progressive. Some 300 colleges and universities agreed to admit graduates of these 30 schools without the usual required subjects.

Curriculum consultants worked with the staff of the schools in redesigning their curricula to include the following general objectives: Greater mastery and continuity of learning; clearer understanding of contemporary social problems; development of a sense of responsibility; freer release of creative energies; greater freedom of choice for students and teachers; and more emphasis on student counseling. In reorganizing their curricula, the various schools used broad fields, correlated, integrated, and problem-type approaches. The study classified as "least progressive" the schools that followed most closely the traditional program of separate subjects and college-preparatory classes, and as "most progressive" those that departed most from this traditional program. An evaluation staff under the direction of Ralph Tyler devised the instruments and procedures to evaluate the results of the experiment.

The first graduates of the 30 participating schools entered college in 1936, and their college careers were followed to discover their success as college students. In this follow-up, 1475 graduates of the 30 schools were paired with 1475 graduates of conventional high schools. The pairs were equated in IQ score, scholastic aptitude, age, sex, and socio-economic background.

Some of the more important conclusions reported by the researchers follow. The graduates of the thirty schools:

1. Earned a slightly higher total grade average
2. Earned higher grade averages in all subject fields except foreign language

3. Specialized in the same academic fields as did the comparison students
4. Did not differ from the comparison group in the number of times they were placed on probation
5. Received slightly more academic honors in each year
6. Were more often judged to possess a high degree of intellectual curiosity and drive
7. Were more often judged to be precise, systematic, and objective in their thinking
8. Were more often judged to have developed clear or well-formulated ideas concerning the meaning of education—especially in the first two years of college
9. More often demonstrated a high degree of resourcefulness in meeting new situations
10. Did not differ from the comparison group in ability to plan their time effectively
11. Had about the same problems of adjustment as the comparison group, but approached their solution with greater effectiveness
12. Participated somewhat more frequently, and more often enjoyed appreciative experiences, in the arts
13. Participated more in all organized student groups except religious and "service" activities
14. Earned in each college year a higher percentage of nonacademic honors (officership in organizations, election to managerial societies, athletic insignia, leading roles in dramatic and musical presentations)
15. Did not differ from the comparison group in the quality of adjustment to their contemporaries
16. Differed only slightly from the comparison group in all kinds of judgments about their schooling
17. Had a somewhat better orientation toward the choice of a vocation
18. Demonstrated a more active concern for what was going on in the world[5]

This study indicated that the usual college-preparatory high school track or course could undergo considerable revision without interfering with the success of students who went to college. Note that most of the items involving academic success showed the two groups to be about equal; those involving nonacademic areas indicated that the graduates from the progressive schools were somewhat superior.

---

[5] Wilford M. Aikin, *The Story of the Eight-Year Study*, Vol. I of *Adventure in American Education*, 5 vols. Copyright 1942, by McGraw-Hill, Inc., pp. 111–112.

PRESENT PATTERNS IN THE ORGANIZATION AND IN THE GROUPING OF STUDENTS FOR LEARNING

In recent decades, several patterns have emerged for organizing the school so that its structure might harmonize with desired educational objectives. One pattern concerns itself with the organization of curriculum by separating subjects into single fields or by combining subject fields in various combinations. A second type of structure, administratively rather than content determined, concerns itself with the provision for individual differences among learners through homogeneous and heterogeneous grouping, team teaching, and nongrading policies.

Such division of organization into content- and activity-determined and administratively determined patterns is, of course, an artificial device to facilitate discussion. Team teaching is employed with separate-subject curriculum as well as with the developmental-activity curriculum. Separate subject fields have traditionally paid attention to intraindividual variability as have core curriculum, or team teaching, or the nongraded school. In reality, the content-determined and the administratively-determined aspects of organization occur in many combinations and permutations.

Present patterns in the organization of the curriculum

For purposes of convenient reference and discussion, Kearney and Cook make two broad classifications of curricula: "(a) subject-matter curriculums, including separate subjects, correlated subjects, and broad fields; and (b) developmental-activity curriculums."[6] They describe the subject-matter curriculum as emphasizing content, facts, and skills. They characterize *developmental-activity curriculums* as emphasizing the need to focus on the needs and development of the individual child and ". . . to fit the scope and sequence of each child's activities and experiences in school to his biological, intellectual, and social growth."[7]

A *subject-matter curriculum* is organized around a specific group of concepts and processes. The classification takes meaning from the unique nature, and the aims and ends, of the subject matter. Thus, composition,

---

[6] Nolan C. Kearney and Walter W. Cook, "Curriculum," in Chester W. Harris, ed., *Encyclopedia of Educational Research*, 3rd ed. (New York: Macmillan, 1960), p. 359.
[7] *Ibid.*

English literature, American literature, dramatics, journalism, speech, creative writing, developmental reading, and remedial reading are distinguished as separate subjects within the broader field of language arts. Such subject matter is often taught five days a week in 40- and 50-minute periods by a specialist in the subject.

A frequent complaint against organization by separate subjects is the rigid compartmentalization of knowledge, the failure to relate one discipline to another. Another complaint is that content, not the needs of the learner or of society, dictates most of what is taught.

Concern for the atomism and rigidity of subject organization has led to attempts to reorganize school programs in ways that might more effectively relate subjects to one another. One such attempt at reorganization has been the *correlated curriculum* in which several separate subjects complement one another. In a correlated curriculum, separate subjects from different fields—American literature and American history, for example—are combined and are studied simultaneously. The separate subjects lose their identity as distinct bodies of conceptions.

Still another way of shaping a program is by a *broad-fields curriculum*. In this type of organization, single subjects in a broad field are combined; formally discrete subject matters are integrated. Thus, reading, writing, listening, and speaking are united into a language arts program; history, economics, sociology, and political science are combined into a broad-fields class known as social studies; specialized courses in science become general, life, and physical science.

Kearney and Cook's second category is the *developmental-activity curriculum*. They say that such organization ". . . takes advantage, upon occasion, of all the aspects of broad-fields, correlated, or subject-matter curriculums, but it goes beyond them in its emphasis on the nature of the learner, on the range of interests and abilities in the classroom, and on problem-solving as the essence of the educative process."[8]

In the secondary school, the developmental-activity concept has sometimes been embodied in *core curriculum*. Core is often said to be curriculum that disregards subject-matter boundaries, and, instead, focuses on learnings fundamentally important to all students. Yet, because the term *core* is used in different ways, it has been necessary

---

[8] *Ibid.*, p. 360.

to give considerable thought to practices termed core in various school systems. Alberty identifies six different designs labeled core programs:

1. The core consists of a number of logically organized subjects or fields of knowledge each one of which is taught independently
2. The core consists of a number of logically organized subjects or fields of knowledge, some or all of which are correlated
3. The core consists of broad problems, units of work, or unifying themes which are chosen because they afford the means of teaching effectively the basic content of certain subjects or fields of knowledge; these subjects or fields retain their identity, but the content is selected and taught with special reference to the unit, theme, or problem
4. The core consists of a number of subjects or fields of knowledge which are unified or fused; usually one subject or field (e.g., history) serves as the unifying center
5. The core consists of learning experiences selected from broad preplanned or problem areas, in terms of the psychobiological and societal needs, problems, and interests of students
6. The core consists of broad teacher-student planned units of work, or activities, in terms of needs, problems, or interests as perceived by the group; no basic curriculum structure is set up[9]

A helpful description of a commonly accepted present-day usage of the term core curriculum is provided by Faunce and Bossing.

1. It seeks to establish relationships among areas of living by the study of problems that challenge the pupil to explore and utilize the knowledge and skills of more than one subject
2. It aims at larger objectives than would characterize any single subject area
3. It involves the joint planning of those objectives, and of the means of achieving them, by both teachers and pupils; it is directly geared to the goal of increased skill in the processes of cooperative planning
4. It requires a block of time longer than the traditional period
5. It involves either a single teacher for two or more periods, or a team of teachers who work together
6. It is dedicated to improved guidance of individuals and groups of pupils
7. Its basic emphasis in instructional planning is the present psychobiological and social needs of the pupils themselves[10]

9 Harold B. Alberty, *Reorganizing the High School Curriculum*, rev. ed. (New York: Macmillan, 1953), pp. 167–168. Reprinted with permission of The Macmillan Company.
10 Roland C. Faunce and Nelson L. Bossing, *Developing the Core Curriculum*, (c) 1951, pp. 8–9. Reprinted by permission of Prentice-Hall, Inc., Englewood Cliffs, New Jersey.

The integration of activities into the altogether too-infrequently-used core program requires careful and detailed planning by the teacher and students, broader understanding and skills than many teachers possess, and close cooperation among the teachers who have the requisite abilities and who can therefore contribute most to the students' experience. If the integration of activities is efficient, it is possible that the various separate-subject areas can be organized by students into more meaningful educative experiences.

NEW PATTERNS IN THE GROUPING OF STUDENTS FOR LEARNING

Several administrative patterns have emerged recently to accommodate the individual learner. One of the concerns of planners has been the horizontal and vertical organization of the means of instruction in the secondary schools.

Vertical organization deals with the way ". . . units are stacked one upon the other, providing for the upward progression of students through a time sequence."[11] Thus, mathematics precedes physics; physics precedes chemistry. A hierarchial pattern is assigned course work; it is assumed that there is a set order for presenting knowledge. Commonly, each course is assigned to a grade level and students move along at a set rate of progression.

Horizontal organization deals with the way in which ". . . segments of these vertical units are arranged side by side providing both a pupil-to-teacher ratio and a basis for assigning students and teachers to available space."[12] Horizontal organization has already been considered in part in the discussion of the patterns of division of the means of instruction. Arranging units side by side according to instructional field is one type of horizontal organization. The combination of related areas of knowledge into a developmental-activity curriculum is still another type.

---

[11] John I. Goodlad, "Individual Differences and Vertical Organization of the School," *Individualizing Instruction*, Sixty-first Yearbook of the National Society for the Study of Education, Part I (Chicago: The University of Chicago Press, 1962), p. 209.
[12] *Ibid.*

One administrative device used in horizontal organization (and in vertical organization, too) is the bringing of students together into homogeneous groups. Such homogeneous grouping often takes the form of the division of students into groups of low, average, and high mental ability. Even though such grouping is often done on the basis of mental ability, the sectioning of age groups into homogeneous sections sometimes uses other criteria of identification: achievement level, interest, and teacher recommendation.

Homogeneously (or, more often, ability) arranged instructional groups are justified on the basis of provision for individual differences. Fast students need no longer be held back by slow students in their progression through subject matter. In homogeneous groups for the academically talented, activities can be enriched or accelerated. In homogeneous, age-graded classes for the slow, attention can be given to basic skills and to remedial work. Such grouping has grown in use in the last decade, and in many schools membership in such a group is fixed and stable for the entire school year.

But homogeneous grouping has not solved all of the problems of opening the way to individualization. Homogeneous grouping is often used to facilitate one type of learning only, academic. And its critics point out its failure to provide for societal needs through the planned interaction of youth of differing intelligence and motivation. Too, the teacher sometimes assumes that homogeneous grouping completely eliminates intraindividual differences. He then paces class members through the same graded textbook at the same rate of speed, using lecture and recitation methods. However, the fact remains that, even after the classification of students on the basis of general aptitude, heterogeneity exists. Tyler, for instance, demonstrates this variability in a seventh-grade group in Table 5.1. Tyler's article, and the other articles in the same yearbook, cautions us that attempts to produce completely homogeneous groups are not very feasible.

Because attempts to attain homogeneity within instructional groups have not been wholly effective, and because research on the great variability—in readiness, in ability to learn, in many traits—of humans has evinced the need to give increasing attention to individual differences, recent innovators have tried to plan more flexible settings and more readily manipulated schedules for learning. Two important innovations of recent times are the nongraded school and team teaching. And much of the exploratory work in seeking new ways of organizing the means of instruction has followed guidelines established by such groups as the Commission on the Experimental Study of the Utilization of the Staff in the Secondary Schools and the conferences at Mt. Kisco, New York.

TABLE 5.1. *Distributions of Grade Equivalents on Achievement Tests for Seventh-Grade Pupils with IQs of 118–122, and with IQs of at least 120.*

Pupils with IQs of 118–122

Grade equivalent	Paragraph meaning	Word meaning	Arithmetic reasoning	Arithmetic computation
11	1	9	...	...
10	10	8	7	10
9	11	6	16	5
8	7	19	11	22
7	14	10	19	13
6	13	5	3	6
5	1	...	1	1

Pupils with IQs of at least 120

Grade equivalent	Paragraph meaning	Word meaning	Arithmetic reasoning	Arithmetic computation
11	6	36	...	10
10	42	32	42	28
9	38	28	47	19
8	30	49	41	76
7	25	11	30	26
6	23	9	6	7
5	1	...	1	1

SOURCE: Adapted from Fred T. Tyler, "Intraindividual Variability," *Individualizing Instruction*, Sixty-first Yearbook of the National Society for the Study of Education, Part I (Chicago: University of Chicago Press, 1962), p. 167. By permission.

Convinced of the ineffectiveness and inflexibility of the organization of classes of 25 to 35 students meeting five days a week, J. Lloyd Trump, as spokesman for the Committee on Staff Utilization, has recommended that schools be organized for large-group instruction, small-group discussion, and individual study. He recommends that some 40 percent of the students' time be spent in large-group instruction, that 20 percent be spent in small-group discussion, and that approximately 40 percent be spent in individual study.[13] Large groups would consist of 100 or more students; small groups of 12 to 15 students.[14]

Another plan for pupil-grouping has been reported by Anderson. He summarizes the ideas of a conference of scholars at Mt. Kisco, New York, as to efficient numbers for groups and as to appropriate teacher-pupil activities in Table 5.2.

TABLE 5.2. Mt. Kisco Conference Recommendations for Pupil-Teacher Ratios and for Time Spent in Various Groupings.

Teachers to students	1964 (percent of time)	1974
0 to 1[a]	20–25	increase
1 to 1[b]	5	same
1 to 6[c]	25	increase
1 to 12[d]	30	decrease
1 to 120	15	increase
1 to 400	1	same

[a] Independent study on the child's own part in library, language laboratory, private study space, project areas
[b] Tutorial or counseling activity
[c] A working, interacting group
[d] Discussion and decision making
SOURCE: Robert H. Anderson, "The Organization and Administration of Team Teaching," in Judson T. Shaplin and Henry F. Olds, Jr., eds. Team Teaching (New York: Harper & Row, 1964), p. 207. By permission.

Such organization of instruction as described by Trump and Anderson tends to call for change in the subject-matter curriculum. It also calls for flexible class schedules, for new roles for teachers, for different pupil-teacher relations, and for school plants oriented to individual work.

Team Teaching

One new organizational plan is team teaching. Team teaching can be defined as an arrangement in which two or more experienced teach-

[13] J. Lloyd Trump, Images of the Future, Commission on the Experimental Study of the Utilization of the Staff in the Secondary School (Washington, D.C.: National Association of Secondary School Principals, 1959), p. 10.
[14] Ibid., pp. 7–10.

ers (hopefully, together with secretarial aides, consultants, and interns) share the responsibility for a common group of students, varying the size of the groups and the teaching procedures according to the objectives of the work at hand and the needs of the students.

John Guy Fowlkes has summed up various advantages of team teaching for classroom teachers and for the pupils assigned to their instructional teams in this manner:

1. The instructional team pattern can make possible teaching children in large groups, small sections, and individually, appropriateness to the subject matter being the criterion. Such an arrangement, for example, would make it possible for the entire learning group to be assembled for one type of lesson, such as in poetry or music appreciation; for other presentations, both large and small groups might be provided.
2. Team leaders can be given continuing relationships with the same children over a period of time by dividing the total learning group into equal-sized subdivisions and having certain staff regularly carry on phases of the instructional program.
3. Students can be brought into contact with highly competent teacher-specialists in both large and small groupings. Academically talented students can be assembled for training in various subject-matter fields, while at the same time those requiring remedial help can be given similarly individualized attention.
4. Professional members of the instructional team can be free to refine their specializations and to contribute their competence to all students in the group while serving as consultants to team associates.
5. Noncertified team personnel can perform such necessary chores as record keeping, testing, checking papers, supervision of halls, playground, lunch rooms; obtaining and making available instructional resources; and other kinds of educational housekeeping, thus freeing professional members for professional responsibilities.
6. Various professional talents of members of the team can be pooled to diagnose students' strengths and weaknesses and to develop appropriate educational programs for individual students.
7. The creation of differentiated staff assignments for teachers can make possible advancement from one professional level to another as competence is achieved.
8. Resources such as closed-circuit or nationally released television lessons can easily be utilized by the large learning group with supplementary follow-up provided by members of the team in smaller subgroups.
9. Greater opportunity can be provided to group students according to such traits as interests, instructional requirements, special talents, for

short periods of time without loss of the benefits that heterogeneity may provide.[15]

Thus, the advantages of team teaching are many. Among the advantages to teachers are maximum utilization of their unique teaching competencies; sharing of the tasks of gathering information, planning, and evaluating; availability of time for more extensive preparation of lessons; avoidance of the duplication of effort that occurs when the teacher presents the same lesson three to five times a day; commitment to curriculum-innovation; and recognition of outstanding teaching ability. Among the advantages to students are the individual attention and the independent study afforded by team teaching designs, the exposure to different master teachers, and so on.

Nongraded schools

Although found more at the elementary than the secondary school level at this date, gradeless schools are a type of vertical school organization for coping with individual differences and for facilitating continuous progress for students. Defining the nongraded school as a school "where the grade levels have been entirely removed from a minimum of two grade levels," Goodlad reports that 40 to 50 communities in the United States operated nongraded schools during the 1957–1958 school year.[16] B. Frank Brown, principal of one of the most well-known nongraded schools—Melbourne High School, Florida—speaks of such a school as ". . . a place which makes arrangements for the individual student to pursue any course in which he is interested, and has the ability to achieve, without regard either to grade level or sequence."[17]

As measured by their performance on nationally standardized tests, the students at Melbourne are grouped into five regular phases (designated numerically) that permit mobility,

Phase 1   Subjects are designed for students who need special assistance in small classes

---

[15] John Guy Fowlkes, "Organizing Schools Toward Maximum Utilization of the Instructional Staff," an address given before the meeting of the American Association of School Administrators, Atlantic City, New Jersey, 1960. By permission.

[16] John I. Goodlad, "Classroom Organization," in Chester W. Harris, ed. *Encyclopedia of Educational Research*, 3rd ed. (New York: Macmillan, 1960), p. 222.

[17] B. Frank Brown, "The Nongraded School," in Ronald Gross and Judith Murphy, eds., *The Revolution in the Schools* (New York: Harcourt, Brace & World, 1964), p. 100. By permission of The Center for Applied Research In Education, Inc.

Phase 2   Subjects are designed for students who need more emphasis on the basic skills

Phase 3   Material is designed for students with average ability in the subject matter

Phase 4   Subject matter is designed for capable students desiring education in depth

Phase 5   Challenging courses are available to students with exceptional ability who are willing to assume responsibility for their own learning and go far beyond the normal high school level[18]

and into two phases (alphabetically designated) in which the student may remain for a semester or for a year:

Phase X   Nonacademic subjects which do not accommodate student mobility; e.g., typing, physical education. These subjects are ungraded but unphased.[19]

Phase Q   (Quest) In this phase a student may research an area in which he is deeply and broadly curious, either to develop creative powers or in quest of knowledge.[20]

Representative schedules of three students of the same age but of different needs and capacities are

Student A

English	Phase 1
Mathematics	Phase 3
World history	Phase 2
Biology	Phase 3
Physical education	Phase X
Typing	Phase X

Student B

English	Phase 3
Mathematics	Phase 2
American history	Phase 4
Chemistry	Phase 3
Band	Phase X
Art	Phase 4

Student C

English	Phase 4
Differential equations	Phase 5
History of Asia	Phase 3
Physics	Phase 5
Spanish	Phase 4
Probability and statistics	Phase Q[21]

[18] *Ibid.*, p. 105.
[19] *Ibid.*, p. 107.
[20] *Ibid.*, p. 111.
[21] *Ibid.*, p. 108.

When de-emphasizing chronological age level, grades, and the time element, such nongraded arrangements tend to eliminate the lock-step system that has characterized education until very recently. They provide for highly diversified education and encourage the student to assume more responsibility for his education.

Generally, experiments in vertical and horizontal organization in the school—in nongrading, in team teaching, in combining subjects, in making longer class periods possible—are undertaken to learn if these programs can meet the needs of students better than can organization by more traditional organizational patterns. Some of the criteria used to evaluate these programs and innovations are

1. Can the teacher understand individual students better?
2. Can the teacher help students more effectively with their academic and personal problems?
3. Can the problems common to a group of students be discovered more accurately and handled more efficiently?
4. Can social interaction and human relations in a democratic society be explored more fully so that students will develop more effective skills in these areas?
5. Can instruction be provided that is more in harmony with the dynamic and continuous nature of the learning process?
6. Can students share in planning, executing, and evaluating learning activities more effectively?
7. Is meaningful learning made possible, such as that involved in problem-solving activities?
8. Are the required subject-matter knowledge and skills learned better when they are used as tools in solving problems or when they are learned through independent or individual study?

PRESENT CONTENT OF COURSES

Basing his work mainly on studies made by the U. S. Office of Education, Kenneth Hovet has attempted to describe what is being taught in our high schools today.[22] Some of his findings are presented in the following paragraphs.

---

[22] Kenneth Hovet, "What Are the High Schools Teaching?," *What Shall the High Schools Teach?* (Washington, D.C.: Association for Supervision and Curriculum Development of the NEA, 1956), 69–94.

For graduation, 16 Carnegie units are commonly required in both required and elective courses in grades 9 through 12. If it were feasible to hazard a national "average" of courses required of all students in the schools, it would be English, three units; social studies, two units; mathematics, one unit; science, one unit; health, one unit. These courses would constitute eight of 16 Carnegie units. The remaining eight units would be obtained partly in these five areas and partly in such fields as business education, homemaking, art, music, industrial arts, agriculture, and foreign languages.

The range of courses offered increases as the total enrollment rises. In grades 7 through 12, some 500 discernibly different courses are given, and a number of activities formerly called extracurricular are now offered as elective courses for credit. Some of the courses offered for the first time in the last several decades include radio speaking and broadcasting, remedial English, creative writing; Latin-American history, consumer education; core; conservation, fundamentals of electricity, advanced general science, advanced biology, advanced chemistry, aeronautics, earth science; Russian, Portuguese; photography, home mechanics, handicrafts, plastics, transportation laboratory; general industrial shops, diversified occupations, vocational radio, aviation trades, cosmetology; cooperative store-training, cooperative office-training, retailing, consumer economics; consumer-buying, home management; safety and driver education; music appreciation, harmony, theory, and practice; school service art; special classes for the handicapped and for the mentally retarded.

The elective system and the wide range in courses are, of course, not limited to the senior high school. In many junior high schools, elective subjects are first offered in the seventh grade, and it is not uncommon to find that less than half of the subjects are required of all the students. The tendency in the junior high school is toward elective courses patterned on those in the senior high school. To the extent that junior high school students take many different "common" and elective subjects taught by many different teachers in short class periods each day, the junior high school may fail to achieve any of the four main functions for which it is designed: (1) To meet the needs peculiar to students, some of whom are still children and others of whom are relatively mature; (2) to provide an educationally sound transition from grades 6 to 7; (3) to develop increasing competence in foundation learnings

—reading, spelling, writing, composition, arithmetic; and (4) to help students learn to participate in a democratic society.

Suggestions for requirements for graduation made by various interested individuals and national groups are having some influence on high school programs and merit consideration. Conant, for example, recommends a general education program for all students that would require that four years of English, three or four years of social studies (to include two years of history), one year of mathematics, and at least one year of science be taken between grades 9 through 12. The elective program for all students would include at least seven additional courses, excluding physical education.[23] The program for the academically talented should, according to Conant, consist of a minimum of four years of mathematics, three years of science, four years of a foreign language, four years of English, and three years of social studies during a four-year period.[24]

PLANNING AND IMPLEMENTING THE CURRICULUM

Who should decide what the curriculum is to be in the junior and senior high school? Who should decide why, when, and how students are to learn a given content or to participate in various activities?

Many people contribute to these decisions. Those who by the nature of their interests, abilities, and preparation should be most qualified to answer the when and how are teachers, curriculum-coordinators, administrators, guidance workers, and other specialists in education. These same personnel, who often have children in school themselves, should also have considerable voice in determining the what and why aspects. But students, parents, and others in the immediate and in the larger community must also contribute their ideas to the what and why and, to a lesser extent, to the when and how. If history has taught us anything, it is that it is unwise to allow any small, relatively homogeneous group to dictate curriculum. As we saw earlier in this chapter, curriculum-recommending groups that were dominated by specialists in

---

[23] James B. Conant, *The American High School Today* (New York: McGraw-Hill, 1959), pp. 47–48.
[24] *Ibid.*, p. 57.

subject-matter fields in our universities favored subjects that were suit-able only for college-bound students with top ability.

At the level of the local school system, various committees work on curriculum theory, and on suggested practices and content. Krug speaks of several kinds of local school system committees, one of which is the central curriculum, or instructional, council. The function of the central curriculum council is to single out problems of common concern to the local school system, to select problems for study by the entire system, and to organize means for the study of common problems. The central curriculum council may, in turn, create system-wide committees to revise curriculum guides and outlines in various instructional fields such as social studies or English.[25] And, in a like manner, curriculum is also developed by planning groups and committees in the individual school. The committees and groups in building units are

1. Schoolwide faculty groups for study of philosophy and/or objectives
2. Editorial subcommittees on school philosophy and/or objectives
3. Groups to recommend policy on school problems
4. Committees on instructional fields
5. Committees on programs for achieving all-school objectives
6. Committees on aspects of the all-school program
7. Case-study discussion and study groups
8. Resource unit construction groups[26]

Of course, not only do local school systems and local school boards play important roles, but so do agencies and institutions at a broader level. Sometimes a state legislature will recommend that such a course as "Americanism versus Communism" be included in the secondary curriculum. State boards of education, using powers delegated by the legislatures, make recommendations on the curriculum. The various regional accrediting associations—such as the North Central Associa-tion of Colleges and Secondary Schools or the Southern Association of Colleges and Secondary Schools—set criteria for educational programs of high quality. Various national curriculum-revision groups, such as the Physical Science Study Committee (PSSC), have introduced new courses of study into the schools.

Indeed, since about 1960, much curriculum-planning has been the work of national subject-matter groups, such as the many regional and

---

[25] Krug, *op. cit.*, pp. 287–288.
[26] *Ibid.*, pp. 288–291.

national committees in science, mathematics, social studies, English, the arts, and foreign languages. One such now-famous curriculum-planning group is the PSSC, sponsored by the NSF, Fund for the Advancement of Education, and the Alfred P. Sloan Foundation. Through the cooperation of college professors and high school teachers, this committee has developed a physics textbook, teachers' guides, laboratory experiments, films, and bibliographies for further reading. The basic physics materials prepared by PSSC—on electricity, optics and waves, mechanics, and the universe in modern physics—were tried in public schools, evaluated, revised, and published commercially. This pattern for curriculum project committees, consisting of scientists as well as teachers, also characterizes the Biological Science Curriculum Study, sponsored by the National Science Foundation and American Institute of Biological Sciences; as well as the Chemical Bond Approach Project and the Chemical Education Materials Study, both sponsored by the National Science Foundation.

In English, to choose another example, solutions for updating curriculum have come from many sources other than local school systems. The Commission on English, appointed by the CEEB, has prepared kinescopes on various problems of teaching English and guides for curriculum study; in 1962, it held summer institutes on 20 different college campuses to discuss curriculum in language, composition, and literature. In NDEA institutes held in the summer of 1965, 103 groups worked on curriculum. Under U.S. Office of Education grants for curriculum centers, a wide range of materials is currently being developed: *An Articulated Program in Composition* (K-13), University of Nebraska; *A Sequential and Cumulative Program in English for Able, College Bound Students* (10-12), Carnegie Institute of Technology; *Development of Reading and English Language Materials for Grades 7–9 in Depressed Areas*, Hunter College; *Teaching English as a Second Language*, Teachers College, Columbia; to list but a few of the titles of some 16 such projects financed by the USOE. Other granting agencies, other titles, could be listed.

Such increased interest in curriculum development by scholars in the teaching fields; such increased emphasis on the disciplines and on content; such reconsideration of the provinces of colleges, universities, and secondary schools; such financing by agencies outside the local school system, suggest the widespread questioning of traditional patterns of curriculum planning. To the extent that textbooks, related instructional materials, and evaluation materials determine what adolescents learn in the secondary schools, curriculum building, which consists of groups of scholars getting together with teachers, writing materials, trying the materials out on a small scale, revising, trying out materials on a larger scale, and distributing the results nationally, occupies an extremely important place in the organization of both old and new content for instruction.

Ultimately, however, any curriculum or series of objectives will fall far short of achievement unless the individual teacher is committed to bringing the curriculum to life in the classroom. To insure his involvement and commitment to making curriculum objectives become realities in the lives of students, the professional teacher will participate in many ways in planning the school curriculum. He will do the best possible job in the classroom by attempting to develop learnings that are considered important. He will want to work with the school committee that is concerned with his major subject-matter interest. He may work with curriculum development at the local, state, or national level. Only as the teacher wills to involve himself in change, acquires training to implement theoretical principles, thinks creatively, and tries out objectives in the classroom will the curriculum objectives be translated into purposeful learning by students.

SUMMARY

Although there is some separation of the means of instruction for administrative purposes, the curriculum consists of all of the experiences that a student has under the guidance of the school. Curriculum planning is a continuous process of evaluating and reformulating educational objectives, of organizing content and proposed learning experiences into course guides, and of providing instructional aids.

Education has progressed far toward meeting the needs of society and of all learners since the establishment of the Latin Grammar School in 1635. The founding in 1874 of the free public high school, an institution closely related to the needs of a people becoming urbanized, marked the real beginning of modern education. The Eight-Year Study demonstrated certain advantages of deviating from the traditional patterns of education by allowing students freer choice of content and by exposing them to less authoritarian teaching procedures.

Much experimentation and innovation in the education of students 12 to 18 years of age has occurred in recent decades, and the tempo of change and experimentation is accelerating. Continuing efforts have been made to better both subject-matter and developmental-activity curricula. Especially in the junior high school, core curriculum has sought to integrate formerly disparate learnings and activities. Concern for organizing schools vertically and horizontally has led to creative, new approaches to education through team teaching and the nongraded school. Evidence on the variability of ability and achievement among students has led to increased attention to developing flexible settings and schedules for students.

Considerable research and experimentation are still needed to demonstrate what learnings students can acquire and how they can acquire these learnings most efficiently; what learnings are valuable to all students and how the learnings can be acquired in the classroom; the extent to which the high school can and should prepare students to meet their future responsibilities as parents, employees, and citizens without further formal education; the extent to which students who are going to college should specialize in narrow subject fields in high school. These are curriculum problems that teachers, because of their education and professional competence, should share in solving by being open-minded about experimentation and by participating in curriculum-decision groups at every level, up to and including the national level. It is in the classroom that the emphasis on the learner, the purposive nature of learning, the ideals of democratic living, and the values of particular subject matter bring out clearly the differences between a good and a poor curriculum.

QUESTIONS AND ACTIVITIES

1 Studying the objectives in the eleventh-grade girl's classes, note whether emphasis is balanced among objectives that arise from the needs of the society or the culture, the needs of the learner, and from the unique content of the various subject-matter areas. If objectives in any area of this tripod need to be supplied, list some additional instructional goals where they are needed most.

2 Compare your own high school transcript with the unit recommendations made by the Committee on College Entrance Requirements, 1899.

3 What helpful ideas about curriculum design do you derive from the Eight-Year Study?

4 Briefly, contrast separate-subject, correlated, broad-fields, and core classes. List the courses taken during your most recent year of college that fit each definition.

5 Compare the relative advantages of using homogeneous rather than heterogeneous grouping. Do you see any drawbacks in using homogeneous grouping?

6 Which generalizations given in Chapter 3 might be implemented more readily in team teaching than in self-contained classrooms?

7 Which of the needs of adolescents discussed in Chapter 2 could be provided for better in a nongraded, rather than in a graded, school?

8 Discuss the role of the principal, teachers, students, parents, state curriculum groups, and national curriculum groups in planning curriculum. Who should decide how students are to be taught?

9 Discuss the generalization that any curriculum or series of objectives will fall far short of achievement unless the individual teacher is committed to bringing the curriculum to life in the classroom.

SUGGESTIONS FOR FURTHER READING

BROWN, B. FRANK, *The Nongraded High School*, Englewood Cliffs, N.J.: Prentice-Hall, 1963.

LEEPER, ROBERT R., ED., *Curriculum Change: Direction and Process*, Washington, D.C.: Association for Supervision and Curriculum Development, 1966.

PASSOW, A. HARRY, *Curriculum Crossroads*, New York: Bureau of Publications, Teachers College, Columbia University, 1962.

SHAPLIN, JUDSON T., AND HENRY F. OLDS, JR., EDS., *Team Teaching*, New York: Harper & Row, 1964.

Strategies of Curriculum Development, compiled by Dan W. Anderson, James B. Macdonald, and Frank B. May, Columbus, Ohio: Merrill, 1965.

TABA, HILDA, *Curriculum Development: Theory and Practice*, New York: Harcourt, Brace & World, 1962.

part II

CREATIVE TEACHING-LEARNING ACTIVITIES

6 Unit and daily planning

*I*n any planning that seeks to direct action, planning such as the architect's blueprint for a building or the scientist's prospectus for an experiment, three stages can be identified: (1) An over-all design or plan for action is outlined. This plan is a clearly defined statement that delimits the total structure of the project or design and that indicates the activities and materials necessary for the desired results. In curriculum-planning, this over-all design or plan may take the form of a *curriculum guide*. (2) The over-all plan is then divided into cohesive units that are outlined in more detail. Although each such unit is relatively independent, it does not vary to such an extent that the total design, the curriculum guide or course of study, will be greatly altered. In curriculum planning in the instructional fields, this planning may take the form of a *resource unit*. (3) Specific details within each unit are outlined. These details account for most of the variation in the planning process and are meant to be readily adaptable to the specific situations and to the resources that are available when the plan is put into effect. In curriculum planning in the instructional fields, these detailed plans are incorporated into a *teaching-learning unit* and, finally, are developed into a *daily plan*.

The unit is a plan for organizing learning experiences. The word *unit* suggests unity, and *unit teaching* suggests an attempt to provide unity within an instructional field. Reviewing a number of generally accepted uses of the term unit, Saylor and Alexander suggest the following meanings:

> (1) A unit is an organization of more experiences than a lesson or period or activity or similar somewhat arbitrary division of experience; (2) a unit is organized in relation to some one of many possible sources of unity . . . —logical divisions of subject matter or social problems or children's needs or others; and (3) a unit involves both a unity organization in planning and its classroom development.[1]

Such a definition may have the virtue of helping avoid teaching-learning activities that are too loose, too narrow, too unrelated. Such a definition should lead you to examine your field for segments of subject matter, for important activities and processes, for ideas, themes, and topics that give a vital context to what might otherwise remain useless, meaningless minutiae to students.

If then we accept the Saylor definition, a unit is always planned for more than one class period. Even though the duration of a unit may be a week, several months, or a semester, one month or one reporting period is frequently used as the basis in planning. The main reason for using a period longer than a day is that it is extremely difficult, if not impossible, for the teacher to use time efficiently when each day's work constitutes a complete learning experience in itself. And the student often cannot discover the relationship between successive unrelated daily experiences. J. N. Hook, warning the English teacher against teaching in snippets, talks of ". . . teaching the semicolon today, *Miniver Cheevy* tomorrow, the complex sentence Wednesday, a short story Thursday, and public speaking Friday. . . ."[2] The student often fails to organize such experiences into a meaningful pattern of learning.

Units can be based on content in a single subject, such as a unit on the folk ballad in a class in literature; on content that crosses single-subject lines into broad fields, such as a unit on the effect of air transportation on social, economic, and political life in a community; on projects or problems that draw upon information from several fields, such as a unit on improving recreational facilities in the school and

[1] J. Galen Saylor and William M. Alexander, *Curriculum Planning for Better Teaching and Learning* (Holt, Rinehart and Winston, 1954), p. 397.

[2] J. N. Hook, *The Teaching of High School English*, 3rd ed. (New York: Ronald, 1965), p. 64.

community; or on skills, such as reading the newspaper in the light of knowledge of propaganda and slanting in a class in journalism. Although it has used various methods such as an inquiry or discovery method, science has traditionally chosen content as the basis for units, blocks of subject matter such as precipitation, radiant energy, or hard and soft water. Mathematics, too, favors topics determined by content: whole number—fundamental questions; common fractions—meanings, fundamental operations. The social sciences frequently use three types of unit: the chronological (Ancient Greece), topical (You and Taxation), and the problems unit (What Is Being Done About the Problems of Population?). The literature program in English also uses units determined by content: organization by topic (Freedom), organization by literary type (Lyric Poetry), organization by chronology (The Anglo-Saxon Period), organization by a single selection (*David Copperfield*), or organization by a controlling idea or theme (The Many Faces of Courage).

Units usually include many different kinds of student activities: Reading from various sources, listening to teacher or classmates, doing individual and committee work, participating in group discussion, making written and oral reports, visiting outside the classroom, constructing objects in which creative and artistic talents are employed, conducting experiments in a laboratory, observing and analyzing films, and so on. In classes such as beginning typing and shorthand, the variety of activities is not so broad as in social studies and English. But variety of activity or experience is one factor in arousing interest in a subject and in assisting the student to learn a skill or attitude.

Learning is usually enhanced when students help plan some details of their work. Therefore, preplanning should include provision for student participation. Student participation in unit planning once the instruction has begun varies widely, however. Its effectiveness depends on the competence of the students, the nature of the learning outcomes desired, and the teacher's competence and preference. Often, the beginning student is not competent to make wise decisions on such matters as sequence of activities and desirable content. Too, the student taking a class intended to develop desirable attitudes and group skills (English, social studies) would have to interact more, participate more, than if he were in a class intended to develop an individual skill (beginning swimming, French, typing). Finally, the teacher's preference and competence seems to be a principal criterion governing the extent to which students share in planning. Some seniors participate less in planning in Problems of Democracy than do seventh-graders in their social studies classes.

All planning, both advance and pupil-teacher, should be intimately related to the general goals of secondary education (see Chapter 1); the characteristics of the learner (see Chapter 2); the nature and conditions of meaningful learning (see Chapter 3); the structure and content of the subject matter (see Chapter 4); the over-all school curriculum (see Chapter 5); and the teacher's skills and competences.

THE RESOURCE UNIT

Klohr has defined the resource unit as ". . . a carefully planned series of suggestions centered in some broad problem, topic, or area of experience and organized to serve as a source of ideas, materials, and procedures to help a teacher in preplanning a learning unit."[3] The resource unit is often prepared by a group of teachers in cooperation with curriculum consultants. It contains more suggestions for learning experiences than does a curriculum guide; its topics are more limited in scope and are more numerous than those in a curriculum guide. The resource unit is often developed as a source of ideas for several schools or school systems. And the general plan, as well as specific parts of it, can be used in a number of different teaching situations.

Krug suggests that the format for a resource unit include the following parts:

   I. Significance of the topic or area
  II. Inventory of possible objectives
 III. Content outline (Expository outline, list of questions or problems, or both)
 IV. Suggested activities
     A. Introductory
     B. Developmental
     C. Culminating
  V. Bibliographies and lists of materials
 VI. Suggested evaluation procedures[4]

---

[3] Saylor and Alexander, *op. cit.*, p. 403.
[4] Edward A. Krug, *Curriculum Planning*, rev. ed. (New York: Harper & Row, 1957), p. 236. By permission.

Resource units developed in this fashion are helpful in planning class activities, in preparing a teaching-learning unit, and in securing a broader understanding of the instructional techniques and materials used by other teachers in the same general instructional field. Working out resource units enables teachers to locate and solve common teaching problems, to secure concrete suggestions that can be put into practice immediately, and to draw up guides for instruction that are sometimes more useful than those in printed curriculum guides.

Excerpts from a resource unit, titled India, written for secondary school social studies teachers, are presented here. As you study the unit, note the many suggestions made in relation to activities and to instructional materials.[5]

INDIA: A RESOURCE UNIT FOR SECONDARY SCHOOLS

The importance of India

1. The world's largest democracy
2. 438 million people, world neighbors of ours; about one person in every seven in the world today
3. Potentially a great industrial nation
4. A country in a stage of dynamic renascence
5. A pivotal "independent" nation of South Asia
6. A demonstration area of the effectiveness of democracies in raising living standards, in competition with Communist China in the eyes of Asians—and others
7. Home of Hinduism, a major religion-civilization
8. Contributor to world culture, past, present, future
9. Developing a unique Community Development Program concerned with the physical, social, and economic needs of village people
10. Leading role in the United Nations
11. Close relations with the United States in the past and present

---

[5] And for further excellent examples of the resource unit, see the *Problems in American Life Series* sponsored by the National Council for the Social Studies and the National Association of Secondary School Principals.

General organization of the unit

This is a resource unit, intended to give background to teachers in junior and senior high schools. It is especially concerned with ninth-graders. Teachers should pull from this unit the materials needed for a specific group.

If a period of 15 to 20 days is spent on India, it is suggested that classes may want to spend four to six days on an introductory study of those aspects of India that all students should know, then six to eight days on committee work, and five or six days on the reports of committees and any culminating activities.

A part of one or two of the days of introduction may well be spent in the initial work of committees, including letters to be written for materials, because it takes considerable time to receive replies to such letters.

General aims of the unit

Specific aims for any group need to be worked out with reference to the needs and interests of that class. They should include behavior, attitudes, skills, general concepts, and knowledge. Some general aims that may prove suggestive follow:

1. To understand the size and importance of India today
2. To appreciate the Indian people
3. To understand the effect of land and resources on India in the past and in the present
4. To learn about ways of living in India in the past and present and the reasons for these ways of living
5. To learn about the religions of India and to remove stereotyped thinking on this topic
6. To understand some of the major values of Indians yesterday and today
7. To understand the place of family life in India
8. To learn about the educational system of India today, with some references to the "growing up" process in the past
9. To learn about the government of India today and a little about government under the British in times past
10. To learn about the economy of India, with special emphasis upon

the current Five-Year Plans, Community Development, and the transition from primitive agriculture to scientific industrialism and farming

11. To appreciate some of the ways in which Indians have fun and enjoy and create beauty, with special emphasis upon music and the dance
12. To understand some of the problems of a country in transition from colonialism to independence
13. To study about some of the great leaders of India—past and present
14. To learn about our contacts with India in the past and present
15. To study the role of India in foreign policy, including its role in the United Nations
16. To learn how to gather information, analyze materials, and record pertinent data
17. To learn to work more effectively in committees and individually
18. To meet at least one Indian or someone who knows India well
19. To participate in some project to aid India
20. To be a "receiver" of some of India's "gifts" to the world

Some possible introductory activities

1. Show a film on India, such as "Asian Earth"
2. View a filmstrip, such as "Pivot of Asia"
3. Discuss current events relating to India
4. View an exhibit of maps, charts, pictures, and objects from and about India
5. Listen to or view a radio or television program on India

General approaches to the unit

Teachers may want to have students pool their information on India, making a record of it to ascertain later to what extent their data were correct. Then they many want to develop a list of questions for which the students will find answers, arranging the questions later by related topics. The teacher may want to decide which topics will be explored by the entire class and which by committees. It is important to have a large map of India on display from the very first.

Common reading

It is often helpful to have one brief account, which all students read, as a common background. Trumbull's booklet, India Since Independence, may be one such common reading.

Land, climate, and resources

What are the important geographical features of India—its terrain, mountains, rivers, deserts, soil, resources, climate? How have these affected India in the past and today? How may they affect her in the future? What is being done to develop these resources?

General background. Huge subcontinent, shaped like kite or triangle. Peninsula jutting out of southern Asia into Indian Ocean. About one half the size of the United States.

Neighbors. Burma, China, Tibet, Nepal, Afghanistan, Ceylon, and Pakistan. Proximity to China and U.S.S.R. and effects.

Rivers. Ganges, Brahmaputra and Jumna in north, Mahanadi, Godavari, Kistna and Cauvery in south. Conflict with Pakistan over water from Kashmir.

Mountains. Giant Himalayas rising to height of five-and-one-half miles. Eastern and western Ghats. Mt. Everest—29,141 feet. Snows from Himalayas provide water for much of India.

Climate and rainfall. Effect of monsoons. Rains of June, July, and August in the north; October, November, December in south. Mild winters except in north.

Deccan Plateau. Triangular plateau south of the Ganges.

Resources. Wheat, tea, sugar, jowar (millet), cotton, silk, rubber, coconut products, wool, jute, rice. Coal and lignite, limestone, manganese, copper, mica (world's largest supplier), aluminum, chromium, nickel, and iron. Large quantities of thorium—important for atomic energy. Now sure of large coal deposits. Think they have important oil deposits. Large supplies of wood. Hides and skins. Large potential hydroelectric power. Use of many resources just beginning.

Some suggested activities

1. Make maps of several kinds
2. Make a study of specific products

3. Report on expeditions to Mt. Everest
4. Make a large products map of India
5. View Indian textiles in a local store

References

Any geography will have some material. *(See also bibliography at end of this section.)*
1. Modak, The Land and People of India. *Chapter 1*
2. Rama Rau, This Is India. *Chapter 10*
3. Rawlinson, The Land and People of India. *Chapters 1 and 2*
4. Spencer, Made in India. *Chapters 10 and 11*
5. Van Loon, Geography. *Chapter 35. For slow readers*

The people of India

Who are the people of India? How fast is the population growing? What is being done about problems of population?

General background. Second largest nation of the world in population. Around 438 million. Very diverse in culture, race, religion. All races represented, although most Indians belong to the white or Caucasion group despite the fact that they are brown. India likened to a deep net into which various races and peoples have drifted.

1. Aryans or Indo-Aryans in north; tall, fair-skinned; language from Sanskrit
2. Dravidians in the south; usually darker, shorter; speak languages different from the north
3. Mongoloids in the northeast; high cheekbones, yellow skin, eye fold, beardless faces
4. 70 to 75 percent in villages
5. Fifteen official languages, including English
6. 85 percent Hindus by religion; Moslems or Muslims second largest group; Christians date back to early days of Christianity
7. Large population increases each year tend to wipe out economic gains; official emphasis on birth control through Family Planning Program

8. Some areas very crowded; 907 persons per square mile in Kerala and 776 per square mile in Bengal; most heavily populated areas have little industry, accentuated problems

Some suggested activities

1. Collect, mount, and show pictures of a variety of Indians
2. Make a study of the population problem in India, with official attempts to solve it
3. Arrange a panel on Indians, with reference to their religions, languages, races, and so on
4. Discuss some of the problems caused by such a wide variety of peoples

References

Most books on India have some material on the people. For specific references see the following:

1. Bothwell, The Story of India, Chapter 8, easy reading
2. Focus magazine, October, 1954, "India's Population Problem," for better readers
3. Kennedy, Here Is India, Chapter 2, "People and Climate"
4. Raman, Let's Read About India, Chapter 8, "The Peoples of India"
5. Rawlinson, The Land and People of India
6. Trease, The Young Traveler in India and Pakistan

. . .

Here are omitted the topics Ways of Living in India, Transportation and Communication, Fun and Beauty—Art, Architecture, Dances, Music, Recreation, Food and Health, Languages, Education, Religion, The Government, The History of India, Industralization and Planning, Relations with the United States and Other Nations, and Some Outstanding Persons in Indian History.

. . .

Some suggested culminating activities

1. Prepare a radio or TV program, with different individuals and committees taking part

2. Conduct a panel discussion on some of the major problems of the unit just completed
3. Invite an Indian to come to the class and share in your final reports, commenting upon them, supplmenting them, adding other topics not covered by you
4. Visit an Indian restaurant, or prepare in cooperation with a homemaking class an Indian meal
5. Make a series of wall charts to display in the school corridors
6. Prepare an Indian program for another class, a school assembly, a PTA meeting or some other group
7. Make a collection of pictures of many phases of life in India and use them in opaque projector, commenting upon them and getting class to ask questions about them
8. Prepare a scrapbook of the information you have collected, poems from India you liked, pictures you found, and so on
9. Visit the Indian delegation to the United Nations
10. Show photographs taken throughout the unit by a student interested in photography

Some possible means of evaluation

1. Discussion by the class of the aims of the unit and which ones were met best, which least
2. Observation by the teacher in the growth of attitudes, skills, knowledge
3. Attitudes test given at the beginning and end of the unit
4. Observation of behavior toward visitor from India
5. An open-ended test on India
6. Comments from librarian, parents, and others on growth of students during the unit
7. Observation of alertness to current events in paper on India
8. Discussion of the "unfinished problems" of India
9. Comments of students on their own growth, especially in committee reporting, note taking, or other skills they have been trying to improve
10. Have pupils keep short diaries of things they are thinking about, working on
11. Do an annotated bibliography of the materials used, suitable for

use by other classes in future years; keep them on 3" x 5" cards, with bibliographical data on one side and comments-reactions on the other

Bibliography

A selected bibliography for teachers and better student readers

Anderson, Howard, ed., Approaches to an Understanding of World Affairs. Washington, D.C.: National Council for the Social Studies, 1954. Chapter 12 on India.

Bowles, Chester, Ambassador's Report. New York: Harper & Row, 1954. 415 pp.

Bowles, Chester, New Dimensions of Peace. New York: Harper & Row, 1955. 391 pp.

Brecher, Michael, The Struggle for Kashmir. New York: Oxford University Press, 1950. 211 pp.

Brown, Norman (ed.), India, Pakistan, Ceylon. Ithaca, N.Y.: Cornell University Press, 1953. 308 pp.

Chakravarty, Amiya, The Indian Testimony. Wallingford, Pa.: Pendle Hill Publications, 1953. 40 pp.

Cormack, Margaret, The Hindu Woman. New York: Teachers College, Columbia University, 1953. 207 pp.

Cressey, George B., Asia's Lands and Peoples. New York: McGraw-Hill, 1951. 608 pp.

Focus, "India's Population Problem." New York: American Geographical Society, October 1954. 6 pp.

Gandhi, Mohandas K., Autobiography. Washington, D.C.: Public Affairs Press, 1948. 640 pp.

Moehlman, Arthur H., and Roucek, Joseph S. Comparative Education. New York: Dryden, 1952. 630 pp.

Moraes, Frank, Jawaharlal Nehru. New York: Macmillan, 1956. 511 pp.

Murphy, Gardner, In the Minds of Men. New York: Basic Books, 1953. 306 pp. Study of tensions in India, undertaken by UNESCO.

Nehru, Jawaharlal, The Discovery of India. New York: John Day, 1946. 595 pp.

Nehru, Jawaharlal, Toward Freedom. New York: John Day, 1946. 445 pp.

Redding, Saunders, An American in India. New York: Harper & Row, 1954.

Rosinger, Lawrence K. India and the United States. New York: Macmillan, 1950. 149 pp.

Saiyidain, K. G., et al., Compulsory Education in India. Paris: UNESCO, 1952. 191 pp. Available from UNESCO Publications, 801 Third Ave., New York 17, N.Y.

Tennyson, Hallam, India's Walking Saint: The Story of Vinoba Bhave. New York: Doubleday, 1955.

Wallbank, T. Walter, India in the New Era. Chicago: Scott, Foresman, 1951. Also available in a Signet-Mentor paperback.

Films

"Asian Earth." Atlantis, 1954. 22 min., black and white. Family life.

"Assignment India." Encyclopaedia Britannica, 1958. 56 min., black and white. An overview.

"The Coconut Tree." India Information Service, undated. 10 min., black and white.

"Dances of India—Bharatnatyam." India Information Service, 1946. 10 min.

"Farmers of India—Ganges Valley." United World, 1949. 20 min., black and white.

"Festival Time." India Information Service, 1951. 10 min., black and white.

"Fifty Miles from Poona." Canadian Film Board, 1960. 20 min., black and white. Story of a Hindu family.

"Freedom Marches On." India Information Service, undated. 10 min., black and white. The story of the first few months of independence.

"Gandhi." Through the Columbia Broadcasting Company (484 Madison Ave., New York 22, N.Y.), 1958. 26 min., black and white. Highly recommended by the Asia Society.

"Hindu Family." Encyclopaedia Britannica, 1952. 10 min., black and white.

"Historic Cities of India." Teaching Film Custodians, 1939. 10 min., black and white.

"Jawaharlal Nehru." Encyclopaedia Britannica, 1958. 30 min., black and white. Nehru talks with Chester Bowles.

"Moti: Child of the New India." Atlantis, 1955. 15 min., color or black and white. Village boy and changes in his village.

"Musical Instruments of India." India Information Service, undated.
10 min., black and white.

"Public Schools of India." India Information Service, undated. 12 min.,
black and white.

"Santiniketan." India Information Service, 1949. 10 min., black and
white.

Records

A few records of Indian music are available from Folkways and Victor.

Pictures

Portfolios of photographs on India may be purchased from the F. A.
Owen Publishing Company, Dansville, N.Y., and from the Fideler Company, Grand Rapids, Mich. Photographs are in black and white.[6]

THE TEACHING-LEARNING UNIT

The teaching-learning unit is a plan made by the teacher in advance
of teaching. Its purpose is to organize ideas for specific uses with a
specific group of learners. It differs from the resource unit in several
ways:

1. A teaching-learning unit takes into consideration the achievements,
   interests, and abilities of specific students
2. A teaching-learning unit is formulated according to one's idea of
   the successive steps, the sequence, most effective in learning concepts, skills, and abilities
3. A teaching-learning unit presents a limited number of concepts,
   skills, and attitudes; the number is determined by the time available, the specific objectives of the unit, the manner and sequence
   in which the concepts will best be learned, and so on
4. A teaching-learning unit is often in a format suitable for and
   usable by students

[6] From *Guide to Social Studies Teaching* by Leonard S. Kenworthy. © 1962, 1966
by Wadsworth Publishing Company, Inc., Belmont, California, pp. 208–229.
Reprinted by permission of the publisher.

Teachers differ as to the amount of student participation occurring in their classes. Some teachers distribute copies of the unit to guide the student's work. These teachers definitely prepare the unit for student use. The teacher clearly specifies the dates on which assignments are to be completed, selections to be read, tests to be given, and class discussion to be held, together with the sequence in which activities are to be completed. These teachers may or may not make provisions for students to choose from various assignments or activities. Other teachers write the unit for their own use and yet incorporate in it provisions for the students to share in defining objectives, deciding content, planning activities, and devising evaluation procedures. Allowing students to participate in planning does not mean that the teacher spends less time in planning. On the contrary, more time is usually required.

Here is a tentative framework for a teaching-learning unit. As you analyze this framework, decide where definite provisions should be made for students to share in planning after instruction is under way.

Framework for a Teaching-Learning Unit

I. Introductory statement
   A. State the age, grade level, and ability grouping, if any, for which the unit is planned
   B. Estimate the length of time that is needed for the unit
   C. Indicate briefly the over-all plan into which this unit fits

II. Outline of objectives
   A. State the specific concepts, facts, and generalizations that students will acquire
   B. List the specific skills that students will develop
   C. List the specific attitudes that students will develop

III. Content outline
   A. Outline the major subject-matter content, and/or
   B. Outline the problems to be solved, and/or
   C. Outline a series of projects to be completed

IV. Learning activities
   A. Initiatory activities
      1. Outline a series of activities that will get the students off to a successful beginning; using your ideas as to how to initiate a good teaching-learning situation, indicate the sequence of these activities

2. Indicate the approximate amount of time required for initiating the unit

B. Developmental activities

1. Outline the activities in which the students will engage to acquire concepts, skills, and attitudes; indicate the successive steps students go through in learning a concept or skill in the order in which you think these best learned

2. Estimate the time for this phase

C. Culminating activities

1. Outline a summarizing activity or group of activities that each student can contribute to, that the whole group will direct its effort toward during the major part of the learning period, that will best satisfy each student's need for approval from classmates and others, and that will promote good attitudes toward classmates, teacher, school, and subject matter

2. Indicate the time needed for this phase, allowing for appropriate student participation

V. Materials and resources

A. Locate reading materials, audio-visual materials, and demonstration and experimentation materials that are needed to make the activities worthwhile

B. Locate and list facilities that will be used in the school (outside the classroom) and in the community

C. Devise procedures for bringing people from the community to the classroom and for taking the students into the community

D. Outline the procedures you will use when it is necessary for students to contact persons or to secure materials outside the classroom

VI. Evaluation procedures

A. Outline the procedures you will employ to determine where students are when the unit starts

B. Outline the methods you will use in assisting students to measure their own progress as the unit develops

C. Outline the procedures you will use to measure student growth in concepts, facts, skills, and attitudes when the unit ends

In using this framework for planning units, you will have to adapt it, by varying the emphasis on the various parts to the learning task proposed and to the characteristics of the adolescents you are teaching.

The various parts of the teaching-learning unit are now presented in greater detail.

Introductory statement

A first step in planning a unit is to consider the interests and achievement levels of the students. The experienced teacher can usually estimate interest and achievement quite accurately. The beginning teacher will have to rely quite heavily on the examination of cumulative records and on discussion with experienced teachers to estimate the mental ability, interest, and achievement levels of the group for which the unit is being organized.

Despite recent trends toward flexible scheduling, the length of time necessary to complete a unit must be estimated because most classes still meet for a specified number of minutes each day, hours each week, and days each month. Learning activities must be completed within these time limits. However, flexibility can still be provided by extending or shortening other units that are to follow. The estimated time for completing a unit should be disregarded when this will facilitate learning.

In order to assure continuity of learning, the teacher must decide how the unit fits into the over-all plan. Units that are well planned and well executed flow smoothly from one to the next; each unit builds on the preceding one and leads to the following one.

Objectives of the unit

Objectives should be socially valid. They should be neither too difficult nor too easy for the students. They should be stated in sufficiently concrete terms to serve as guides for evaluation.

Social validity here refers to educational objectives from the standpoint of what society considers valuable and worthwhile. We can determine the social validity of objectives by examining some of the general goals of secondary education outlined in Chapter 1. If we accept these societal goals as valuable and worthwhile, our objectives might be prefaced by three words: "All youths need. . . ." Many high school students have withdrawn from school because sufficient consideration has not been given to these words in formulating objectives and in actual teaching.

It is difficult to predict accurately the degree of understanding and skill that students will achieve during a given time. Furthermore, students vary widely in ability and achievement. Therefore, no unit plan should fix an average level of attainment because, if rigidly followed in practice, the fixed level will eliminate some learners and will retard others. Instead, objectives should be expressed in terms of the general level of performance anticipated, on the assumption that each student will progress to a higher level than he was on when the unit began.

The objectives should be stated in a form that will serve as the basis of evaluation. And they should be stated in concrete terms where possible. If the acquisition of concepts, skills, and attitudes can be expressed in terms of student behavior, for example, the teacher can then ascertain whether a certain student is achieving the desired behavior, as well as the degree to which he is achieving it. In writing an objective in terms of student behavior, it is a convention to begin with a verb and to use the student as the understood subject of that verb.

Sample objectives, expressed as skills and attitudes that meet all three of the criteria expressed in the first paragraph of this section, are now presented. One social skill to be developed in a unit on improving recreational facilities in the school and the community is, "The student works cooperatively with classmates." This objective needs further definition for evaluation purposes. What distinguishes the student who cooperates from the one who does not? [The student who cooperates:]

1. Volunteers his own ideas in his group
2. Listens attentively to others
3. Remains calm in discussions
4. Is courteous
5. Secures information for his group
6. Completes group-appointed tasks
7. Assumes responsibility for his own contributions to the group
8. Assumes responsibility for getting the group's work completed

Although these eight objectives do not include all of the possible behaviors of students who are learning to work cooperatively, they are sufficiently specific to provide a basis for teacher and students to evaluate progress.

How can a specific attitude be expressed clearly? "Prefers good music" is an attitude to be developed in a class in vocal music. What does the student do to develop a favorable attitude toward good music? [The student:]

1. Participates in singing good music
2. Memorizes words and melodies
3. Listens attentively to records in class
4. Criticizes records on the basis of the criteria for good music
5. Listens to broadcasts of good music
6. Attends concerts and recitals whenever possible
7. Reads biographies of composers
8. Buys good records
9. Joins school music organizations
10. Brings good music into the home and into other social groups as recreation

Although they may not cover everything you would include, these ten objectives are sufficiently clear to provide criteria for evaluation. You will probably agree that the students will necessarily show some of these behaviors if the desired attitude is being formed in this music class. If none of the ten is apparent, the instruction is not contributing toward developing the attitude.

The groups of objectives at the beginning of Chapter 5 provide further illustrations of how teachers state unit objectives in various subject fields.

Content outline

A statement of the objectives of a unit, if clearly expressed, indicates content: Concepts and generalizations indicate the facts and information required of the student; skills indicate the methodology. But although a listing of concepts, skills, and attitudes may suggest the content of a unit, it is not usually sufficiently specific to permit omitting this section of a unit plan.

Content may be organized by a topical outline of the subject matter; by an outline of the developmental sequence of a skill; by a statement of developmental problems; by an outline of projects; by any of the techniques discussed at the beginning of this chapter; or by a combination of these. A content outline for a unit in United States history might be arranged according to major problems for study, with an outline of the subject matter and a breakdown of the social skills to be developed, or it might follow a chronological arrangement. The particular way a content guide is organized depends upon the specific outcomes sought. The degree to which very specific content should be incorporated in this section of the unit depends largely upon the teacher's mastery of the field. Generally, a brief statement of the major emphases in the unit, leaving the specifics to be covered for daily planning, is effective for the experienced teacher. The beginning teacher may want to outline specific concepts in some detail. The main purpose of the content guide is to make certain that major areas are not omitted and that minor aspects are not overemphasized.

Unit activities

Activities in a unit are planned on the basis of a developmental sequence: They follow an initiatory, developmental, and culminating pattern. Unit activities are treated in more detail in Chapter 7.

Initiatory activities are planned and organized so that students:
1. Focus attention on the teacher and the desired outcomes
2. Secure an overview of the unit
3. Discover values they can gain
4. Feel the need to exert themselves in carrying out individual or group activities or both
5. Plan, with the teacher, procedures for particular activities
6. Establish group and individual objectives

During this initial period, the teacher needs to learn to know each student as an individual; to study group characteristics, particularly diverse interests, range in achievement, and range in abilities; and to establish a good emotional atmosphere in the classroom.

Developmental activities follow smoothly from the initiatory and are so organized that the students:
1. Continue to be interested in their work
2. Gain a clearer perspective of goals and of methods for achieving them
3. Develop concepts, skills, and attitudes while successfully completing the developmental activities

The teacher provides appropriately for individual differences so that each student can attain his potential in relation to the unit. Except in the case of highly homogeneous groups, developmental activities should be designed to provide for a wide range in final achievement.

Culminating activities are designed to help students:

1. Summarize their experiences
2. Find further ways to use their new concepts and skills
3. Acquire favorable attitudes
4. Discover new goals

The culminating activity is usually planned before the unit is initiated, and the developmental activities are planned so that all students will experience some success in the culminating activities. In other words, in teaching there is no sharp break between any two of these stages; one moves smoothly into the next.

Resources and materials

Four types of materials and resources were listed in the framework for a teaching-learning unit: (1) reading materials, (2) audio-visual materials, (3) demonstration and experimentation materials, and (4) school-community resources including personnel. The materials and resources required are determined by the learning activities, because every kind of learning activity requires particular materials and resources if it is to be made meaningful to the students. Sources of materials should be explored in planning the unit. Two important phases of unit-planning are (1) planning how you can secure materials and resources before starting the teaching and (2) discussing with the students how they can assist you in obtaining materials.

Many learning activities are somewhat less than successful because the necessary materials are not available and because school and community resources are not fully utilized. The teacher who limits unit activities to those possible with the materials available in the classroom often overlooks activities that are clearly worthwhile. Imagination and resourcefulness in supplementing classroom resources with those available in the school and in the community pay good dividends. It is generally good to plan class trips into the community or into other school areas, such as the library, well in advance. Thus, the teacher who secures the necessary materials in advance, who has students assist in obtaining additional materials, and who plans in detail for the effective use of all materials, will be successful in attaining his teaching objectives.

Evaluation procedures

Evaluation procedures measure the extent to which objectives are achieved and to which students derive value from the learning experiences. Evaluation is concerned with the following steps: (1) Objectives are formulated; (2) activities are organized to achieve these objectives; (3) materials and resources required to make the activities meaningful are secured; (4) student behaviors that indicate growth in concepts, skills, and attitudes are identified; (5) instruments that include written tests, informal appraisal devices based on observation and conferences, and ratings based on student self-appraisal are utilized to obtain data concerning student growth; and (6) these data are analyzed. This analysis enables the teacher to determine the students' strengths and weaknesses, plus the special problems that need further attention. The analysis helps the teacher to ascertain the extent to which the objectives have been achieved, the degree to which the various activities were effective, and the extent to which the group profited from them.

Thus, evaluation is an integral part of the teaching-learning process. In planning, evaluation begins with the teacher's attempt to identify and express valid objectives. In teaching, evaluation begins with the teacher's attempt to determine where students are at the beginning of the unit. The primary purpose for evaluation during and after completion of the unit is to facilitate learning. Evaluation of this continuing and varied type is sufficiently comprehensive to provide a basis for marking the student and for reporting to parents. The marking and the reporting may be on an individual or a comparative basis, whichever the specific situation demands. A more detailed treatment of evaluation procedures is presented in Chapter 13.

A sample unit

Here is a sample teaching-learning unit. Its format and ordering differ from those suggested in this chapter: Aims are stated as aims rather than as objectives; and the understandings, skills, and appreciations begin with infinitives rather than with finite verbs. Yet, you will note that it provides for all of the major headings and subheadings in the framework. The chief way in which the *Macbeth* unit departs from the over-all view of planning held in this chapter is that it makes little provision for students to assist in planning the unit. As you read the *Macbeth* unit, try to decide whether it would be improved by provisions for student-teacher planning or whether it is an excellent example of planning as it stands.

MACBETH:[7] A UNIT FOR GRADE ELEVEN OR TWELVE

Overview

Every curriculum has elements of requirement and elements of free choice. This unit is offered as an example of the former. Designed for a class of students ranging in ability from average to gifted, it is largely teacher-planned and teacher-directed. Because of the nature of the class —individuals sensitive to appreciation on different levels—and because of the teacher's purpose—to help students re-create a dramatic and a literary experience—individual projects are disregarded so that attention can be centered solely on the play. Students are not asked to read in advance, assignments are concerned with explorations to probe the depths of actions and lines already heard in context. Thus, the necessary compression of time helps students sense the headlong rush of the action and feel the tensions the play creates. . . . the individual experiences—reading, listening, speaking, and writing—achieve unity through the literary work. However, no teaching time is spent on any skill but reading.

Appreciation for form can be enhanced by the study of Macbeth— one of those desirable models Wilder might recommend for youth. More than any drama widely studied at the secondary level, it gives students a chance to experience what is meant by "suspense of form— the incompleteness of a known completion." This suspense, occurring not because of the reader's eagerness to discover what will happen next but because of the artistic structure in which the playwright has cast his work, creates a tension between the past and the future meeting in*

---

[7] From *Teaching Language and Literature* by Walter Loban, Margaret Ryan, and James R. Squire, © 1961, pp. 405–413, by Harcourt, Brace & World, Inc. and reprinted with their permission.

* Charles Morgan, "The Dramatic Illusion," quoted by Susanne K. Langer, *Feeling and Form* (New York: Scribner's, 1953), p. 309.

the present and conveys a sense of destiny. This suspense of form, rather than suspenseful development of plot or characters, accounts for the pleasure derived from repeated rereadings of this literary work.

Aims

Understandings. To perceive the development of the major theme; to recognize how minor concepts support major.

Skills. To discover the implications of lines; to develop awareness of dramatic reasons for action; to comprehend the subtleties in the revelation of character.

Appreciations. To respond to Shakespeare's poetry—its rhythm and imagery; to sharpen sensitivity to the contribution made by symbolism; to sense the force of the dramatic irony underlying the play; to heighten awareness of form in relation to content.

Time: three weeks
Form in relation to content

Appreciation of the esthetic form—its degree depending upon the sensitivity of the reader—is first absorbed subconsciously as the play is quickly read; the discussions following the reading can help students discover how the author has ordered his material to create the total effect.

Two perfectly integrated elements, initiated by the same act—the murder of a king—and moving simultaneously toward an inevitable conclusion: the destruction of harmonious order within a state, the disintegration of two human beings—the murderers.

The economy and logic of the sequence of events

Presented in three stages and directed toward a destined end:

The beginning to Duncan's murder shows an established society with a good king surrounded by his loyal subjects, among them the able Macbeth, each contributing to the welfare of all; but the disorder to come is foreshadowed in the opening scene—"Fair is foul and foul is fair"—and in the discontinuity of Macbeth's speeches as soon as he actually conceives the murder.

The scenes from Duncan's death to the senseless murder of Macduff's family show the change which takes place both in a society and in an individual when disorder replaces harmony.

The final stage shows the disintegration of the two murderers as well as the restoration of harmony within the kingdom by the reinstatement of the gracious Malcolm (Act IV, scene 3 establishes his character) with the help of another good king, Edward of England.

The controversial Porter scene: not primarily a humorous interlude for audience relief, but an integral part of the play's design, heightening tension because it contrasts with the preceding world of darkness and hallucination and represents the reality the two murderers must immediately face.

The symbolism

Planting. Signifying growth, the healthy aspects of life, the future: A symbol of fertility and fruition as it pertains to Duncan, changing to one of sterility and decay in the lines of Macbeth, and returning to its original significance as used by Malcolm in the last speech of the play.

Darkness. The atmosphere of the play relieved only twice: Once in the beginning when Duncan approaches Macbeth's castle and again at the end when the kingship is restored to Malcolm; between is the darkness of evil.

Masking. Symbolizing the disguises assumed to hide from oneself and others, a complex interweaving of many strands: inappropriate garments, borrowed robes, drunken hope as a dress, a giant's robe stolen by a dwarf; the innocence of the flower concealing the serpent, the eye winking at what the hand does, darkness as a protective covering for crime, the smoke of hell concealing the wound from the knife: This imagery is used in the beginning in a sense complimentary to Macbeth; then for the greater part of the play, to represent his desire to mask his evil from himself and others; and finally, contemptuously by Malcolm's followers in referring to Macbeth as one unfit to wear kingly robes.

The Babe. Symbolizing both the unpredictable future and those compassionate qualities in man that make him human; children appearing again and again throughout the play in various guises—as characters, metaphors, and symbols; highlighting the irony of Macbeth's attempts to control a future he believes the witches already know in order to establish a dynasty—a desire that makes him human.

These symbols, often combined in a single passage, are closely inter-woven into the fabric of the drama.

The Language. Its discriminating rhythms and images reflecting the repose or inner conflicts of the different characters.

These elements of form may be discussed briefly with students during the initial reading and synthesized in reviewing passages after the play has been read. Such preparation will make the artistic unity of the whole more understandable as the class finally listens to a recording of the play.

Concepts

Major. The disintegration of a state by the evils resulting from the overthrow of a lawful order; Duncan, Malcolm, and Edward as symbols of that order.

Supporting. The disintegration of the human personality by the disruption of inner order and harmony, which is delineated in the story of two human beings, Macbeth and Lady Macbeth.

The conflict of good and evil forces, universal in its implications—the witches symbolizing the projection of evil already existing in the human heart.

Contrast in the immediate reactions of Banquo and Macbeth to the meeting with the witches:

Banquo: Concerned with externals, questioning the evidence of his senses—"Were such things here . . . ?"

Macbeth: Interested in what has been said— ". . . tell me more. . . . Speak, I charge you."

Contrast in the moral predisposition of each: Banquo thinks of the witches as an evil influence,

> "What, can the Devil speak true?"
> ". . . But 'tis strange.
> And oftentimes, to win us to our harm,
> The instruments of darkness tell us truths,
> Win us with honest trifles, to betray 's
> In deepest consequence."

Macbeth is psychologically and morally ready for the evil suggestion:

> ". . . why do I yield to that suggestion
> Whose horrid image doth unfix my hair
> And make my seated heart knock at my ribs,

Against the use of nature?"
"If chance will have me king, why
chance will crown me,
Without my stir."

Each time Macbeth meets the witches, he seeks not help, but assurance of success. At no time does he blame the witches or Lady Macbeth for his crimes; implicit in his every line is his belief that he acts of his own volition.

Complementary natures of Macbeth and his wife form the perfect instrument for the embodiment of the conflict which Shakespeare envisioned: Macbeth, physically brave: Shown consistently from the first report of him in Act I to his last words to Macduff; hypersensitive and imaginative: The majority of his lines are the poetry of a disturbed imagination, heaping one image upon another (Act II, scene 2, lines 36–40 contain six images for sleep); always more concerned with what might happen than with things as they are,

"Present fears
Are less than horrible imaginings."

Lady Macbeth, practical: Quick to "catch the nearest way"; when awake, nothing impresses her but immediate facts as she sees them; most of her lines are sharp and incisive, without the imaginative concepts that Shakespeare gives to Macbeth; lacking in foresight and reflective powers: ". . . we'll not fail."

"Who dares receive it other,
As we shall make our griefs and clamor roar
Upon his death?"

". . . the attempt and not the deed
Confounds us."

Shrewd. Understanding her husband's nature, she hurries him along without giving him time to retreat, showing him his own arguments against the crime are really arguments for it.

Launching the unit

Sensing the Predominant Mood. Sometime before the study of Macbeth begins, students, as motivation for impressionistic writing, may listen to the Richard Strauss tone poem, "Macbeth," which is not identified; although responses will vary, the mood communicated by the music is so intense that the words war, conflict, struggle, storm, fear, will be found in most of the papers. On the day texts of Macbeth are given out, several student papers—impressions invoked by the Strauss work—may be read to the class and the title of the music given; then students are told that one critic has described Shakespeare's Macbeth as a "tempest set to music"; the class discusses the criticism in reference to the feeling conveyed by the tone poem.

Understanding the background. To avoid stopping as the play is being read, the teacher sees that the class has the following information:

Approximate time of Macbeth's reign—1040–1058—ending shortly before the Norman invasion.

The relationship between Duncan and Macbeth—to show that Macbeth's hopes of eventually becoming king were not without foundation.

Unrest in Scotland—the revolt, the invasion—with the names of the king's generals and the opposing forces written on the board.

Two attitudes—toward war and toward witches—which have substantially changed since Shakespeare's day.

Developing the unit—first reading of the play

Aims. To help students understand the action, expressed in terms of human beings and a story; see and hear each scene as theater; appreciate the gradual development of character; recognize individual images and symbols and thus prepare for their cumulative force as the play unfolds; and respond intellectually and emotionally to the poetry.

General plan. Reading aloud of entire play by teacher and those students willing to give time for practice, discussion of each scene after reading; and writing of brief papers designed to probe the thinking and to spark imagination.

Analyzing Act I

The analysis of Act I calls attention to concepts the play develops; poses some of the questions students should consider as they read;

suggests a procedure for conducting the first reading of the four remaining acts. Lack of space prevents giving an analysis of the entire play; teachers will find that both Brooks and Traversi, referred to at the end of the unit, give valuable help on interpretation.

Scene 1. If you were staging this scene, how would you set it? What colors? What lighting? Listen to the sound of the lines. What movement would you suggest to actors to help an audience see what it hears? What is the purpose of the scene? What is the meaning of "Fair is foul, and foul is fair"? (The purpose of such a question is to direct attention to a salient point; a definitive answer cannot be given until the play has been read.)

Scene 2. What do we learn of Macbeth and Banquo from the report of the battle? How is Macbeth to be rewarded for his support of the king? Why is he marked for honor when Banquo apparently conducted himself with equal ability and loyalty? Logical reason? Dramatic reason?

Scene 3. Notice the difference in the language used by the witches when speaking among themselves and when speaking to Macbeth. Dramatic reason? (Among themselves the witches speak as women of the lowest class, for that was the class to which they were thought to belong; to Macbeth they speak in the lofty tones and cryptic utterances commonly associated with oracles. One purpose, an element of the dramatic irony underlying the play, is to confuse Macbeth, making fair things seem foul, and foul things fair. This purpose is not clearly stated until Act III, scene v, lines 26–33.)

Macbeth in his first lines uses fair and foul to describe the day, apparently referring to the outcome of the battle and to the weather, respectively. Dramatic reason? What is the significance of the effect of the witches' prophecy upon Banquo as compared with its effect upon Macbeth? What is the dramatic purpose of Macbeth's being made thane of Cawdor at this particular time? (To establish his belief in the power of the witches as supernatural beings.)

Consider the symbolism: lines 86 and 118 (these references to children are not symbolic, but should be pointed out as indicating Macbeth's concern, not yet obsessive, for the future); lines 108–109 and 144–146 (because they belong to the wearer, the clothes are not ill-fitting here, in contrast to most of the garment metaphors appearing later); lines 58–59 (planting as a symbol of the unpredictability of the future is introduced here).

Scene 4. What is the dramatic purpose of Duncan's naming Malcolm his successor at this time? Notice examples of dramatic irony: lines 11–21, lines 54–58. Consider the symbols of planting, lines 28–33, and of masking, lines 50–53.

Scene 5. How does Lady Macbeth characterize her husband? (Examine the validity of this characterization as the play proceeds, finally determining to what extent her description of her husband fits herself.) What is the meaning of Lady Macbeth's line, "I feel now the future in the instant"? (Later, determine how much of the future she was really aware of.) Another example of the masking metaphor occurs in lines 52–56.

Scene 6. Notice the example of dramatic irony in the lyrical description of the castle, contrasting with the scene of horror which preceded. Contrast Lady Macbeth's greeting to Duncan—its formality, stilted phrasing, emphasis on duty—with the warmth of Duncan's remarks. Notice how Shakespeare indicates Lady Macbeth's feelings by the labored rhythm of the lines.

Scene 7. Compare the sense of values, methods of thinking of Macbeth and Lady Macbeth. She does not foresee the consequences of the king's murder; he does, but hopes to avoid them. Notice how each uses the same facts to arrive at different conclusions. Is either more logical than the other? Is either more sensitive to the feelings of others? Analyze this scene for evidence of their somewhat complementary natures.

What is the significance of lines 51–54? Throughout this scene Lady Macbeth, as she has promised, gives an exhibition of her skill in chastising with the valor of her tongue; notice the range of the appeals by which she attempts to move her husband to act.

The symbol is further developed: the child, signifying both the humanity of man and his insurance for the future, lines 21–25 and 54–59; variants of the masking imagery, lines 32–35, lines 35–38, and lines 81–82.

Writing

As the reading of the play progresses, students may be asked to write briefly on selected topics which probe their thinking concerning the implications of lines and scenes significant to concepts being developed. Illustrations from the first two acts will serve as examples.

Act I. (1) What impression have you formed of Lady Macbeth? (The obvious one at this time is that she is a fiend, but later developments may suggest a woman, consciously steeling herself to commit an act against nature.) (2) "There is no way to partition off the continuum of time; the future is implicit in the present."† Explain. Do you agree with this statement? Do you think Macbeth would? Discuss in reference to his speech, scene 7, lines 1–28.

Act II. (1) Does Lady Macbeth really faint or only pretend to ? (If she is a fiend, the faint may be pretense; however, the murder of the guards is evidently a surprise to her, the first evidence that she has unleashed a power she cannot control. The shock of knowing the king's murder is not the end but the beginning may well have caused her to faint.) (2) In scene 2, lines 73 and 74, Macbeth says, "Wake Duncan with thy knocking! I would thou could'st!" Is the wish sincere? Consider in relation to his character as portrayed thus far. (3) If you were staging the play, would you use a real dagger in scene 1, lines 33–49? Give reasons.

Audio-visual activities

After the reading of each act, it is helpful to have students listen to some of the key speeches (not the entire act) spoken by accomplished actors; the recording with Maurice Evans and Judith Anderson, still available in some schools, is ideal for this purpose; unfortunately, it is no longer available on the market; selections from the Old Vic recording might be used the same way.

After the first reading of the play, some teachers use the film, "Shakespeare's Theater," which suggests a method of staging the last act of Macbeth.

Second reading of the play

Purpose. To help students understand the interrelation of the various elements which make up the whole.

---

† Cleanth Brooks, The Well Wrought Urn, p. 2. (See resources for teachers at the end of this unit.)

Procedure. Using the section "Form in Relation to Content" as a guide, the teacher reads significant but brief passages to illustrate the interweaving of the various elements in each act; if this is to serve its purpose, it must be done quickly without belaboring points and with no effort to make every student see the significance of each.

Culminating experiences

Synthesis

Group Work. In preparation for the final discussion, the class may be divided into six committees, each to review the evidence concerning one aspect of the play. (Necessarily, because the various aspects are well integrated, the evidence of one overlaps that of the others.)

The Witches: Symbolic role in the play; the prophecies and the manner of their fulfillment.

Macbeth: The course of his crimes; his impelling motives; his increasing tension.

Lady Macbeth: Her intellectual processes in regard to the crimes to which she is accessory; the development of her emotional experiences.

The "Fair is foul, and foul is fair" Theme: Passages where it is stated, implied, illustrated.

Symbolism. Use of babes on various levels—as characters, symbols, and elements of metaphor. The garment and masking symbolism—from Macbeth's initial impulse to reject "borrowed robes" to Angus' description of him in the last act as a "dwarfish thief" trying to wear a "giant's robes." The plant symbolism, reflecting the development of the play— from the early references to seeds and planting, symbolic of the fertility surrounding Duncan, to Macbeth's lament that his life "is fall'n into the sear, the yellow leaf."

Dramatic Irony. During the reading, the Oedipus myth may be discussed in relation to similarities and contrasts with Macbeth; Oedipus struggled to overcome a fate which had already been decided; Macbeth, although he believed the witches possessed "more than mortal knowledge," tried to impose a plan on the future, contrary to that which they had predicted.

Discussions. Led by the teacher, the final discussion should attempt to integrate the evidence of these various elements into a unified whole.

Writing

In writing the final essay, students may be allowed to choose any one of the following topics.

The Prophecies (highest possible grade, C). A factual account of the substance of the prophecies and of the manner of their fulfillment.

Ideal Partners in Crime (highest possible grade, B). An analysis of the complementary natures of Macbeth and Lady Macbeth, supported by specific examples.

Dramatic Irony (possible grade, A). Critics have compared the structure of dramatic irony underlying Macbeth with that of the Oedipus myth. Discuss dramatic irony as it operates in each case, noting the similarities and contrasts in the two situations.

Symbolism as an Integrating Force (possible grade, A). Select any one of the series of symbols that run throughout the play—masking, seeds and planting, the Babe; explain its contribution to the drama; give specific examples.

Final reading

The students follow in their books as they listen to the Old Vic recording of the play.

Viewing Macbeth

The Hallmark TV production of Macbeth with Maurice Evans and Judith Anderson is available on loan, free of charge, from Associated Films, 347 Madison Ave., New York 17, N.Y. The Evans-Anderson 1960 TV version, filmed in Scotland, is markedly superior; undoubtedly it will soon be available to schools.

Evaluation

Appreciations. Genuine appreciation of the play as a dramatic and literary experience cannot be evaluated exactly; the teacher has to depend upon observations of personal reactions.

Skills and Understandings. The teacher has class discussions, the short papers written as the reading progresses, and the final essay which may be used for purposes of evaluation.

Brief key quotations, listed in scrambled order, to be arranged in proper sequence, prove useful in testing some of the more subtle understandings of the development of the drama; for each, a short explanation of the significance of the sequence the student selects should be required. Quotations that could be used are lines from Macbeth's speeches showing his mental and emotional states as his affairs grow progressively worse, or lines containing symbols—especially the masking and planting metaphors—which change in their application as events in the play change.

Aftermath

After the completion of the unit, the students may enjoy hearing one of their number read James Thurber's essay, "The Macbeth Murder Mystery."

Resources for teachers

Cleanth Brooks, The Well Wrought Urn. New York: Harcourt, Brace, 1947. See especially Chapter 2, "The Naked Babe and the Cloak of Manliness."

Robert Ornstein, Shakespeare in the Classroom. Urbana, Ill.: Education Illustrators, 1960. Available from National Council of Teachers of English.

James Thurber, My World and Welcome to It. New York: Harcourt, Brace, 1942.

D. A. Traversi, An Approach to Shakespeare. Garden City, New York: Doubleday Anchor, 1956. See especially pp. 150–181.

Margaret Webster, Shakespeare Without Tears. Original edition, 1942. New York: Fawcett, 1957. See especially Chapter 10, "The Tragic Essence."

DAILY PLANNING IMPLEMENTS THE UNIT

After a teaching-learning unit has been organized, daily planning is still necessary, but it is now in proper focus. It is unnecessary to project a series of daily plans far into the future when a unit has already been planned. Instead, daily plans are organized to fit into the unit; in fact, they are essential for carrying out the details of it. As shown in the accompanying framework for a daily plan, the major purposes in daily planning are to insure efficient handling of routine, to outline the day's activities, to make certain that necessary materials are ready for use, and to indicate the approximate use of time. The teaching-learning unit itself contains estimates of the approximate length of time necessary for the various activities. Such estimates are purposefully flexible to avoid rigidity in timing that would shorten or prolong a particular activity unduly. Daily planning enables activities to be adjusted to the students' rate of learning and provides the details necessary to achieve the objectives of the unit.

FRAMEWORK FOR A DAILY PLAN

Class   Date

Major objectives for the day:

Activities in progress or problems under investigation

Anticipated use of time	Activity	Teacher participation	Student participation
	Routine		
	Initiatory activities		
	Major activities		
	Summarizing activities		
	Planning for the next day		

Outline of materials, including subject-matter understandings and related skills:

Evaluation:

Handling routine

The particular methods of handling routine need careful attention in daily planning because many class periods begin with routine details. Most teachers are concerned with calling the roll for reporting attendance; adjusting such physical aspects of the classroom as light, ventilation, heat, and seating arrangement; securing needed materials from storage; and making announcements. Two considerations are immediately apparent in connection with these routine details: (1) Time must be utilized efficiently, and (2) student participation in routine tasks should be a worthwhile experience. Both of these considerations are important. When the teacher spends from three to ten minutes at the beginning of the period on routine details, adolescents do not sit quietly and do nothing. Usually, they talk with one another. The longer the period of inactivity, the louder and more restless they become. Many beginning teachers cannot gain the attention of the class for the remainder of a period because they have failed to plan carefully for routine details.

Experienced teachers allocate routine duties to various members of the class, using as many students as possible. When students know that they are responsible for these duties, they come to the classroom before the bell rings so that materials and supplies will be ready and so that all other details are taken care of. This leaves the teacher free to greet the class pleasantly and to set the tone of interaction for the students.

Initiatory activities

In daily planning, be specific in outlining the questions you will ask, the review of preceding activities you will give or the questions you will use to elicit such review, the suggestions you will make, and the methods by which you will utilize the chalkboard and other illustrative materials and supplies. One frequent student criticism of secondary school teachers is that their questions and suggestions are not readily understandable. In framing the oral part of your daily plan, select your terminology as carefully as if you were writing a business letter.

In getting off to a good start, present an idea, a question, material, or a demonstration that attracts the attention of the entire class and that at the same time initiates mental activity on the part of each student. A teacher can stimulate mental activity by calling attention to a prominent display or to demonstration material; by asking a "how" or "why" question that cannot be answered in one or two words; by putting major ideas on the chalkboard for the students' consideration; by reading a brief, very interesting report related to a class activity; or by presenting a short, quick-moving summary of previous activities.

Major activities

The methods utilized in directing major activities should assist students in establishing clearer understandings, in reaching higher levels of skills, and in attaining desirable attitudes.

Outline the major activities to be undertaken by you and the class. Be specific in analyzing practice procedures. Whether the practice is highly specific as in typing, moderately specific as in problem-solving, or generalized as in group discussion, the following questions will be helpful in deciding on method:

1. Do the students feel the need for this practice?
2. Do they have a general understanding of the whole process?
3. Is provision made for detecting and eliminating errors and poor form?
4. Do the methods, including length of the practice period, make allowance for individual differences?
5. Which part of the class period can be used most efficiently for practice?
6. What student behaviors indicating fatigue or boredom will the teacher look for?

Summarizing activities and planning for the next day

Summarizing activities and making plans for the next day become one when the daily plans are part of a cohesive unit. A summary for today should lead into what will be accomplished tomorrow. Each student needs to know what comes next, why it is to be done, and what he can do to prepare for it. For many years this has been called the *assignment*. Assignment, as usually interpreted, means a teacher-stated direction. Because the assignment must be clear, specific, and easily understood, teachers are prone to give hasty assignments such as the following:

"Each of you do the odd-numbered problems in your text, pages 67 to 68, and hand them in at the beginning of class tomorrow." "Tomorrow we will discuss civil service in our state, so read pages 138 to 150 in your textbook, which outline our system." "Tomorrow we will review for the monthly test. Each of you is to bring to class twelve questions, two from each of the six chapters that we have finished. Make these questions the kind that can be answered in one or two words." Such assignments do not motivate students well. They are weak in providing for individual differences. They do not do a good job of telling how to do the assignment.

Three generalizations to guide planning for subsequent days may be stated as follows: (1) When students share in planning their activities, they will put forth greater effort in carrying out these plans. (2) The same assignment for all the class usually fails to provide for a given student's unique needs. (3) Each student needs to know what comes next and how it is to be done. Regardless of the additional time involved, careful consideration of the role both teacher and students will take in subsequent planning pays large dividends.

Materials outline

In all teaching fields, having materials and supplies available and ready for use is an important part of daily planning. Many teacher demonstrations lose their effectiveness because at a crucial moment, when interest should be at its peak, some material is missing. Securing it diverts the students' attention from the demonstration. Science teachers are generally agreed that every classroom demonstration should be rehearsed by the teacher before the class meets and that the teacher's comments during the demonstration should be written or thought out prior to class. This holds true for all other types of demonstration. Radio programs, sound films, and television hold our attention because of the great amount of skilled effort that has been put into planning the programs.

Subject matter should also be outlined. The outline should include the important concepts and skills in the form and sequence in which they will be studied by the students. That is, the ideas should be arranged in the order most meaningful to the pupils and should be expressed in carefully chosen terms that the students will understand. It is usually better, in selecting terminology, to have in mind the students of the lowest ability and achievement in the class so that everyone will understand what is being said. Whenever new terms are a necessary part of developing skills, attitudes, and concepts, the students should be given the opportunity to examine the terms before the teacher uses them as part of the new subject matter.

Timing the daily plan

When the daily plan is part of a larger unit, flexibility in using time is possible, for the bell that ends a particular period does not halt the learning experience. And the more interest students show in activities, the more complicated the timing of the learning experience becomes. But when the daily plan is to be used to present a complete learning experience in itself, planning the use of time is extremely difficult. Flexibility is impossible: The learning experience must end although the students are excited about the lesson; or the learning experience must continue to the end of the hour despite complete student apathy.

Turn back to the framework for a daily plan and note that space is allotted for anticipated use of time. The device of anticipating the division of the period is not intended to set inflexible time barriers but rather to indicate, in preplanning, how much of the period will be used by the teacher and how much by the students. In filling in the proposed time, activity, and teacher-student participation, add up the time you have allotted yourself for explaining, lecturing, reading, asking questions, or demonstrating and the time you have allotted the students for having major responsibility for various activities. For example, if you plan to lecture for 40 minutes, put "lecture" under teacher participation and "listen" or "take notes" under student participation. Do this for all of the day's activities, routine and otherwise, and be sure to include what the students do. It often happens that when experienced teachers check anticipated and actual use of time, they find that they were much more active for a longer period of the day than they had planned.

Evaluation

When planning the teaching-learning unit, the teacher outlines briefly a method whereby students can measure their own progress. This method is then treated in detail in daily planning. For instance, the unit may include a multiple-choice test to appraise the acquisition of concepts. The daily planning is then concerned with specific instructions for administering the test: Distributing copies of it; giving directions for answering questions; determining the extent to which students will be helped; anticipating the time allowed for completion after the first student finishes; explaining the method of scoring when students assist in it; and returning the tests and answer sheets.

One frequently overlooked phase of evaluation in daily planning is an analysis of the strengths and weaknesses of the day's teaching. Teachers often evaluate mentally but make no written comments. Not recording evaluation means that many effective teaching procedures go unrecorded and that many ineffective practices are repeated. Keeping a log of daily evaluations is profitable for the beginning teacher especially. A loose-leaf notebook that contains daily lesson plans and that provides space for making daily evaluations is excellent for this purpose. Such evaluations also provide a cumulative record of the progress of the unit.

Aside

At this point, you are probably wondering how you can plan for a year, then write several units during a semester, and, finally, draw up a series of daily plans. One approach is to write your over-all plan first; to outline a teaching-learning unit or two before you start to teach; and, finally, to organize the lesson plans for the first day. Make subsequent adjustments in the teaching-learning unit and the daily plans as you proceed. The job is time-consuming, but extremely worthwhile. Once you have planned a group of units, discovered successful student activities, and found the teaching procedures best for you, you will have time to supplement and rework the units and to experiment with new methods and materials.

SUMMARY

Preplanning is necessary to guide both teacher and students in beginning and completing learning activities successfully. The preplanning may take the form of a resource unit or a teaching-learning unit.

In a resource unit, many ideas on suggested activities and materials are organized around a certain topic, a topic that can lead to a variety of possible teaching-learning units. Such a resource unit can be the basis for advance planning in several schools or school systems.

In a teaching-learning unit, objectives are expressed as the concepts, skills, and attitudes to be acquired by a specific group of students. Sequential activities, calling for both student and teacher participation, are outlined in a framework of initiatory, developmental, and culminating activities. The materials required for these activities are located, and plans are made for their use and for the direction of student activities. Procedures are outlined for appraising the extent to which the objectives are achieved.

The daily plan incorporates the specific details required for the units. Its major purposes are to assure that the classroom is managed well, to outline specific methods for the day's activities, to insure that needed materials are available and ready for use, and to utilize time efficiently.

QUESTIONS AND ACTIVITIES

1 Compare the major characteristics of a resource unit with the characteristics of a teaching-learning unit.
2 Discuss class activities in which students should share in planning.
3 Write a teaching-learning unit related to your area of subject-matter interest.
4 Recalling what you studied in Chapter 3, "Conditions of Learning," apply some of the generalizations on learning and human abilities to initiatory, developmental, and culminating activities.
5 How does daily planning differ from planning a teaching-learning unit?
6 Write a lesson plan for the first day on which you meet a new group of students.
7 Outline some procedures that you might advocate for handling routine details such as returning papers, taking roll, and so on.
8 What kind of record should the teacher make of his own progress in conducting learning activities?
9 Describe a teaching situation in which the teacher might not need written plans.
10 To what extent might a recent innovation such as team teaching call for different strategies within the various phases of the teaching-learning unit? In what ways would the unit planned by a teaching team resemble the unit planned for a self-contained classroom?

SUGGESTIONS FOR FURTHER READING

BATCHELDER, HOWARD T., MAURICE MC GLASSON, AND RALEIGH SCHORL-ING, *Student Teaching in the Secondary Schools*, 4th ed., New York: McGraw-Hill, 1964.

CALLAHAN, STERLING G., *Successful Teaching in Secondary Schools*, Chicago: Scott, Foresman, 1966.

MAGER, ROBERT F., *Preparing Instructional Objectives*, Palo Alto, Calif.: Fearon, 1962.

NORDBERG, H. ORVILLE, JAMES M. BRADFIELD, AND WILLIAM C. ODELL, *Secondary School Teaching*, New York: Macmillan, 1962.

RIVLIN, HARRY N., *Teaching Adolescents in Secondary School*, 2nd ed., New York: Appleton-Century-Crofts, 1961.

7 *Organizing meaningf*

arning activities through unit-teaching

$\mathcal{T}$he word *unit* is used in several ways. In the last chapter, we spoke of a resource unit, an outline made by professionals of many possible objectives, activities, teaching materials, evaluative techniques, and references. The resource unit often presents *institutional* objectives, the objectives of a whole system or of teachers within one school building. Also, in the last chapter, we spoke of a teaching-learning unit, organized by a teacher and his students, containing objectives, activities, lists of materials, and so on, for a specific group of students. The teaching-learning unit can be said to present *instructional* objectives, objectives of a classroom.

We might now point out that there are several types of teaching-learning units. One type is often called a *subject-matter unit*; the instructional objectives are the teacher's. The other type of teaching-learning unit is sometimes called an *activity unit*; the instructional objectives are both the teacher's and the students'. For the remainder of this chapter, the discussion of organizing meaningful learning activities is based on a preference for the activity unit, for instructional objectives developed by an individual teacher and his students in a given classroom. When the expression unit-teaching appears here, it is intended to refer to activity units, as well as to subject-matter units.

Many of our best experienced teachers use unit-teaching and attain excellent results one year after another. Unit-teaching puts more emphasis on the students' learning and organizing, relatively less emphasis on the teacher's talking and on his planning of all details. You may find, too, that some of your most vivid recollections of high school classes focus on activities that you and other students planned with the teacher. The activities probably followed the same sequence that we will discuss in this chapter: initiatory, developmental, and culminating activities. Culminating activities are usually remembered longest and with the most pleasure.

Although we will artificially divide unit-teaching into three stages— initiatory, developmental, and culminating activities—you should realize that in the actual teaching of daily lessons there are no finite divisions. One stage flows smoothly into the next. Similarly, in a semester's or a year's curriculum, one unit should lead into another; it should not stand alone as a separate, and, consequently, meaningless activity.

INITIATING UNIT ACTIVITIES

In initiating unit activities, you might find several principles particularly helpful. A teacher should
1. Focus the students' attention on the teacher and on the proposed learning outcomes
2. Establish the main objectives of the unit
3. Organize developmental activities
4. Assess student characteristics
5. Establish a good emotional atmosphere.

As we have mentioned before, learning is more effective when the student himself has helped to establish goals and to organize activities. You should keep this in mind in following through with the second and third principles.

Focus the students' attention on the teacher and on the proposed learning outcomes

The teacher's immediate concern in initiating a unit acitvity or a daily lesson is to involve the student in the proposed work. There are several methods that can be used to achieve this, although the exact method used for any one unit depends on the type of unit, the learning objectives of the unit, the characteristics of the class, and the personal preference and ingenuity of the teacher. In Chapter 6, we said that the teacher might focus attention by presenting an idea or a lead question, by directing interest to a display, or by reading a relevant article or report. Conducting a demonstration, such as the one presented here, is another effective way to gain class attention. This demonstration for an eighth-grade science class begins a unit on the nature of water.

> You see on this table a jar of water capped with a one-hole stopper that has a small glass tube in it. I am going to attach one end of this rubber tubing to the glass tube and the other end to a pump underneath the table. In a few minutes you are going to see the water in the jar actually boil without ever having been heated. What is making this happen?

In courses such as music, art, printing, and mechanics, a good way to create interest is to familiarize the students with the tools and materials that they will be using. The following illustration is taken from the first meeting of a seventh-grade sewing class.

> Because you will be working with this type of sewing machine nearly every day, you should be very familiar with its operation. Today I shall teach you the names of its parts and show you how to thread it. When I have finished, you can practice threading it and sewing on these scraps of material.

Some courses, such as history, English, and social science, are not always suitable for a demonstration-type approach. Instead, the teacher might present a visual aid, such as a picture, chart, or travel poster. On the first day of a unit in a tenth-grade world history class, a teacher, projecting a page from a colorfully illustrated book with an opaque projector, began in this way:

> Because we decided last week that we would like to begin our study of the ancient civilizations with a look at Egyptian culture, I have brought with me today this book on ancient Egypt. I am going to leave it here for you to look at later on, but now I would like you to examine carefully some pictures which I have selected to see what is in them that raises questions about life in ancient Egypt.

Classes in modern foreign languages are particularly adaptable to a student participation approach. Direct conversation immediately interests the entire class.

—Bonjour, mes amies.
—Bonjour, madame.
—Et comment allez-vous, Jean?
—Très bien, merci. Et vous?
—Pas mal. Et Étienne, avez-vous apporté aujourd'hui vos photos de France?
—Oui, madame. Ils sont ici.
—Bon! Vous ne les avez pas oubliés.

Although each of the methods we have illustrated attacks the problem of focusing student attention in a different way, all of them have at least two practices in common. They immediately involve the entire class in activity, and they make use of sensory devices to add interest and color. Usually, material that appeals to the five senses will attract attention and arouse curiosity.

Unfortunately, students are also attracted by extraneous sounds and sights: Traffic noises in the street, the second-period gym class running past the window, and the aroma of baking-powder biscuits. Or, again, a cluttered, disorganized bulletin board, or one that exhibits irrelevant material, is more distraction than an aid. Realizing that interference from external sources cannot be controlled completely, an alert teacher will do what he can to eliminate distractions within the classroom.

If the classroom contains movable desks, the seating arrangement can be modified to lessen distractions during initiatory activities. Because a circular arrangement permits everyone to hear and see everyone else, there is little opportunity for students to become engrossed in one another. In addition, because the circle will also include the teacher, a cooperative tone is set, rather than the usual formal lecturer-audience atmosphere. Although the circular arrangement is conducive to holding attention, many classrooms are not equipped with movable desks. The teacher, knowing that Tom in the back row is going to become bored if he cannot see or hear what is happening, should stand where eye-contact can be made with every student, even though this may not necessarily be the front of the room.

After gaining attention and interest through various techniques, the teacher is ready to discuss the objectives of the unit with the students.

Establish the main objectives of the unit

In planning a unit, the teacher identifies valid objectives suited to the developmental levels of the class. It is the teacher's responsibility to offer an overview of the unit in order to help students clarify the goals of which they are already aware and to help clarify those objectives that may be new. Once the unit has begun, the amount of student participation in setting goals depends on the students, the teacher, and the desired learning outcomes. Because of personal preference or teaching style, some teachers permit their students little opportunity to share in setting objectives. Students whose objectives have always been prescribed for them must be trained to set intelligent, realistic goals. Those who often need the most guidance are the high-ability students satisfied with low performance, and the students who, having experienced many failures, erratically set their goals too high or too low. Through the teacher, a student must discover values, learning outcomes, and larger goals that are relevant to his life.

One way in which a teacher can guide the formulation of objectives is to lead an informal discussion based on a carefully chosen question. The initial statement of the teacher beginning the unit on ancient Egypt poses the type of motivating activity that could easily lead to a guided, but informal, setting of instructional objectives. How much the class is willing to participate actively depends on its past experience in discussing ideas with a teacher and on the emotional atmosphere established in the classroom. Many students are wary of a teacher who says that "we" are going to decide. Time and positive experiences will assure them that you are sincere.

A second method for clarifying objectives is to use anecdotes, cartoons, or illustrations that depict people using or misusing certain skills and understandings. During discussion, the teacher must be sure that the class accepts the implied objectives and states them clearly. This may be done in several ways: Listing suggested objectives on the board; assigning small groups to compile a list of possible outcomes that might be considered by the entire class; or making a written assignment of a paragraph or two in length.

Constructing a questionnaire or checklist is yet another way to include the class in the setting of objectives. Each item included should, of course, concern a possible objective of the unit. Here is a sample list for an English class. Students are to rank the items from one to ten according to which items they feel would be most helpful to them.

——————— Learning to read with greater comprehension
——————— Learning to evaluate the popular arts (for example, television, films, or radio)
——————— Learning the proprieties of capitalization, spelling, and usage
——————— Getting acquainted with the library and knowing the sources of information it offers
——————— Becoming acquainted with the literature of other countries
——————— Knowing how to organize ideas in speaking
——————— Learning something about language history, language families, and sound systems
——————— Learning how to judge the quality of literature
——————— Increasing powers of clarity, organization, and self-expression

——————————————————————————————————————

(Your own suggestion)

A teacher can also use a diagnostic test that will show the level of performance or development already acquired by each student. Before administering such a test, the teacher should assure the class that the results are informative only and that they will have no bearing on grades in class. In typing classes, a diagnostic test can take the form of a short speed test or of demonstrating knowledge of the format for a business letter. Questions on a diagnostic test in history can be worded so that the answers will tell the teacher something about the students' attitudes or about possible misconceptions they might have.

Because objectives are not always clear or realistic to some students at the beginning of a unit, devices such as the diagnostic test and the checklist may prove valuable in setting individual goals. The specific method you choose depends on the content of the unit. In some classes, such as home economics, shop, art, typing, bookkeeping, and music, the process of identifying and stating specific objectives is not too difficult. For example, an art student may have as a short-range goal the completion of several small-scale projects in color experimentation; as a more distant goal, the final showing of several more ambitious projects. In other courses, such as English, social studies, and mathematics, students may find it more difficult to formulate individual goals. Because some class objectives seem artificial and impersonal, the objectives are not accepted, and consequently little learning takes place. This is especially true when the teacher not only does all the evaluating himself but also marks each student on the basis of a comparative performance with the rest of the class. Most students will accept objectives, however, when they realize that they will gain something of personal relevance: completing a project that means a great deal to them, learning a skill that may help them at work, understanding a process that arouses their curiosity, gaining social approval, or satisfying the needs to know and understand and to achieve mastery over things, including subject matter.

Organize developmental activities

At this point in the initiatory stage, definite plans are made for activities that will lead to the objectives. The teacher's main responsibility in organizing is to help the class analyze possible activities and to establish working procedures. The amount of time allotted to such organization depends on the type of objective. Little time will be spent in a group discussion of activities if the main objective is the development of a skill such as playing the piano, typing 50 words per minute, or baking palatable brownies. However, less concrete objectives may consume more cooperative planning time. In social studies, organizing activities for a study of the intelligent use of leisure time might consume several class periods.

In organizing activities, as well as in setting unit objectives, a teacher chooses the amount of direct guidance he wishes to assume. A teacher who feels uncomfortable in an informal, cooperative situation might distribute a detailed outline of activities for the entire unit and then review the outline, explaining how the unit is organized and setting various time limits for specific projects. Although the outline appears fairly rigid, student suggestions for other activities might be incorporated into the unit if possible.

An effective method for organizing activities after the objectives are stated is to present the problem and to ask students for possible solutions. In guiding the subsequent discussion, the teacher might keep in mind these steps of problem-solving:

1. What is the problem? What questions could we ask that would clarify or pinpoint the problem?

2. What do we already know about the problem?
3. What additional information do we need? Where can we get this information?
4. What is the most efficient way to record the information? Graphs, maps, charts, illustrations?
5. What is the best way to summarize or analyze the information?
6. How can our conclusions be tested?
7. What applications or implications do our conclusions have?

Understandably, all of these questions cannot be answered at the outset of unit activities. Answering one through three would give an extensive basis from which to start class projects, to assign information-finding committees, and to organize work groups. As individual projects begin to take shape, the class will want to answer questions four and five. Six and seven lead into and might well form the framework for culminating activities.

We might consider a third method, which is a workable combination of the first two, for cooperative planning activities. Here, instead of delineating the unit in detail, the teacher simply outlines its broader aspects. The students then help to plan specific activities. This method is less time-consuming than asking students to find solutions for problems, but it also gives the students less practice in planning and in thinking through a problem.

Assess student characteristics

In order to plan activities suitable for each person in the classroom, a teacher must become familiar with the characteristics of his students as quickly as possible. An assessment of individual characteristics involves the answering of such questions as: How well does this student get along with his peers? What is his attitude toward school and toward this particular class? Does he have any unusual problems with his family? What particular interests, hobbies, experiences, or knowledge does he have that I could utilize in this class? How well has he achieved in the past?

A teacher has at his disposal several means for securing this type of personal information. The most obvious source, and the one often relied on too heavily at times, is the student's cumulative record. We are all familiar with the type of information shown on office and guidance records: previous grades, attendance, IQ, performance on achievement tests, physical defects, emotional problems, and in some cases, character traits. Much of this information, of course, is relevant to a particular time in the past and should be evaluated as such. Too much reliance on past records, especially on achievement as reflected in grades given by former teachers, can be damaging to the student.

An informal conversation with a school counselor, the principal, or the student himself can give a teacher a great deal of insight into the student with whom he will be working. An assigned paragraph or questionnaire written at the beginning of the year may be useful in obtaining information on a student's interests and on his use of nonschool time. Becoming familiar with less tangible qualities, such as social and emotional adjustment, requires a perceptive, sensitive teacher, one who can mentally jot down the answer to questions such as these:

1. How does the student respond when he does not get the attention he seeks?
2. How do his classmates react to him?
3. How much control does he have over others? Himself?
4. Does he need a great deal of guidance?
5. Does he show a willingness to participate, or is he reluctant to say anything?

Sometimes it can be helpful to appraise the work methods of individual students. Such information may result in an improvement in working techniques, so that individuals do not lose interest or do not fall far behind the pace set by the rest of the class. In appraising work methods, you might ask such questions as these:

1. Does the student start to work immediately?
2. How long can he concentrate without yielding to minor distractions?
3. Does he accept the suggestions of the teacher or class?
4. Does he complete the task, or does he have the tendency to start several jobs and finish none?
5. Does he need guidance in attacking a particular problem?

The characteristics of individuals in a group interact to give the group itself certain prominent characteristics. For example, the students of one classroom may work well together: The group is cohesive, and the enthusiasm of the good workers is strong enough to support the reluctant ones. Another class, composed of smaller, exclusive cliques, will have a much more difficult time cooperating.

A teacher, unfamiliar with the group dynamics of a class, will soon discover which students are already established as leaders. Because students follow their own leaders quite willingly, it is important to utilize the cooperation of these leaders as soon as possible. One way to involve leaders is to appoint them as chairmen of committees or to give them other leadership responsibilities. However, because constant delegation of responsibility to the same people tends to isolate other students, it is not feasible to focus on the same leaders throughout the year. Yet, in initiatory activities, the cooperation of established leaders insures that the class will work well in groups.

What to do about small cliques that might be disruptive is at times a problem, especially if the groups are held together by such factors as peculiar ways of dressing or antisocial behavior. The teacher's first concern is whether or not to break up the clique. Separating a group with the hope that other students would influence its individual members may work in some cases, but it may also alienate the clique even further. On the other hand, by allowing the clique to remain together, the teacher undertakes to change the behavior of the entire group at once. Which alternative to choose depends on the intensity of feelings among the members, the amount of disruption they cause, and the degree of influence a particular teacher exerts. Usually it is not wise to break up a closely knit clique until desirable attitudes and worthwhile goals are established.

In nearly every class, we find one or two students who always seem isolated, either by choice or by class prejudice. These are the "loners" of the group, the ones who do not have many friends, who rarely volunteer, or who may daydream too much. Isolates need special attention when one of the objectives of the unit is to help all students develop the social skills required to organize and to carry out an activity cooperatively. Isolates may be absorbed into a group more easily if the teacher can discover in them some special skill or talent that holds prestige value for other students. Giving the isolate a responsibility that has in the past been delegated to publicly acknowledged leaders may be one way to do this. Any technique used, however, depends entirely on the nature of the student and the class. When group prejudice is involved, the attitude of the entire class must be overcome.

All of the information gathered on each student and on the class as a whole has little value if it is not utilized in planning subsequent activities. When no follow-up occurs, or when the information has no effect on teaching methods, all of the time spent compiling the information has been wasted.

Establish a good emotional atmosphere ✓

To help students form favorable attitudes toward school and toward learning, a teacher should try to build a pleasant and stable emotional atmosphere. A classroom fraught with tension, anxiety, and dislike is not pleasant either for teacher or student and is not conducive to learning. As was pointed out earlier, the emotional tone of any working group is greatly influenced by the interactions of the personalities involved. Because of this, one teacher-class combination may work together harmoniously whereas another may foster uncomfortable feelings of tension and unease.

If a classroom is to become an emotionally secure environment in which to work, a teacher must keep several principles in mind. As a teacher, you must learn not only to control your own emotions but to accept those emotions of your students that may appear to you as erratic or unreasonable. Normal adolescent behavior is often unpredictable. Tempers may flare, or humor may intrude where least expected. The boy who walks into class cheerful and accepting may suddenly become hostile and aggressive if angered by what seems to be a minor provocation. In some instances, accepting the spontaneous but often uncontrolled emotions of adolescents without inflicting harsh punishment is a first step toward developing an emotionally secure group. In other instances, the teacher may have to punish to maintain group morale or to help the student achieve self-discipline.

Adolescents, as well as adults, want to be accepted as individuals. Although this seems to be a paradox when we recall their need to belong to a group, it is not puzzling when we realize that above all adolescents are trying to find and to be themselves. Ignoring individuality by constantly comparing one student or one group with another serves to alienate as well as to motivate. Each of us has at one time heard comments such as, "Look at Joan's paper. It shows careful thought for mechanics and neatness," or "Class, you should not be having such trouble with your outside reading. Why, do you realize that the college-preparatory classes have to read twice as many books as you do?" Often, teachers making statements such as these believe that they are giving their students the strongest motivation, when in reality, they are only creating feelings of hostility, resentment, or insecurity. All students, whether children, adolescents, or adults, wish to be recognized and accepted as individuals.

Teachers, in a position of authority and power, often forget that students are human beings with sensitive human emotions. Respecting the feelings of others is a courtesy not to be forgotten in the classroom. Using sarcasm, treating students like children, and criticizing them harshly before the entire group are sure to win resentment and create anger. Cooperation in a relaxed atmosphere is gained through gracious adult behavior such as accepting students as adolescents, as individuals, and as human beings.

You, as a teacher, are a controlling factor in the establishment of a good classroom atmosphere. In addition to accepting your students and their limitations, you need to have the personal self-control to listen earnestly to what they say and to give the leadership that will let them see you as a model of desired social behavior. All of these qualities, in addition to those listed in Table 8.1 of Chapter 8, are necessary for creating a warm, receptive class and for getting unit activities off to a good start.

DEVELOPING UNIT ACTIVITIES

Once the main objectives of a unit are established and a tentative outline of activities is agreed on, the plan for carrying out the unit moves smoothly into the second, or developmental, stage. The exact activities undertaken at this point depend on the type of problem being solved, the nature of the class, and the nature of the instructional objectives. In some units, such as the unit on water in general science, where problem-solving techniques are followed, the next steps after initiatory activities are to gather and analyze information, to set up and test hypotheses, and to apply new knowledge. In a class such as sewing or shorthand, however, developmental activities are quite different. Here the main goal of the class is to develop a specific skill. In the daily activities in sewing and shorthand then, the emphasis is on repeated, meaningful practice. At the developmental stage, as at any other stage, no one single method for proceeding can be prescribed. In deciding the exact teaching techniques to be used in developmental activities, much depends on the goal of the learner and the individual differences among learners. There are some principles, however, that will apply to all types of units and to all teaching situations intended to develop concepts, skills, knowledge, and attitudes. The teacher should

1. Implement a developmental sequence in learning
2. Maintain a high degree of interest
3. Clarify objectives and procedures
4. Provide for individual differences

Implement a developmental sequence

Briefly stated, the developmental sequence in learning that has been discussed in Chapter 3 includes (1) setting a goal, (2) directing activities toward achieving that goal, (3) refining the old methods or discovering new methods of reaching the goal, (4) applying previous experience to the development of new skills and understandings, and (5) applying the confirmed knowledge. Because steps 1 and 2 refer to initiatory activities, and step 5 refers to culminating activities, it is with steps 3 and 4 that we are concerned during developmental activities. We are immediately involved with methods of reaching the goal and with developing new skills, attitudes, and concepts. The following unit suggests several ways to do this.

A unit in general science in the junior high school

This unit is organized around the central theme "How Can We Conserve Plant and Animal Life in This Area?" The junior high school, located in a small town near the Rocky Mountains, draws its student population from both the town and surrounding farms. This eight-week unit is designed for a science class of about 30 students. The activities of week one may be considered as initiatory; weeks two through seven, as developmental; and week eight, as culminating. As you read through

this outline, consider how you would improve the instructional procedures or adapt them to your own field.

WEEK ONE

Presenting an overview; stating the problems; and recognizing the need
for their study.

1. Introduce the theme of the unit and discuss its relation to the
preceding unit—conserving human resources in the community. Ask
students to relate their own experiences with conservation. Write new
words related to conservation on the board and examine them in the
basic textbook.

2. Show a film on conservation. In discussion, define the new terminology and the problems that the film presents.

3. Invite a forest ranger to talk to the class about conservation practices
in national forests and mountain parks.

4. Help the students clarify and list the specific problems of conservation in the area by (a) assigning reading in the basic text, (b) discussing
activities of the first three days, and (c) discussing problems suggested
by the students on the basis of their own experiences.

5. Administer a short test of concepts and generalizations to discover
where individuals stand; have each student check and rate the three
problems in which he is most interested.

WEEK TWO

Defining the problem more specifically and making preliminary plans
for the culminating activity.

1. Discuss the major plant and animal resources in the area. Refer
students to the basic textbook, supplementary references, and special
books in the library for information concerning the value of plant and
animal life. Use specific questions to relate this knowledge to previous
discussions and to the original list of problems. Ask students to bring
in any other information, especially pictures, graphs, and charts, that is
suitable for a study display.

2. Discuss the materials the students bring in. Organize the class into
four committees on the basis of its preferences: conservation of city parks;
conservation on the farm; conservation in the residential and industrial
areas of the city; and conservation in mountain parks and forests. Have
each committee elect a chairman to be responsible for future study
displays.

3. Hold a general class discussion of the procedures in organizing
committees and in the assigning of responsibility for work within committees. Discuss the kind of information needed, where it may be

obtained, who would obtain it, how records about it will be kept, and how it will be presented.

4. Break up into small groups. Supervise each committee so that no wide departures from procedures occur. Have each committee consider the problems discussed yesterday in connection with its particular area of interest.

5. Discuss the culminating activity—a demonstration of the conservation practices by means of posters, graphs, charts, pictures, and models of water-conservation systems. The demonstration is to be given at a science club meeting six weeks hence, and the posters and models will be on display during that entire week.

WEEK THREE

Gathering information and making a preliminary analysis of it.

1. Give the entire class reading assignments in the basic text and in supplementary reference sources; give help as needed in interpreting charts, graphs, and so on. Allot part of the class period for individual reading.

2. Plan a field trip to the surrounding rural area. Outline specific types of information to be obtained. Assign student responsibilities for the trip (local contacts, and so on).

3. Discuss library assignments. Outline and demonstrate the resources available for locating specific kinds of information, taking notes, and making a bibliography. Spend nearly an entire period in library.

4. Discuss any problems encountered yesterday in locating information. Set up procedures for recording the information for committee discussion.

5. Make the field trip. Note irrigated farming, dry farming, strip cropping, crop rotation, natural and artificial windbreaks, grazing practices, animal feeding, insect control, and so on.

WEEK FOUR

1. Summarize what was learned on the rural field trip. Make plans for and conduct a similar trip to an urban area to study the parks, recreational facilities, residential and industrial landscaping arrangements relating to conservation and irrigation methods.

2. Continue reading in text and supplementary sources.

3. Continue library research and committee work.

WEEK FIVE

Gathering information and planning for committee projects.

1. Make a field trip to the national forest. With the help of a forest ranger, plan and carry out a field trip to the national forest. Study the natural storage of water, water diversion, reservoir systems, and the role of water in generating electricity. Record any information about plant

conservation, such as controlled grazing areas, tree cutting, insect and fire control.

2. Make final plans and gather art materials for preparing posters, models, charts, and graphs.

WEEKS SIX AND SEVEN

Analyzing information gathered from various sources; planning committee presentations; preparing exhibits.

1. Allot several days to committee work. Discuss with the entire class any new problems that arise or any changes that might be made in the original plans. Give help to individuals on reading, locating sources, organizing information, and so on.

2. While projects are taking final form, set up a schedule for whole-class discussion, committee presentation, and individual reports.

WEEK EIGHT

Presenting conclusions; appraising and applying new concepts. Continue committee reports. Set up an exhibit in the school and give the demonstration to the science club. Repeat the concepts test given at the end of the first week. Give a problems test to discover how well the class understands and is able to apply new information. On the final day summarize the unit and conduct a class appraisal of the success of activities.

Although this specific unit was planned for a general science class, it contains certain activities that can be used in the developmental stage of any unit. In gathering information, the teacher and class took advantage of a variety of available sources: personal experience; commercial films; textbooks; other books, pamphlets, or magazines provided by the library; community personnel (farmers, forest rangers, and city dwellers); and the immediate environment. Social amenities and cooperative skills were practiced: Deciding on specific goals; organizing committees; parceling out tasks and responsibilities; listening to and questioning outside speakers and local personnel; making arrangements for the field trips; contributing to class and committee discussions; and participating in the final activities. Because of the variety of sources and materials that a teacher can use, nearly every type of unit offers students the opportunity to develop skills not directly related to the instructional objectives of the unit. For example, synthesizing information in the form of graphs and charts teaches a class to read, understand, and draw logical conclusions from other graphs they may encounter. Other related skills are reading efficiently, locating source material, listening and conversing intelligently, taking useful notes, and learning the techniques for making a graph or for building models and displays.

The learning outcome of the science unit was primarily the development of concepts needed for the understanding of local conservation problems. For a unit whose main outcome is the learning of a specific skill, developmental activities will be somewhat different from those of the science unit. In teaching skills such as those involved in modern dancing, sewing, or swimming, the teacher's main task is to know the correct form or procedure and the best sequence for presentation. The majority of time spent at the developmental stage will be allotted to steady, well-planned practice of the skill. As time goes by, the amount of practice increases and a certain block of time is set aside for individual work. At this stage, it is important for the student to become more independent in analyzing his own performance and in overcoming his difficulties.

When a change or refinement of an attitude is a chief outcome of a unit, the emphasis during developmental activities might be on maintaining a good emotional atmosphere. If a person's experience is pleasant and satisfying, his attitude will probably be favorable. On the other hand, if a student experiences unpleasant feelings, such as anxiety, fear, or embarrassment, his attitude toward that particular situation and everything connected with it may be very unfavorable. An adolescent boy whose voice suddenly fails during a crucial speech in the class play will not be favorably disposed toward taking part in another play that year. When a teacher's main goal is attitude-formation, the immediate task is to provide a variety of pleasant, rewarding experiences and to create a classroom free from anxiety, pressure, and harsh emotions. The following principles might be helpful for the teacher. A teacher wishing to influence his students' attitudes should

1. Express the desired attitude in his own actions and speech
2. Make the classroom environment as attractive as possible
3. Provide an abundance of pleasant experiences without disruptive incidents or outside interference
4. Appeal to as many sensory perceptions as possible
5. Minimize the amount of verbal analysis of activities
6. Conclude activities when enjoyment is high

The specific methods and activities that you choose can be very similar to those of the science unit. For example, if you are a social studies teacher planning a unit on laws and law enforcement, you might wish to develop a favorable attitude toward law enforcement agencies. As part of your unit activities, you might consider asking a personable, interested policeman to talk with the class or taking a tour through the local police station, observing an open court case, and so on. In implementing a developmental sequence for any unit, the exact unit activities, of course, depend on the inventiveness of the teacher and the needs, abilities, and interests of the class.

Maintain a high degree of interest

At any point in the developmental stage of a unit activity, there is the chance that the interest of the class or of several students will markedly decrease. Adolescents, like many adults, may begin work on certain projects with an amazing amount of zest yet completely lose their enthusiasm a few days later. As the work becomes more concentrated and complicated, the teacher has to put forth more effort to prevent discouragement and a total loss of interest. An entire week spent building interest is lost if nothing is done in the following weeks to maintain that interest. In Chapter 3, we discussed in detail several of the more important principles of motivation. Now we need only to apply them to unit activities. Two principles, focusing student attention and creating a warm atmosphere, have already been covered in the section on initiating activities.

As you know, setting goals toward which to work is a very important procedure in initiatory unit activities. Equally important is the ability to adjust and to reorient these goals according to class progress and achievement. Because the reorientation toward goals is taken up in the following section, we will mention here only the necessity for the teacher to provide incentives as a means of maintaining interest. Because a student's desire to reach a main objective of a unit may not be strong enough to carry him through intervening developmental activities, a teacher should offer other rewards: Frequent approval and praise, constructive criticism, or certain privileges, such as free time or additional desired responsibility.

Closely related to the practice of providing small incentives is the idea that a student's knowledge of his own progress is essential for motivation. A high level of interest cannot be maintained unless the class is aware of the progress it has made in relation to its final objective. A secondary developmental activity might be the establishment of criteria or techniques for evaluating class activities. In a short group discussion, for example, a class can decide whether the committees' working procedures are as efficient as they might be, and, if not, how to improve them. Daily or weekly records can be kept of improvement in reading rate, typing speed, test scores, and so on. A student who feels that he has accomplished something each day is not likely to lose interest in what he is doing. It is important for the teacher to remember that students' experiencing success at any task, no matter how insignificant that task may seem, is probably the best incentive for further work. Accordingly, the teacher should arrange class activities so that each individual has a chance to feel that he has succeeded at something.

In addition to capitalizing on the students' desire to succeed, a teacher can also use human curiosity as one way to strengthen interest. The introduction of novel, unexpected ideas or unfamiliar material bolsters class motivation and makes intriguing an activity that could otherwise have been boring and dull. New material adds variety when the class seems to be bogged down by a monotonous day-after-day activity. Apathy and lack of interest grow when students can predict for days ahead exactly what will happen simply because each day's activity is the same. Field trips, outdoor experiences, and informal discussions with people of the community all provide variety and take advantage of the natural curiosity that can be so helpful in maintaining interest.

Clarify objectives and procedures

Each activity has an objective, a certain skill or level of performance to be achieved at a given time. One of the characteristics of realistic goal-setting is the ability to modify objectives if necessary. As developmental activities progress, the teacher and the class may feel the need to clarify and possibly to reorient their objectives. Two procedures, in particular, are effective in analyzing the need for a change of objectives. In the first, the teacher evaluates the students' performance by discussing progress with individuals, with committees, or with the entire class. Specific evaluating devices may be personal observation, checklists or rating scales, or small tests designed to give information on progress. In the second procedure, the student is helped to formulate his own criteria for evaluating his performance in relation to the objectives that were set. Committees can be given checklists, or individuals can get together to discuss their progress and possibly realign their goals. No matter what procedure is used, the teacher should make sure that the specific goals are suited to individual students as well as to the entire class.

Frequently a teacher will set a definite task or a level of performance to be achieved by each student at a specific time. As developmental activities progress, however, several factors may indicate that plans should be altered.

1. The students' ability or achievement in relation to the objectives has been over- or underestimated
2. A great range in individual differences becomes apparent
3. The students' goals are not in accordance with the teacher's goals

When it is obvious that the previous objectives need to be modified, both the teacher and the class should have the flexibility to realign their planned activities and time schedules. Because students might be made insecure by a constant change of objectives, a teacher must use a great deal of judgment in deciding when it is feasible to modify plans. Often the class will suggest that more time is needed or that emphasis is being placed on an unimportant area while another activity has more to offer. When suggestions like this are sincere, the teacher has at least two alternatives. One is not to modify plans but to make certain that students see a relationship between the outcomes of the activity and themselves. Quite naturally, interest in achieving an objective is going to wane if the class sees no immediate or future application for what it is learning. A second approach, one that too many teachers do not consider, is the possibility of modifying the final objectives. Throughout our lives, we must constantly alter our goals according to the situation and to external circumstances. Teaching the student a mature, realistic attitude toward setting goals and toward facing the possibility that those goals may have to be altered is an invaluable outcome of any unit activity.

Provide for individual differences

Although the importance of providing for differences among individuals has been mentioned several times throughout this chapter, we have not yet explicitly talked about the exact practices a teacher can use to insure that each activity is suited to each student. Perhaps it is not necessary to go into detail on the procedures, yet the subject is so important that it warrants particular attention. In preplanning a unit, a teacher roughly outlines the final instructional objectives, the content to be included, the rate at which activities will proceed, and the activities themselves. At each of these stages there must be an adequate amount of leeway to allow for individual differences. A teacher must be prepared to modify any aspect of a unit whether it is the objectives, the content, the activities, the material and sources, or the evaluating procedures.

Modify content and activities

A teacher should never demand that a class master a certain amount of subject matter without first considering the individual learning rates of the students. At the end of a week, a unit may have been "covered" by the teacher, but it will not necessarily have been learned by the students. If the range between high-, middle-, and low-ability students increases to such an extent that each group hinders the progress of the other, the type of material and the time allowed to cover it may have to be considerably altered. For instance, if middle- and low-ability students have difficulty keeping up with the rest of the class on assigned reading, they may be given a programed text that covers comparable content but that can be used at an individual rate. We have already discussed the effectiveness of allowing students to help in planning activities. Even when the cooperative activities are well under way, the teacher should keep in mind the characteristics of each separate student. The shy, retiring girl who does not feel comfortable when attention is focused on her should not be a committee chairman or the first person to give a report. In assigning specific tasks to be accomplished during developmental activities, the special interests of individual students can be used to good advantage. If Ben has an interest in landscaping and works part-time for a local nursery, he would be the most logical person to take the responsibility for arranging the urban field trip for the general science class. Steve, who is artistically talented, might become interested in portraying Chaucer's characters in *The Canterbury Tales*. Although the preplanning of content and activities gives a unit structure and offers security, a teacher must be prepared to adjust plans according to the individuals involved.

Adapt materials and resources

The materials used for one unit may be entirely inappropriate for another. Similarly, the materials used for one class or one student may fail with a second. Reading a programed text might annoy Betty, the highest achiever in the class, yet the same text will be the ideal method for holding the attention of Jon, a student of average achievement. Asking students to bring in newspaper clippings or magazine articles will not be an effective device with those students in whose homes magazines and newspapers do not appear. A teacher who is familiar with family circumstances can avoid embarrassing and humiliating incidents by tactfully suggesting alternate activities or by supplying the necessary materials. The choice of movies, records, field trips, guest speakers, and so on should depend on the character of a class, its ability, attention span, and motivation level.

Modify evaluation procedures

Certainly we are all aware that in one class there can be a wide range of ability and interest. Because of this, a teacher should be prepared to accept a wide range in final achievement also. Not everyone will be able to attain a perfect score on the final spelling test. And, therefore, not everyone should be expected to or even encouraged to perform perfectly. A realistic setting of goals plays an important part in final evaluation procedures. It is quite unrealistic to expect that a low-ability student will spell each word correctly or use each verb according to standard dialect. However, it might, for example, be reasonable for the teacher and a given student to agree that 50 percent improvement is a worthwhile goal. The student would then be evaluated on the basis of his own comparative scores, not on how well he ranks with others. We should remember that one of the most important functions of evaluating and testing is to guide students in their self-appraisal. All evaluation devices should be considered to have a dual role: One is testing; the other is teaching. Here again time schedules may have to be changed in order to accommodate both roles. The specific day set for testing may have to be postponed because, of course, students cannot be expected to perform when they have not yet learned. Also, an extra day or two may have to be taken to give students all the assistance and guidance possible.

CULMINATING UNIT ACTIVITIES

During the final activities of a unit, both the teacher and class realize the objectives set in the initial planning stage. Although specific goals may have been modified in the developmental activities, they nevertheless retain their same general character and require some kind of summarizing activity. The exact type of activity and the amount of time spent on it, of course, depend on the established objectives; and no one can specify the best method for culminating a unit. It is as unfeasible to dictate this as it is to recommend a single best procedure for initiating or developing a unit. In a sewing class, the culminating activity might be relatively simple: The completion of a dress, a suit, or another specific project. Or it might be slightly more elaborate and complex: Producing an all-school style show or completing costumes for the school play. The general science unit that we outlined in detail had as its culminating activities the completion of committee projects for presentation to the entire class, the school exhibit, the demonstration for the science club, and an informal unit evaluation discussion. Whatever final activities are planned, the teacher should attempt to

1. Summarize experiences meaningfully
2. Elicit suggestions for applying the new concepts
3. Suggest new goals

Summarize experiences meaningfully

As mentioned before, culminating activities should be completed when interest is still strong. Never should a unit be allowed to become overly boring and repetitious.

In order to give coherence to a unit, the teacher should guide the class through a general summary of what has been accomplished in a number of ways: An informal class discussion and evaluation conducted by either the teacher or students, a panel discussion, a role-playing situation, a dramatization, a written assignment in which students analyze unfamiliar material in the light of what they have just learned, and so on.

The culminating activities listed here were planned for a thematic unit on the tragic sense in literature. In initiatory and developmental activities, the students had done a variety of projects involving the definition and nature of tragedy as experienced in their lives, in movies they had seen, and in books, newspapers, and magazines they had read. Final activities might be

1. To summarize the tragic element, referring in particular to the specific works studied in class
2. To select three tragic heroes and write on their effectiveness as tragic heroes in terms of characterization
3. To identify with a character and defend his actions
4. To write papers on or to discuss problems suggested by the works studied, questions such as:
   a. Is Creon the actual tragic hero of *Antigone*? Why?
   b. What inconsistencies exist in the characterization of Hamlet?
   c. What qualities made Duncan a poor leader?
5. To dramatize a scene from a classic tragedy in modern style and dress
6. To follow a tragic theme through a poem, a short story, a play, and a novel
7. To analyze an unfamiliar work as tragedy or comedy
8. To write the ending to an incomplete short story

No matter what type of summarizing activity you prefer, it is important to remember that a unit should be given an emphatic ending that offers a feeling of success and accomplishment.

Elicit suggestions for applying the new concepts

All teaching-learning situations are intended to have an effect on the lives of students. If students see nothing in a unit that is pertinent or of value to them and their interests, the unit will be meaningless. The recognition that what one is learning has an immediate or future application is itself an ability that must be learned. A teacher, therefore, should prompt suggestions of how new concepts, skills, or attitudes can be applied to everyday life, to work, to an intelligent use of leisure time, or to future plans. An age-old complaint by students is that school has no relation to "real life." It is up to the creative teacher to insure that the activities of a unit are made pertinent to the students' lives and are not merely an arbitrary section of content that should be "covered."

Suggest new goals

Directly connected with the application of new knowledge and skills is the importance of placing units within a larger framework, of providing relationships between units so that each has something in common with the next. A smooth transition between activities insures that a unit does not stand alone as a separate segment of learning. Ideally, solving a certain problem and reaching an established goal should serve as a basis for asking further questions and for suggesting new objectives. When units are interrelated, when the culmination of one unit leads to the initiation of the next, students see meaning and purpose in objectives. By objectives we mean not just instructional objectives but personal and individual goals as well. A question raised at the completion of a unit may stimulate independent study and individual goal setting.

SUMMARY

Unit-teaching is organized in three overlapping stages: initiating, developing, and culminating activities. In initiating a new unit, the teacher's main tasks are to secure the attention of the class, to help students set concrete goals for the unit, to begin plans for subsequent learning activities, to become familiar with the characteristics of the class and of individual students, and to establish a warm, businesslike rapport with the class. The exact techniques used to accomplish these tasks depend on the desired outcome of the unit, the nature and background of students, and the preferences and competence of the teacher.

Like initiatory activities, developmental activities are also dependent on numerous factors, such as the nature of the objectives, the degree of motivation in the class, and the range of individual differences. In addition to implementing a developmental sequence of learning, a teacher must also be concerned with each of the factors alone. By over- or underestimating the amount of progress that can be made in a certain time period, a group can often set unrealistic objectives. Because of this, both the class and teacher must be flexible enough to modify objectives if necessary. When asked what is their main classroom problem, a majority of teachers will answer "Motivation." Although interest in a unit may be quite encouraging at first, it can wane rapidly unless the teacher works hard to help the students maintain enthusiasm. Some suggested ways for keeping student interest and work output at a high level are to offer short-range incentives and rewards, to give the student knowledge of his progress through teacher- or self-evaluation, and to capitalize on curiosity and the need for a variety of experiences.

At every stage in unit-teaching, the importance of providing for individual differences cannot be overemphasized. Considering student characteristics is as important in culminating activities as in developmental activities; and a teacher must be prepared to modify content, materials, and evaluation procedures in order to make them suitable for all students. A wide range in final achievement is to be expected, and culminating activities should be planned accordingly. The main purpose of the culminating stage is to summarize experiences and new learning meaningfully. However, in culminating activities, students also realize that what they have learned in a given field has applications to other fields and to other areas of life.

QUESTIONS AND ACTIVITIES

1 Distinguish between institutional objectives and instructional objectives.
2 What are the values of using concrete materials and familiar activities in initiating a unit?
3 Suggest procedures for helping students set instructional goals.
4 Discuss some of the major advantages and disadvantages in student-teacher planning of activities.
5 Discuss some of the factors that might prevent a teacher's knowing his students as individuals.
6 List at least five major attitudes or understandings important in your subject-matter field that students might gain over a given period of time. Outline the developmental activities you might use. Which skills and attitudes should be developed simultaneously?
7 Compare and contrast culminating activities in two or more different fields, such as mathematics and fine arts.

8 List some means by which teachers can relate classroom activities to everyday life, to work, to intelligent use of leisure time, or to future plans.

9 Using your own learning experiences, give your opinion of the importance of continuous high motivation.

10 List some of the important reasons for providing relationships between units and for helping students place units within a larger framework of knowledge, skills, and attitudes.

SUGGESTIONS FOR FURTHER READING

BATCHELDER, HOWARD T., MAURICE MC GLASSON, AND RALEIGH SCHORLING, *Student Teaching in Secondary Schools*, 4th ed., New York:McGraw-Hill, 1964.

BROWN, EDWIN J., AND ARTHUR T. PHELPS, *Managing the Classroom*, New York: Ronald, 1961.

LIFTON, WALTER M., *Working with Groups*, New York: Wiley, 1961.

MCKEAN, ROBERT C., *Principles and Methods in Secondary Education*, Columbus, Ohio: Merrill, 1962.

WELLINGTON, C. BURLEIGH, AND JEAN WELLINGTON, *Teaching for Critical Thinking*, New York: McGraw-Hill, 1960.

8 Conducting group and individual work

$\mathcal{I}$t is not possible to champion any existent instructional method as clearly superior to any other. Each teaching method, and each strategy for forming groups, has its own unique strengths and weaknesses. And appropriate teaching activities depend on many factors: Societal needs, as stated in the school's curriculum; the nature of the structure of the subject fields; educational objectives (affective, cognitive, and psychomotor); teacher characteristics (personality, background, and abilities); learning principles; learner characteristics; various administrative and curriculum arrangements within the school; available instructional media; size of instructional groups; and so on.

We have seen that various large- and small-group arrangements and pupil-teacher ratios are obtainable under a team teaching organization, and that some of these flexible arrangements can be made within the self-contained classroom. However, no absolute decision can be made as to whether individual work or group work is of more value except in terms of the objectives sought. Some objectives require individual work; others require group activities.

Although certain instructional fields employ more individual than group work, or more group than individual work, a careful balance of whole-class, small-group, and individual activities is essential in the now prevalent class group of 25 to 35 students. Certain whole-class activities (lectures, demonstrations, films, recitation, planning, evaluation) are justifiable in terms of efficiency and economy, as well as in terms of extension of learning. Other whole-class activities (large-group discussion, projects, field trips) help each student become an accepted member of a group, develop goals in common with someone else, and share information and solve problems with the group. While achieving some of the objectives of whole-class activities, small-group work (panel discussion, socio-drama, small-group discussion) helps meet the varying abilities, interests, and needs of smaller groups within the total class. Individualized activities (tutorial, independent study, laboratory work) are essential if students are to develop certain skills and attitudes, and if they are to learn independent work and study methods. Individual work also provides for the wide differences among students.

Whole-class, small-group, and individual forms of activities will now be discussed according to the specific methods of organizing and conducting groups to achieve specified objectives.

WHOLE-CLASS ACTIVITIES

The more important values that can be secured by a balanced use of whole-class activities include developing a feeling of belongingness, security, and worthwhileness on the part of all students; establishing group goals; securing and sharing information with the entire group; practicing communication skills; developing leadership abilities; and formulating codes for group conduct. Even though some of these values can be attained in small-group activities, none is so readily achieved in solely individual activity.

Objectives attainable with whole-class activities will now be discussed in the subsequent analyses of whole-class discussion; whole-class projects; sound films, records, radio, and television; field trips; recitation; and lecture. Although it is true that each of these, particularly the first two, can be used with groups smaller than the entire class, each is commonly employed with large-group instruction.

The discussion method (whole class)

Frequently, an entire class works as a unit during which time interest is aroused and students become involved in and motivated for the learning experience and for small-group and individual work. During this time, the teacher can help students decide what strategies are best for solving the problems posed by the content and what methods students can use to relate the learning activities to their own experiences. Discussion is appropriate to obtain such goals.

It is difficult to define *discussion method* in a way that accurately describes its use in all classrooms. In part, the term takes its meaning as the opposite of the lecture method. In a class conducted by the lecture method, the student listens and takes notes as the teacher defines, explains, classifies, and infers. In a class conducted by discussion method, the student himself can pose questions, answer questions, and interact with other students. However, discussion may vary from the teacher's demand for tasks involving memory only, at one extreme, to his requiring what Guilford has called divergent thinking and evaluation, at the other extreme. Too, the teacher may dominate the group in an authoritarian manner, initiating problems and receiving answers to all questions posed, in a one-to-one relationship. But, still within a discussion frame, the teacher may feel his role to be to create an atmosphere in which students can discuss freely, in which they can have an uninhibited interchange of ideas. And he may see his role to be to help make areas of agreement and disagreement clear; to help students identify their own assumptions, stock responses, and prejudices; to help students realize alternative solutions; and to guide discussion so that all major concepts are carefully considered.

Some reasons for using discussion technique are given by McKeachie, who says that discussion is appropriate when the teacher wants

1. To give students opportunities to formulate principles in their own words and to formulate applications of these principles
2. To get prompt feedback on how well his objectives are being attained
3. To help students learn to think in terms of the subject matter by giving them practice in thinking
4. To help students become aware of and to formulate problems which necessitate information to be gained from readings or lectures[1]

Other advantages of whole-group discussion are these: If the teacher's goal includes going beyond the acquisition of knowledge, the student

[1] Wilbert McKeachie, *Teaching Tips: A Guide-Book for the Beginning College Teacher*, 3rd ed. (Ann Arbor, Mich.: George Wahr, 1956), p. 18.

can derive a sense of belonging to a group. The student can improve communication skills (listening and speaking) from participating in whole-class discussion. He can work toward the development of a mature socialized personality through cooperative group processes. Also, he can obtain information to get an activity under way, to arrive at conclusions, or to formulate generalizations, important parts of school learning.

In a tenth-grade history class, for example, the teacher and students consider keeping up with contemporary world events a worthwhile educational activity. The teacher initiates the project with an informal class discussion of how information will be obtained, how it will be presented to the whole class, how much time will be devoted to it each week, and how it is to be related to their study of history. The class decides to divide the world into major geographical subdivisions. Each student lists the three regions in which he is most interested. On the basis of these choices, committees are formed, and each committee is responsible for posting pertinent information about a particular region on a designated area of the study display each week. At a given time each week, the entire class discusses the display, and one or two members of each committee give the class an oral report on the more significant events in an area. Whenever a student on another area committee finds material not included in the report, he presents it himself.

Had there been no opportunity for the students to discuss the problem, the methods of securing materials, the sources of information, and the quality of graphic and oral presentations, the interest of the class, the group morale, and the amount of information would have decreased considerably. The teacher had, of course, considered this project carefully before its initiation and had stimulated student participation during the project by asking significant, thought-provoking questions.

Informal class discussion usually does not occur spontaneously. Students do not improve their discussion techniques without teacher direction and guidance and without consideration of the process of discussion and communication. To get a discussion started, the teacher asks "how" and "why" questions (as opposed to "who," "when," "where" questions) relevant to the subject matter under investigation. And to insure student growth, the "how" or "why" question should seek to elicit a response that is more than a recitation of textbook material or a recall of the teacher's lectures. To assure progress in a student-centered discussion, the instructor helps students appraise the relevance and importance of contributions, effectiveness of expression, success of communication, and consideration shown other students' ideas. In an informal class discussion, students might observe the following principles:

1. Be acknowledged by the chairman or teacher before speaking
2. Speak clearly so that everyone hears
3. Word questions carefully and clearly
4. Be certain that statements are related to the problem
5. Participate in the discussion without monopolizing it
6. Defend statements and ideas when they can be supported by facts but avoid arguing
7. Take part in a discussion expecting to learn from classmates
8. Take responsibility for summarizing a discussion if the summary will help the group think more clearly
9. Be courteous and respect the rights of others
10. Listen attentively to all speakers
11. Make notes of new points and of points with which you disagree
12. Recognize that most problems of living together are solved by groups of people who are trying to work them out together

A circular or semicircular seating arrangement is usually best for keeping the attention of the whole group on the discussion. Requiring students to stand up when they speak impedes rather than facilitates discussion. However, it is wise for a student chairman or for the teacher to recognize the student who wishes to speak if the group has ten or more members.

The lecture method

The lecture is a teaching method in which the teacher talks according to a preplanned, structured scheme, expecting the student to listen and to make careful notes. Lecturers differ as to the degree of formality of their presentations and as to tolerance for audience obtrusion, but usually there are few student interruptions of the expository-didactic process. And such interruptions as occur are usually not for purposes of discussion of a higher order, but rather for seeking to clarify questions of fact.

Lectures are appropriate to introduce a topic or unit (The Reformation Movement in Germany, Old Stories That Live Today, Elizabethan England). Lectures are well used to summarize and synthesize important information that cannot be found in the textbook or in readily available sources. They are valuable in clarifying discussion, explaining a process, presenting a point of view, or summarizing progress.

There is probably no instructional field in the secondary school in which lecturing should be used exclusively or even as the major instructional technique. Research suggests that although the lecture leads to an initial acquisition of information, other methods facilitate the retention of information better.[2] Research suggests that the lecture is less effective than other methods in its impact on attitudes and on social learnings.[3] Lecturing, as it is often observed, makes little or no provision for reinforcement. It makes little provision for differing responses, for utilizing student curiosity, or for providing knowledge of progress in learning. Lecturing is not the best way to help the student with critical thinking or with processes of inquiry or cognition. Lecturing thwarts the exploratory aspects of learning because the student is supposed to accept the reliability of the information in the lecture. It affords the student no opportunity to practice communication skills. And, finally, lecturing does not utilize the generalization that learning is best accomplished through active participation, not through passive reception, that learning is best accomplished and best internalized when the student is experiencing, doing, and reacting.

Quality lecturing will be carefully planned and may involve some of these steps:

1. Consider the instructional objectives to be achieved. If your goal is to convey knowledge (specific facts, terminology), a carefully sequenced lecture may be meritorious; but, if your aim is to teach reflective thinking, application of facts and principles, values and attitudes, another method may be more appropriate.
2. Consider the material from the students' point of view. Analysis of the audience is an important part of any attempt at communication. What level or variety of English usage is most appropriate?

[2] Thomas F. Stovall, "Lecture Versus Discussion," *Phi Delta Kappan*, XXXIX (March, 1958), 255–258.
[3] *Ibid.*

What syntactical structures? What rhetorical devices? What terms need extended definition?

3. Use concrete language, illustrative materials, and demonstrations, but consciously try to make some movement from concrete to abstract and from abstract to concrete. Many lecturers become frozen at one or another end of the continuum. Freezing at the very concrete level will mean that your students get the educational objectives listed at the bottom of the Bloom taxonomy. Freezing at the abstract, however, does not insure that the students will learn higher order processes.

4. Help the student see the rhetorical devices and logic of your exposition: induction, deduction, cause and effect, extended definition, chronology, and so on.

5. Outline important concepts on the chalkboard.

6. Talk fluently and clearly. Use your voice in such a manner as to indicate the main points and the sequence of your presentation.

7. Do not use your notes too frequently; do not actually read your material.

8. Summarize at the end of the lecture.

9. Use films, overhead projector, and recordings when possible.

A teacher can usually get his best results by lecturing for only a part of a class period. The remaining time can be spent in whole-class discussion or in small-group work, in creating a learning environment in which students are encouraged to ask questions or to add to the information presented in the lecture.

Sound films, records, radio, and television

As will be seen in Chapter 10, phonograph records and sound motion pictures are widely used with whole-class groups, and television is being used increasingly. At the present time, these media are used more with the whole class than with small groups within the class.

The motion-picture and television programs produced for school use are generally attention-getting and interest-holding; hence, they offer considerable opportunity for making learning activities meaningful to a whole group. Although these presentations have some value in themselves, preparation for them and follow-up discussions make them particularly worthwhile.

Recitation method

Perhaps the most commonly used method, recitation, involves three steps: (1) The teacher assigns textbook passages or other printed matter; (2) the student studies the text material during a class study period or at home; (3) and then the teacher questions the student on the material. The teacher's major purpose in questioning is to discover the extent to which the students know the correct answers called for by the assignment. It is not uncommon to find teachers devoting half of the instructional period to rapid-fire factual questions to be answered by the students.

The recitation method has several weaknesses. It often fails to create a favorable feeling between teacher and students because the class regards the teacher as an inquisitor rather than as a helper. It frequently creates tension among the students because, although the teacher may be tactful, his approval is given for correct responses and incorrect responses elicit his disapproval. Furthermore, the recitation technique is of little use in building cooperative attitudes and values; more likely, it will promote highly individualistic, competitive attitudes. It is inefficient in developing interaction in oral discussion or in improving listening habits. In reality, many teachers must resort to devices such as marking, arbitrary seating arrangements, and various rewards and punishments to get students to recite or to pay attention in class. Because the task confronting the student is to give the answer the teacher wants or the textbook gives, the recitation method is not conducive to acquiring problem-solving attitudes or skills. Finally, the recitation method does not provide the student with self-appraisal techniques because the teacher does all, or most of, the appraising.

However, recitation does have its values if not overused. Some students may learn the correct answer from hearing another student recite. A student who knows an answer already may remember it longer because he has given it orally. The student obtains immediate knowledge of the correctness or incorrectness of his response (feedback). And a student may study the assignment more carefully than he would ordinarily if he knows that he may be asked for some answers during a brief recitation period. Some of these values can be obtained with a short, fast-moving review by question-and-answer recitation on factual materials such as foreign-language vocabulary, the plot of a novel, or various mathematical processes.

Whole-class projects

There are a number of projects that can be undertaken by classroom groups. An English class might produce a school assembly program; a science class might prepare a display for the PTA; a music appreciation class might conduct a concert hour for the teaching staff. Such a variety of projects has wide appeal to adolescents and has great value in creating feelings of belongingness and importance in the group.

Not all projects are entirely successful, of course. Sometimes, the difficulty lies in the leadership; at other times, it lies in the characteristics of the group and its members. For a project to be successful, the teacher must make sure that the students consider it worthwhile. He must assist students in planning, without dominating them; and he must supervise closely enough throughout the project to make certain what various students are doing. Whole-class discussions are needed to enable the students to secure the necessary information and to help them learn how to accept responsibility.

Field trips

One of the better methods for securing information about the geography, business, history, public health, recreational facilities, vocational opportunities, governmental services, music, and art of a community is provided by field trips. Regarded by some as a waste of time, the field trip is invaluable for escaping from excessive verbalism and abstraction into concrete experience. What textbook material can substitute for studying the heavens at a planetarium, for observing the balance of nature in an arboretum, for seeing a Picasso canvas? Certainly, an educational excursion is not misspent time if it falls within the objectives of the unit at hand, if students are prepared for what they are to see, and if carefully prepared follow-through activities lead to group discussion, reading, and study.

Field trips are generally considered to be of significant value in building a better understanding of the community, in developing student responsibilities for their own actions, and in bringing school and community programs into closer relationship. Usually, the entire class makes the excursion. However, students who become quite interested in a problem may make field trips outside of school hours and assume responsibility for their activities. Today, throughout the country, high school students are making long-term community surveys that involve traveling long distances (for example, trips by Midwestern students to Washington, D.C.).

Unless field trips are carefully planned and executed, little purposeful learning will occur. Before pupil-teacher planning of any trip, the teacher should give careful consideration to its probable educational values. If students are to obtain valuable information, their curiosity and interest must be aroused and the trip must be related to class goals. A teacher-led discussion may establish the need for the trip, orient the members of the group to the field situation, put forward a series of questions to be answered or things to be observed, outline a system for recording information during a trip or immediately afterward, and formulate a procedure for appraising the information gained. The last step (reviewing, appraising, following-through) is frequently overlooked, but is extremely important because students will look for and record information more efficiently when they know how the newly acquired experience will be utilized and appraised.

Unless field trips are carefully planned, they may lead to serious misunderstandings between school and community. Certainly, when repeated field trips are undertaken, as in making a community survey, the plans involving the people in the community should be given special emphasis. To avoid problems, the teacher should make the necessary arrangements with the person or persons who will be host at the place being visited, obtain parental consent, arrange for transportation, consult the school's principal about the trip, and talk to the students regarding their conduct. If, in classroom discussion, students are unwilling or unable to exercise the control and judgment necessary in formulating reasonably adequate standards of conduct, it is likely that the field trip will be hazardous for all concerned. Further, if specific procedures are not carefully worked out with the guide or host at the destination, the best-behaved students will profit little from the trip.

SMALL-GROUP ACTIVITIES

Small-group activities sometimes meet the varying abilities, interests, and needs of students better than do large-group activities. This is especially true in subjects required of all students in a grade (for example, English and social studies), in heterogeneous, age-graded classes. Although it is common for the administration to divide students into classes according to ability to attain or according to actual achievement, separating the bright and the slow from the average, there will still be variability within a class when various academic, intellectual, physical, and social traits are considered. Of course, even in honors sections, interests and needs will require small-group work; and, certainly, the more heterogeneous sections of students of average ability will need group activities. No means of grouping has yet been found that completely eliminates the need for some individualization, individualization that can be attained in small groups of two to twelve.

The teacher's attitude, and the pattern of behavior by which he was taught, is sometimes a primary factor in determining whether class time is spent in group activities. Many high school teachers, when they were in grades 1 through 12, were never in a class where group projects were planned and completed by the students themselves. At the present time, nursery schools and kindergarten give attention to socializing activities, but children of this age are not ready to join any but quite small groups. The elementary school then gives some attention to continuing group activities such as play period, care of pets, painting murals, and so on. But in the junior high school heavy emphasis is placed on subject-specialization. Teachers who are expert in various areas of knowledge teach these subjects; and the students go from one room to another, one teacher to another, to get ready to meet the academic requirements for high school. In the senior high school, the students drill on college-entrance requirements; and, thus, high school becomes a preparation for further schooling. Teachers who are the product of such schooling and who have profited in their higher education from such experiences find it difficult to organize group activities in which students can learn to participate effectively with others.

Yet, participation with others at home and in school—in all social groups—is requisite for developing the competencies and qualities necessary for living in our complex culture. One learns democratic values, tolerance, cooperation, and skills for collective thinking by participating in many activities in which goals are formulated by a group, projects are planned by a group, and rules are made by a group.

Bases of small-group formation

There are several bases for forming small groups in age-graded classes. Depending upon the outcomes desired, the chief bases are (1) mechanical, (2) friendship, and (3) interest groupings; (4) achievement level; and (5) differential ability.

Mechanical grouping is often used to help students get acquainted and to encourage them to work cooperatively with other class members. In forming these groups, the teacher may use the letters of the alphabet with which the students' names begin or he may use the rows in which the students sit. He may also have the students count off from one to 30 and divide them into groups according to number. Except by accident, mechanical grouping does not secure groups that are homogeneous in any ability or characteristic.

Friendship grouping is used to get students to work together efficiently as quickly as possible or to deal with cliques as groups. Friends do not need time to get acquainted; and, having already worked together in the school, home, or neighborhood, they can get started quickly. It is probably better to keep members of cliques together at first rather than to distribute them among several groups, for clique members can disrupt small-group efforts. To the extent that similar interests and abilities are related to the formation of friendship, friendship groupings are more homogeneous than are groups based on mechanical arrangements.

Interest grouping is widely used in unit-teaching. When a larger project or culminating activity is planned, smaller projects and other activities are identified, and the students volunteer for them on the basis of interest. Interest grouping is found not only in the single class but in the entire program of the school. Student selection of tracks or programs, elective subjects, and cocurricular activities is based on interest, although other factors, including friendship and ability enter in. There is probably no better way of getting a working group formed than to have students identify an interest themselves and then explore it fully with other students.

Achievement-level grouping is used widely in the required subjects in the high school, especially in the heterogeneous, age-graded class and in the homogeneous "average" sections. (In these average sections will be bright students who elect not to enter honors classes and slow students who work very hard to obtain their achievement level.) In this type of grouping, each student's level in the particular area of achievement is identified. Thus, where achievement in reading, composition, or logical reasoning is closely related to learning efficiently in any class, the students are grouped on the basis of their achievement level and go from one to another group as necessary. This may mean from two to five groups within a class. For example, in eighth-grade arithmetic, there might be three groups—low achievers, middle achievers, and high achievers. When reading is an important means of acquiring information, as in English, social studies, or science, groups are formed on the basis of achievement level in reading, and reading materials and instructional techniques are varied as necessary for the various groups.

Differential-ability grouping enables a teacher to place students who differ in ability in one of several smaller groups. For example, in an American history class, five committees are formed to secure and present information on federal support of education during each of the last five government administrations. The teacher wants each committee to include a student who can lead discussions well and who can get the group going in the desired direction, another student who reads and writes well and who knows how to use the library well, and still another student who can visualize information well. He will also include one or two students who cannot do any of these things particularly well but who need to learn. Differential-ability grouping in heterogeneous classes provides for differences and capitalizes upon strengths.

Forms of small-group activities

Of the many forms of small-group activities, only the study of textbooks and references, British-style debate, panel discussion and reporting, and sociodrama and informal role-playing are discussed.

The study of text and reference materials

When students manifest a considerable range in ability to use a basic text, small-group work can be used to good advantage. For example, students in a geometry class are divided into groups of three or four sections of students varying widely in ability. The teacher assigns each group a number of problems to solve, perhaps the same within each group. The students do the assignment together, using the chalkboard and other available materials. The same procedure can be used in foreign language, science, or English classes when the basic text can serve as the basis of daily work assignments.

In such classes as social studies and literature, where the basic text is organized into units, each of which contains several chapters, the class is frequently divided into groups to work on specific chapters. This enables the student to attain considerable information in a relatively short time. Various types of oral, written, and graphic presentation are used for group reports to the class.

In studying a topic that requires reference books and current printed information, groups are frequently organized within the class to do the research. Each group assumes responsibility for investigating one aspect of a topic or one type of source material.

The chief criticisms of having students work together on an assignment are that better students are held back by slower ones, that most of the work is done by one student, that the group does not learn how to study and work individually, and that the classroom is noisy. Certainly, all these conditions are present when group work is poorly organized. But they can be avoided if there is sufficient teacher-student planning so that the students recognize their responsibility to their group and to the class for doing a fair portion of the work, so that they share in deciding what to do and how to do it, decide on rules of conduct for group work, and devise techniques for appraising individual contributions to the group and group contributions to the class. Whether the better students should help the slower cannot be answered dogmatically. However, civilized group life is based on the assumption that the strong will help the weak, that anarchy flourishes when group life is based on the survival of the fittest.

When two sections of the same class are relatively equal in achievement, the teacher can discover for himself the relative merits of small-group work by an action-research approach, by a pragmatic attempt to evaluate day-by-day and unit activities. The classroom teacher can begin this type of problem-solving by giving an achievement test at the beginning of a reporting period. During the reporting period, whole-class activities can be used in one section and group work in the other. The other factors—films used, discussions, explanations made by the teacher, and so on—are held constant. The test is repeated at the end of the period. The scores made by the two sections are compared, and the teacher notes especially the average or mean score, the range in scores, and the amount of progress made by the students scoring highest and lowest. Also, at the end of the period, the teacher has the students in each group demonstrate their ability to work together in planning such activities as a class party or a field trip and evaluates their effectiveness in such planning. This kind of classroom research is often much more meaningful to the teacher than is the reading of research carried out by professors of education and by their Ph.D. candidates.

British-style debate

The British-style debate, based on House of Commons procedures, brings the audience into the debate. A problem is formulated and a speaker for the affirmative and a speaker for the negative each make a five- to eight-minute formal presentation. A second member from each side then gives a shorter talk. The two speakers may then yield to a question or a contribution from the floor or audience. This is followed by an open period in which the floor may speak or ask questions of a debater or of someone in the audience who has already spoken. These speeches, however, must be in an affirmative-negative sequence so that an equal number of people speak on each side of the question. A speaker from each side then makes a summary presentation, after which members of the audience may speak again.

For eliciting audience interest, participation, and identification with the problem, the British type of debate is far superior to the more formal style. A good way to adapt this type of debate to classroom use is to limit debate to half the period and to use the remaining time for whole-class or small-group discussion of what has been said.

Panel discussion and panel reporting

Panel discussion is often more natural and less formal than debate. A class may be organized into panels—that is, groups of from four to eight members—to secure and discuss information and to present concepts, facts, generalizations, and conclusions to the rest of the class. In one form of panel discussion, each student makes a short formal presentation related to the subject under investigation. In another form, the chairman states the topic, and the panel members then respond informally. With this latter procedure, the students speak from notes only and contribute more frequently to the discussion than if they were merely reading or reciting previously constructed statements.

The chairman of the panel has much of the responsibility for its success. If a class is unfamiliar with panel procedures, it is advisable for the teacher to act as chairman of the first panel.

Here are the main jobs the teacher should do in planning a panel:

1. Have the topic discussed by the whole class to make sure that the students understand it clearly and are interested in getting and presenting information
2. Help the students organize into panel groups and select a chairman to guide the panel in securing information
3. Help the chairman and group members allot responsibility for securing information and for devising graphic aids and demonstrations in the presentation
4. Aid the class in devising forms for recording information
5. Help the students develop a conversational style in committee meetings
6. Assist the chairman and students in drawing up a presentation plan based on each member's specific responsibility for an area of information
7. Help the chairman plan his presentation, including:
   a. A clear statement of the topic and brief introductory remarks about it
   b. Introduction of the panel members and the special area of concern of each member
   c. Statement of the first question to be responded to by a panel member
   d. A method for accepting questions from the floor
   e. A method for bringing each panel member into the discussion
   f. A method for summarizing when needed
   g. A method for keeping the remarks focused on the topic
   h. The closing remarks

8. Work out with the entire class techniques for evaluating the panel on:
   a. Clarity of the discussion
   b. Relevance of materials presented
   c. Effectiveness of presentation of the individual students
   d. The chairman's effectiveness
   e. The conduct of the audience
   f. The appropriateness of the contributions from the floor

Tape recordings of a panel discussion are excellent evaluation devices.

Sociodrama and informal role-playing

Sociodrama is unrehearsed dramatization dealing with social problems. It is a spontaneous experience that is effective with various learning situations requiring insight into other human beings. In sociodrama, students play their roles using only the information they already possess as to how the part should be played: There is no script, no rehearsal, and no memorizing of lines. The presentation is brief, often five to ten minutes in length.

Sociodrama is one type of role-playing. (Another type of role-playing is psychodrama, a technique used in therapy.) The distinction that is often drawn between sociodrama and role-playing is that sociodrama centers chiefly on a social problem whereas informal role-playing emphasizes self-concept, insight into self.

The techniques of sociodrama can be adapted to a variety of situations. For instance, a class may decide to give a party that is not on the school's already crowded social calendar and someone from the class must secure the approval of the director of student activities. The teacher initiates a discussion on what the student might say to the adviser, and several alternatives are given—that the student be timid, or aggressive, or straightforward and courteous. One student volunteers to act as adviser; another, as petitioner. The players step outside the classroom briefly to decide how to act out the roles, and then the situation is dramatized. When a student in the audience suggests how a role might be portrayed more effectively, the teacher asks him to take the role. (This replacement is frequent in groups that are accustomed to sociodrama.) Following the presentation, there is a general class discussion, and one student is selected to obtain the adviser's approval for the party.

Other social situations, involving alternative courses of action to solve problems, in which role-playing works well are an applicant for a job interviews an employer, a student seeks information from a community leader, a salesman talks with a customer, a high school sophomore asks her parents' permission to attend her first dance, or a student discusses a test score or semester mark with his teacher. Playing shy, aggressive, cooperative, friendly, objective, and thoughtful roles gives all these situations reality and helps the student learn the preferred way of behaving. And, of course, the student who can play the preferred role easily in the presence of his teacher and classmates will meet actual situations with greater ease and self-confidence.

Role-playing is also of value in demonstrating concepts and attitudes acquired in courses that are largely content-centered. For instance, after studying a novel, play, or historical event, the class identifies the leading characters. The action and setting are reviewed briefly, and the students are selected for the various roles. As he plays his part, each student reveals his attitudes toward the character, his awareness of the psychological order of events, his understanding of how experience modifies character, and so on. The audience also has ideas about how the roles should be played and will want to discuss possible inferences on the verisimilitude of the treatment of character.

Some suggestions that may prove useful in organizing and directing informal role-playing and sociodrama for the first time are

1. Select a situation that the class understands well. Generally, such situations arise in informal discussion of the topic being studied.
2. Allow sufficient time for setting up the situation so that the setting and the roles are understood by the entire class.
3. Emphasize the fact that the student is playing a role, not portraying his own feelings and attitudes. He is not supposed to act as he really feels about the situation.
4. Attempt to get students to volunteer for all of the roles. In case none do, select students who are not shy or easily upset.
5. Prepare the audience for observing. An effective technique is to say, "Notice how Helen and David play their roles. If you would do differently, you will have a chance after they finish. Treat

Helen and David as you want them to treat you when you play the role."

6. Stop a student when he steps out of the role or when he cannot continue with success. Some students volunteer in an attempt to overcome their feelings of insecurity with braggadocio but become inadequate and sometimes paralyzed in the situation.

7. Get a second group of students to play the roles when the first group has finished.

8. Expect students to be nervous when playing a role for the first time.

9. Summarize role-playing presentations in a short class discussion when this is feasible. Compare and contrast the varying interpretations of the first and second group of role-players.

Some of the more important values derived by students from role-playing and sociodrama are practice in using new ideas, heightened interest in the course content, further bases for discussion, an increased awareness of alternative strategies for action, deeper insight into a social problem, motivation to prepare materials more carefully, increased ability in communication skills, and a high degree of transfer of learning to the actual situation being dramatized.

INDIVIDUAL ACTIVITY; INDEPENDENT, SELF-DIRECTED STUDY

Whole-class and small-group activities are useful in achieving certain objectives, but they should not be thought of as replacing individual work and effort. The group activities discussed here attain the desired outcomes through the interaction of individuals, which in turn means that individuals must contribute to the group effort. The need of students to acquire understandings and independent skills, and the obligation of the teacher to meet the problem of adjusting to human variability, requires individual activity.

Some forms of individual study or practice are particularly needed in acquiring skills: in reading, writing, and mathematics, for instance. Individual experience is necessary in achieving certain cognitive learning outcomes: problem-solving, evaluating, creating and integrating. Individual experience is, of course, also necessary in acquiring specialized uses of psychomotor abilities, in typewriting, in playing a musical instrument, in dancing, and so on. Individual study and practice are needed if the student is to formulate desirable attitudes toward individual effort and performance, and if he is to satisfy the need for mastery of content.

Many individual methods of instruction have been created in past decades. Space limitations preclude a description of each plan. But among the many plans for individualized instruction are the Pueblo Laboratory Plan and the Winnetka Plan in both of which students are assigned work individually according to interests, needs, and abilities, and in which students progress at individual rates of learning in a public school situation.[4]

Of the many forms of class activities that are focused on individual study, the four most widely used are (1) supervised study and individual projects, (2) library work, (3) learning by teaching machine and programs for self-instruction, (4) laboratory work, and (5) discovery learning.

Supervised study and individual projects

In a directed or supervised study period, students work on teacher-made assignments and on many kinds of self-initiated individual projects. The teacher helps each student with his work, posing questions, answering questions, serving as consultant, noting convergent and divergent thinking. In many classrooms, half, and sometimes more than half, of the instructional period is used for supervised study; the remainder, for discussion, lecture, films, and the like.

Supervised study has proved to be one of the better teaching techniques, for it provides for dissimilarities in student characteristics and, at the same time, helps students acquire individual skills and work methods. The teacher-student contacts during supervised study periods help the teacher gather data on individual background, ability, and need. The supervised period has gained in favor, also, because apparently many students profit little from unguided, mechanical homework.

Various methods of making assignments in supervised study have

---

[4] For a brief treatment of various ways of meeting individual differences that gives brief single-paragraph descriptions of 31 plans, see Harold G. Shane, "Grouping in the Elementary School," *Phi Delta Kappan*, XLI (April, 1960), 313–319.

been devised to fit the characteristics of different groups. Among these methods are the common assignment, the achievement-level assignment, and the flexible, individual assignment.

The common assignment

In classes where the level of student achievement is relatively heterogeneous, a common assignment is often given to the class. Frequently, when the assignment consists of silent reading, the teacher provides the students with a list of questions or with study guides. And as the individual student encounters difficulties, the teacher helps him. This help should be both diagnostic and evaluative in nature so that the difficulties are identified and methods of overcoming them are devised. Merely giving correct solutions is not good practice.

Carefully directed common assignments may be useful in teaching students to read charts and maps, to get meaning from paragraphs, to identify key ideas in an assignment, to identify unfamiliar words, to organize a complete assignment into a meaningful pattern, and to practice skills.

The achievement-level assignment

In heterogeneous classes in such areas as English and arithmetic, the students can be expected to vary considerably in their levels of achievement. Therefore, the teacher determines each student's achievement level, divides the class into groups for purposes of making differential assignments, and sets up a supervised study period. In arithmetic, to choose one example, the assignment to each group might consist of problems involving percentage, ratio, or fractions. But the assignments would vary both in type and in difficulty as achievement levels dictate. For low-achievers, the problems would be stated very simply and would deal with concrete situations; for advanced students, the problems could well be more difficult and abstract.

In literature study in an eighth-grade English class, to choose still another example, the same general ideas hold true. Thus, the slow-learning students might be assigned junior novels, novels written for and about adolescents, such as James Summers' *Prom Trouble*, or Henry

Gregor Felsen's *Hot Rod.* Advanced students might read Mark Twain's *Tom Sawyer* or Esther Forbes' *Johnny Tremain.* If the unit centered about such a theme as "The Conflict of Youth and Age," there might be a common core of readings in short stories, essays, and poetry for all students so that there could be a common background of readings for whole-class discussion. This core of common readings, useful for motivating the further reading of novels, would be selected for the average reading-achievement level, in the knowledge that the faster students would be provided other more adult titles and that students of lesser ability would need considerable help from the teacher and would read only fairly simply written selections.

As may readily be surmised, the teacher's task in organizing assignments at three or four levels of difficulty, while providing a core of common activities in which the whole class participates, is both time-consuming and difficult. It requires thorough familiarity with the characteristics of the students and with the instructional materials, as well as a sound basis in the principles of learning. And unless the students complete most of the assignments, achievement-level study periods will not prove of value.

The flexible, individual assignment

Some teachers prefer flexible, individual assignments that make the students responsible for choosing from among various activities in accordance with their interests and abilities.

To be effective, the flexible assignment must incorporate a broad range of activities and must provide for student initiative to operate in selecting them. The English teacher who uses the flexible assignment in a literature unit might present a list of readings representing different genre and different levels of difficulty. Students would have the opportunity to suggest still other titles. Apart from a minimum core of assignments required of all students, each student then makes his selection and reads as much as he can. During the supervised study period, the teacher helps the student improve his method of attack in selecting the main thought of a passage, in drawing inferences, in determining the author's intent and point of view.

Library work

The central school library is a place to read for delight, to listen to records, to do reference work, to study and work at tables. With its variety of newspapers, current periodicals, books, and reference materials, the school library can meet the interest and ability levels of all children in the secondary schools. It is particularly valuable for students who learn easily through reading.

The librarian will help adolescents expand their interests to continually more varied authors, subjects, and genre. She will advise the teacher as to readability levels of books. She will be available to help students with reference work at such time as their instruction in library skills is no longer sufficient to lead them to all possible sources. However, the student should not ask the librarian to do all of the locating of materials, because he, not the librarian, is the learner.

Many central school libraries have good collections of records with the necessary sound equipment, including earphones, so that individual students can listen without interfering with other pupils who are studying. The academically talented student will gain many cultural or literary values from a varied selection of records. The less able student who does not find reading a play or discussing a printed speech very meaningful may gain greatly from listening to a recording of it.

Autoinstruction

Although not completely tested in classroom situations at this date, autoinstruction, including programed instruction, holds high promise for improving learning through facilitating the individualization of instruction. In the next few decades, the teaching machine, or various programs for self-instruction, may be the chief media for presentation of fundamental skills. Use of the machine for information at a low level of abstraction will free the teacher to work with his students in higher-order cognitive functions—creative thinking, valuating, synthesizing—and with the affective domain—attitudes and values.

Basically, the teaching machine presents programed materials to the student in a series of small steps. At each step, an effort is made to enable the student to make a correct or adequate response before proceeding to the next step. Thus, the teaching machine provides immediate checks and a constant evaluation of student performance and facilitates the student's working at his own pace.

More will be said in Chapter 9 of the ideas underlying programed materials.

Laboratory work

Laboratory work was strongly emphasized in the 1920s and 1930s. This emphasis decreased later, as group work and group projects came to the fore, but the recent need for more engineers and scientists has revived interest in it. Throughout this entire period, however, certain areas of instruction—home economics, agriculture, various fields in vocational education, business education, and the secondary school sciences—continued to stress the need for doing, seeing, and thinking— not merely reading, talking, and thinking—if students were to learn efficiently, if they were to apply learnings.

More classes in various subject-matter fields can and probably should include laboratory-type individual activities, at the same time providing for a variety of whole-class and small-group activities. Whether in social studies, English, or calculus, situations can be arranged for laboratory-type activities. Students in an English class would probably profit as much from experimentation and the collection of data to attain concepts—from examining various materials, reconstructing plots on the chalkboard, taking the part of characters for the tape recorder, and manipulating punctuation marks on glass slides—as do students in biology or in cooking. And many students with little interest in reading, listening, and speaking might become greatly interested in a variety of laboratory activities—doing, manipulating activities.

Discovery learning

Another method, discussed earlier in this book, that can be used with the individual or with groups of various sizes is the so-called discovery learning. Providing real and meaningful problems, encouraging and guiding students as they collect information, and providing prompt,

---

5 Joseph R. Suchman, "The Child and the Inquiry Process," in A. H. Passow, ed., *Intellectual Development: Another Look* (Washington, D.C.: Association for Supervision and Curriculum Development, 1964), pp. 59–77.

TABLE 8.1. *Comparisons of Teacher Leadership Behavior and Learning Outcomes.*

Teacher behavior

Warmth

Sentimental; personal identification with students	Warm; understanding; self-controlling; listens attentively; accepts feelings; accepts students' ideas; observes students' reactions skillfully; asks questions; praises and encourages	Aloof; egocentric; fearful; anxious

Planning and execution of classroom behavior

Unplanned; slipshod	Responsible; business-like; systematic; flexible; integrative; orderly; work-oriented; explains things clearly; rewards fairly; explains reasons for criticism	Dominative; prescribes arbitrarily; uses power and coercion indiscriminately; asks for more than students can do; uses nonconstructive criticism

Approach to student behavior and subject matter

Impulsive; turbulent; variable	Stimulating; imaginative; surgent	Dull; routine

Related instructional procedures

May handle one type reasonably well; perhaps independent study best	Effective with group discussion; lectures; recitation; and independent activities	May handle one type well; perhaps lecturing best

Student behavior

Related subject-matter achievement of students

Inconsistent, varying with interest and ability of the students; insecure students do not learn well	High and consistent when procedures are selected in terms of objectives and student characteristics	May be high in outcomes emphasized by the teacher; rebellious students do not learn well

Related emotional security

Low for already unhappy children; might be high for a child who identifies with the teacher	High, when balance of direction and freedom is maintained in various activities	Low for most children

SOURCE: Herbert J. Klausmeier and William Goodwin, *Learning and Human Abilities*, 2nd ed. (New York: Harper & Row, 1966), p. 193. By permission.

accurate feedback, the teacher guides the student to attain various concepts and generalizations himself.[5] The student raises questions and finds his own answers. The student's question is not answered before he has had a chance to seek for the answer or solution himself. Such a method tends to facilitate a permanent attitude of inquiry toward learning.

COMPARISON OF TEACHER LEADERSHIP BEHAVIOR AND LEARNING OUTCOMES

Klausmeier and Goodwin demonstrate the interaction between the teaching method, or teacher leadership behavior, and student behavior and learning on several dimensions (Table 8.1). They compare the teacher's warmth, planning and execution of classroom behavior, approach to student behavior and subject matter, and related instructional procedures to the students' achievement of subject matter and of emotional security. Cautioning the reader that teacher behavior exists on a continuum, rather than being discontinuous or clearly delimited, Klausmeier and Goodwin suggest that teachers whose behavior patterns are toward the middle of the continuum are able to use a variety of instructional procedures. Warm and understanding, responsible and businesslike, stimulating and imaginative teachers will vary procedures —using lecture, question-and-answer recitation, group activities and independent work. Aloof, egocentric, and dominative teachers tend to use lecture and recitation to the exclusion of other methods. Teachers whose behavior patterns are toward the middle of the continuum are more likely to select methods in terms of instructional objectives as they relate to student characteristics than are teachers at either extreme of the continuum. However, personality (here, teacher leadership behavior) is an elusive concept: Behavior patterns are seldom pure types. Any teacher may well find himself toward one or the other pole on any dimension. Teachers have strengths and weaknesses, perform better in some areas than in others, and affect students differently.[6] There is little evidence that a teacher can change easily from one pattern of behavior

---

[6] Herbert J. Klausmeier and William Goodwin, *Learning and Human Abilities*, 2nd ed. (New York: Harper & Row, 1966), pp. 192–195.

to another. Ultimately, the teaching method must be congenial to the teacher's typical behavior patterns.

SUMMARY

Whole-class, small-group, and individual activities should be organized to help students acquire the content of the subjects and to relate content to cognitive processes. They should help students become well-balanced, socially conscious people who operate efficiently as members of a group and as individuals. No single grouping arrangement or method of teaching is superior to another in all cases. Instead, the potentialities that inhere in various sized class groupings and instructional procedures should be utilized.

Of the whole-class activities, discussion helps make the student an active participant in learning. Field trips help escape unnecessary verbalism about observable concrete referents of words. Recordings, television, and sound films convey instruction in vivid, dramatic forms. The lecture is valuable for coverage of content, and for transmitting one person's knowledge. Question-and-answer recitation is helpful in motivating student learnings by competition and in providing for reinforcements, rewards and punishments. Some methods are especially valuable for transmitting the fund of knowledge of a discipline. Other methods help each student feel that he is an accepted, worthwhile member of the class; they help the group develop common goals and cooperate in obtaining and sharing information. Typically, whole-class activities are the beginning of small-group activities: Specific individual or small-group activities originate as students read materials in common, discuss content, go on educational excursions, or watch sound motion pictures or instructional television.

Small-group activities are required for fostering individualized learning opportunities for smaller groups within the class, according to the abilities, interests, and needs of such groups. Subgroupings within a class are usually organized on the basis of seating arrangement of alphabet, friendship, interest, level of achievement, or differential ability. Sometimes, membership in a group is relatively fixed for the year—as when students are grouped by reading level. At other times, groups are temporary—as when students work on a brief report or project. Four of the many activities that enhance opportunities for learning in small numbers are the study of text and reference materials, British-style debate, panel discussion and reporting, and sociodrama.

Individual activities are essential for developing individual skills, independent study and work methods, and desirable attitudes toward individual effort and performance. They satisfy the adolescent's need for mastery over things and provide for wide individual differences among students. Supervised study and individual projects, library work, laboratory work, autoinstruction, and discovery-learning are among the most important of individualized methods. The supervised or directed study period during the regular class period is widely used to assist students, by means of independent study and practice, to reach their maximum achievement. Discovery-learning, as it results in a questioning or searching attitude, is favorable to the acquisition of new concepts and to the broadening of partially developed concepts.

Certain types of teacher leadership behavior are associated with effective instructional methods and with high student achievement. Although no teacher can be totally effective with all children, nor can he effectively employ all teaching methods, it is clear that some teachers are far better than other teachers.

QUESTIONS AND ACTIVITIES

1 Which objectives in your area of teaching might best be served in large-group instruction? In small-group? In individual study?
2 Compare the advantages and disadvantages of the discussion method (whole-class) with those of the lecture method.
3 Discuss the purposes for which you might use recitation in your classroom.
4 Some teachers say that field trips are a complete waste of time. Give your opinion on whether or not the field trip is misspent time.
5 Describe situations in which you might use each of these bases for forming small groups: mechanical, friendship, interest, achievement level, and differential ability.
6 Set up a sociodrama in which one person takes the role of an administrator who strongly favors whole-class activities; another, the role of an administrator who favors small-group activities; a third, the role of an administrator who favors individual activities; and a fourth, the role of an inexperienced teacher seeking information.

7 Which educational objectives are best achieved through independent, self-directed study?
8 What is the opposite of discovery-learning? Give your opinion of the possible strengths and weaknesses of discovery-learning.
9 Discuss any possible restrictions upon teacher leadership that might be most difficult for a teacher to change or to modify.

SUGGESTIONS FOR FURTHER READING

ASCD 1964 YEARBOOK COMMITTEE, *Individualizing Instruction*, Edited by Ronald C. Doll, Washington, D.C.: Association for Supervision and Curriculum Development, 1964.

HENRY, NELSON B., ED., *Individualizing Instruction*, Sixty-first Yearbook of the National Society for the Study of Education, Part I, Chicago: University of Chicago Press, 1962.

INLOW, GAIL M., *Maturity in High School Teaching*, Englewood Cliffs, N.J.: Prentice-Hall, 1963.

NOAR, GERTRUDE, *Teaching and Learning the Democratic Way*, Englewood Cliffs, N.J.: Prentice-Hall, 1963.

WALLEN, NORMAN E., AND ROBERT M. W. TRAVERS, "Analysis and Investigation of Teaching Methods," in *Handbook of Research on Teaching*, Chicago: Rand McNally, 1963, pp. 448–505.

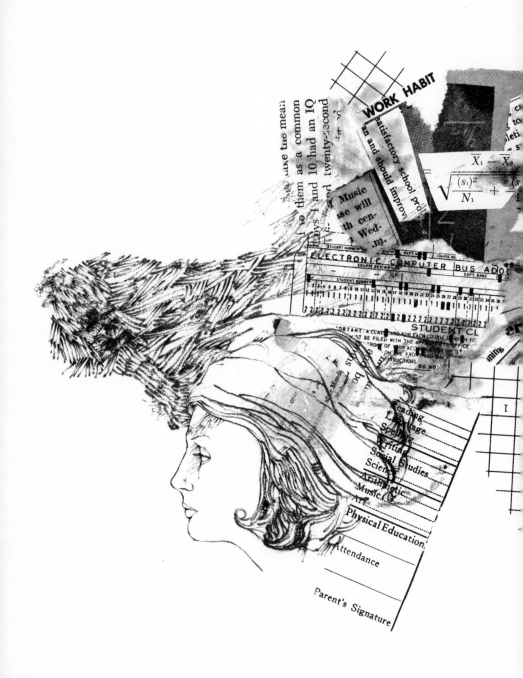

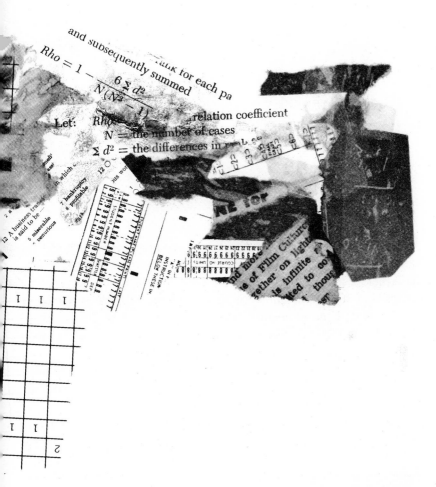

9 Textbooks and autoinstructional materials

$\mathcal{E}$ven after American presses began to produce schoolbooks in sufficient quantity to eliminate the need for importing textbooks, they, nevertheless, remained scarce for the whole of the Colonial era. Large numbers of students might work with as few as a half-dozen copies of a book. And, if no more appropriate volume were available, copies of the Bible, Addison and Steele, or Goldsmith might be pressed into service for instruction in reading, spelling, and writing.

During the Colonial period, books called spelling manuals contained materials for the entire course of study—spelling, reading, grammar, script samples, arithmetic, religious dogma, and so on. Such books, for the most part, lacked the various learning and teaching aids common to today's textbook—appendices, indexes, illustrations, notes, questions.

Soon after the Revolution, textbooks for separate study areas began to appear: Individual spellers, grammars, readers, and geographies were published. But up until the twentieth century (that is, for as long a period as the school population consisted largely of college-preparatory students), textbook writing was dominated and influenced for several generations by a few names: William McGuffey (readers), Lindley Murray (grammar), Hugh Blair (rhetoric), Joseph Ray (arithmetic), Jedidiah Morse (geography), and Noah Webster (spelling). The selection of learning material was still a relatively simple process.

Today, the classroom teacher's desk is stacked high with examination copies of or brochures on well-written, handsomely illustrated, beautifully bound textbooks, books written and edited by some of the foremost teacher-scholars of our time. But in the midst of such plenty, many people concerned with high-quality education sometimes scorn "textbook education." How are textbooks best used? To what ends and through what procedures? How can the teacher assist students in using textbooks effectively? What are some criteria for selecting textbooks?

Too, various autoinstructional materials show promise of having an impact on conventional classroom instruction. What do we know as of this date of the uses and effectiveness of existent autoinstructional devices and materials?

TEXTBOOKS

Table 10.1, found in the following chapter, indicates some of the instructional functions of printed matter. Printed media is said to function well in directing attention, in presenting a model of the student's performance, in guiding thinking, and in giving feedback.[1] Gagné has said,

> Assuming that the student possesses the necessary prerequisite knowledge, instruction by means of a book is usually a remarkably rapid and efficient process. Although no figures are available, the amount of time required for oral communication must surely be three or four times as much as that needed for instruction by means of a book. For the vast range of subject matter that is taught following the primary school years, printed communication can certainly be the major medium of instruction, and often is. When pictures and diagrams are combined with printed text (as, for example, in a good high school physics text), the dangers of excessive verbalism can largely be overcome, and the book can impart a great deal of instruction in a relatively short time, when used by a suitably prepared student who can read. At this level of schooling, in fact, whatever ineffectiveness books possess as instructional media may often be attributed to difficulties that are not inherent in the medium itself: Either the student has not acquired the necessary background knowledge or he has not learned how to read, or both.[2]

---

[1] Robert M. Gagné, *The Conditions of Learning* (New York: Holt, Rinehart and Winston, 1965), p. 284.

[2] *Ibid.*, pp. 276–277.

Three principles involved in the efficient use of textbooks are (1) the teacher selects textbooks carefully and considers their value as tools, as creative resources, that can be used to change behavior; (2) the teacher assists his students in the use of textbooks; and (3) the teacher considers the use of advance organizers as they seem appropriate.

Select textbooks carefully and consider their value as tools or resources

Books can and do change behavior. The biography of great men often attests the enormous impact of printed matter: As Keats discovers belles-lettres; as Lincoln aspires to statesmanship; or as Dickens becomes engrossed in *Tom Jones, Roderick Random,* or the *Arabian Nights.*

Textbooks, as well as belles-lettres, can produce growth in behavior or learnings. They can and do teach well, in part, because they are often written specifically for students at various levels of schooling in terms of what is known of format, interest, up-to-date content, readability, learning theory, and so on. They present subject matter in a logical arrangement to achieve specified aims. They more or less guarantee to cover important concepts, principles, or other content of a subject sequentially. They contain many teaching aids: suggestions for further reading, test items, discussion questions, vocabulary sections, and so on.

However, the suggestion that the textbook be viewed as a tool suggests that it is a means, not an end. Too often in secondary education, the textbook has dominated or determined curriculum. Class work has often been dominated by the goal of mastery and recall of textbook materials. And venerated though textbooks have been, their weaknesses are several. Textbooks are often inadequate in providing for discovery, inquiry, or problem-solving techniques. They do not always give sufficient attention to the need to provide for intraindividual variability. They sometimes oversimplify complex skills, concepts, and behaviors. They often pretend to a final truth that is deceiving. The reading level, the vocabulary load, and the concepts are often beyond the grasp of a student of average ability in a given grade.

However, as a tool in teaching, the textbook does have its values. To the extent that one goal of teaching might be coverage, the standard textbook does attempt to cover important materials sequentially. All students are exposed to a common body of knowledge. Textbooks can arouse curiosity and can motivate. Textbooks can help guide thinking and can help the student assess his learnings. The textbook provides material that the classroom teacher lacks time to create. If a student reads well and brings a sufficient background of knowledge to his reading, a textbook can instruct.

To insure that textbooks are suitable for his classroom, the teacher will want to play a role in the adoption of materials. Fortunately, the statewide adoption of textbooks by state committees, by the state superintendent, or by laymen is now less common than it once was. Local selection and adoption is increasingly prevalent. And it is assumed that the teacher, rather than the layman, is best qualified to determine how faithful the text is to the subject matter and how well it provides for the needs of his students.

Chief factors in selecting a textbook—factors that the teacher is well qualified to evaluate—are the qualifications of the author(s), the faithfulness of the content to current scholarship, and the appropriateness and interest of the content for learners.

In determining whether the scholarship of a textbook is authoritative, the teacher should consider the qualifications of the author. Is he an authority in the subject field in which he is writing? Is his presentation based on his own study, reflection, and experience; or is it hastily or carelessly conceived? Does he distort or give misinformation? Many scholars cannot or do not write for young people; to make the scholar's findings available, popularizers rewrite complex ideas so that they are simple and so that they are of high interest. An inept popularizer, failing to grasp his subject matter fully, can misinform.

Obviously, another important consideration in examining a textbook is the quality of the material as judged by your own opinion and by the opinion of reviewers writing in your professional journals. Such evaluation will consider the agreement of the text material with current scholarship and research.

Another important concern of the classroom teacher in selecting a text is that it teach the knowledge, skills, and values contained in institutional and instructional objectives. The teacher will often try to ascertain the extent to which the authors present mere facts, the extent to which the book encourages creativity, discovery, inductive reasoning, application of knowledge, synthesis of knowledge, and so on. Clearly, if the goals of the textbook writer are not in accord with those of the teacher, learning will be inefficient. The teacher might especially ask whether the textbook is suited to the potentialities of all students and whether it presents a balanced program for each individual.

The teacher will also want to examine the author's rationale in the placement of subject matter. In a period characterized by many new curriculum developments, the teacher must select textbooks with great care. Controversies over such trends as the introduction of mathematical logic as early as grades 5 and 6, or the efforts to combine mathematics and science, are reflected in a wide range of newly developed textbooks and other instructional materials. Choosing among available materials brings serious responsibilities to the teacher and requires his thoughtful consideration of new insights into the structure of subject matter and into cognitive organization and motivation.

The teacher will also want to examine some of the factors that enter into a consideration of the readability of the text—the appropriateness of the style for the audience for which it is intended, the possible interest of content for the reader, the past experience that the reader will bring to the book.

Still other factors in choosing a textbook will be the cost, the durability of the binding, the worthwhileness of photographs and illustrations, the quality of the paper; and readability factors such as length of line, size of type, interlinear space, and color of ink and paper.

The creative teacher will want to ask himself to what extent other media should supplement or replace sections of the textbook. Chapter 10, "Using Audio-Visual Materials," will consider the functions of motion pictures, television, flat pictures, and so on, in classroom instruction. Often, audio-visual materials serve as invaluable adjuncts to textbooks. Many publishers are now marketing recordings, films, transparencies for overhead projectors, and units containing many different paperbacks to accompany the textbook—all of which are intended to constitute a single package for use in the classroom. Such teaching materials— films, recordings, pamphlets, slides, posters, models, and tests—are sometimes called *instructional program packages*.

The teacher, in selecting a textbook, might also ask himself whether it serves instructional objectives as well as, or better than, other printed materials. Sometimes magazines, newspapers, pamphlets, brochures, or classroom sets of paperback books may meet objectives better than a single textbook could. Sometimes, instead of a single textbook, the teacher will want sets of textbooks of various levels of difficulty in order to provide for exceptional children as well as for children of average ability. Sometimes a basic textbook may be a focal point in initiating the study of a problem but will, as interest develops, lead to wide use of the schoolwide library. Or, again, the teacher may feel that, finding no text to serve the needs and abilities of his students, he will want to prepare some of his own teaching materials.

Certainly, the availability of inexpensive paperbacks is a boon to the classroom teacher—whether he teaches science, social studies, mathematics, or fine arts. *Paperbound Books in Print*, revised several times annually, lists many titles in each area of study, titles that facilitate an individualized approach to learning or that readily supplement the basic textbook. Such inexpensive books put a personal library within the reach of every student and possibly serve, in part, to insure that students form lifetime reading habits.

Some publishers now package paperbacks in units. One such unit, a thematic unit designed primarily for seventh-grade students and appropriate for both English and social studies classes, is entitled *Small World*. *Small World* employs a three-phase organizational plan to provide books according to those interests important in the daily affairs of youth and to use these existing interests to develop still others through learning tasks appropriate to the abilities of the learner. Phase I calls for classwide reading in a unit anthology, *Small World*, which contains prose and poetry by such writers as Margaret Mead, Leo Tolstoy, Leigh Hunt, George and Helen Papashvily, William Saroyan, and Robert Frost. Phase II is in small groups and involves such titles as Pearl Buck's *The Big Wave*, John Carson's *The 23rd Street Crusaders*, Catherine Marshall's *Julie's Heritage*, Barbara Reynolds' *Emily San*, and Ian Serraillier's *Escape from Warsaw*. Phase III involves individual, extensive reading from such books as Arora's *Tiger on the Mountain*, Benary-Isbert's *The Long Way Home*, Bryant's *The Lost Kingdom*, Canfield's *Understood Betsy*, Gates' *Blue Willow*, McSwigan's *Snow Treasure*, Mowat's *Two Against the North*, Seymour's *When the Dikes Broke*, Twain's *The Prince and the Pauper* (abridged), and Whitney's *The Highest Dream*. A chief goal of these readings is to demonstrate the possibility for better understanding the customs and beliefs of others in a world that daily becomes increasingly smaller.[3] Such units

---

[3] Robert Smith, Jane Sprague, and Stephen Dunning, eds., *Small World* (Englewood Cliffs, N.J.: Scholastic Book Services, 1964).

of instructional materials are good in providing for differences attributable to sex, home background, and differing rates of learning ability and help in the acquisition of knowledge, skills, and attitudes.

Still other publishers present instructional materials in kits, boxes, or laboratories that facilitate a multilevel, indivdualized program. For example, Science Research Associates (SRA) offers reading laboratories —in editions from elementary grades to the senior year of high school and beyond. The reading laboratory provides a wide range of reading materials designed according to pupil interest and ability. Materials are often designed to be pupil-operated in order to afford the teacher more time to work with each student individually.[4] SRA also publishes laboratories on writing skills, computational skills, and so on. Still another publisher offers a kit to improve student speaking and writing, *Individualized English: Set J.* These teaching materials permit the diagnosis of each student's level of achievement, present programed instructional materials to help the student overcome any problems, and test the student's progress. In using *Individualized English*, each student can pursue an individual course of study determined by his mastery of the subject matter.[5]

There are no longer a few well-established textbooks that dominate the secondary school curriculum. Textbooks are now available with many emphases, many shades of opinion. They are excellent tools and resources for teaching and for learning. However, to avoid the rigidity of a textbook-dominated course and to show flexibility, inventiveness, and creativity, the teacher can use the textbook creatively, letting a topic in the book lead to use of other mediums of instruction. He can employ various audio-visual aids. He can use the textbook flexibly, not feeling compelled to cover every unit presented. He can write his own materials when time permits. He can use multiple textbooks to provide for a wide range of student needs and interests and for a more truthful presentation of content. He can supplement textbooks with adjunct programed materials. He can remember that there are books in the central school library that are within the reach of every student. In all fields, the teacher can build classroom libraries of paperbacks. And he

---

[4] See, for example Don H. Parker and Genevieve Scannell, *SRA Reading Laboratory Ic.* (Chicago: Science Research Associates, 1961).

[5] J. N. Hook and William H. Evans, *Individualized English: Set J* (Chicago: Follett, 1964).

can also consider the best uses of instructional program packages, of laboratories of printed material, and of various kits and units.

Assist students in the use of textbooks

When a textbook is to be used as the basic instructional material, the teacher should assist the students in getting an overview of the content of the textbook, the purposes the textbook serves, and the best uses of the textbook. To accomplish this, the teacher should guide students in a preliminary survey of the entire textbook and should use advance organizers where appropriate.

Previewing the textbook

Students are helped to use a textbook by previewing it under the teacher's direction. To begin the preview, the teacher might ask, "Where can we find a listing of the major topics and of the subtopics under each major topic?" After this survey of the table of contents, the teacher might refer the students to the general introduction to the book and pose these questions: "Why did the author write the book?" or "For what audience did he write the book?" Next, the teacher might direct the students' attention to the index and help them locate information there under the subdivisions of main entries. For example, he might show the students that entries for almanacs, atlases and gazeteers, biographical dictionaries, encyclopedias, and yearbooks might be listed as subdivisions of the main entry, reference books. In this way, he would assist the student in learning which key entries in the index are important in finding a subdivision with ease and with speed.

In a rapid skimming of the textbook, the teacher might also indicate the placement and uses of keys, appendices, cross references, footnotes, and glossaries.

Surveying a chapter

Next, the teacher might assist the students in surveying a representative chapter in some detail. A rapid skimming might involve looking at the material in italicized print and at summaries. A more careful survey of a chapter would include noting the visual cues for identifying the major concepts, generalizations, and principles of a chapter: Cues such as boldface, italics, marginal notes, numerical or alphabetical listing of items, chapter headings, center headings, and side headings.

The teacher should remind the students that the introductory paragraphs often outline the major ideas in a chapter, that the summary presents conclusions about the major ideas, and that the introductions and summaries can also provide for continuity of chapters.

Too, in building student readiness, the teacher should introduce the student to unknown words and to words that, although well known, have specialized meanings in the chapter. The teacher should help set the purposes for reading the chapter and should suggest adjustments in the reading rate required by the range and the complexity of the materials that the chapter contains. The teacher might note how important it is to jot down important concepts or to write a brief summary of the chapter during a first reading. He might point out the values of the end-of-chapter questions and suggested readings for extending the students' knowledge of the content.

The chapter survey should be closely related to classwork. Thus, after a class viewing and discussion of a film on water pollution, the teacher may say, "We have seen and discussed the effects of the pollution of our rivers, lakes, and streams. Your textbook also discusses water pollution. In which chapter and on which pages is this information given?" After the chapter title, section, and page are located, the teacher proceeds, "Does your textbook add any new information to what we have already said of the causes and effects of water pollution? How can we find the information quickly?" These questions will refer the students to introductory paragraphs or to summaries and will require them to note visual cues.

The teacher may assign a silent reading of material, guiding the reading with the single question, "What are the main points presented in this chapter?" Or he may ask quite detailed questions. Oral reading of short introductory paragraphs may also be helpful.

When a chapter contains charts, diagrams, graphs, maps, or pictures, the teacher should ask specific questions that can be answered only by the correct interpretation of the materials. A commonly used method of handling this phase of the chapter survey is to divide the class into three or four groups and to give a task. For example, you might say, "The graph on page 37 shows the values of crops lost each year because of floods. The figures in the left margin are the years. The figures at the bottom show the value of the crops. Answer these questions from the graph: (1) In which year were losses heaviest? (2) In which year were losses smallest? (3) Which year appears to be average? (4) What main conclusions about flood damage have you obtained from the graph?" The first three questions, directed to different groups after they have studied the graph, should produce uniform answers. The answers to the last question should indicate the extent to which the students have grasped the significance of the information and how much further assistance they need. Whenever new graphic materials are introduced, the teacher should devise methods to insure their accurate interpretation.

Consider using advance organizers

In Chapter 3, "Conditions of Learning," you read of the advance organizer, designed to facilitate the learning and retention of factual material. The advance organizer consists of a group of principles or of superordinate concepts of high abstraction and generality, stated as nearly as possible in terms already familiar to the learner, to which the learner can relate new concepts and subconcepts that are less inclusive and less abstract than those in the advance organizer. The advance organizer can assist the learner in discriminating between what has been learned and the new material, and in relating previously learned and new material.[6]

In using advance organizers, a classroom teacher would present central, unifying ideas before specific ones; he would present the essential concepts to which to relate new content. He would assist the learner in noting similarities and differences between related concepts.

An example of an advance organizer is given here. (The lesson that it is intended to help the student learn is presented later in this chapter in the section on linear programing.) Note that the organizer is at a higher level of generality and inclusiveness than is the new material (lesson 1) and that it provides a general overview of the new material that follows. Note that the writer of the advance organizer has included discriminations, analogies, and comparisons to help the student learn the new material better.

---

[6] David P. Ausubel, *The Psychology of Meaningful Verbal Learning* (New York: Grune & Stratton, 1963).

Lesson 1

In order to describe something, we usually look at the whole thing and then look at the parts. Knowing the parts and how they fit together helps us in our description. If we are dealing with a number of things, we frequently put them into groups in order to make our description clearer and more organized. During the next two weeks, you will be using this approach in learning to describe English sentences.

One of the first things you will learn is that all sentences can be described in terms of certain basic sentence patterns. There are nine basic sentence patterns in the English language. These nine patterns might be compared to the primary colors that an artist uses. All hues can be obtained from mixtures of red, blue, and yellow which are the three primary colors. Similarly, every sentence you read can be described as taking the form of one of the nine basic sentence patterns, or as a combination or rearrangement of the nine basic sentence patterns. Here are two groups of sentences:

Group 1	Group 2
< John is president.>	< John is older. >
< The boys are a team. >	< The boys are tall. >
< All of the men were police- men. >	< All of the men were happy. >

Although each of these sentences is different, we can classify Group 1 as belonging to one of the nine basic sentence patterns and Group 2 as belonging to another.

Let's look at the sentences again in another way:

< John + is president. >	< John + is older. >
< The boys + are a team. >	< The boys + are tall. >
< All of the men + were police- men.>	< All of the men +were happy. >

These sentences, like every sentence which may be constructed in the English language, can be divided into two main parts. You will learn to call the part to the left of the + sign the subject group and the part to the right of the + sign the predicate group. For this first lesson you will work with the subject group. In all nine basic sentences, the subject group is always a noun phrase. In other sentences, which are rearrangements or combinations of basic sentences, the subject group may or may not be a noun phrase; in basic sentences it is always a noun phrase.

As you learn about noun phrases, you will discover that the last word in all noun phrases is a noun. What is a noun? Rather than depending on the traditional definition of noun as the "name of a person, place, or thing," you will learn to use the noun test-sentence. If a word fits in the noun test-sentence, it can be used as a noun. In a later lesson, you will be given other ways which will help you identify nouns.

These pages you have just read are meant to give you a brief overview of today's lesson. Now that you have an idea of what you will be learning, you are ready to begin Lesson 1.[7]

As was suggested in the section on advance organizers in Chapter 3, there is little evidence as to the frequency with which organizers should be used. However, if a year's work consists of a series of related, sequential teaching-learning units, the teacher might begin instruction with an organizer for the total material. Then he might begin each unit (here, perhaps a given chapter in a textbook) with an organizer which would enable the student to compare and to differentiate ideas contained in the unit just completed and the unit being initiated.

AUTOINSTRUCTIONAL DEVICES, MATERIALS, AND TECHNIQUES

Materials of instruction presented by automated teaching devices often have these characteristics:

1. Series or sequences of concepts, discriminations, generalizations, or chains are presented to the student in the form of items, steps, or frames. An item, step, or frame may present a statement of information; it may pose a question; or it may both inform and question.
2. The student responds to each item, often by an overt action or active response, such as attempting to identify a correct response or to construct a correct response.

---

[7] Materials for research in concept-learning, developed by Herbert J. Klausmeier, Research and Development Center for Learning and Re-education, University of Wisconsin, Madison, Wisc., pursuant to a contract with the U.S. Office of Education, Department of Health, Education, and Welfare, under the provisions of the Cooperative Research Program, Center No. C-03/Contract OE 5-10-154.

3. As the student responds to an item, he is given information that allows him to determine whether his response is correct or incorrect, or whether communication was successful or unsuccessful.

The device that conducts or controls such teaching is known as an autoinstructional device. Autoinstructional devices may be textbooks with special formats, or, at the other extreme of complexity, they may be computer teaching machines systems.

At this date, there is no unanimous agreement on the techniques of programing or on the learning-theory positions that underlie programed instruction. The teaching machine and program may present series of concepts, discriminations, or generalizations in a fixed sequence or in a sequence that varies with the student's response to an item. In addition to variation in the method of sequencing frames, the programing techniques may vary according to the types of responses required of the student or the conceptualizations of the learning process that are reflected in the programs.

The most important systems of programing methodology are to be seen in the work of three scholars: N. A. Crowder, S. L. Pressey, and B. F. Skinner. Crowder's style of programing is called intrinsic, or branching, programing; Pressey's, adjunct programing; and Skinner's, linear programing.

Linear programing

Probably the most widely used approach to programing has been the linear style proposed by B. F. Skinner. From the findings of carefully controlled research in the behavior of lower organisms conducted in the laboratory, Skinner has advanced certain suggestions for use in the control of the learning process and has described certain shortcomings in traditional classrooms.

He speaks of the importance of arranging what he terms *contingencies of reinforcement,* the relations between a given behavior and the consequences of the behavior. If it follows a response immediately, a satisfying consequence, a positive reinforcement, facilitates the permanent acquisition of a response. A lapse between a response and reinforcement diminishes the effect of the reinforcement. The days that pass as the teacher evaluates papers or the minutes that elapse before the teacher studies the student's work at his desk vitiate the necessary reinforcement of the student's responses. Reinforcements should be immediate.

Skinner does not think that efficient contingencies of reinforcement can be arranged without mechanical devices:

> An organism is affected by subtle details of contingencies which are beyond the capacity of the human organism to arrange. Mechanical and electrical devices must be used. Mechanical help is also demanded by the sheer number of contingencies which may be used efficiently in a single experimental session. . . . The simple fact is that, as a mere reinforcing mechanism, the teacher is out of date.[8]

He also asserts that reinforcements by mechanical aids will avoid the aversive controls—censure, displeasure, sarcasm—sometimes used by the teacher in an effort to bring about learning, and that the devices using programed materials avoid the anxiety created by a teacher's threat of punishment.

Skinner says that a long series of contingencies, presented in small steps, is necessary in acquisition of complex patterns of behavior:

> The whole process of becoming competent in any field must be divided into a very large number of very small steps, and reinforcement must be contingent upon the accomplishment of each step. This solution to the problem of creating a complex repertoire of behavior also solves the problem of maintaining the behavior in strength. We could, of course, resort to the techniques of scheduling already developed in the study of other organisms but in the present state of our knowledge of educational practices, scheduling appears to be most effectively arranged through the design of the material to be learned. By making each successive step as small as possible, the frequency of reinforcement can be raised to a maximum, while the possibly aversive consequences of being wrong are reduced to a minimum.[9]

To obtain optimal learning, programers following Skinner's approach often use the following techniques: Each student is required to go through an identical sequence of small steps. Each student responds to each step and is immediately reinforced. Each student's performance is as nearly without error as possible, as the result, in part, of the use of various cueing techniques such as giving prominence to a given word

[8] B. F. Skinner, "The Science of Learning and the Art of Teaching," in Arthur A. Lumsdaine and Robert Glaser, eds., *Teaching Machines and Programmed Learning* (Washington, D.C.: Department of Audiovisual Instruction, NEA, 1960), p. 109. By permission.

[9] *Ibid.*, pp. 108–109.

by using boldface type, color keying, and so on, or such as employing words possessing a high association value. So that each student must recall, rather than recognize, he is required to construct a response rather than to select a response from alternatives.

The teaching material that follows is an example of a variation of linear programing. The 60 frames are the first of 22 lessons presenting selected concepts from structural and transformational grammars. (You studied the advance organizer for this lesson earlier in this chapter.) Note the frames that review, utilize, or require recall of the concepts presented in earlier frames—concepts such as basic sentence, subject group, and predicate group. Note cueing techniques—such as the use of boldface type in frame 10. Note that the stimulus discrimination in frame 16 involves a multiple-choice response, whereas previous frames have called for a constructed response. Note that the material is being presented in small steps, with frequent repetition and with information as to the adequacy of responses.

LESSON 1: A LOOK AT BASIC SENTENCES

1. The English language has nine types of very simple sentences. These are called **BASIC SENTENCES.** They may be used alone, or they may be combined. All more complicated sentences which you read and write are combinations of these nine _____ sentences.	
2. < Some pianists are women.> is an example of one of the _____ types of basic sentences. (How many?)	basic
3. < The umbrella is black.> is also a basic s _____.	nine
4. < Turkeys gobble.> is another _____ _____.	sentence
5. < The umbrella + is black.> < Turkeys + gobble.> These basic sentences have _____ main parts. (How many?)	basic sentence

---

6. How many main parts does this basic sentence have?   two
   < Our team + won the match.>

---

7. < The umbrella + is black.>   two
   < Our team   + won the match.>
   All English sentences, whether they are basic or not,
   have two main parts. In < Most rabbits eat carrots.>
   we would put a + after _____ to show the
   two main parts.

---

8. To show the two main parts of   rabbits
   < Don looked happy.>, we would put a + after

   _____ .

---

9. < The chicken + seemed sick.>   Don
   This basic sentence, like all English sentences, has
   _____ main parts.

---

10. We would save a lot of words and time if we could   two
    refer to the two parts by single terms, instead of say-
    ing "the part to the left (or right) of the + sign."
    Let's call the part to the *left* of the + sign the SUB-
    JECT GROUP.
    In < Two mice + were behind the stove.> *Two
    mice* is the _____ group.

---

11. < Some of my books + are at home.>   subject
    Here *Some of my books* is the subject _____ .

---

12. We will be using the term *group* in a very special way.   group
    You are used to thinking of a group as having two or
    more items, but here a group may have only one
    word. For instance, in < Joan + was upset.> the
    subject group has only _____ word.
                     (How many?)

---

13. In the basic sentence < Those chairs + are antique.>   one
    the subject group is *Those chairs* because it is the
    part of the sentence to the _____ of the +
    sign.

---

14. In < Skunks + are friendly.> *Skunks* is the   left

    _____ _____ .

---

15. The term we use for the second part of the sentence
is **PREDICATE GROUP.**
< Skateboards + are fun.>
In this basic sentence *are fun* is the _____
group.

subject
group

16. The predicate group is that part of a sentence to the
(left/right) of the + sign.
[Choose one]

predicate

17. What is the predicate group in this sentence?
< These oysters + are raw.>

right

18. A predicate group may also have only one word. For
example, in < Someone sneezed.> *sneezed* is the
_____ _____.

are raw

19. The subject group is to the left of the + sign, and
the predicate group is to the _____ of the +
sign.

predicate
group

20. < My goldfish is dead.>
After what word would you put a + to separate the
subject and predicate groups?

right

21. < My goldfish + is dead.>
What is the first word in the predicate group?

goldfish

22. The first word in the predicate group of
< Two anteaters + are in the zoo.> is _____.

is

23. *Is* and *are* are forms of the word *be.* Here is a list
of all the forms of *be: am, is, are, was, were, been,*
and *being.*

Which of these basic sentences has a form of *be?*
(Write only the letter of the sentence.)
a. < Two hawks shrieked.>
b. < The stranger was a doctor.>
c. < John hit his sister.>

are

24. Let's look more closely at these sentences.
< My goldfish + is dead.>
< Two anteaters + are in the zoo.>
< The stranger + was a doctor.>

b.

One similarity among these sentences is that the first word in the predicate group is a form of _____.

25. For a little while we will be working only with the first three types of basic sentences. All three must have a form of *be* in the predicate group. For the remainder of Lesson 1 we'll look a little more closely at the subject group and then in the next lesson at the predicate group. What is the subject group in this sentence? < Tomatoes + are tasty.>	be
26. < Two worms + were in his pocket.> The subject group here is made up of two words. What are they?	Tomatoes
27. < Many of the settlers + were outlaws.> Here *Many of the settlers* is the _____ _____.	Two worms
28. Tomatoes Two worms Many of the settlers In time you will learn how to construct many kinds of subject groups. But for now, while we are working only with basic sentences, the subject group is always what we call a NOUN PHRASE. Each of the subject groups above is a _____ phrase.	subject group
29. < The sidewalk will be icy.> Here *The sidewalk* is used as the n_____ p_____ in the subject group.	noun
30. We will abbreviate *noun phrase* as NP. The subject group of all basic sentences is a _____.	noun phrase
31. A NP may be many words, or it may be only _____ word, as in < Telephones are handy.>	NP
32. < Two of the three screens are loose.> The NP in this sentence has _____ words. (How many?)	one

33. NP stands for ――――― ――――― .	five
34. In basic sentences the ――――― group is always a NP.	noun phrase
35. You have been identifying the subject and predicate groups and marking them with a + sign. We can also use a + to separate the two main parts of a NP. < These doughnuts + are homemade.> What is the NP subject group?	subject

36. The NP *These doughnuts* is made of two words:
    These + doughnuts
The NP *Several of the carnivals* has four words:
    Several of the + ――――――
	These doughnuts

37. Two of my shirts To mark the two main parts of this NP, we put a + between *my* and ――――― .	carnivals
38. These *doughnuts* Several of the *carnivals* + predicate group Two of my *shirts* Each one of these NP's may be the subject group of a basic sentence. The underlined word in each NP is called a NOUN. In basic sentences the last word in a NP is a ―――――― .	shirts
39. *Doughnuts, carnivals,* and *shirts* are nouns. In < Your house + is very modern.> *house* is the ―――――― .	noun
40. < Newspapers + were everywhere.> What is the noun here?	noun
41. You will learn later that nouns and NP's may be used in several places in the sentence. So far you know that a noun is the (first/last) word in the NP.	News-papers
42. A good way to recognize a noun is to see if the word will fill the noun position in this TEST-SENTENCE. < (The) ―――――― is/are here.> To test the word *butterfly*, for example, we would say: < The butterfly is here.> *Butterfly* is a noun; it completes the noun t -s ――――― ――――― .	last

43. The ( ) around a word mean that the word does not always have to be used. < (The) ——————— is/are here.> If we wanted to test the word *Joe* in the noun test-sentence, would we use *The?*	test-sentence
44. What marks do we use to show that a word does not always have to be used?	No (We would simply say < Joe is here.>.)
45. *Joe* and *butterfly* can be called nouns because they fill the noun position in the test-sentence. < (The) ——————— is/are here.> Test the word *tractor* by putting it in the noun position in the test-sentence. Would we call *tractor* a noun?	( )

46. Which of these words will complete the noun test-sentence?
    < (The) ——————is/are here.>
      a. always
      b. calendar
      c. organize
      d. chalky
	Yes (<The tractor is here.>)

47. Now write the noun test-sentence.	b.
48. < (The) ——————— is/are here.> All English sentences have two main parts: a subject group and a predicate group. The blank in this test-sentence indicates a noun position in the ——————— group.	< (The) ——————— is/are here.>
49. < Her records were on the floor.> What part of this sentence have we underlined, the subject group or the predicate group?	subject
50 < Her records were on the floor.> We have been working only with basic sentences that have a form of *be*. What form of *be* is used in the sentence above?	the predicate group
51. < Her records were on the floor.> is a ᵇ——————— sentence.	were

52. < The kittens are in the petunias.> is also a basic sentence. To separate the subject and predicate groups, we would put a + after the word _____.

basic

53. < The kittens + are in the petunias.>
The subject group of all basic sentences is a NP. In this sentence *The kittens* is a _____.

kittens

54. NP stands for _____ _____.

NP

55. What is the NP in < This rabbit is muddy.>?

noun phrase

56. The NP *This rabbit* has two words. Other NP's may have only one word, or they may have many more. How many words are in the NP of
< Many of these pencils are too short.>?

This rabbit

57.   This rabbit
Many of these pencils
In a basic sentence the last word of the NP is called a noun. *Rabbit* and *pencils* are _____

four (Many of these pencils)

58. If we are not sure which word is the noun, we can use the noun test-sentence, which is _____ _____.

nouns

59. < (The) _____ is/are here.>
What marks in the test-sentence indicate that a word is not always used?

< (The) _____ is/are here.>

60. < (The) _____ is/are here.>
Which of the following words would you call a noun because it will complete the test-sentence?
        a. naturally
        b. chooses
        c. giraffes
        d. very

( )

c.[10]

[10] Materials for instruction in English syntax developed by Nathan S. Blount, Research and Development Center for Learning and Re-education, University of Wisconsin, Madison, Wisc., pursuant to a contract with the U.S. Office of Education, Department of Health, Education, and Welfare, under the provisions of the Cooperative Research Program, Center No. C-03/Contract OE 5-10-154.

Intrinsic, or branching, programing

Growing out of research on training troubleshooters in electronic equipment and a desire to reproduce a tutorial teaching situation, the work of Norman A. Crowder has been with a style of programing known as intrinsic, or branching, programing.

Central to Crowder's approach is the use of the student's response to a multiple-choice question to determine which material the student need work with next. If the student selects a preferred response, he proceeds to the next sequence of information and to another question. If the student selects an inadequate response, he is referred to a review of the material that attempts to explain his error to him and he is then tested on the concept again.

Knowing that misunderstandings do occur during learning, Crowder sees the function of a program to be to resolve a given student's misunderstanding before the student moves on to new concepts or information. To this end, Crowder has developed a scrambled text in which, according to the response to a question, students are directed to different pages in the text. Such a style simulates a tutorial method of teaching. Students of high mental ability and high achievement move rapidly through the units without the need for corrective passages. Students having difficulties are referred to correctional material.[11]

Limitations of space prevent reproducing many pages of a branching program here, but Figure 6 presents material designed to teach basic skills in reading to elementary school students. Note that the first sequence of material (labeled with the number 1 in boldface in the upper left-hand corner) lists three choices for the student's response. If the student chooses the correct response, he goes to 15 and then proceeds to the next sequence of information, new information (sequence 7; not reproduced in this text). If the student elects 4 or 8 (incorrect responses), he is referred back to the original sequence of information, 1.

Crowder believes that such a style of programing provides more effectively for individual differences among students than does a linear

[11] Norman A. Crowder, "Automatic Tutoring by Intrinsic Programming," in Arthur A. Lumsdaine and Robert Glaser, eds., *Teaching Machines and Programmed Learning* (Washington, D.C.: NEA, 1960), pp. 286–298.

15

wind

Yes! The happy face shows that you are right. You found the last word in the second sentence of the story.

Because you are right, you can go to the next lesson.

As you work in this book, remember to use the Student Record Sheet. Always put a circle around your answer numbers. That is the way you keep your place.

Go to No. 7 in this book.

4

book

Sorry. The sad face tells you that you are wrong. You did not find the right answer. The word **book** is not the last word in the second sentence of the story. It is the last word in the last sentence.

One of the other answers in No. 1 is right. You must look for it there. Read the lesson again and find the right answer.

Go back now to No. 1

8

day

Sorry to say, this answer is not right. The sad face shows it. The word **day** is not the last word in the second sentence of the story. It is the last word in the first sentence.

One of the other answers in No. 1 is right. You must look for it. Put a circle around your new answer number on the Student Record Sheet.

Go back now to No. 1.

1

Here is the first part of the story:

PART 1

Snow had been falling all day. By evening it was piled into big drifts by the wind. Through the blizzard, lights could be seen. They came from houses that were warm and snug against the storm. At Mike's house, dinner was over. As they left the table, his father said to him, "Don't read too late." Mike went to his room and closed the door. He drew the curtains across the window. "It's a good night to be indoors," he thought. Then he sat down in the big chair with his new book.

Find the second sentence of the story above. Then find the last word in that sentence.

What is the last word in the second sentence?

The right answer is one of the words below:

book   (No. 4)
day   (No. 8)
wind   (No. 15)

Find the word that is the right answer. Then look at the front of the Student Record Sheet. You will be told there what to do next. Do not make any marks in this book!

FIG. 6 Examples of intrinsic programing. (Grace-carol Bostwick, Lessons for Self-Instruction in Basic Skills, Reading Interpretations I, Read to Know, Series A–B, Del Monte Research Park, Monterey, California: California Test Bureau, a Division of McGraw-Hill Book Company, 1965, frame numbers 1, 4, 8, and 15. Used by permission.)

style of programing. Such programing can move beyond basic concepts, skills, and facts to more complex cognitive and affective goals.

Adjunct programing

Sidney L. Pressey, often credited with devising the first teaching machine, has been a pioneer in the technology and theory of programed instruction. Recently, Pressey has had misgivings about the direction that autoinstruction has taken. He feels that the animal-laboratory-based experimentation of recent years needs careful scrutiny. He has advocated the use of programed materials in an adjunct or facilitating, rather than in a primary, role. The beginning of a learning unit for a student, according to Pressey's new techniques, might be to study a substantial amount of material such as an entire chapter in a textbook. Only after the studying of the chapter would autoinstructional materials be used; and they would be used ". . . to enhance the clarity and stability of cognitive structure by correcting misconceptions and deferring the instruction of new matter until there had been such clarification and elucidation."[12] The adjunct program might function as a device by which the student might evaluate his knowledge of the unit, or review or relearn material, or discriminate between similar concepts.

The adjunct program has an advantage over the linear program in that it maintains the meaningful structure of the subject matter. And in adjunct programs, the programer can provide advance organizers, outlines of topics, and classification schemes to facilitate the student's perceiving relationships among parts.

Computer-based teaching machines

Instructional systems now exist that can teach using computer-based teaching machines. These instructional systems are capable of individualizing instruction or of using instruction paced for groups.

One example of a computer-based system is seen in the Automated Teaching Project sponsored by the System Development Corporation (SDC). There are three major units in the SDC teaching machine: (1)

---

[12] Sidney L. Pressey, "Teaching Machine (and Learning Theory) Crisis," *Journal of Applied Psychology*, XLVII (February, 1963), 3.

a Bendix G-15 computer; (2) a random access slide projector; and (3) an electric typewriter. The Bendix G-15 is the central control unit; it determines which teaching materials the student will use and it analyzes the student's responses. The projector, using instructions from the computer, displays instructional materials for the student. The typewriter is used for the student to respond to multiple-choice questions and for the computer to provide feedback to the student. In selecting instructional slides, the computer considers the student's errors, the student's speed, the student's opinion of his performance, and certain background information on the student such as prior achievement, personality, and mental ability. The computer can omit material when the student is performing well and can supply remedial material when the student has difficulty.[13]

Uses and effectiveness of autoinstruction

At this date, a number of programs are becoming available in several subject-matter areas. *Teaching Machines and Programed Learning, II,* contains discussions of autoinstruction in mathematics and logic, science, reading, English, and in second-language learning. Hanson and Komoski cite research that says that, during the 1962–1963 school year, programs in mathematics were the most available and the most used.[14]

Hanson and Komoski also report that, in 1962–1963, 79 percent of the users of programed material in the schools used the material without any machine. They also say that 60 percent of the users employed a teacher as an active supplement to the program.[15] As a result of looking at the uses of programed instruction in specific schools, Hanson and Komoski present some frequently cited advantages and trends that suggest that programed instruction can be used in the schools with some assurance:

1. It is the student whose activity is under observation
2. With most programed materials, an unusual opportunity exists for

---

[13] Harry F. Silberman and John E. Coulson, "Automated Teaching," in Harold Barko, ed., *Computer Applications in the Behavioral Sciences* (Englewood Cliffs, N.J.: Prentice-Hall, 1962), pp. 309–335.

[14] Lincoln F. Hanson and P. Kenneth Komoski, "School Use of Programed Instruction," in Robert Glaser, ed., *Teaching Machines and Programed Learning, II* (Washington, D.C.: Department of Audiovisual Instruction, NEA, 1965), p. 649.

[15] *Ibid.*, pp. 649–650.

obtaining and maintaining extensive records of the responses of the students

3. The diagnostic potential of such records is considerable
4. The teacher is relieved from most of the straightforward textual transmission and is at the same time freed to be more sensitive in attending to individual student needs
5. A program or a unit that successfully achieves its goal, however small, can be readily retained and shared, whereas material that is not satisfactory may be dropped or locally revised until it approaches its goal
6. Because of the student activity and records obtained, these materials tend to improve with successive trials; over the years new and better programing techniques will make their contribution
7. The continuing evaluation of experimental materials against the longest range educational goals will almost surely become a more conscious process[16]

Other critics mention some of the limitations of autoinstruction. Feldhusen reports that some researchers have found signs of boredom and dissatisfaction after long periods of study.[17] Stark notes that of the many objectives—instructional objectives involving content, process, and skill—programers have to date limited themselves to as few objectives as possible. He deplores this "unwise emphasis on single-purpose programs" and urges the programer to accept responsibility for more objectives, including creativity and evaluative activities. Stark also says that programs are organized according to the logic of the learning process rather than according to the logic of the subject-matter content and that programed teaching materials are not good sources for use as reference materials. Stark also notes the assumption underlying many autoinstructional materials that identical materials are suitable for all learners. He cautions that autoinstructional materials need to be individualized; ideally, such individualization would provide a separate program for each student.[18]

Although there is little research evidence to suggest that one type of program is clearly superior to another, most of the current programs are of a small-step, rather than of a branching, variety.[19] It is possible

---

[16] *Ibid.*, pp. 682–683. By permission.
[17] John F. Feldhusen, "Taps for Teaching Machines," *Phi Delta Kappan*, XLIV (March, 1963), 265–267.
[18] Robert E. Stark, "The Teaching Machine: Tool of the Future or Passing Fancy," *Phi Delta Kappan*, XLIV (March, 1963), 247–249.
[19] "Criteria for Assessing Programmed Instructional Materials," *Programmed Learning*, I (July, 1964), 100.

CLASSIFICATION

1

When we write, we try to convey our thoughts to others by means of words. To do that, we cannot just write down ideas as they come to our minds; we must put them in such an order that our reader knows what we are talking about. One kind of order is called *classification*. By this we mean that a writer looks at a group of things or ideas and sees a connection between them. When he states what connection he sees, he has classified his details.

Go on to frame 2

CLASSIFICATION

2

When we classify things, we put them together according to some connection which we see between them. For example, if we put an apple, a pear, and a peach together, we might classify them under the word *fruit*. The word *fruit*, then, is the classification under which we may list apple, pear, and peach.

What is a two-word classification or phrase for: a baseball glove, a football, a skate, and a soccer ball? (Write your answer below.)

Answer: _____

CLASSIFICATION

3

ANSWER: athletic equipment or sports equipment

From the following list, choose and copy below four items which could be classified under the term *automobile parts:*

muffler, driver, roads, driveways, matches, hats, wheel, stop sign on the road, carburetor, gloves, coat, tail light, garage.

Answer: _____

CLASSIFICATION

4

ANSWER: muffler, wheel, carburetor, tail light

Divide the following list into two separate groups and write each word under the proper classification: pen, frying pan, stove, ink, recipe, pad of paper, egg beater, pencil, coffee pot, eraser.

Answer: writing equipment	cooking equipment
1. ___	1. ___
2. ___	2. ___
3. ___	3. ___
4. ___	4. ___
5. ___	5. ___

CLASSIFICATION

5

ANSWER: writing equipment	cooking equipment
pen	frying pan
ink	stove
pad of paper	recipe
pencil	egg beater
eraser	coffee pot

Divide the following list into three columns according to the principle of classification. In the space provided at the head of each column, fill in a term which will classify the items listed in that column.

bed, muffler, cat, bureau, deer, coat, table, dog, hat, lamp, shirt, pig, chair, tie, cow

Classification:

1. ___
2. ___
3. ___
4. ___
5. ___

FIG. 7 *Example of programed materials. (Edward J. Gordon, Gary Burgard, and Prudence A. M. Young, A Programed Approach to Writing: Book Two, Boston: Ginn, 1965, pp. 1, 3, 5, 7, 9. By permission.)*

that different types of programs may prove to be useful for particular instructional and institutional objectives, and that eventually different styles of programing may be combined with success in a single program. The writers have noted that many published programed materials cannot be categorized as pure types of intrinsic or linear programing. Here is programed material designed to teach writing (Figure 7). Note how the material departs from the Skinnerian style. The steps might sometimes be characterized as relatively large, rather than as small. Frame 1 calls for no response. Frame 2 gives no cues to insure the fact that all learners give a single best response. Frames 3 and 4 would elicit the same responses, but the categories called for in frame 5 could differ from reader to reader. Such item writing—involving now large, now small, steps and several alternative correct responses—may be a trend in writing autoinstructional materials in the next several decades. In the meanwhile, research needs to continue to be conducted to determine the best possible uses of programed learning and of teaching machines.

SUMMARY

The teacher is the person most qualified to select textbooks for his students and to assist students in using textbooks. In selecting a textbook, the teacher should ask, "Will it contribute effectively to achieving the objectives of the course or program?" "Is the scholarship authoritative?" "Is the content suitable for the specific purposes?" And so on. The teacher should consider the value of textbooks as tools, as creative resources, that can be used to change behavior. Sometimes, he will use textbooks as an adjunct in teaching: He will not let the textbook be the entire course of study; he will not let the textbook set the learning objectives in his classroom. To assist students in the use of textbooks, the teacher should help students preview the entire textbook and survey a representative chapter. Providing advance organizers is another technique that helps students read and study textbooks and other expository materials efficiently.

Programs can be presented in the form of programed textbooks, by machines, or by complex computer teaching machines systems. At this date, there are three important programing methodologies: intrinsic, or branching, programing; adjunct programing; and linear programing.

However, the authors believe that many published programed materials cannot be categorized as pure types of intrinsic or linear programing. Although much research needs to be done with autoinstructional materials, such materials seem to have potential for permitting students to progress through materials at individual rates, for achieving the student's active participation in learning, and so on.

QUESTIONS AND ACTIVITIES

1 Compare the textbook with such audio-visual devices as movies and television as to their effectiveness as instructional media.
2 Write several two-page book reviews on textbooks in your subject-matter area. In your reviews, comment on the qualifications of the author, the quality of the material, and the appropriateness of the material for students at the level for which the textbook was written.
3 What factors other than those listed in this chapter should go into consideration of the readability of a textbook?
4 Make a list of inexpensive paperbacks that you might use with your classes when you begin teaching.
5 Using this textbook, or another of your textbooks, evaluate the procedure for previewing a textbook.
6 Make a rough outline of units for a semester's study in your area in the secondary school. Indicate the points at which advance organizers might be used.
7 Compare the programing methodologies of linear programing and intrinsic programing.
8 Discuss the ways in which the programed material in English syntax does not follow Skinnerian techniques of programing.
9 Read about and discuss other recent computer-based teaching machines.
10 Which generalizations given in Chapter 3 might be implemented more readily with autoinstructional materials than without them?

SUGGESTIONS FOR FURTHER READING

BRETHOWER, DALE M., *Programed Instruction: A Manual of Programing Techniques*, Chicago: Educational Methods, 1963.

BUTMAN, ALEXANDER, DONALD REIS, AND DAVID SOHN, EDS., *Paperbacks in the Schools*, New York: Bantam, 1963.

CARPENTER, CHARLES, *History of American Schoolbooks*, Philadelphia: University of Pennsylvania Press, 1963.

CRONBACH, LEE JOSEPH, ED., *Text Materials in Modern Education: A Comprehensive Theory and Platforms for Research,* Urbana: University of Illinois Press, 1955.

ELSON, RUTH MILLER, *Guardians of Tradition, American Schoolbooks of the Nineteenth Century,* Lincoln: University of Nebraska Press, 1964.

FRY, EDWARD B., *Teaching Machines and Programmed Instruction: An Introduction,* New York: McGraw-Hill, 1963.

GLASER, ROBERT, ED., *Teaching Machines and Programed Learning, II,* Washington, D.C.: Department of Audiovisual Instruction, National Education Association, 1965.

LUMSDAINE, A. A., AND ROBERT GLASER, EDS., *Teaching Machines and Programmed Learning: A Source Book,* Washington, D.C.: Department of Audio-Visual Instruction, National Education Association, 1960.

LYNCH, JAMES J., AND BERTRAND EVANS. *High School English Textbooks: A Critical Examination,* Boston: Little, Brown, 1963.

LYSAUGHT, JEROME P., AND CLARENCE M. WILLIAMS. *A Guide to Programmed Instruction,* New York: Wiley, 1963.

SCHRAMM, WILBUR L., *Programed Instruction, Today and Tomorrow,* New York: Fund for the Advancement of Education, 1962.

10 *Using audio-visual materials*

*A*uditory and visual materials have played an increasingly significant role in American education during the past several decades. Listed in the current *Educational Media Index* are over 60,000 entries of nonbook instructional materials, including kinescopes, flat pictures, graphs, maps, charts, films, records, slides, video tapes, and transparencies for the overhead projector. Each year, more records, tapes, and transcriptions are produced for use in the schools. Dozens of businesses and corporations distribute free or inexpensive pictures and graphics: charts, flat pictures, and posters. Some 50 educational television stations, operating on UHF and VHF channels, devote time to lessons televised for use in school classrooms; airborne television now serves one wide geographic area. The use of teaching machines and programed materials has mushroomed. Encouraged by both federal and private grants, educators have engaged in unprecedented research on the instruments and media of instruction. And the further importance of these films, records, machines for projecting visual materials, machines for reproducing auditory materials, machines for autoinstruction, and so on, is attested to by the increasing number of centers within school systems for storing, producing, and distributing audio-visual materials and by the increasing amount of money spent per pupil for equipment.

How important are audio-visual materials in learning? Visiting a school for the blind and for the partially seeing demonstrates the importance of hearing in learning. Similarly, spending a day in a classroom for the deaf and for the partially hearing demonstrates the importance of visual experiences in learning. Observing young children suggests that direct sensory experiences—seeing, hearing, touching, tasting, and smelling—are the bases for the subsequent development of abstractions, for the manipulation and interpretation of words and other symbols, and for the understanding of figural, semantic, or symbolic content. The direct contact that the individual has with the world outside him is through the sense organs. Sensory experiences are essential to cognitive learning. Although thinking and imagining may occur in the absence of direct and immediate sensory experiences, the content of thought and imagination is to an extent based on previous experiences. The multitudinous sensory experiences that the individual continuously experiences from within and without are the raw materials of learning, and the individual both seeks and responds to such sensory stimulation.

Many students in grades 7 through 12 cannot get sufficient meaning from reading alone. They lack direct experiences with many concepts, skills, and attitudes. They would profit from the seeing and hearing, looking and listening experiences made possible with those audio-visual materials that concretize the abstract. Although audio-visual materials cannot replace the teacher's face-to-face leadership of learning activities, or the student's independent reading and direct experiencing, or small-group and whole-class discussions, or problem-solving, or undisturbed reflective thinking, most students can learn certain concepts, skills, and processes better through audio-visual instruction than through reading and discussing alone.

MEANINGFUL LEARNING THROUGH VISUAL MATERIALS

A significant advance in the effectiveness of classroom instruction has resulted from the widespread use of visual aids in learning. Reading printed materials, which some authorities classify as visual education, and listening to discussions or explanations are more interesting when supplemented with visual aids. Events, concepts, and processes become more meaningful to the student when visual aids are used to help him better conceptualize what the printed or spoken words attempt to describe.

Because they vary in their usefulness in achieving educational objectives, visual aids must be selected in terms of the learning outcomes desired. Some of the purposes served by visual aids follow:

1. They provide visual presentations of events, concepts, or processes that often cannot be studied firsthand or that cannot be understood easily by reading and listening alone; for example, a meeting of the United Nations Security Council, the metamorphosis of the fruit fly, the functioning of the human reproductive system

2. To the extent that students come to feel a desire for further study, visual aids have motivational value in the various content areas

3. As they enable students to understand concepts and processes that are extremely important in their daily living, visual aids help realize societal objectives

4. Visual aids provide a common experience or group of concepts that form the basis for later study

5. Because facts and information are retained better when presented to the student in different settings, visual aids promote retention

6. Visual aids introduce variety into teaching; variety itself stimulates a zest for learning and discourages boredom

7. Because some materials can be learned more quickly visually than in any other way, visual aids save time for both teacher and students

The chalkboard

The slate that was so important an instructional material in schools up until the past few decades has been replaced by the chalkboard found today in almost every classroom, including the office of the principal and the counselor. In the newest classrooms, the chalkboard, as well as the tackboard, is sometimes used for movable partitioning. And movable chalkboards are available for rooms that have none.

How can the teacher best use the chalkboard in English or in the language arts, history or social studies, mathematics, and science, four areas of instruction common to students in grades 7 to 12? He could use it in these ways, among others: To present questions that structure purposes; to give instructions to the class; to summarize class discussion;

to indicate the major steps in a project; to draw attention to the differences and likenesses in the spelling of certain words and in mathematical processes; to diagram scientific specimens and processes; and to show relationships that can be visualized with lines and words. Materials on the chalkboard are quite adaptable to change: to correction, enlargement, and substitution.

Students, too, can use the chalkboard in many ways, either singly or in small groups, particularly for graphs, charts, caricatures, and outlines. Frequently, they can handle chalk as well as the teacher can. Not to be overlooked is the adolescent's need for physical activity. In their successive class periods, students usually sit a great part of the time. It is wise for the teacher who has a class the last period in the morning or afternoon to provide some form of physical activity. To the extent that the students can learn as efficiently using the chalkboard as sitting in their seats, the teacher may have them work at the board in small groups. One of the principal reasons that junior high school students like board work is that it satisfies their need for physical activity.

Flat pictures, cartoons, posters

The increased interest in photography and the excellent photographs available in magazines such as *Life, Holiday,* and *National Geographic* provide the teacher and his class with good pictures that can make classroom activities meaningful to many students. And, in view of the availability of colored and of black-and-white pictures at little cost, it is doubtful that any visual material can be more versatile than the flat picture. Flat pictures present life-like ideas and impressions. They cover a wide range of subjects and convey meanings that often cannot be expressed in words. They present unfamiliar and novel phenomena to the viewer as they attract and hold interest. When used in a combined pictorial-verbal presentation, they afford one of the best interest-getting techniques in teaching. If stored properly, they can be kept for use from year to year. Even though a 5 x 8 inch flat picture cannot be seen well by the entire class, it can be looked at and studied by individuals and by small groups, or it can be projected with the opaque projector. Of course, the teacher must initiate and control the use of flat pictures if they are to fulfill sound educational objectives.

Cartoons and posters, secured from outside sources or made by the teacher and students, have high interest appeal for adolescents. Cartoons showing the struggle between labor and management, posters relating to various vocational fields, caricatures illustrating good manners—these suggest only a few of the many excellent uses of cartoons and posters. Securing the facts needed for authentic presentations encourages purposeful learning.

A prospective teacher who collects visual materials and becomes skilled in displaying and using them while in college will find many uses for them in his first teaching position. Dark and colorless classrooms can be made bright, interesting, and colorful at very low cost; and a study display carefully planned by the teacher and students can itself teach.

Graphs

Bar graphs, circle graphs, and line graphs are used to summarize detailed information. They provide a quick, simple way to compare quantitative information.

Although relatively simple to construct, a bar graph is useful for the visual presentation of such facts as the school population each decade since 1890; the number of automobile accidents in the community in each of the past ten years; or the cost of a given item of clothing in the last decade. For any information that can be presented in a series of ratios, for making comparisons and contrasts, the bar graph is effective for presenting the summarized data visually.

A circle graph is used to best advantage to show the relationship both of the parts to a whole and of the parts to each other. It is an excellent way of showing the distribution of values. For example, ask a student to compute how he spends his money during a given month. He calculates the expenditures for the various items—food, clothing, movies, ball games, transportation—and then figures these items as percentages of the total expenditure. He uses a circle to represent the total amount of money spent—100 percent. He then enters the cost of individual items on the circle as fractional parts, with clear-cut dividing lines or with different colors for the various segments.

Line graphs show variability, trends, and the relationships of one or more factors—for example, precipitation and barometric pressure during a week. To record barometric pressure and rainfall at six-hour intervals each day, the student enters the days of the week, divided into six-hour periods, on the horizontal line. He records units of precipitation on the left vertical line and units of barometric pressure on the right vertical line.

Because a great deal of information is presented graphically in newspapers, magazines, and books, students should learn to interpret graphs. The best way to teach this skill is to have the students themselves secure information, summarize it, and present it as a graph. They can place the information on a slide for projection, or they can project the original graph in an appropriate size and color. You will find that high school students often need considerable individual assistance in plotting a simple circle graph or a bar graph.

Maps and globes

One has only to spend a single day in a modern secondary school to realize the variety of information that is presented by means of maps. Political maps, political-physical maps, and special purpose maps that show current events, rainfall, temperature, population, products, and literary information are prominently displayed in classrooms and corridors.

Modern map-makers have greatly improved map coloring, legibility, simplicity, and use of symbols. They have devised better methods for showing size, location, distance, and direction.

Maps are prepared for specific purposes. The form, projection, color, and symbols employed by the map-maker depend on the kind of information the map is intended to convey. For example, the major emphasis of a current events map is on the broad sweep of events in the various political regions of the world. The paper for such a map is relatively cheap, and the projection distorts both distance and size slightly. The map is not intended to show minute details of distance and size perfectly. Again, a modern air map with the North Pole at its center shows distance and size in the Northern Hemisphere in the proper perspective, but the same features are somewhat distorted for land masses in the Southern Hemisphere. Thus, in selecting maps for classroom use, the teacher should know what purpose the map is designed to achieve.

Because the earth is a sphere, a globe represents it most accurately.

The chief types of globe are political, physical-political, and slated outline globes. These range in size from the small desk globe to the large globe that can be seen by the entire class. The physical-political globe with boundaries, land elevations, and ocean depths indicated by color and the slated outline globe on which the teacher and students can write are especially useful for pupil activity in secondary schools. Because they are now available at relatively little cost, transparent globes are becoming widely used. No other teaching aid can satisfactorily replace the globe for accurate teaching about the earth's rotation, time zones, the international date line, and great-circle routes. No other aid can convey so precisely ideas of area, shape, location, direction, and distance on the earth's surface.

The opaque and the overhead projector

An opaque projector can project onto a screen, enlarged, any nontransparent flat picture, printed matter, or small object. The picture or print can be mounted or unmounted; it can be projected directly from a book or a magazine. Thus, the opaque projector increases the variety and flexibility of uses of flat pictures, cartoons, posters, and so on. The projector can be used effectively for any activity in which learning is enhanced by pictorial or reading materials: to introduce topics, to clarify lectures and discussion, to review materials, and to test. Handwritten material is immediately available to the whole class. Two possible limitations on the use of the opaque projector are that (1) the classroom must be at least partially darkened because the projector uses reflected light; and (2) if the teacher faces the class, he cannot see the material that is being projected, or else he stands where he sees only the students' backs.

Another device for communicating visually with your class is the overhead projector, a compact, lightweight, easily operated machine. The material projected consists of a transparency, made of film, that can be purchased ready-made from various publishers or that can be reproduced from your own written document, map, or diagram by a copying machine such as the well-known Thermo-fax machine. Once made, a transparency can be used repeatedly.

The overhead projector can be used in a completely lighted room.

The teacher can face his audience at all times, maintaining eye contact and noting audience reaction, while the material is projected onto a screen above or to one side of him. Because the material being projected is right side up, the teacher can refer to it easily himself; he can emphasize specific items by pointing; he can use the transparency as a chalkboard, writing with a grease pencil. The teacher can reveal one item at a time, blocking out the remaining area; he can alter the order of transparencies, comment, and return to a previously viewed transparency. With registered components, he can use overlays for step-by-step presentation. The social studies teacher could add overlays of rivers, cities, counties, one at a time, to the transparency of a state. The English teacher could superimpose sentence modifiers, prepositional phrases, adjective and adverb clauses on a basic, or skeletal, sentence to show growth toward a mature prose style.

Silent films, film strips, slides

The commercial production of silent films ended when it became possible to transmit sound simultaneously with the projection of visual images. Although silent films are of limited educational value, one should not overlook the fact that many high school students have movie cameras and take excellent pictures. Students are generally interested in their own activities and those of their friends; hence, student-made movies are often stimulating. The production and use of these movies bring about good motivation, creativeness, and healthy school-community relations. Motion pictures that show how a teacher gives a group test, how students set up an experiment in chemistry, how a homeroom is decorated for American Education Week are only a few of the everyday occurrences that can be filmed and shown to new students and teachers, to parents and community groups. Too, a highly meaningful use of silent films is seen in the coaching of athletics.

Filmstrips consist of a sequential series of photographs that show characteristic situations or definite steps in a process. They are particularly valuable in science classes, for showing the steps of an experiment, various stages in life processes, or pictures of plant and animal life for detailed consideration. The major features of an industrial plant can be identified by means of filmstrips before a social studies class makes a field trip. Designs in leather or metal can be shown in art classes. The operating parts of a carburetor can be shown in a class in automobile mechanics. Basic information on the operation and use of the library can be presented to an English class.

One possible value of the filmstrip over the moving picture is that closer and more sustained attention is possible. The filmstrip can be projected for any length of time to permit questions and discussion, and it can be looked at as often as desired. The filmstrip is economical and is probably as effective as the silent motion picture.

Glass slides serve almost the same purposes that filmstrips do. A song can be projected in a music class. Phrases and sentences can be projected for a decreasing period of time to help acquire speed in reading. A business letter can be projected and its form clarified. The chief disadvantages of glass slides are the difficulty of their production, the space required for storage, and the danger of breakage.

Filmstrips and slides are used widely in many subject fields and at all grade levels because they provide a true representation of processes and objects. They permit careful examination and restudy, do not require expensive projection equipment, and can be prepared by the students and teacher.

Study displays and three-dimensional materials

An uncluttered, attractively arranged, frequently changed bulletin board can be an effective teaching device and can provide activities in which each student can participate. A partial list of visual aids to learning that can be displayed on a bulletin board or on a similar flat area follows:

cartoons	maps
charts	paintings
diagrams	photographs
drawings	postage stamps
graphics	postcards
graphs	

All of these aids can be purchased; some can be made at small cost or collected at no cost by the students and teachers.

Psychological timing, artistic arrangement, and use of color and lettering are important factors in setting up a display. Creativity on the part of both students and teacher is required to set up a display that attracts and holds attention.

MEANINGFUL LEARNING THROUGH AUDIO MATERIALS

Educational radio, phonograph records and transcriptions, tape recordings, and language laboratories are the major audio aids to learning. In the sections that follow we shall try to suggest the advantages and limitations of each aid.

Educational radio

Although supplanted in part by television, educational radio continues to be used for basic instructional experiences, as well as for enrichment. It continues to be a major audio aid to learning: Through news and special events reports; through its musical programs, which have a large daily audience; and through various school-of-the-air broadcasts.

Beginning its thirty-fifth year of regularly scheduled informational broadcasts in September, 1965, WHA-AM, -FM, in programs broadcast by state stations throughout Wisconsin, provides a variety of specialists in various fields of knowledge who help supplement student learning through radio teaching. Among the established favorites of public school students are *Wonderful World of Nature, It Happened When, Young Experimenters, Let's Draw, Let's Find Out, Let's Sing, Let's Write, Exploring the News, Rhythm and Games,* and *Book Trails.* For each of the series, with the exception of *Exploring the News,* teacher manuals are available. In addition to programs for school classrooms, WHA also provides adult education services with homemakers' programs, book reviews, chamber music, opera, symphony, university lecture series, broadcasts giving ethnic and historical information on the state, and so on. Such scheduling is typical of a number of educational broadcasting systems throughout the nation.

To make effective use of radio facilities, the teacher must plan his work well in advance. One difficulty in using educational radio is that, because of its predetermined time schedule, the program most suitable to a given learning activity is sometimes not broadcast when needed.

When the programs correlate with units of study, the teacher will often recommend listening to programs outside the school to overcome this difficulty.

Here is an example of the possible use of radio as an aid in instruction. Let us imagine that students in an American history class are studying political platforms and candidates during a national campaign. Among the questions raised in discussion are (1) What are the platforms of each party? (2) Who are the candidates for President and Vice-President? (3) How does each candidate state his own views in relation to his party's program? (4) Which party's platform is best? (5) Which is the best candidate to vote for?

The class obtains some information on platforms from the newspapers. Radio schedules are studied in class, and programs are assigned to various class members. Then the information obtained from these programs is brought to class and discussed, the students comparing radio presentations with newspaper presentations. Students are given specific writing assignments based on radio programs, writing that includes outlining the speeches they have heard, evaluating the accuracy of the information heard, and speculating why, at certain times, candidates have made statements contrary to their party's platform. To help decide which man to vote for, the students play the roles of the candidates in sociodrama. Panels of students, representing candidates for various offices in the same party, discuss legislation that might be enacted if they were elected. As a result of these activities, there is preparation for the radio programs, supervision by the teacher to help ascertain the fact that the students listen to the programs, close correlation with the unit being studied, and effective follow-up activities.

Or, again, in addition to other projects, an agriculture class might be studying livestock marketing. Each day the class listens to a short radio program that carries reports of livestock prices. Committees of students, responsible for listing the various prices, make line graphs of the daily prices of cattle, hogs, sheep, and poultry. The findings of these committees are correlated with published studies on the preparation of livestock for shipment, handling livestock in transit, reports on supply and demand, expositions on the government's price-support program and the effect of international events on livestock prices. Students analyze charts to discover times at which shipments were at a peak but at which prices were correspondingly low. Such analysis helps students estimate whether the same pattern would probably hold true in the future.

Other uses of radio in the school would include a student production of a broadcast for a commercial station, a school-operated station, a school public-address system, or ham short-wave systems. Among the various kinds of programs produced might be musicals, with student performers; recorded music, with students acting as disk jockeys; dramatic presentations, with a student cast; and school news reports. The values of participation in such kinds of radio programs are that:

1. Students are motivated and learn to write clearly and creatively
2. They learn standards of speech performance and have extensive practice to facilitate the development of speech skills
3. They acquire listening skills, as they listen attentively to radio programs and to class discussion about radio programs
4. They learn to work within carefully specified time limitations
5. They acquire basic facts about the production of radio programs
6. They become further interested in educational broadcasts
7. As a result of pupil-pupil interactions in creating *their* program, they acquire feelings of affiliation and belonging
8. Such broadcasts help unify many aspects of school life, including the instructional program
9. Such broadcasts better school-community relations

Language laboratories

Title III of the National Defense Education Act of 1958 gave momentum to the utilization of language laboratories in the secondary schools. Although there are today some 9000 to 10,000 laboratories in use in various areas such as speech correction, music appreciation, and vocabulary improvement, the chief use of the language laboratory has been by foreign language teachers in the development of aural-oral proficiency in non-native speakers of modern and classical languages.

There are different and varied types of language laboratories, but two principal arrangements of equipment are common today. One setup permits listening only. In this laboratory, the components consist of listening stations equipped with plug-in jacks for headphones with volume control and, sometimes, with channel selectors. A second arrangement permits the student both to listen and to record. The components of this arrangement, for each working position, are the tape recorder, earphones, microphone, volume control, and, possibly, a selector switch for different levels of the master program. In this second arrangement, the student hears a master voice, repeats the sound, and records his response. He can then replay his tape for comparison with the master tape; he can replay the tape for review or to see his progress. A monitor and an intercommunication system enable the teacher to listen to students and to speak with them. Such a laboratory can use a master tape for each position or can use one tape for an entire class.

The language laboratory makes available to the student excellent models of speech and of intonation by native speakers or by highly trained teachers. It is excellent for pattern practice and for studying idiom and vocabulary. It permits each student in a class simultaneous participation in listening or in listening-speaking skills. It can help each student proceed at his own pace. It frees the teacher from presenting repetitive drill materials. It permits the teacher to work with one student without interrupting all of the other students. It is in itself a stimulus to students fascinated by equipment. It provides for repetition, for overlearning.

Records and transcriptions

Records and transcriptions are more useful in the school than is radio because important speeches, plays, and musical productions are being recorded and made available at relatively low cost. The records can be stored easily and then used at the most opportune time.

For English classes, excellent recordings of well-known novels, poems, and short stories are available. On record, Robert Frost reads his *Mending Wall, Birches, Mowing,* and other poems. William Faulkner reads from his Nobel Prize acceptance speech and from *A Fable, As I Lay Dying,* and *The Old Man.* Judith Anderson and Anthony Quayle lead the cast in *Medea.* Arthur Miller analyzes methods of characterization and reads from *The Glass Menagerie, Some Poems Meant for Music,* and *The Yellow Bird.*

The teacher of speech and language classes can obtain records of various dialects used in this country and in Britain. Records are also available for the self-improvement of speech and for learning to speak various modern foreign languages.

In social studies, a series of recorded programs dramatized by leading performers, titled *Immigrants All; Americans All*, includes *Our English Heritage, Our Hispanic Heritage, Willing Freedom, The Negro, Social Progress, A New England Town*, and *An Industrial City*. Also in social studies, *Voices of Yesterday* presents 24 historic figures. Included are representations of Florence Nightingale *Addressing Her Comrades*; William Jennings Bryan *On Freedom for the Philippines*; Admiral Robert E. Peary *On His Discovery of the North Pole*; Theodore Roosevelt *In a Message to the American Boy*; and Will Rogers *On Politics*.

Tape recordings

The tape recorder is well used to record various events in the school and in the classroom and to appraise student progress in conduct, skills, concepts, and appreciations. It is a versatile device for creative teaching.

After discussing with students the desirability of entering the classroom quietly and starting work, the teacher finds that they continue being noisy. Unnoticed by the students, he records the noise they make until he quiets them. He then tells them about the recording and asks them to listen to it quietly. At the next class meeting, he again records the first few minutes without their knowledge. This time he plays both recordings and leads a class discussion of the improvement. Meetings, panels, and discussion sessions can also be recorded and played back for evaluation.

Progress in speaking a foreign language can also be shown by tape recordings. Thus, at the beginning of the fourth week of a class in Spanish, the teacher records a ten-minute student conversation in Spanish. Within four to eight weeks, he records another ten-minute conversation. Both are then played back so that the students can evaluate their progress and, with the teacher's help, determine the areas that need improvement. Musical performances, dramatic readings, voice correction exercises, and the like can be evaluated similarly.

In addition, tape recordings serve well to inform parents of a pupil's progress. The teacher can play a recording of the student's first attempts in singing, reading, or speaking a foreign language, or of playing a musical instrument at the beginning of a semester as compared with a performance two or even ten months later. The progress is evident to the parents. There is little need for the teacher to say anything more.

A mathematics teacher has introduced the concept of equations. How well do the students understand the concept after a ten-minute presentation? Tape recording their answers to the questions he asks provides the teacher a partial answer. After the students have done more work with equations, another tape recording provides the comparison needed to determine their progress.

One of the principal purposes of the study of literature is to heighten appreciation; that is, to develop desirable attitudes toward good literature. The extent to which this purpose is being achieved can be shown by a tape recording in the third and tenth week of the students' responses to the teacher's questions: "What purpose did the author have in writing the novel you have read?" "How well did he accomplish his purpose?"

There are, of course, many sources for expertly prepared, prerecorded tapes. Commercial firms market many selections: classical music, jazz, folk music, theatre, and so on. The current *National Tape Recording Catalogue* lists magnetic tape recordings in the National Tape Repository, available at a minimum fee, on such varied topics as literature (*Death of a Salesman, Canterbury Tales*), ballet music, harmony, tone color, utilizing the atom, and the values of exercise. Prerecorded tapes are central to the use of language laboratories in the study of modern language.

Tapes are not subject to damage by dust and scratching as are disk recordings. Tape recordings are easily made in the classroom with equipment that is portable. Tapes can be reused, can be edited, and can be stored easily.

SOUND MOTION PICTURE AND TELEVISION: TWO COMBINATIONS OF MEANINGFUL SENSORY EXPERIENCE

The sound motion picture and television are two of the most valuable instructional media used in classrooms today. They provide more self-contained instruction than any other audio-visual material discussed in this chapter. But, of course, they cannot replace books and direct experience; they cannot achieve all of the desired objectives of secondary education.

Sound motion pictures

The success of educational films has been widely attested to by expert opinion and by various research findings. Films have been shown to be instrumental in developing mental, physical, and social skills. Sixteen-millimeter sound films, frequently in color, with dialogue, narration, music, and sound effects have an impact comparable to actual field trips, demonstrations, and lectures. Today's equipment consists of easily operated, self-threading projectors and of projectors that use cartridge units. An enormous number of films are available from various producers and distributors. The current *Educator's Guide to Free Films*, alone, lists 4071 sponsored and commercial free films. The current edition of the *Educational Film Guide* and its semiannual supplements list over 10,000 films. Complete courses are available on film (chiefly in mathematics and science), and researchers constantly seek to overcome its limitations. For example, the one-way communication process and the passivity of the learner, drawbacks until now, are being combatted by having instructional films that intersperse question-and-answer sessions or that introduce other exercises in which the students participate between sections of a film.

Slow-motion photography embodies a process in which movements too rapid for the human eye to see are caught by the camera and slowed down for an observable demonstration. Such a film can teach better than if actions are projected at normal speed.

Photomicrography permits the photographing of phenomena that cannot be seen by the human eye. Erosion and the growth and division of human cells and of other microscopic plant and animal life are among the processes and objects that can be seen clearly by means of photomicrographs.

Animation in motion-picture photography has now reached a high level of development. Concepts that are difficult or impossible to photograph, such as prenatal growth, atom-splitting, H-bomb devastation, and air currents, can be visualized in drawings and then photographed and shown in rapid sequence to give the effect of movement or animation. Many of the mysterious processes that are so challenging to the adolescent imagination—photosynthesis and energy conservation, for example—are revealed in animated motion pictures available in many subject fields.

Among the other values of sound motion pictures are these: The motion picture can record history; it can be shown repeatedly; it can make what would otherwise be abstract concrete; it can present fantasy as well as realism; it can make demonstrations by experts available to many students at a single time; and it can teach while entertaining. For these reasons, sound films offer opportunities for improving learning that are impossible when sound recordings or silent movies are used alone.

Television

The two principal types of live television instruction are by closed-circuit and open-circuit, or regular, transmission systems. Open-circuit television is transmitted on Very High Frequency (VHF) or Ultra High Frequency (UHF) channels and is licensed by the Federal Communications Commission (FCC). Closed-circuit television is transmitted directly from a camera by cable to its receivers; the broadcast can be seen only by viewers of the receivers within the circuit.

Any live televised program can be recorded for later use. A kinescope recorder, a special camera that photographs images from a television monitor, can make a sound film of a television program. This film can then be packaged as a 16-millimeter kinescope that can be shown in any classroom on a 16-millimeter sound motion picture projector. Video tape is still another device for recording television programs. The tape, although requiring expensive equipment to produce, is suitable for immediate playback and for repeated playback; it can be erased and reused. The better commercial and educational television productions are now being recorded on kinescope and video tape and are available for use in the schools.

Single-room television, in which camera, receivers, and controls are located within the classroom or large lecture hall, has many applications. It can be used to administer standardized tests to several hundred students. It can be used as a magnifying device for three-dimensional objects, as well as for a complete teaching aid, in laboratory demonstrations. It can be used to replace opaque and overhead transparency projectors.

Studio television, open- or closed-circuit, can be used as a supplementary teaching aid, as a major resource, as an enrichment device, or for total teaching. The amount and kind of television used depends on the type of material to be presented, the abilities and attitudes of the student, the facilities available for television reception, and the need to have access to resources that are not normally available. Often, the decision to use television is made on such practical considerations as availability of teachers and on cost. Once a school system has installed television equipment and instruction is handled through television for 250 or more students, the cost is less than for self-contained classrooms.

One of the best longitudinal studies using closed-circuit television as one variable was conducted at Miami University in Ohio. Among the findings were (1) that large-group instruction (including television) produces as high an achievement level as small-group instruction produces, and (2) that subject-matter retention is not affected by instructional procedure. The students involved in the experiment at Miami University said that they preferred small classes to large classes or to television courses, but their motivation and interest were not adversely affected.[1]

Many questions remain to be answered on the use of educational television. Which human abilities and characteristics can be nurtured most effectively through television? For example, can aural-oral skills in a foreign language be nurtured as well in hundreds or thousands of students simultaneously viewing and responding to televised instruction as by the use of the language laboratory, managed by one or more teachers, within each school building? Can it present facts on such an area of information as Victorian England as well as can the teacher in the self-contained classroom? Can it affect attitudes toward the value of life-long reading habits as well as can the individual English teacher? How well can it develop skills other than seeing and listening? Is television equally appropriate for teaching divergent as well as convergent thinking?

Although experts might disagree on the answers to these questions, evidence suggests many values for educational television. Television is efficient where one presentation must be taught in a number of classrooms. Goals appropriate to large-group instruction can be achieved by television without adversely affecting student achievement and

---

[1] F. Glenn Macomber and Laurence Siegel, *Experimental Study in Instructional Procedures* (Oxford, Ohio: Miami University, 1960), pp. 5–7.

interest. Television can and does bring cultural, educational, entertaining, and informational broadcasts from many sources utilizing nationally known content specialists. Television does realize the values of a number of other audio-visual materials: Flat pictures, models, chalkboard, sound films, and so on. It can free the classroom teacher to devote more time to individual students. It can broaden the curriculum of smaller schools that are unable to finance the educational programs that they want. However, unless schools support experimentation with educational television, an intelligent decision cannot be reached as to its most efficient uses.

Experts do not predict that television instruction will eliminate the need for good classroom teachers. They believe that television will make the efforts of master teachers more productive. To the end of more productive teaching, assistance in the form of special texts, study guides, and other materials is being given the classroom teacher so that he can make maximum use of televised instruction.

The teacher continues to be the key person in the educative process. The more information, skills, and attitudes adolescents learn through television, through autoinstructional materials and machines, through educational films and other audio-visual devices, the more time the teacher will have to humanize education, to help each child achieve self-realization.

AUDIO-VISUAL INSTRUCTIONAL MATERIALS MUST BE USED INTELLIGENTLY

Sufficient examples of classroom use of audio-visual materials have been given to suggest six main principles for their intelligent use:
1. Select the material in terms of the learning goals
2. Prepare the students for use of audio-visual materials
3. Prepare for operation of the equipment
4. Provide opportunities for the student to participate
5. Provide follow-up activities
6. Evaluate the outcomes

Each of these principles will now be discussed briefly in terms of educational films alone. Each applies, of course, equally well to video tapes and to kinescopes, and suggests some of the uses of other audio-visual materials.

Select the material in terms of the learning goals

The best procedure for selecting films in a school is to organize a committee of teachers under the chairmanship of the school, city, or county supervisor or coordinator of audio-visual materials. The committee examines the list of films owned by the school, recent educational film catalogues, and listings of films that can be rented from a central school office or a community or a state agency. The teachers then select films for preview. While previewing a film, they might consider these questions:

1. What specific instructional purposes does this film serve?
2. How and where does it fit into our teaching-learning units?
3. Is the film suited to the mental, social, and emotional maturity of the students?
4. Does the film present its message clearly and accurately?
5. Is the film sufficiently realistic to capture and hold the interest of adolescents?

One good reason for previewing films is to make better selections and to allocate the films to various classes. Information presented in some films sweeps across subject lines with apparent purpose. Thus, the films *How to Read a Book* and *Act Your Age* can be used advantageously in many high school classrooms during the first week of school. But students should not be required to see the same film in three or four classes during a short period of time. Articulation is necessary.

Ultimately, each film should be previewed by the classroom teacher in his role as a content specialist. One of these authors still remembers his embarrassment at the laughter that accompanied the showing of a film on Macbeth. Previewing would have shown him that sublime tragedy was made farcical by poor directing and acting.

Prepare the students to use the material

Before a film is shown, the teacher should provide his students with a motivational set. During his preview, the teacher notes the main features of the film, any terms that might be difficult for the students, any totally new concepts, and any questions or problems directly related to the current classroom activity. Class discussion before the showing of the film makes the reason for seeing the film apparent to the students. Also helpful is a list of questions or features placed on the chalkboard or distributed in mimeographed form.

Such introductory activities are extremely valuable to the students. To show a film such as *Human Reproduction* or *And Now Miguel* without this preparation is to misuse the film badly. Some schools often show an educational film to the whole school in an assembly without giving teachers and students any opportunity for advance preparation. Obviously, although entertainment films can be used in this manner, the probability of misuse in the case of educational films is great.

Plan for the operation of the equipment

In most high schools, the teacher is responsible for having the classroom and equipment in readiness for showing the film. In larger schools, students who are interested in giving service to the school often operate the projectors and are trained by audio-visual experts to do so. But every teacher should be able to operate projection equipment and to teach students how to operate it.

Provide techniques for the student to participate

Try to establish procedures that foster active student response and participation during the showing of the film. Some general conclusions on the value of student participation techniques have been summarized by Allen as:

1. Learner participation during a film showing will result in greatly increased learning from the film
2. The overt verbalization of responses by the learner during the film increases learning
3. The furnishing of "knowledge of results" of the learner's overt response during a film also aids learning
4. If participation during a film requires the practice of a skill demonstrated, the taking of notes, or the performance of any other activity that may divide the attention between the observation of the film and the performance of the activity, the film must be paced slowly enough to eliminate the distraction caused by such division of attention

5. Mental practice of skills demonstrated, information communicated, or questions asked during or after a film showing will increase the learning under certain conditions[2]

Provide follow-up activities

Educational films require appropriate follow-up. If a film is valuable, it should lead to the discussion or further study of a related problem or topic. Follow-up activities are determined by the type of film, but some general follow-up activities for a film might include the following: (1) Lead discussion on the major points presented in the films and on any questions posed by your students. (2) Give specific assignments based on the film. (3) Note how the students do these assignments; discuss any problems that arise. (4) Show the film again to help the students evaluate their performances or to increase learning. (5) Use ideas from the film in later class activities.

Identifying the main points in a film, discussing them very briefly with the class, putting these main points in question form, and presenting the questions to the students before showing the film help focus student attention. After the film, the teacher can then divide the class into small groups and assign a question to each group for discussion and for subsequent reporting to the entire class. Or, with other films, he can ask questions and then follow the film with whole-class discussion. Both procedures work very well.

Evaluate the outcomes

The purpose of evaluation is to determine the extent to which goals or objectives have been achieved. It is important for the beginning teacher to become aware of the importance of evaluation and to learn the techniques of evaluation: To this end, Chapter 12 will treat measuring and evaluating pupil progress.

Although evaluation will be treated more extensively later, here are some questions that suggest what you might want to consider in evaluating your uses of audio-visual aids. Is the material suitable to the achieve-

---

[2] William H. Allen, "Audio-Visual Communication," in Chester W. Harris, ed., *Encyclopedia of Educational Research*, 3rd ed. (New York: Macmillan, 1960), p. 125.

ment level, general intellectual ability, and special abilities of the student? Do the materials tend to have a favorable impact on student attitudes, preferences, values, and sets to learn? Are the materials efficient? Are the aids worth the time and the expense involved? Do the materials present concepts in relatively concrete, highly meaningful ways? Does the equipment lend itself to effective, economical use in your subject-field? Do the materials aid in inquiry process and in discovery techniques? Are the pictures of high quality? Is the sound of high quality? And so on.

TABLE 10.1. *Instructional Functions of Various Media.*

Media

Function	Objects; demonstration	Oral communication	Printed media	Still pictures	Moving pictures	Sound movies	Teaching machines
Presenting the stimulus	Yes	Limited	Limited	Yes	Yes	Yes	Yes
Directing attention and other activity	No	Yes	Yes	No	No	Yes	Yes
Providing a model of expected performance	Limited	Yes	Yes	Limited	Limited	Yes	Yes
Furnishing external prompts	Limited	Yes	Yes	Limited	Limited	Yes	Yes
Guiding thinking	No	Yes	Yes	No	No	Yes	Yes
Inducing transfer	Limited	Yes	Limited	Limited	Limited	Limited	Limited
Assessing attainments	No	Yes	Yes	No	No	Yes	Yes
Providing feedback	Limited	Yes	Yes	No	Limited	Yes	Yes

SOURCE: Robert M. Gagné, *The Conditions of Learning* (New York: Holt, Rinehart and Winston, 1965), p. 284. By permission.

FUNCTIONS OF VARIOUS MEDIA
FOR INSTRUCTION

Robert Gagné has summarized the instructional functions of various media in a form reproduced here as Table 10.1. The summary should help you utilize your knowledge of the learning process (Chapter 3) and of conducting individual and group work (Chapter 8) in using audio-visual materials.

Reading down column 3, you will note that oral communication serves well all of the instructional functions with the exception of presentation of the stimulus. In addition to oral communication, the most effective stimulus presentation might include various visual devices: flat pictures, graphs, maps, objects, models, and so on. In a like manner, examination of column 8 suggests that teaching machines perform all instructional functions well with the exception of inducing transfer. Gagné suggests that transfer is better facilitated through oral communication (for example, discussion.)[3]

SUMMARY

The intelligent selection and use of the many audio-visual materials of instruction are important for the modern teacher. Visual materials and devices such as the chalkboard, flat picture, graph, map, opaque and overhead projector, film strip, and study display facilitate the learning that is accomplished by means of sight. Educational radio, language laboratories, records, and tape recordings have demonstrated their value in facilitating learning that is accomplished by means of hearing.

Television and sound motion pictures facilitate more efficient learning because they combine hearing and seeing. The sound motion picture is widely used in secondary schools today with excellent results. Television gives promise of having a more powerful impact on education than any other audio-visual resource—perhaps as strong an impact as commercial television has had on our recreational, reading, and other daily habits.

---

[3] Robert M. Gagné, *The Conditions of Learning* (New York: Holt, Rinehart and Winston, 1965), pp. 283–284.

Audio-visual materials, including television, should be considered as materials of instruction. Even television cannot substitute for the teacher's face-to-face leadership of the learning activities, for the independent reading and direct experiencing of students, or for small-group and whole-class discussions, problem-solving, and undisturbed reflective thinking.

All audio-visual materials must be used intelligently. To achieve the desired results, the teacher must select material in terms of the learning goals sought; the students must be prepared for the meaningful use of the material; appropriate learning activities must follow the use of audio-visual materials; and outcomes must be evaluated.

QUESTIONS AND ACTIVITIES

1 Rank in order of descending importance the visual aids discussed in this chapter on the basis of educational value, cost, ease of use, and ease of making in class.
2 Begin to collect some visual aids that might help you when you begin teaching.
3 Compare the uses of the opaque and overhead projector.
4 Prepare some materials that you think might best be presented through overlays for step-by-step presentation on the overhead projector.
5 List some instructional objectives best served by audio materials.
6 Preview a film appropriate for a unit in your area. Outline a plan for using the film.
7 Give your opinion of why educational radio has not been completely supplanted by educational television.
8 Describe the possible impact of language laboratories on the learning of a modern foreign language.
9 Is it likely that instruction by television will ever largely replace instruction by individual classroom teachers?
10 According to Gagné, which instructional media are best for presentation of the stimulus? For inducing transfer? For providing a model of expected performance?

SUGGESTIONS FOR FURTHER READING

BROWN, JAMES W., RICHARD B. LEWIS, AND FRED F. HARCLEROAD, *A-V Instruction: Materials and Methods*, 2nd ed., New York: McGraw-Hill, 1964.

COSTELLO, LAWRENCE F., AND GEORGE N. GORDON, *Teach with Television*, 2nd ed., New York: Hastings House, 1965.

DE KIEFFER, ROBERT E., *Audiovisual Instruction*, New York: Center for Applied Research in Education, 1965.

DIAMOND, ROBERT M., ED., *A Guide to Instructional Television*, New York: McGraw-Hill, 1964.

ERICKSON, CARLTON W., *Fundamentals of Teaching with Audio-Visual Technology*, New York: Macmillan, 1965.

HERMAN, LEWIS, *Educational Films*, New York: Crown, 1965.

KINDER, JAMES S., *Using Audio-Visual Materials in Education*, New York: American Book, 1965.

LUMSDAINE, A. A., "Instruments and Media of Instruction," in *Handbook of Research on Teaching*, Chicago: Rand McNally, 1963, pp. 448–505.

SCHRAMM, WILBUR, ED., *The Impact of Educational Television*, Urbana: University of Illinois Press, 1960.

WILLIAMS, CATHARINE, *Learning from Pictures*; Washington, D.C.: Department of Audio-Visual Instruction, National Education Association, 1963.

WITTICH, WALTER A., AND CHARLES F. SCHULLER, *Audiovisual Materials: Their Nature and Use*, 4th ed., New York: Harper & Row, 1967.

11 *Improving work and study methods*

*A*s early as the seventh grade, students are often given an assignment or task without any help in how to do it. As a result, they acquire independent work and study methods on a trial-and-error basis. Because some of the students often experience failure rather than success, such methods can lead to inefficiency and, much worse, to lack of interest in independent study or work. Most high school and college students, including graduate students, frequently need their teachers' assistance in starting a task quickly and correctly, in identifying and using materials well, in concentrating, and in completing the task successfully. The teacher's daily pattern of instruction should include this assistance.

Listed here are some principles by which you might help students improve their work and study methods, attitudes, and conditions. Although some of the suggestions to be discussed do not apply so readily in certain subject-matter areas, every secondary school teacher in any subject field or cocurricular activity can put most of them to use.

1. Student readiness is increased
2. The physical and psychological environment is made conducive to study
3. Students learn to read more efficiently
4. Students learn to write more effectively
5. Students learn to listen better

6. Students are helped with study and work schedules

7. Provisions are made for students who have special needs

Special attention is given to reading, writing, and listening in sections of this chapter because reading is still the principal means of acquiring information through independent effort; writing is still the principal means of conveying information, opinions, or emotions in a permanent form; and listening is the most frequently used communication skill. Little attention is given group discussion and oral presentations because they are treated in Chapter 8.

STUDENT READINESS IS INCREASED

Have you ever tried to concentrate on reading complex expository writing, such as income tax directions, when you felt ill? Have you ever tried to take a long examination or to write a theme when a member of your family was in the hospital seriously ill? Have you ever taken an advanced course in college without having had the prerequisite courses? Have you ever tried to construct components for a stereo set or to learn to play a musical instrument when you felt certain that you did not have the necessary abilities? A person's physical condition and his social, emotional, and mental characteristics, together with his previous achievements and his present work habits, are important in determining how efficiently any task is begun and completed. The following discussion analyzes these factors briefly.

Physical condition

A child who has a vision or hearing acuity loss, or any physical defect that is uncorrected or not compensated for, who becomes fatigued too readily, who is malnourished, or who does not get sufficient rest is incapable of effective school work. The teacher should be well informed on the health records and health habits of his students.

Some school systems have a school physician who creates a program for the appraisal of the health of all children. In other schools, the family physician and dentist conduct examinations of health status. In almost all schools, there is a public health nurse who acts as liaison between school and home.

In the school nurse's office will be cumulative health records for each student. These records will include entries on absences, various deficiencies, immunization, illnesses, surgical experiences, accidents, home visits by the nurse, and unusual personal traits. The nurse will confer with you on students who need special attention because of epilepsy, poor vision, poor hearing, diabetes, and so on.

The teacher should note left-handedness and provide for it; he should note the student's physical size and seat him accordingly. He should look for students who hold printed matter unusually near or far from their eyes so that he can detect near-sightedness and far-sightedness and assign seats accordingly. He should note students who cup a hand to their ear or who have difficulty in following a class discussion so that he can identify the hard-of-hearing. To identify students with poor health habits, the teacher should also watch for sleepiness and for lack of interest in the work.

The teacher is an important person in helping students overcome physical handicaps, in encouraging good health habits, in teaching accident prevention, and in preventing the spread of communicable diseases. Many young people may be enabled to study more efficiently if unusual physical development, minor defects, and minor physiological malfunctioning are identified and provided for in the classroom. Of course, serious conditions should be referred to the parents and to a family physician, or to the school physician.

Social and emotional adjustment

Does a student have one or two good friends in the class, or is he an isolate? Whether or not it appears to be the case in the classroom, adolescents are interested in how others react to them. If they are to become well-adjusted adults, adolescents must learn to make and keep friends. A student who has no friends in class and who does not get along well with his teacher may not study effectively.

When a person feels that he belongs to a group, he takes part in its activities. When he feels that he is not wanted by the group, he remains aloof and isolated and, thus, loses the opportunity to learn from the group. Three developmental needs of adolescents—making satisfactory heterosexual adjustments, achieving emotional maturity, and gaining independence from adult control—require interaction with peers. To become socialized, the individual must learn socially approved behavior. He can do this more effectively through group activities than through individualized activities.

Each student acquires a feeling of worthwhileness when school activities are organized in a manner enabling him to pursue a special interest or ability that has a prestige value for other adolescents. Telling a class that everyone is equal and worthwhile is ineffective; but organizing classroom experiences that allow each pupil to contribute something to the class and that clarify the many different ways of making such contributions creates status feelings for everyone in the class. One sure means of making many students lose status is to reward only one kind of performance, such as reciting perfectly in class, making high scores on tests, or reading rapidly.

Social adjustment can be appraised by observing students during discussion and committee work, during individual and group reports, and during oral responses to the teacher. Students with extreme degrees of the following characteristics should be identified: seclusiveness, withdrawal, aggression, daydreaming and phantasy, and anxiety. Because such characteristics are on a continuum, we cannot categorize all students on such bases; but students exhibiting the traits to an extreme degree should be identified, and methods appropriate to help overcome the deficiencies should be found.

Emotional and social adjustment are closely related. Emotions originate and are expressed, for the most part, in an individual's interactions with other people. Unfortunately, anger, jealousy, fear, and affection are not always readily identifiable in adolescents because many have already learned to hide their true feelings. Nor are continuous worry and anxiety about physical development, friends, school work, or home conditions easily recognized. Yet, anxiety that persists for relatively long periods of time is very destructive to any kind of concentrated effort. Hence, the teacher needs to observe the expression of adolescent emotions and to analyze the conditions under which the emotion originates. Some problems engendered by an inappropriate curriculum—lack of provision for individual differences, repeated failure of the student— are clearly within the school's province to solve; other problems are clearly the province of the therapist only.

Previous achievement

The subject matter taught in the school becomes increasingly difficult for the student because new content or skills are based on already acquired concepts, facts, principles, and skills. Thus, concepts in a series of social studies or mathematics textbooks increase in difficulty at each grade level. So do skills in typing, shorthand, music, and physical education. A student's work methods in any educational experience are efficient to the extent to which he can draw on his previous achievement for present purposes and to the degree to which the work requirements set by the teacher correspond with the student's present achievement level.

Achievement tests can be standardized or teacher-made. They measure the specific learnings that the student brings to his present work or the extent to which a student has met the objectives of a particular class. Factors in the construction of paper-and-pencil objective tests of achievement will be a subject treated in Chapter 12.

In any class activity, a teacher needs to devise appraisal techniques for determining where his students are. He then needs to use teaching procedures that will get students off to a good start from that point. Unless previous achievement is given consideration, students cannot develop effective study habits at the beginning of the unit of study, and they will drop progressively further behind as the work progresses.

Established study habits

Since early childhood, high school students have been acquiring attitudes toward work and study methods. Some of these attitudes are good; others are not. When one student comes across a new word, he adds it to a list, finds its meaning in a dictionary, and uses it in his writing and speech. Another student skips over new words, quickly loses interest in reading because he does not understand what he is reading, and quits. One youngster has learned to do certain things at home— to keep his room tidy, to get up for school on time, to take care of his clothing, and to keep the lawn mowed. He does these tasks promptly and without prodding and considers himself remiss unless he has completed them on schedule. Another adolescent may have indulgent parents who do everything for him, or parents who lead such lives that they cannot get any semblance of order in the home for themselves or for their children.

In a school environment, the teacher can appraise the student's work habits by noting how long he takes to get started, how he cares for and uses materials, how well he concentrates, how well he employs various approaches in problem-solving, and how well he completes his work. The teacher should begin to familiarize himself with the students' established work habits early in the year. He might well give flexible, rather than common, assignments until he has had sufficient opportunity to help each student study most efficiently.

General intellectual ability

Two assumptions on intelligence have prevailed in the present century: One is that the individual's potential for all types of intellectual activity is determined by heredity and remains constant from birth throughout life. The second is that heredity and environment interact in such a fashion that intellectual ability is not constant but is modifiable, and that aptitudes are the result of prior experience and physical development as well as of biological endowment. The tendency now is to place greater meaning upon environmental influences than was formerly the case, especially environmental influences during the early years of life.

An impoverished childhood environment might retard an individual's development to an extent that he might find difficult to remedy. An enriched environment might accelerate his development. Perhaps too much emphasis has been placed on IQ scores on the assumption that IQ is unchangeable or that there is a perfect correlation between IQ and achievement in any school subject. It is highly probable that intelligence tests are not equally valid measures of intelligence for students from all types of socioeconomic backgrounds. Predicting how well a student may do in a subject must include knowledge of his performance thus far in the subject. Adding the knowledge of the present level of achievement to the knowledge of general intellectual ability improves the prediction of performance.

The student with high general intellectual ability may not start to work as quickly or to concentrate as persistently as the student with average or low general intellectual ability. However, the student with high ability does not need as much help in learning to attack verbal and abstract problems as other students need. In general, the brightest students can memorize rapidly, have large vocabularies, read rapidly, manipulate abstract concepts readily, have good school records, and make original contributions to classroom discussions. However, qualities like these are on a continuum: There are no sharp differentiations between bright, average, and slow students. The teacher needs to be especially alert to discover those students who learn easily and those who learn very slowly. And he needs to give all pupils any help needed in forming efficient study methods if they are to reach their maximum potential for learning.

THE PHYSICAL AND PSYCHOLOGICAL ENVIRONMENT IS MADE CONDUCIVE TO STUDY

In one classroom the students get to work quickly and devote the whole period to work; in another the same students dawdle, draw pictures, daydream, attract their classmates' attention, and leave most assignments uncompleted. Such differences may be due in part to whether or not the teacher makes the classroom situation conducive to study.

Physical environment

Classroom conditions such as lighting, ventilation, adequate seating capacity, cleanliness, color, and decorations all affect work methods. Although the effects of these conditions are too obvious to warrant extended discussion, it is true, nevertheless, that teachers often become accustomed to furniture, decorations, seats, and lighting facilities. Because they are comfortable in the classroom and because it is familiar and homelike to them, these teachers fail to recognize that the setting may not be conducive to maximum learning.

The optimal physical setting for independent work, such as supervised study periods in the regular classroom, includes these features: A well-lighted, pleasantly decorated room that is free from distracting noises; comfortable, moveable student desks; storage space; reading and project areas; classroom library; mechanical aids; and other materials required for concentrated work.

Teacher qualities

Teacher personality, interests, attitudes, and values are also important factors determining whether or not a student will work and study effectively. Even though a wide variety of personal and professional characteristics exist and produce meaningful learning, teachers who are, for instance, cheerful, friendly, and sympathetic are more likely to achieve success than are teachers characterized by the opposite traits.

Some qualities that produce conditions of teacher-learner interaction conducive to learning and development, qualities characteristic of "high" group members of the teaching profession, are summarized in Table 11.1. The efficiency of pupil learning—motivation to study and to learn —is enhanced when guided by a teacher who enjoys working with young people, who is intelligent, who is well prepared in the subject matter, who is well adjusted emotionally, and who has an adequate self-concept.

Interesting activities

No one attacks a task energetically unless he is interested in it. A student does not continue to work unless he feels that he is making progress. Interest thrives on success and dies with failure.

To stimulate interest in a given activity, the teacher can (1) help students see the value of the work in relation to their immediate life or their vocational plans; (2) help them see the significance of the work as it affects their success and happiness in school; (3) use interesting and challenging materials and activities; (4) start with relatively easy materials and assignments; and (5) devise methods whereby students can measure their progress. Unless the learning situation can be arranged so that it will arouse and maintain interest, students will not study well or work consistently.

The teacher's methods

Students learn to study and to work effectively if the teacher guides them in such learning. The teacher who is unconcerned about how his students study or who is impatient with them is not likely to teach them essential study and work skills. Study skills, like other skills, are acquired gradually and continuously. It is each teacher's responsibility

TABLE 11.1. *Personal Qualities that Appear to Distinguish Teachers Selected to be "High" and "Low" with Respect to Over-All Classroom Behavior.*

Elementary teachers	Secondary teachers	Elementary-secondary teachers combined
	Characteristics of "high" group teachers	
A. "High" group members more frequently (than "low"):	A. "High" group members more frequently (than "low"):	A. "High" group members more frequently (than "low"):
1. Manifest extreme generosity in appraisals of the behavior and motives of other persons; express friendly feelings for others.	1. Manifest extreme generosity in appraisals of the behavior and motives of other persons; express friendly feelings for others.	1. Manifest extreme generosity in appraisals of the behavior and motives of other persons; express friendly feelings for others.
2. Indicate strong interest in reading and in literary matters.	2. Indicate strong interest in reading and in literary matters.	2. Indicate strong interest in reading and in literary matters.
3. Indicate interest in music, painting, and the arts in general.	3. Indicate interest in music, painting, and the arts in general.	3. Indicate interest in music, painting, and the arts in general.
4. Report participation in high school and college social groups.	4. Report participation in high school and college social groups.	4. Report participation in high school and college social groups.
5. Manifest prominent social service ideals.	5. Judge selves high in ambition and initiative.	5. Judge selves high in ambition and initiative.
6. Indicate preferences for activities that involve contact with people.	6. Report teaching experience of 4–9 years.	
7. Indicate interest in science and scientific matters.	7. Report teaching-type activities during childhood and adolescence.	
8. Report liking for outdoor activities.	8. Indicate preference for student-centered learning situations.	
9. Are young, or middle-aged.	9. Manifest independence, though not aggressiveness.	
10. Are married.		
11. Report that parental homes provided above-average cultural advantages.		
B. "High" group (compared with "low" group):	B. "High" group (compared with "low" group):	B. "High" group (compared with "low" group):

pupil opinions).
2. Indicates greater preference for non-directive classroom procedures.
3. Is superior in verbal intelligence.
4. Is more satisfactory with regard to emotional adjustment.

A. "Low" group members more frequently (than "high"):
   1. Are from older age groups.
   2. Are restricted and critical in appraisals of the behavior and motives of other persons.
   3. Are unmarried.
   4. Indicate preferences for activities that do *not* involve close contacts with people.

B. "Low" group (compared with "high" group):
   1. Is less favorable in expressed opinions of pupils.
   2. Is less high with regard to verbal intelligence.
   3. Is less satisfactory with regard to emotional adjustment.

Characteristics of "low" group teachers

A. "Low" group members more frequently (than "high"):
   1. Are from older age groups.
   2. Are restricted and critical in appraisals of the behavior and motives of other persons.
   3. Indicate preference for teacher-directed learning situations.
   4. Value exactness, orderliness, and "practical" things.
   5. Indicate preferences for activities that do *not* involve close contacts with people.

B. "Low" group (compared with "high" group):
   1. Is less favorable in expressed opinions of pupils.
   2. Is less high with regard to verbal intelligence.
   3. Is less satisfactory with regard to emotional adjustment.

pupil opinions).
2. Indicates greater preference for non-directive classroom procedures.
3. Is superior in verbal intelligence.
4. Is more satisfactory with regard to emotional adjustment.

A. "Low" group members more frequently (than "high"):
   1. Are from older age groups.
   2. Are restricted and critical in appraisals of the behavior and motives of other persons.
   3. Value exactness, orderliness, and "practical" things.
   4. Indicate preferences for activities that do *not* involve close contacts with people.

B. "Low" group (compared with "high" group):
   1. Is less favorable in expressed opinions of pupils.
   2. Is less high with regard to verbal intelligence.
   3. Is less satisfactory with regard to emotional adjustment.

SOURCE: David G. Ryans, *Characteristics of Teachers: Their Description, Comparison, and Appraisal* (Washington, D.C.: American Council of Education, 1960), pp. 360–361. By permission.

to help his students acquire the study skills that they need in order to profit most from the work.

Teaching students how to study is as important as teaching subject information and facts. However, teaching study skills should be done in a functional setting. It is easier to teach adolescents study methods in individual classes in English or in algebra than it is to form a special class to teach more generalized methods of study.

It is not always necessary to tell students exactly what to do and how, when, and why to do it. But the teacher can usually give helpful brief instructions before his students begin a task. He can help the students recall relevant knowledge, help them determine the abilities or skills needed for the new task, or help them have a clear idea of the final outcome desired. It is the teacher's responsibility to make sure that all of his students understand the components of a learning activity. When they do not understand, there is much confusion and little learning.

STUDENTS LEARN TO READ MORE EFFICIENTLY

Some college teachers contend that high school teachers do not teach students to read rapidly with meaning; high school teachers then hold the elementary schools responsible for failing to do a good job. The elementary school teacher, in turn, says that the child's home conditions were such as to prevent his being taught to read well; finally, the parents maintain that the schools failed them when they were students so they cannot do a better job with their children. Thus, the circle is closed, and nothing is done to improve the situation.

Although the instruction of students with serious retardation and difficulty in reading is clearly the province of highly specialized teachers, all teachers in the secondary school, not just the reading or English teacher, should share the responsibility for basic instruction in reading and for instruction in adjusting skills to the demands of the content fields. The learning process in reading is never completed: Everyone can improve certain skills. Guided reading in the various curriculum areas can give experiences that lead to growth and to a full use of abilities. Some of the skills common to the various content fields, skills that should be given attention by each teacher, are word-identification techniques; reading with meaning; practice for vocabulary; practice for concentration; flexibility in rate of reading; locational skills; critical and creative reading; and expanding interests and improving tastes. Even though students will have had instruction in these skills in elementary school, the junior or senior high school teacher needs to see that such skills are maintained, developed further, or mastered better.

Word-identification techniques

The principal word-identification techniques, employed with an unfamiliar word by adults and young people alike, are the use of: (1) context clues, (2) word-structure analysis, (3) use of phonics, and (4) dictionary usage. Using context clues involves reading the phrase, clause, sentence, or paragraph that contains the new word as a means of trying to grasp the word's correct meaning. Using structural analysis involves the division of the word into its known parts (prefix, root, stem, suffix, and various affixes). The use of phonics involves the reader's associating sounds with the appropriate letter symbols and his blending the sound in a whole word to improve word perception and independence in word recognition. Because the pronunciation of many words differs from the aggregate pronunciation of each letter in the word, a combined attack is often employed—using the context, breaking the word into known parts, and using phonics.

Some students can recognize, understand, and use most of the words that they encounter in classroom reading. Other students need the same kind of intensive instruction that elementary teachers give in the intermediate grades. Some students need to be taught phonics; some, word-structure analysis; and so on. Each teacher in the secondary school needs preparation in teaching developmental reading, and, here, word-attack skills, in his professional training.

Reading with meaning

Understanding what one reads is the best assurance that the material will be remembered. Poorly understood materials must be memorized if they are to be reproduced; poorly understood materials are quickly forgotten. Students vary widely in their ability to comprehend. Most of them, however, can be taught to improve their reading comprehension. Practice to increase reading comprehension should be included at appropriate intervals in the general class activities rather than set up as an unrelated drill.

Practice for comprehension must be adapted to what is being read. Material of the kind usually contained in textbooks is generally aimed at presenting and clarifying a number of basic concepts, generalizations, or processes. Several major tasks in finding the meaning of such material are identifying the major concepts, grasping relationships necessary in understanding the generalization, and organizing the material into a meaningful pattern that will be remembered. Several types of practice are suitable for this type of material—practice with the sentence, with the paragraph, and with larger units of prose.

Sentence meaning

As a word itself may be a barrier to comprehension, so may the syntax of a sentence, especially the syntax of a sentence that has many layers of modification or inverted order, be a barrier to understanding an author's meaning. Students need an understanding of the basic, or kernel, sentence patterns of which all sentences, no matter how complicated, are built. Students need an understanding of the kinds of subject-predicate word groupings that constitute sentences in written English. They need to understand techniques of subordination, coordination, and modification. Their comprehension will involve being able to deal with inverted word order and with pronoun references. They need to understand that the function of a word (as a noun, verb, adjective, or adverb) changes as the word is used in different sentence positions. They need to know the function of the marks of punctuation, of capitalization, italics, and so on.

Practice for paragraph meaning

The paragraph is one basic structure for conveying unified ideas. Students need to recognize methods by which paragraphs are developed: By details or example, by extended definition, by cause and effect, by a chronological pattern, by comparison and contrast, and so on. They need to recognize a topic sentence, if one exists, or the main idea of the paragraph.

Practice for unit meaning

Paragraphs are related one to another to present a more complete statement of a subject. Usually, a whole series of paragraphs must be read to understand a topic. In giving students practice for unit meaning, select a series of short paragraphs that are relatively complete in themselves and that can be read in a brief period of time. Give a real purpose for thoughtful reading. Formulate a series of questions whose answers lead to understanding the major concept, generalization, process, or event. Have the student focus on guide words; encourage him to separate the important from the unimportant.

Practice for vocabulary

Vocabulary practice can be held before, during, or after the reading assignment, depending on how many new words are introduced and how well their meaning can be understood from the context. However the practice is carried out, growth in acquiring technical terminology is the responsibility of each subject-matter teacher.

Students can keep notebooks in which they enter new words, with synonyms, definitions, and sentences in which the new words are used. They should try to use new words in speech and should acquire permanent habits of using the dictionary.

Practice for concentration

Reading with concentration becomes easier if it is related to a specific purpose. A question that is to be answered on the basis of what is read arouses the student's interest, gets him started immediately, and keeps him at work until the question is answered.

The material used in practicing for concentration should be of moderate length and medium difficulty. If they are to concentrate, students should feel that they are making progress. And long, difficult selections that are almost impossible to read even with sustained attention definitely discourage concentration.

Flexibility in rate of reading

Many students read most printed matter at the same rate whether it is a detective story, a western, a psychology textbook, or a treatise on nuclear physics. They assume that each person uses one reading rate in all situations. Many students worry about improving speed in reading when they should be adjusting their reading speed to different situations.

When a student does need to speed up his reading, tachistoscopes and other mechanical devices for exposing reading text, while controlling time, may be helpful. If such machines are not available or are not feasible, the teacher and student can use flash cards to improve the ability to concentrate and to form associations rapidly. Or students can pace their own reading by moving a card in which a window is cut across or down the page. Of course, reading speed is meaningless unless it is accompanied by comprehension, word-attack skills, and so on.

Techniques of skimming are helpful to the student in getting an overview of a section or chapter and in noting the relation of key ideas to larger topics. Sometimes, students waste time in reading materials that need only a quick survey; skimming would save them a great deal of time. Skimming skills are valuable for finding answers to specific questions on names, dates, places, and events. They help the student select content that he wants to read in depth.

Locational skills

Locational skills involve the extension and development of skills already practiced to some degree in the elementary school. These skills include knowing how to read and study textbooks; how to use the library; how to use the dictionary; how to use basic references, including atlases, encyclopedias, and the various indexes.

Instruction in how to use the textbook most effectively was discussed in Chapter 9. You will recall that the student was asked to survey the textbook and various chapters quickly, noting general organization; noting boldface titles and subtitles; noting the use of any charts and graphs; and studying the index, table of contents, glossary, bibliography, and appendixes.

No teacher should assume that the secondary school student knows how to use a library to maximum efficiency or that he can evaluate well the information he secures there. On the contrary, many people need assistance in locating, using, and evaluating information throughout life.

A professional school librarian will often be available to orient your students to the use of the reference resources of the library and to the arrangement of books in the library. However, if the trained librarian lacks the time for orientation sessions, there are a number of activities that you can follow. You can prepare floor outlines of the central school library and the public library—noting where reference books, fiction, the card catalogue, periodicals, and so on, are housed. You can write the Dewey Decimal Classification System, the most common system of book arrangement in school libraries, on the chalkboard and discuss the ten classes of books in this system:

000–009	General Works
100–199	Philosophy
200–299	Religion
300–399	Social Sciences
400–499	Linguistics
500–599	Pure Science
600–699	Technology
700–799	Arts and Recreation
800–899	Literature
900–999	History, Geography, Travel, Biography

Explain that works of fiction are often shelved in a separate area with appropriate signs on the shelves.

To teach the skills for reading the cards found in a card catalogue, bring to class some exact reproductions of some of the cards. Discuss one of these cards, noting the information it contains about the book —call number, author, title, subject, date of publication, number of pages, illustrations, and so on. Emphasize the significance of the call number as the key to locating books on the shelves. Next, identify the three types of cards—author card, title card, and subject card—so that the students know which card to look for in terms of the information that they possess. Then take the students to the library to examine the card catalogue. Ask each student to find the cards that are identical to his author, title, and subject cards. Ask him to note related books indexed by guide words such as *study, physical education,* or *cars.* Next, take the students to the stacks and show them how books are located by their call numbers. Ask each student to find the book designated on his cards.

Magazines constitute a large part of the contemporary American's reading. Knowledge of the use of indexes to periodicals is important to the student in finding up-to-date materials on subjects of interest and value to him. The magazine index that is found most often in central school libraries is the *Reader's Guide to Periodical Literature*. Among other indexes, limited to special subjects, are the *Agricultural Index, Art Index, Education Index*, and *International Index*. The index to *The New York Times* newspaper will also prove a valuable source in locating information on various events and people.

An unabridged dictionary is valuable both as a source of information and as an aid to reading. Used properly, it helps students find word meanings, thus improving reading comprehension; it helps them pronounce correctly, thus improving oral expression; and it helps students spell, punctuate, and divide words into syllables, thus improving written performance. Two frequently used unabridged dictionaries are *Webster's Third New International Dictionary* and *Funk & Wagnalls New Standard Dictionary*.

If time is available, a quick survey of the various parts of an abridged dictionary is a good starting point for learning how to use the dictionary best. Have the students note the parts of the entries in the dictionary: the vocabulary entry; pronunciation; the part of speech; inflectional forms; etymology; definitions and their ordering; cross entries; synonyms; and antonyms. Have them examine the pronunciation key and the abbreviations used in the work. Point out which desk dictionaries contain sections on signs and symbols; biographical names; a gazetteer; rules of orthography; accepted standards for capitals, compounds, and punctuation; and so on.

The dictionary is, of course, the best guide to the correct spelling, or alternative spelling, of any word. However, many students cannot locate a word. This happens because the English language uses nonphonemic devices—for example, $/\check{s}/$ is represented by the graphemes $<$sh$>$ $<$ch$>$ $<$che$>$ $<$sch$>$ $<$s$>$ $<$ci$>$ $<$ti$>$ $<$sci$>$ $<$ssi$>$ and so on —so that spelling can be difficult, even for adults. A major task in helping students find a correct spelling in the dictionary is getting them to persist until they find the word. Assistance from the teacher must be available, particularly when a student becomes discouraged and wants to quit.

Students also need to know of the existence and uses of the various encyclopedias and other reference resources. This knowledge can be taught best by the subject-matter teacher in the context of actual units of study. Thus, the music teacher may direct students to *Composers of Yesterday* or *Living Musicians;* the English teacher, to *American Authors: 1600–1900* or *Twentieth Century Authors;* the French teacher, to Cassell's *New French Dictionary French-English and English-French;* and the social studies teacher, to the *Encyclopedia of the Social Sciences, Goode's World Atlas,* the *Statesman's Yearbook,* and the *World Almanac.*

The reference books that will be used most frequently should be previewed in the classroom, as the dictionary was. The purpose of previewing is to become familiar with the organization of the work, to be able to find specific information, and to determine which source is most valuable for securing a particular type of information.

After the survey of encyclopedias and other resource references, specific assignments may be given. Depending upon the students' familiarity with the reference books, assignments might include such questions as: (1) Which countries lead the world in the production of oil? (2) Who was William Watson? (3) Who wrote the lyrics for the musical comedy *Hello, Dolly!?* (4) How much did the population of the United States increase between 1950 and 1960? In these assignments, the students must be helped, when necessary, to select the best sources, and to find the information in them. For a class that has had little practice, it is better to investigate one reference book at a time and to give assignments that call for locating specific information in it.

Critical and creative reading

Up to this point, much emphasis has been given to competences that help the student locate and get ideas and meaning from what he reads. Another competence in which the student needs training is to check ideas and information obtained from a given source with his own experiences, to read and evaluate materials critically and creatively.

Different writers have used the term *critical reading* differently. Russell and Fea, examining different uses of the term, conclude, "Through most definitions runs the idea of not accepting as true everything that one sees in print, but, instead, trying to judge or evaluate the source, the ideas, the argument, and the conclusions in the light of one's other experiences."[1]

One first step in critical awareness is to determine the authority of an author to write as an expert on a subject. You might ask students questions such as, "What qualifications did Otto Jespersen have to write a grammar of English?" "What special training and knowledge did H. L. Mencken have to write authoritatively of the spelling and pronunciation of words in America?" Students, and many adults, have a tendency to believe that because a statement appears in print it must be true, and that all authors are authorities on whatever they write about.

Another, and related, step is attempting to determine the writer's purpose. What is Dickens saying about nineteenth-century business enterprise and social philosophy in the character of Mr. Dombey or in the figure of good Mrs. Brown? What is Remarque's attitude toward heroism in *All Quiet on the Western Front*? How does Steinbeck want the reader to feel about the plight of the migrant worker in *The Grapes of Wrath*? Or, in nonliterary works, what do the prefaces, forewords, and introductions show to be the author's over-all intent? What biases and attitudes are reflected in the total work?

Students need to read using some knowledge of the inductive and/or deductive process. Does an extended piece of persuasive writing rest solely on a generalization that is not always true? Is enough evidence given to permit arriving at a given generalization?

Too, students will read critically only when they are aware of such abuses of logic as card-stacking, the red herring, quoting material out of context, oversimplification, false analogy, *post hoc ergo propter hoc* fallacy, and question-begging—propagandistic snares for the too-gullible reader.

Students should be aware of the affective use of words, of connotation. What different effects are created by choosing one of these words rather than another—plump, fat, obese, overweight, adipose? Do these

---

[1] David H. Russell and Henry R. Fea, "Research on Teaching Reading," in N. L. Gage, ed., *Handbook of Research on Teaching* (Chicago: Rand McNally, 1963), p. 902. By permission.

words, in the context of a sentence, serve more to inform or to make the reader experience a certain attitude?

To help students develop critical abilities supply them with a brief article from which you have omitted the conclusion and see what logical conclusions they draw. Have students bring to class and discuss editorials on the same event from two different newspapers. Encourage students to question the reasoning found in lessons in their textbooks. Have a committee maintain a study display containing abuses of logic encountered in magazine advertising or containing statistical evidence distorted by being removed from its context.

In creative reading, a reader "combines or uses the ideas of the writer in a fresh, original way"; " 'creates' from the ideas presented on the printed page"; "goes beyond literal comprehension of ideas explicitly stated by the author to 'reading between the lines' or to an individual uncopied, novel response to the material."[2]

Such creative reading requires a knowledge of the uses of metaphor, symbol, allusion, paradox, irony, and ambiguity. It involves bringing the experiences of the reader to bear on a reading. It involves what Guilford has termed divergent thinking, or what Bloom has termed translation, synthesis, and evaluation. It involves organizing material into new concepts, new generalizations.

Comparing the material read with one's own experience, comparing different treatments of the same topic, and discussing the material with classmates, teachers, and other adults are the main techniques by which secondary school students can evaluate what they read. Discussing reading materials with other students and with the teacher, knowing of alternative readings, helps creative reading.

Expanding interests and improving tastes

Dora V. Smith has said,

Left to themselves, young people tend to read within a narrow area and in materials which afford them little real challenge. They need the guidance of sympathetic and widely read adults in identifying, extending, and intensifying their interests. Many of them have problems which they could solve if they were but aware of them. Others have latent

---

[2] *Ibid.*, p. 903. By permission.

interests which need only to be challenged. Still others know specifically what their interests are but are unaware of materials for pursuing them.[3]

If students are to continue to grow in reading skills in an area, if they are to develop independent habits, if they are to continue reading in an area throughout their lives, all teachers must assume some responsibility for developing tastes and interests.

Knowing that he is helping students make a transition between elementary and secondary school, the junior high school teacher will understand the student's choice of easily read materials that often have action and suspense—even though the teacher himself may consider the books trash. The junior high school student is at the peak of the amount of free reading that he will do in his lifetime. The teacher should capitalize upon the student's interest and abilities in an out-of-class reading progam. The social studies teacher will understand that a student must often read such books as Means' *Shuttered Windows* and Allen's *The New Broome Experiment* before reading Llewellyn's *How Green Was My Valley*, Paton's *Cry the Beloved Country*, or Lee's *To Kill a Mockingbird*. The English teacher needs to realize that many students need some experience with Benson's *Junior Miss* and Felsen's *Hot Rod* as they grow, in part through the teacher's guidance, toward adult materials such as Conrad's *Heart of Darkness* or Hardy's *Return of the Native*.

To help students expand interests, the teacher should himself show enthusiasm for reading, should enjoy books, and should listen carefully to what students have to say about books. In all of his actions and words, the teacher should demonstrate that he reads for enjoyment, for insight into human experience, and for vicarious experience. He should make the learning environment pleasant and provide opportunities for wide free reading in books chosen by the student with his guidance.

---

[3] Dora V. Smith, "Guiding Individual Reading," *Reading in the High School and College,* Forty-seventh Yearbook of the National Society for the Study of Education, Part 2 (Chicago: University of Chicago Press, 1948), p. 180.

STUDENTS LEARN TO WRITE MORE EFFECTIVELY

The teacher of science, psychology, or agriculture complains that his students cannot write up an experiment or observation, saying that the English teacher is at fault for not teaching students how to write well. Yet, if reporting information and writing well-conceived opinions are skills required in all classes, the English teacher cannot be responsible for all of the teaching of composition in the school; nor is he likely to succeed if the standards and guidelines that he suggests in his class are not also used by other teachers.

Not only English teachers but every teacher whose students do written work should be concerned with assisting students to write well. As is the case with reading, it is not enough simply to tell students to write well. They need assistance, assistance at the appropriate level. Most students need instruction in mechanics—capitalization, punctuation, and spelling—in usage, and in various forms of writing—exposition, persuasion, and description. Ideally, this instruction is provided by all teachers in connection with current class activities.

Fowler has suggested four basic principles for a writing program:

1. Writing is a two-way process
2. Writing is based on experience
3. Writing improves through practice
4. Meaning comes before form[4]

That writing is a two-way process suggests that the student needs an audience—his peers, the teacher, other adults—with whom he wants to communicate something that is of interest to him. An awareness of his audience helps the writer select his subject for a particular occasion and purpose. It helps him with his choice of words (colloquial, literary, or scientific) for the occasion. Rather than being perceived as busywork, writing for a well-defined audience should help the student write with more clarity and precision.

That writing is based on experience is a premise suggesting that only as a writer draws on his own background of personal experience, his background of vicarious experience, his background of reading, can he write with clarity, honesty, and persuasion. The writing may be based

---

[4] Mary Elizabeth Fowler, *Teaching Language, Composition, and Literature* (New York: McGraw-Hill, 1965), p. 134.

"One Hectic Day"

To start this out, I guess I had better back up a

little. Last week end, some friends, my parents, one of

my girlfriends, and I went up to the snow. My parents

decided that instead of trying to battle traffic on the way

home Sunday we would leave early Monday morning and be home

by 11 o'clock. So we got up at six in the morning so we

could have breakfast before leaving. We finally got away

at 7:15 and hadn't been gone over an hour when I noticed

there was quite a bit of blue smoke coming out of the tail

pipe. I mentioned it to my Dad, but he just kept on driving.

We passed a gas station but he wouldn't stop, so about ten

minutes later the car started missing and more exhaust came

out of the tail pipe. Then Dad decided to stop. When he

stopped and put the hood up the smoke was so bad that you

would have thought there was a miniture bonfire there in

the motor.

My Dad just stood there for a few minutes and shook

his head. None of us were intrested in saying I told you

so. Then he waved a passing car down and asked them if

they would mind, when going into the first town, to get us

a tow truck as we were having trouble with our car. They

said, "No, they wouldn't mind," so off they went.

There we sat, out in the desilate country with

nothing around us but fields, with a few scattered cows

and chirping birds in the trees.

In about an hour we saw a big tow truck coming down the

Handwritten annotations:

Is your title really a quotation?

What parts of your sentence does this comma separate?
C + (idea)
C – (mechanics)

Find the one word in this phrase that makes the whole first sentence unnecessary.

Do you need both?

It certainly must have been a hectic day, Fred. Now try to make your readers appreciate how bad it really was.
Suggestions:
① Tell more of the hectic details; omit the unhectic.
② make your sentences easier to read by putting only one main idea in each and by providing each pronoun with an antecedent.

Do you like the "50's"?

How many separate ideas have you crammed into this one sentence?

why?

not a brand name

why would a comma here be of help to the reader?

sp.
good comparison

sp.
why?

why?

Do you need to say this?

Are these their exact words?

I like this part! Tell us more. How did the others act?

Please get these cows down out of the trees!

FIG. 8 *Marking to teach writing and thinking.* (A Guide: English in Florida Secondary Schools, *Bulletin 35A, Tallahassee, Fla: State Department of Education, 1962, p. 72. By permission.)*

on academic or nonacademic experiences, but it must not be a poorly assimilated, half-misunderstood, semiparaphrased paper largely copied from one or two encyclopedias.

Writing does improve through practice. Giving brief and accurate descriptions of processes, defining terms, grappling with cause-effect relations, trying to bring a reader to one's own point of view, and writing frequently can all help a student overcome his fear of expressing himself on paper.

That meaning comes before form is almost axiomatic. No good writing comes until the writer wants to say something. Once a student has a controlling purpose for his paper, then a teacher can help him with matters of sentence length, style, semantics, logic, and so on, but not until then.

Six sequential steps by which a teacher and his students produce a finished composition are listed by Fowler as these:

1. Generating ideas
2. Composing and prevision
3. Marking papers
4. Discussing
5. Teaching
6. Revising papers[5]

The subject-matter teacher must help the students ask the right questions about the content, help them find a theme, help them narrow the questions into manageable forms. Once the subject is well stated, the teacher can help the students anticipate problems that might occur in the writing (prevision) and can help them avoid errors. (At the beginning of the course, the teacher should discuss minimal standards for format, spelling, punctuation, footnoting, and so on.) Next, the teacher marks the paper. The preferred practice is that the teacher not confine himself to inserting commas and to correcting spelling errors and usage in red pencil. The preferred practice in grading is that the teacher treat the student's good points more than his weaknesses, that he show the student how to improve his logic and use of rhetorical devices, and that he show students excellent examples of other student writing and of professional writing.[6] Figure 8 presents an example of grading designed

---

[5] *Ibid.*, pp. 135–146.
[6] An excellent guide to theme annotation is Ednah Shepard Thomas' *Evaluating Student Themes* (Madison, Wis.: University of Wisconsin Press, 1962).

to teach. Ideally, the teacher will discuss compositions with the student in individual conferences. Next, the teacher concerns himself with teaching some of the aspects of rhetoric and organization:

1. Stating an idea clearly and concisely
2. Supporting an idea
3. Discriminating between facts and judgments
4. Using concrete detail
5. Teaching economy, sensitivity, and clarity
6. Mastering the "speaking voice"[7]

Finally, the teacher, rather than permitting the students to throw the compositions in the wastebasket after looking at the grade, encourages each student to revise his paper, to say what is said with increased unity, emphasis, and coherence.

Ideally, there should be schoolwide standards for writing, especially for usage. One excellent guide for the items that should be studied in usage has been given by Robert C. Pooley. He recommends the following items as essential to accuracy of communication and to minimal standards of social acceptability:

1. The elimination of all baby-talk and "cute" expressions
2. The correct use of *I, me, he, him, she, her, they, them* (Exception, *it's me*)
3. The correct uses of *is, are, was, were* with respect to number and tense
4. Correct past tenses of common irregular verbs such as *saw, gave, took, brought, bought, stuck*
5. Correct use of past participles of the same verbs and similar verbs after auxiliaries
6. Elimination of the double negative: *We don't have no apples*, etc.
7. Elimination of analogical forms: *ain't, hisn, hern, ourn, theirselves*, etc.
8. Correct use of possessive pronouns: *my, mine, his, hers, theirs, ours*
9. Mastery of the distinction between *its*, possessive pronoun, and *it's, it is*
10. Placement of *have* or its reduction to *'ve* between I and a past participle
11. Elimination of *them* as a demonstrative pronoun
12. Elimination of *this here* and *that there*
13. Mastery of use of *a* and *an* as articles
14. Correct use of personal pronouns in compound constructions; as

---

[7] Fowler, *op. cit.*, pp. 141–145.

subject (*Mary and I*), as object (*Mary and me*), as object of preposition (*to Mary and me*)

15. The use of *we* before an appositional noun when subject; *us* when object
16. Correct number agreement with the phrases *there is, there are, there was, there were*
17. Elimination of *he don't, she don't, it don't*
18. Elimination of *learn* for *teach, leave* for *let*
19. Elimination of pleonastic subjects: *my brother he; my mother she; that fellow he*
20. Proper agreement in number with antecedent pronouns *one* and *anyone, everyone, each, no one*; with *everybody* and *none* some tolerance of number seems acceptable now
21. The use of *who* and *whom* as reference to persons (but note, *Who did he give it to?* is tolerated in all but very formal situations, in which *To whom did he give it?* is preferable)
22. Accurate use of *said* in reporting the words of a speaker in the past
23. Correction of *lay down* to *lie down*
24. The distinction between *good* as adjective and *well* as adverb; e.g., *He spoke well*
25. Elimination from writing of *can't hardly, all the farther* (for *as far as*) and *Where is he* (*she, it*) *at?*[8]

Pooley lists as borderline usages:

1. Making no distinction between *shall* and *will*
2. The split infinitive
3. The use of *like* as a conjunction
4. The use of "different than" as in "He's different than me"
5. The pattern "she is one of those girls who are"
6. The pattern "The reason I did this *is because* . . ."
7. The pattern *myself* as a substitute for *me* in, "I understand you will meet Mrs. Jones and *myself* at the station"
8. Not using the possessive case with the gerund: "What do you think of Jean coming here?"[9]

Only as the teacher provides an occasion on which a student has something that he wants to say and only as the teacher helps the student say what is to be said will the student write in a manner that will result in the improvement of his skills for expressing himself clearly, effectively, and with integrity.

---

[8] Robert C. Pooley, "What Is Correct English?" *National Education Association Journal*, XLIX (December, 1960), 18–19. By permission.
[9] *Ibid.*, 19.

STUDENTS LEARN TO LISTEN BETTER

The average individual spends more time each day listening than reading, writing, or speaking: Almost one third of the hours he is awake is spent in listening. Beseiged by increasing numbers of sounds and by the mass media, the average adolescent has learned to insulate himself from much of the speech and sound that assail him.

The evidence is rather clear that students who are taught listening skills improve; those who are not taught do not improve.

> Studies also suggest . . . that listening is subtly modified by attitudes toward the speaker, the situation, and the audience, that mass listening is modified by the social nature of the situation (the same listener responds variously to the same speech in different audience contexts), that poor listening with or without hearing impairment retards normal language development, and that listening is so important in business and industry that many large enterprises have offered to their employees (at all levels) training courses in listening.[10]

Some of the general attitudes and skills characteristic of the good listener are,

> The good listener brings the following attitudes to the listening situation:
> 1. He wants to listen
> 2. He finds a personal reason for listening
> 3. He is willing to do his part in the listening situation
>
> The good listener brings the following attitudes toward the speaker or speech event:
> 1. He is receptive—willing to "hear out" the event in search of whatever meaning it may contain
> 2. He is friendly and sympathetic toward the speaker, respecting him as a person, and respecting his right to a good audience
> 3. He is aware of the possible effects of his own bias or prejudice or previous experience on his reaction to the listening situation
>
> The good listener prepares to listen in the following ways:
> 1. He tries to learn about subject, speaker, and situation in advance
> 2. He sits where he can see and hear
> 3. He tries to eliminate distractions in his environment
> 4. He is ready to take notes when appropriate

---

[10] National Council of Teachers of English, *The English Language Arts in the Secondary School*, prepared by the Commission on the English Curriculum (New York: Appleton-Century-Crofts, 1956), pp. 253–254. By permission.

The good listener does the following things while listening:

1. He gives the speaking event his full time attention, using his spare thinking time to support and extend the meaning of the event rather than to think about irrelevant matters

2. He keeps in mind the purpose of this speaking event and does not try to force his own purposes upon others participating in the event

3. He is alert to all clues to meaning contained in the speaking situation such as the setting and/or staging of the event; the introductions, program notes, and the like; key words and the particular meaning given to them by their context; the clues given by inflection, rate, emphasis, action, vocal quality, and the like

4. He prepares to respond in an appropriate manner to the situation by preparing questions if questions are to follow; by taking notes if key ideas or information are to be retained; by judging evidence and reasoning if a controversial opinion is under discusion; by lending himself to the mood, attitude and experience of the characters in a play, or the experiences of imaginative literature[11]

The teacher needs to provide opportunities for the student to evaluate his ability to listen for information, his ability to listen as an aesthetic experience, and his ability to listen critically. In previewing films or lectures, the teacher can indicate the general plan of the exposition. He can point out the necessity for suspending judgment, for tolerating points of view not his own. He can teach propaganda devices. He can teach note-taking. The teacher can devise diagnostic tests from lectures, discussion, films, and recordings. Or he can administer the *Brown-Carlsen Listening Comprehension Test* to measure the student's listening ability. Ultimately, however, his great responsibility must be to motivate the student to listen well by showing the contribution of listening to personal, social, and occupational competence.

STUDENTS ARE HELPED WITH STUDY AND WORK SCHEDULES

Most adolescents have several hours of relatively free time each week. These students, as well as those whose time is taken up with many activities, can profit from help in learning to manage their time. Some students may resent such help, but others will appreciate it.

---

[11] *A Guide to the Teaching of Reading, Listening, Viewing: Grades 7–12* (Minneapolis, Minn.: Minneapolis Public Schools, 1959), p. 40.

The teacher can give the student a form on which to record a general schedule of use of time from getting up in the morning to going to bed at night. The teacher then consults with individual students or with small groups and helps each student decide whether he is giving enough time to study. Many students will be amazed at how much time is wasted through lack of organization and planning. Many will find that a regular daily study schedule—for instance, a couple of hours each evening—helps get work done better and helps avoid the tension and anxiety accompanying the attempt to meet deadlines at the last possible moment. Generally, students have more time for recreation and feel more comfortable about their school work when they stick to an orderly plan for getting the necessary work done. This work on scheduling enables the teacher to discover students who are doing too much— perhaps carrying an outside job, taking part in too many cocurricular activities, or taking too many academic courses.

PROVISIONS ARE MADE FOR STUDENTS WHO HAVE SPECIAL NEEDS

In any age group, there will be a small number of children that cannot or do not profit from instruction in regular classes. Three classifications of children who need special provisions because of general intellectual ability are (1) slow-learning children, (2) educable mentally retarded children, and (3) trainable mentally retarded children. The characteristics of exceptional children and the special provisions for their education will be discussed in Chapter 14. Most of you will, in the course of your career, teach adolescents in the first group, and it is very important that our best teachers work with slow-learning children as well as with the gifted. Few of you will work with the second or third groups unless you enter specialized programs of training.

Two other groups sometimes singled out for special attention in the secondary schools are (1) culturally disadvantaged children and (2) delinquents. Culturally disadvantaged children are often the product of impoverished neighborhoods, or are members of large families, or are born of illiterate parents. Lacking a middle-class orientation, lacking a rich background of language experiences, lacking experiences with many of the concepts usually common to the middle-class, lacking motivation to master the content of traditional courses, these children can, nevertheless, be reasonably well educated if the schools are committed to the task. Delinquents are legal minors who repeatedly commit acts in violation of the law or of municipal ordinance. The school has a responsibility to find ways to make education rewarding and meaningful for potentially delinquent students.

SUMMARY

To study efficiently, a student must be ready to study, know what to study, have a desirable setting and the necessary materials for study, and know how to go about studying effectively. In most classrooms, this means that the teacher must consider the readiness of his students and increase their readiness in relation to particular activities. The physical and psychological environment must be made conducive to study, the work must be made interesting, the student must understand what he is to do, and the teacher must give attention to teaching *how* to work and study as well as to *what* to learn and study.

The teacher should not assume that students in grades 7 through 12 can read, write, and listen perfectly. All students need some instruction in the communication skills of reading, writing, and listening. Whenever reading is called for, students may need help in word-identification techniques, reading with meaning, flexibility in the rate of reading, locational skills, or critical and creative reading. Writing can be improved through the efforts of all the teachers in the school, as can listening.

Teachers also need to work with students on making study and work schedules. And they need to make special provisions so that the slow-learning student, the culturally disadvantaged student, and the potentially delinquent student can realize his full potential.

QUESTIONS AND ACTIVITIES

1 Think of a teacher whom you have held in high regard. List the personal qualities of this teacher and compare them with the characteristics of

"high" group teachers as discussed in this chapter. Do the same for a teacher whom you have held in low esteem.

2 Write a narrative paragraph in which you explain to a low-ability student the value for his life of a concept that you know well.

3 Discuss the merit of the statement that every teacher in the secondary school should share the responsibility for basic instruction in reading.

4 From your own recent reading, select several paragraphs that you might use to help students practice for unit-meaning. List questions that you would ask to lead students to an understanding of the major concept, generalization, process, or event.

5 Using the *Education Index*, locate and then read several articles on the teaching of vocabulary in your own, or a closely related, field. Discuss whether vocabulary is best learned from lists of words given all students at a given level or from lists of words compiled by the individual student of words that he thinks he might need or use.

6 Compile a list of reference works in your own field that could be used with your students when you begin teaching.

7 To what extent do you think it is possible to teach "creative" reading?

8 To what extent should all teachers in the secondary school be responsible for teaching composition? Are some aspects of composition better left to the English teacher?

9 Are you committed to the point of view that direct teaching of how to listen is necessary in secondary school?

10 List conditions that might prevent students' concentrating. Suggest ways to create a learning environment in which maximum concentration is possible.

11 Observe three or four students in a junior or senior high school classroom. For each student, note (a) the amount of time used in starting an assignment, (b) the amount of time actually spent in work, (c) the amount of time not spent in work, and (d) the degree of efficiency with which the students use material and tools.

12 Try to help one of your fellow college students, who is not achieving as well as he thinks he can, acquire better study habits and a more efficient work schedule. Write a brief description of the suggestions that you make and of the results of your suggestions.

SUGGESTIONS FOR FURTHER READING

AUSTIN, MARY C., CLIFFORD L. BUSH, AND MILDRED H. HUEBNER, *Reading Evaluation*, New York: Ronald, 1961.

BARBE, WALTER B., *Teaching Reading: Selected Materials*, New York: Oxford University Press, 1965.

CROW, LESTER D., AND ALICE CROW, *How to Study*, New York: Collier Books, 1963.

FRIES, CHARLES C., *Linguistics and Reading*, New York: Holt, Rinehart and Winston, 1962.

JUDINE, SISTER M., I.H.M., ED., *A Guide for Evaluating Student Composition*, Champaign, Ill.: National Council of Teachers of English, 1965.

KRANYIK, ROBERT, AND FLORENCE V. SHANKMAN, *How to Teach Study Skills*, Englewood Cliffs, N.J.: Teachers Practical Press, 1963.

OTTO, WAYNE, AND RICHARD A. MC MENEMY, *Corrective and Remedial Teaching*, Boston: Houghton Mifflin, 1966.

SHANE, HAROLD G., AND JUNE GRANT MULRY, *Improving Language Arts Instruction through Research*, Washington, D.C.: Association for Supervision and Curriculum Development, National Education Association, 1963.

SPACHE, GEORGE D., *Toward Better Reading*, Champaign, Ill.: Garrard, 1963.

12 Measuring and evaluating

Of the two terms in this chapter heading, evaluation is the more inclusive. Evaluation requires making judgments about the relative desirability of something in terms of a standard. For example, we evaluate how well a student is performing in a subject, his conduct in the gym, his motives, and the like. Measurement deals with the administration and scoring of tests of all types. We can measure through administering and scoring an achievement test. We can count the errors in capitalization, spelling, punctuation, and sentence structure in a theme. The number of correct exercises on an algebra assignment can be counted. These measurements are useful in subsequent evaluations. For example, an achievement test is administered and scored at the beginning and end of a semester. This measurement helps us in evaluating the progress made by the student.

Measuring and evaluating are important teacher responsibilities. Just as we decide what we want to measure outside educational settings, such as the length of a garment or the weight of a cut of meat, before developing or selecting measuring tools, so also we must determine educational objectives before deciding upon the measuring instruments. Statements of educational objectives were indicated previously in Chapter 1. In the next section of this chapter, different objectives are stated that were designed specifically to be related to evaluation in any subject field. This statement provides a framework for the subsequent discussions of teacher-made and standardized tests.

A TAXONOMY OF OBJECTIVES IN THE COGNITIVE DOMAIN

Educational objectives were formulated by Bloom[1] in terms of processes. The goal was to organize learner behavior into a relatively small number of categories that could be applied to all subject fields at all school levels. The principal part of this taxonomy deals with knowledge and five processes, called intellectual abilities or skills. Table 12.1 lists the main entries of the taxonomy.

---

[1] Benjamin S. Bloom, ed., *Taxonomy of Educational Objectives: Handbook I: Cognitive Domain* (New York: McKay, 1956), pp. 201–207.

TABLE 12.1. *Intellectual Abilities and Skills.*

1.00 Knowledge
    1.10 Knowledge of specifics
    1.20 Knowledge of ways and means of dealing with specifics
    1.30 Knowledge of the universals and abstractions in a field

2.00 Comprehension
    2.10 Translation
    2.20 Interpretation
    2.30 Extrapolation

3.00 Application

4.00 Analysis
    4.10 Analysis of elements
    4.20 Analysis of relationships
    4.30 Analysis of organizational principles

5.00 Synthesis
    5.10 Production of a unique communication
    5.20 Production of a plan, or proposed set of operations
    5.30 Derivation of a set of abstract relations

6.00 Evaluation
    6.10 Judgments in terms of internal evidence
    6.20 Judgments in terms of external criteria

SOURCE: Based on Benjamin S. Bloom, ed., *Taxonomy of Educational Objectives: Handbook I: Cognitive Domain* (New York: McKay, 1956), pp. 201–207. By permission.

How can schools move from these abstract statements to educational practices designed to develop these abilities in students? A good example is provided by the work of Sanders. Besides teaching social studies classes, Sanders works with teachers in improving their use of questions so that students will achieve more of the higher-level abilities. His main approach is through a systematic consideration of those teacher activities that require students not simply to remember information, concepts, and theories but to use them.

In his early work with teachers, Sanders clarified the terminology related to objectives with these examples:

1. *Memory:* The student recalls or recognizes information . . .
2. *Translation:* The student changes information into a different symbolic form or language
3. *Interpretation:* The student discovers relationships among facts, generalizations, definitions, values, and skills
4. *Application:* The student solves a life-like problem that requires the identification of the issue and the selection and use of appropriate generalizations and skills
5. *Analysis:* The student solves a problem in the light of conscious knowledge of the parts and forms of thinking
6. *Synthesis:* The student solves a problem that requires original, creative thinking
7. *Evaluation:* The student makes a judgment of good or bad, right or wrong, according to standards he designates[2]

These objectives are properly stated in terms of student behavior. As teachers arrange activities to achieve the objectives, they move from having students memorize information to having them use it in a variety of situations. In the process, they improve higher-level abilities. A possible procedure that a teacher might use for each process shows the relationship between the processes and the teacher-learning activities:

Memory: What is meant by *gerrymandering?* (The student is asked to recall the definition given to him earlier.)

Translation: The Encyclopedia of the Social Sciences defines gerrymander in this way:

> Gerrymander is a term to describe the abuse of power whereby the political party dominant at the time in a legislature arranges

[2] Norris M. Sanders, *Classroom Questions: What Kinds?* (New York: Harper & Row, 1966), p. 3. By permission.

constituencies unequally so that its voting strength may count for as much as possible at elections and that of the other party or parties for as little as possible.

Restate this definition in your own words.

Interpretation: Each county in the diagram of the mythical state has about the same population and is dominated by the designated political party A or B. The state must be divided into five voting districts of about equal population. Each district must contain three counties.

A	B	B	A	A
A	A	B	A	B
A	A	B	A	B

What is the greatest number of districts that party A could control if it is in charge of the redistricting and chooses to gerrymander? What is the greatest number of districts that party B could control if it is in charge of the redistricting and chooses to gerrymander? (The students have previously been given a definition of gerrymandering.)

Application: The mayor recently appointed a committee to study the fairness of the boundaries of the election districts in our community. Gather information about the present districts and the population in each. Determine whether the present city election districts are adequate. (The student is expected to apply principles of democracy studied in class to this new problem.)

Analysis: Analyze the reasoning in this quotation: "Human beings lack the ability to be fair when their own interests are involved. Party X controls the legislature and now it has taken upon itself the responsibility of redrawing the boundaries of the legislative election districts. We know in advance that our party will suffer."

Synthesis: (This question must follow the preceding application question.) If current election districts in our community are inadequate, suggest how they might be redrawn.

Evaluation: Would you favor having your political party engage in gerrymandering if it had the opportunity?[3]

You note that the activities and questions after "memory" involve thought processes different from mere recall or recognition. An additional example deals with the synthesis of information. Here is an initial suggestion to teachers about how to get started:

---

[3] *Ibid.*, pp. 3–5.

Directions: Which in this list do you believe are legitimate questions for collective bargaining?

A. How much should workers of various skills be paid?
B. How much should managers be paid?
C. How much vacation should workers have?
D. How fast should the assembly line move?
E. Is a particular worker incompetent and deserving of being discharged?
F. For what price should the products be offered for sale?
G. Who should be selected as officers of a company?
H. Should a new plant be constructed to expand production?
I. How much should be paid the owners of the company in dividends?
J. What new products should be produced?
K. How many laborers are required to do a certain job? . . .

. . . After studying this list, students are presented with this synthesis problem: *What principles or standards can you devise that would be helpful in determining which of the above questions should be decided by collective bargaining?*[4]

Sanders notes that the synthesis problem could be presented for individual study or for class discussion. The following ideas resulted from a class discussion:

A. Workers should have the right to bargain on questions that immediately and directly affect wages, hours, and working conditions. Current law gives them this right.
B. Managers should make decisions in which there is little or no conflict of interest with workers.
C. Manager and workers should participate in those decisions in which they have a special competency that the other side does not possess or possesses to a lesser degree.
D. A principle of capitalism gives owners a right to initiate and operate a business. Under laissez-faire capitalism this right was almost absolute, but it has been limited to an indefinite degree.[5]

The preceding ideas of the students resulted from their synthesis of other information, not from their having read and memorized the statements of someone else. Sanders does not indicate how much previous experience is needed to secure these responses. He cites several other examples of questions and activities that teachers in many subject fields use to facilitate the development of the higher-level abilities.

---

[4] *Ibid.*, pp. 132–133.
[5] *Ibid.*, p. 133.

TEACHER-MADE TESTS

The measurement and evaluation of student performances related to the previous objectives take many forms. For example, the performance or conduct of a student while engaged in study or some other activity can be observed and rated. Also, themes, exercises in mathematics, typing, an art object, and other samples of student work can be turned in to the teacher and evaluated. Objective and essay tests can be written, administered, and scored. All of these procedures are widely used and merit careful consideration.

Observation and rating

Teachers observe student performances; also in most school systems, they are required to rate and to report their ratings to the students, parents, and school officials. Frequently the school system incorporates its main objectives in the report form submitted to the student and parents. Although the main purpose of teacher observation and the subsequent rating of performances is not to provide information to the students and parents, the report forms appearing in Chapter 13 indicate the need for careful observation and subsequent rating. You may wish to turn to them before proceeding further to examine the behaviors and performances that are observed and rated rather than measured with a test of some type.

A rating scale provides for the results of observation to be put in numerical form. The simplest rating scales indicate two degrees, for example, excellent and poor. More discriminating scales incorporate more ratings—as many as the rater can reliably differentiate.

The accuracy of ratings is determined by the exactness with which a performance being rated is defined, the discrimination with which the various ratings are made, and the competence of the person performing the rating. A scale can be devised for rating any performance —a theme, a painting, the playing of a musical instrument; and for rating conduct—behavior toward the opposite and own sex, domination and withdrawal, and the like.

These guides may be useful in constructing rating scales:

1. Select qualities and performances for rating in relation to instruc-

tional objectives. Generally, it is unwise to rate students on a quality or performance that you do not attempt to develop in class.

2. Use rating scales for important objectives that cannot be appraised by other means. It is better to rate performance related to one or two objectives, and to do it well, than to organize many scales that might result in snap judgments.

---

1. APPEARANCE

well groomed; in good taste; exceptionally attractive	good appearance; appropriately dressed	noticeably ill-groomed; sloppy; careless; poor appearance

2. VOICE AND DICTION

| notably pleasant; well modulated; expressive | clear; adequate for good teaching; sufficiently expressive | inaudible; weak |
| | | obvious and annoying defects in quality, pitch, rate, articulation |

3. USE OF ENGLISH

| excellent word choice; exceptional accuracy, clarity, force in expression of ideas, in pronunciation, in usage | adequate command of language; ideas are understandable; good pronunciation and usage | ideas often hazy; meager vocabulary; habitual errors of usage, pronunciation |

FIG. 9 Student-teacher participator rating scale.

3. Carefully describe each rating in terms of your ability to discriminate performance and behavior related to it. It is better to use only three ratings—excellent, average, poor—that you can discriminate than to further subdivide into five, eight, or ten ratings with which you might have difficulty in discriminating.

4. Compare your ratings of an individual's performance with the ratings of another teacher who understands the scale and performs the rating at the same time.

5. Make your scales understandable to students so that they will aspire to achieve higher performances and so that they can rate themselves. Along with the usual areas of achievement and conduct, self-rating scales facilitate learning and self-evaluation by the students.

The first three items of a rating scale used by supervisors of student teachers are given in Figure 9. First rate yourself on each of the items, or traits. Study again the verbal descriptions of the ratings provided for each item. Do the verbal descriptions facilitate the rating? Study the items carefully and estimate which of the guides for constructing a rating scale were followed most effectively.

Checklists are similar to rating scales; however, they do not require evaluation in terms of a standard as do most rating scales. The checklist used in the count down when firing a manned spaceship is complex, requiring the use of a computer. It serves the purpose of checking things off according to a fixed schedule that must be followed if the firing is to be successful. In the assembly of classroom equipment, a checklist also is used. The teacher does not devise elaborate instruments; however, whether the student is making a dress or conducting an experiment, the teacher often has developed a checklist, either mentally or explicitly in written form. While observing the students' performances, he checks the sequence and accuracy of their activities. This checklist, of course, can become a rating scale if each step is rated on two or more bases such as right-wrong or appropriate-inappropriate.

Figure 10 is a combined checklist and rating scale. Notice the major four-phase sequence of Planning, Work Procedure, Product, and Clean Up. Within each phase are pertinent items on which the student is to rate herself and on which the teacher rates the student's performance. Refer back to the five guides for constructing a rating scale and evaluate this combined checklist and rating scale in terms of the guides. Consider, too, whether most teachers could develop a similar instrument that would be helpful to students in determining some of their main goals and in assuming responsibility for attaining them.

FOODS LABORATORY CHECK LIST
AND RATING SCALE

"To the Student: Study this check list carefully. I will answer any questions that you may have about it. Under Student's Score, put a 1, 2, 3, or 4 to mean:

1. Excellent
2. Very good
3. Satisfactory
4. Experienced difficulty

I will also give you a score and we will compare scores."

	Student's score	Teacher's score
PLANNING		
1. Were your plans complete—including an estimate of time and means of serving?	_____	_____
2. Did you save steps by assembling the supplies and equipment before you began work?	_____	_____
3. Did you select utensils and equipment suitable in size and type?	_____	_____
4. Did you use a reasonable amount of equipment?	_____	_____
5. Were you familiar with your recipe and methods?	_____	_____
WORK PROCEDURE		
1. Were you properly dressed and clean before starting your work?	_____	_____
2. Did you follow the directions and the plans you had made?	_____	_____
3. Did you help out if someone got behind?	_____	_____
4. Did you work cooperatively, quietly, and finish on time?	_____	_____
5. Did you dovetail work of preparation, serving, and clean-up?	_____	_____
6. Did you use small labor savers as trays, paper, brushes, etc.?	_____	_____
PRODUCT		
1. Was your garnishing and service appropriate and adequate?	_____	_____
2. Did your product come up to the standards you had decided upon?	_____	_____
3. If not, where did you make errors?	_____	_____
4. If so, what principles did you follow?		
5. What would you do differently?		
CLEAN UP		
1. Did you store your leftovers properly?	_____	_____
2. Did you properly wash the dishes and put them away?	_____	_____
3. Did you clean all of the equipment and put it away in its proper place?	_____	_____
4. Did you clean all soiled counters, table tops, sinks and stoves?	_____	_____
5. Did you finish clean-up on time?	_____	_____

FIG. 10 *Rating scale in food laboratory.*

Work samples

Work samples rather than written tests are used by many teachers. In business education, samples of typing, shorthand, and bookkeeping comprise adequate bases for evaluation. The student hands in work according to the instructions of the teacher; this constitutes the test. In mathematics, students are assigned work to be performed; they turn it in and the teacher scores or otherwise marks it. An outline map is given to the student in geography on which he places the names of countries, cities, rivers, products, and the like. If there are 30 entries, the teacher can simply count each correct entry to arrive at a total score. In the natural sciences, work samples are handled in the same manner. The work sample yields as useful evaluative information as any written test. The work sample can be arranged to measure a variety of educational outcomes and can be scored objectively.

Objective tests

The objective test was rarely used in American education at the turn of the century. Traditional essay tests were in general use. The situation is reversed today, even though many criticisms have been properly raised against objective tests that require only the recall of information. Objective tests can be written to measure recall. Although more difficult to write, they can also measure higher-level abilities such as application and evaluation. The principal types of objective test items are alternate choice, multiple choice, matching, and completion.

Alternate choice

An alternative-choice item requires the student to choose one of two answers as being more nearly correct.
Two Option:
   The revised Stanford-Binet Scale is administered (1) individually, (2) to groups.
   The Kuder Preference Record measures (1) interest, (2) aptitude.
True–False:
   Evaluation is more comprehensive than is measurement.
   Discovering the relative position of students in the class is a primary purpose of evaluation.

Yes–No:

Are all tests reported in *The Fifth Mental Measurements Yearbook* standardized?

Do both the Revised Stanford-Binet Scale and the Wechsler Intelligence Scale for Children yield a total IQ?

Right–Wrong:

A primary purpose of evaluation is to help students progress on learning tasks.

The Strong Interest Blank for Men is a self-report inventory.

Agree–Disagree:

The Rorschach technique is widely used by teachers.

The Iowa Test of Basic Skills is a standardized educational achievement test.

Same–Different:

Ratio IQ–Deviation IQ

General Intellectual Ability–Scholastic Aptitude

Examine these true–false items to discover poor construction:

Standardized tests scarcely ever have reliability coefficients of 1.00.

Essay tests should not be used infrequently in any course.

Aptitude and *ability* are synonymous.

We can agree that "scarcely ever" is vague; "not infrequently" makes the second item difficult to answer; and "aptitude" and "ability" usually have different meanings but may not always, depending on the context in which they are used.

The merits of alternate-choice tests are that they can be adapted to testing in many classes, a great deal of material can be tested in a short time, and they are easily scored. The weaknesses of alternate-choice tests are apparent: Guessing is encouraged; the learner is presented with a wrong as well as a right response; and it is extremely difficult to construct alternate-choice items in which either choice is always correct or always incorrect. When some items in the test are usually true and others are always true, the student is faced with the problem of deciding whether a usually true item should be marked true or false.

Multiple choice and multiple response

The multiple-choice item is used widely in standardized educational achievement tests because it is adaptable to measuring such outcomes as facts, understanding of concepts, the ability to apply information, and the ability to evaluate. Multiple-response items require the student to choose all the correct choices in a series. The following are examples of multiple-choice and multiple-response items:

Multiple choice

(Intended to test the ability to analyze information.)

> *Statement of facts:* The following table represents the relationship between the yearly income of certain families and the medical attention they receive.

Family income	Percent of family members who received no medical attention during the year
Under $1200	47
$1200 to $3000	40
$3000 to $5000	33
$5000 to $10,000	24
Over $10,000	14

> *Conclusion:* Members of families with small incomes are healthier than members of families with large incomes.
> *Assumption* (Select one):
> 1. Wealthy families had more money to spend for medical care.
> 2. All members of families who needed medical attention received it.
> 3. Many members of families with low incomes were not able to pay their doctor bills.
> 4. Members of families with low incomes did not receive medical attention.[6]

If it is assumed that the data and the problem are essentially new to the student, it requires that the student be able to identify the assumption which must be made to support the conclusion in relation to the data.

Multiple response

Which of the following are indicated by both Bloom and Sanders as educational abilities or skills that may serve as objectives?

---

[6] Nelson B. Henry, ed., *The Measurement of Understanding,* Forty-fifth Yearbook of the National Society for the Study of Education, Part I (Chicago: University of Chicago Press, 1946), p. 127. By permission.

1. Knowledge
2. Memory
3. Comprehension
4. Application
5. Synthesis

Multiple-choice and multiple-response items are more difficult to construct than are alternate-choice. Here are some guides that can be used as a checklist in making multiple-choice tests:

1. Select for each test item a concept or generalization of significance
2. Word the introductory statement and the choices clearly and concisely
3. Avoid use of identical words in the introductory statement and the correct choice
4. Include at least four choices to minimize guessing
5. Make the choices parallel in English construction; for example, start all choices with a verb, a noun, or a preposition
6. Make only one choice correct; in part this is accomplished through careful wording of the introductory statement
7. Make all choices plausible; choices readily recognized as incorrect are useless for testing purposes
8. Make the choices of equal length; when the correct choice is longer or shorter than the incorrect choices, the student may select it for that reason

Matching

Matching items call for pairing an item in the first column with a word or phrase in the second column. Some learning involves associating two things. Matching items measure whether the association has been made and whether the student recognizes it, not the extent to which meaning has been established. Matching items may have no distracters or several, as can be seen in the following examples:

Matching items with no distracter:
Match each item with the proper entry, A–D.

1. Denying the existence of some troublesome drive	A. Rationalization
2. Taking pride in the success of someone else	B. Identification

3. Accusing others of sins that tempt us   C. Repression
4. Finding excuses for our behavior that   D. Projection
   we know is improper

Matching items with a distracter:
Match each item with the proper entry, A–E. (Based on 1937 Revision
of Stanford-Binet Scale.)

1. Includes about 45 percent of the   A. IQ 70 and lower
   population
2. Includes about 2 percent of the   B. IQ 115–130
   population
3. Includes about 14 percent of the   C. IQ 90–110
   population   D. IQ 45–65
4. Can learn to read at a low level   E. IQ 24–45

Related materials should be used within groups of items to be
matched. For example, if association of synonyms and association of
men and events are to be tested, use two sets of items—the first dealing
with synonyms and the second with men and events. Also, do not
provide clues to the answers. Notice in the example with no distracter
that each item begins with a verbal and the things to be matched are
all nouns.

The possibility of guessing correctly is decreased through the use of
a distracter. Thus, in the example with no distracter if the student knows
two of the answers, he then has a 50–50 chance of guessing the other
two correctly. Furthermore, he may give the same answer for both
unknowns, thus assuring himself that one is correct. The same is not
possible with the distracter.

Completion

In completion items, words or phrases have been omitted; the student is to fill in the omitted word or phrases. This kind of test can
measure ability to recall or to perceive relationships. Here is a sample
of each:

Standardized tests that are consistent, that is, give similar results over
time, are said to be _____.
An aptitude test that predicts accurately college achievement has high
predictive _____.

The following are examples of poorly constructed completion items.

A _____ test score is meaningless until converted into a derived score.

The _____ Test measures intelligence.

_____ tests can be grouped into categories: _____.

In the first poorly constructed item, the use of the article A gives a clue to the answer; the second is vague and indefinite and any one of several answers is correct; and the third has so many missing words that it is impossible to tell what is wanted.

Guides for constructing objective tests

Teachers are accustomed to using a checklist or outline for preparing lesson plans or unit plans. A similar idea works for constructing objective tests. Stanley gives a meaningful group of guides for constructing classroom tests of achievement, most of them self-explanatory in terms of the previous discussion.

A. *Planning the Test*
   1. Adequate provision should be made for evaluating all the important outcomes of instruction
   2. The test should reflect the approximate proportion of emphasis in the course
   3. The nature of the test must reflect its purpose
   4. The nature of the test must reflect the conditions under which it will be administered

B. *Preparing the Test*
   1. Begin the preliminary draft of the test as soon as possible
   2. The test may include more than one type of item
   3. Most of the items in the final test should be of approximately 50 percent difficulty
   4. It is usually desirable to include more items in the first draft of the test than will be needed in the final form
   5. After some time has elapsed, the test should be subjected to a critical revision
   6. The item should be phrased so that the content, rather than the form of the statement, will determine the answer
   7. An item should be so worded that its whole content functions in determining the answer, rather than only a part of it
   8. All the items of a particular type should be placed together in the test
   9. The items of any particular type in the test should be arranged in ascending order of difficulty

10. A regular sequence in the pattern of correct responses should be avoided
11. Provision should be made for a convenient written record of the pupil's responses
12. The directions to the pupil should be as clear, complete, and concise as possible

C. *Trying Out the Test*
  1. Every reasonable precaution should be taken to insure excellent testing conditions
  2. The time allowance for the test should be generous
  3. The scoring procedure should be fairly simple
  4. Before the actual scoring begins, prepare answer keys and scoring rules

D. *Evaluating the Test*
  1. The difficulty of the test is a rough indication of its adequacy
  2. Individual items in the test should discriminate between pupils who rank high and those who rank low on the test as a whole
  3. It is a good practice to have the items interpreted and criticized by persons who have taken the test
  4. Whenever possible, the results on the test should be checked against an outside criterion
  5. It is sometimes desirable to estimate the reliability of the test[7]

Three of the guides warrant further discussion. Number 3 under "Preparing the Test" implies that the average score made by all students who take the test should be about 50 percent. This is desirable when the intent is to devise a test that spreads the scores from very low to very high. In many cases, however, the teacher wants to find out how well the students have learned what has been taught, for example, 20 spelling words during the week. In this case, the test is comprised of the 20 words, and if every student scores 100 percent the teacher is satisfied with the test. If the average score is 50 percent, the teacher is properly dissatisfied with his teaching methods or with the performances of the pupils.

The same idea applies to number 1 under "Evaluating the Test." A test, of course, has a low reliability coefficient when many students get most of the items correct. This in itself, however, is not adequate cause for selecting items that have not been taught or that the teacher thinks many students cannot for any other reason answer correctly.

---

[7] Julian C. Stanley, *Measurement in Today's Schools*, 4th ed., © 1964, pp. 171–201. Reprinted by permission of Prentice-Hall, Inc., Englewood Cliffs, New Jersey.

Under "Evaluating the Test," number 5 indicates the desirability of obtaining a reliability coefficient. Without computing a reliability coefficient, one can get a rough estimate of reliability by the following procedure: First, construct the best test possible and administer it. Secondly, score first the odd-numbered items and then the even-numbered items. Thirdly, record the score on the odd-numbered items and then on the even-numbered items for each individual. Now, if the two scores for each individual are exactly the same, your test is 100 percent reliable. Suppose it is a 100-item test and many individuals have differences in scores of four or more on the two parts, some scoring higher and some lower on part two as compared with their part one scores. Your test is not highly reliable. Suppose a student made a score of 38 on the 50 odd-numbered items and a score of 33 on the 50 even-numbered items. The percent correct for each part of the test is 76 and 66, respectively. Suppose 70 percent is a passing mark. Which of the two scores should be used to decide whether the student passed? Your marking system should not have finer limits than the reliability limits of the tests used in arriving at the scores.

Essay tests

An essay test item may be responded to in a few minutes, during a class period, or during a longer period of time. Inasmuch as objective type items can be constructed readily to measure such abilities as recall of information and comprehension, essay testing can be focused on assessing higher-level abilities, such as application, analysis, synthesis, and evaluation. Essay questions that utilize prior material in this chapter illustrate items designed to measure these abilities.

Application. Using the eight guides for constructing multiple-choice items previously listed, write four items based on the content of this chapter and specify how each guide was applied in one or more of the items.

Analysis. Analyze the reasoning in this statement: "The results of teacher-made tests have been used unwisely in failing students, causing them to drop out; therefore, teacher-made tests should be discontinued."

Synthesis. Based on your study of the eight guides for writing multiple-choice items and the actual writing of a few items, restate the guides so that they could be applied more readily by teachers in the subject field in which you are most interested.

Evaluation. Rearrange the eight guides for constructing multiple-choice items from first to last on the basis of their applicability to testing the subject matter of your major field. Justify your ordering.

Besides measuring higher-level abilities, essay tests also may enable the student to acquire better methods of studying in preparing for an essay test than for an objective test. English and other teachers use essay tests to encourage organizational abilities and to gain insight into the cognitive abilities of students.

Essay tests also have weaknesses. They may not cover a comprehensive area of the subject field and thus may have low content validity. Quality of handwriting and use of English may affect the tester's estimate of what is being measured. Essay tests may have low reliability, partly because only a few items can be answered during the test period and also because subjectivity enters into the scoring. Validity and reliability can be improved by constructing test items carefully, defining the criteria for scoring the tests, and comparing the marks given with those given by another competent teacher. Although essay tests take less time to write, they require much more time to score than do objective tests.

Self-reporting devices

Self-reporting devices include the questionnaire, checklist, autobiography, interview, and sociometric test. A common purpose of these devices is to secure information which will be useful in gaining a better understanding of the student as a person. The reader has undoubtedly supplied information about himself through responding to one or more of these devices and is thus aware of the accuracy of his responses. Also he may have questioned the use made of the responses and the extent to which the responses were held confidential.

Increasingly the public and teachers are concerned about privacy, including privacy for students. There seems to be little objection to having students express their opinions about any aspect of the instructional program, especially when the responses are summarized and each student's identity is thus "lost." Opinions and information about sex, race, religion, home conditions, and politics comprise a more sensitive area. Caution is justified in this connection, not because of public sentiment but because of respect for the privacy of the individual.

Obviously, research to improve education requires securing sensitive information at times. An individual student can also be understood better by the teacher when certain information is available. Although this is the case, we should carefully examine all information sought of a student to make certain that it is necessary and will be used to improve education for him. More information regarding the construction of self-reporting devices and also some cautions regarding their use and the use of published personality tests and inventories are presented by Klausmeier and Goodwin.[8]

STANDARDIZED TESTS

Two types of widely used standardized tests are those designed to measure general intellectual ability and those designed to measure educational achievement. Less widely used are tests of specific intellectual abilities, interest inventories, and personality tests. Standardized tests, regardless of what they are intended to measure, have some distinguishing characteristics.

Characteristics of standardized tests

Standardized tests have some readily identifiable features. Teachers at times are unaware of these for they do not receive copies of the manuals accompanying the tests. Therefore, we shall review four main characteristics of standardized tests: First, the items are carefully selected. If certain technical recommendations concerning an evaluative instrument have been followed, a systematic study has been made to determine the reliability, validity, and usability of the test. The type of validity and reliability is reported in the test manual.

A second characteristic of a standardized test is the instructions regarding administration. These instructions are in the manual for the guidance of the test administrator and, as necessary, on the test copy for the person being tested. The exact words to use in administering the test, the amount of time to allow for completion, and the type and amount of help and encouragement to give are clearly specified. For

---

[8] Herbert J. Klausmeier and William Goodwin, *Learning and Human Abilities,* 2nd ed. (New York: Harper & Row, 1966), Chapters 16, 17.

example, an older edition of the *Teacher's Manual, Iowa Tests of Basic Skills,* gives a brief overview of the test and then instructions for preparing to administer the test, including advance arrangements about seating, pencils, and scratch paper; administering the entire battery of tests within a time schedule; distributing and collecting test materials; timing the tests; marking the tests properly; and preparing the pupils for taking the tests.[9] (These are also important in preparing to administer a test that the teacher has constructed.)

Specific instructions for opening the first test period are given next. After these appear the instructions for pupils' putting their names on the answer sheets and for marking the answer sheets properly. The directions for administering the vocabulary test start as follows, with the first paragraph for the teacher's information and the next paragraph to be read to the pupils:

This test requires 17 minutes of actual working time. It should be administered immediately after giving instructions to pupils for marking the answer sheets, as directed in the preceding section.

(1) Begin by saying:

"We are now ready to begin work on the first test. This is a vocabulary test like the practice test we just studied. Find the section labeled Test V, Vocabulary, on your answer sheet near the top on the front side. (Pause.) Now place your answer sheet beside page 3 of your test booklet. (Pause.) We will read the directions at the top of page 3 to remind you of what you are to do. Read them silently while I read them aloud. They say:

"In each exercise, you are to decide which one of the four words has most nearly the same meaning as the word in heavy black type above them. Then, on the answer sheet, find the row of circles numbered the same as the exercise you are working on. You are to fill in the circle on the answer sheet that has the same number as the answer you picked. The sample exercise in the box at the right has already been marked correctly on the answer sheet."[10]

Next, instructions are given whereby the test administrator makes certain that the procedures are clearly understood by the pupils and that they get started properly with the first test item.

A third feature of a standardized test is the standardized scoring.

---

[9] E. F. Lindquist and Albert N. Hieronymus, *Manual for Administrators, Supervisors, and Counselors, Iowa Tests of Basic Skills* (Boston: Houghton Mifflin, 1956).

[10] *Ibid.,* p. 9.

Whether the student enters his response on the test copy or answer sheet, a scoring key is provided. For tests in which the items cannot be scored as right or wrong the instructions needed for making judgments are given. The *Handbook for Essay Tests, Level 1, College Sequential Tests of Educational Progress* suggests that students' essays be rated from one to seven, seven being the highest rating.[11] In the initial scoring on which the subsequent norms are based, the readers score on the basis of three factors: quality of thought—50 percent; style—30 percent; and conventions—20 percent.

Quality of thought was defined as ". . . the selection and the adequacy of ideas and supplementary details, and the manner of their organization (that is, the way in which their connections are derived from the arrangement of parts)."

Style was defined as ". . . clearness, effectiveness, and appropriateness, including matters of structure and diction, emphasis, the *means* of transition between ideas, and the finer points of simplicity, economy, variety, and exactness of expression."

Conventions was defined as ". . . the properties of mechanical form, including grammar and usage, capitalization, punctuation, and the mechanical aspects of the structure of sentences." A number of essays are then presented in the handbook with ratings and comments to guide the rater in making his judgments.

A fourth characteristic of standardized tests is the presence of established norms with which test scores can be interpreted in terms of grade equivalent, percentile, or other forms of derived scores. A norm is not a standard to be reached, but a range of values or scores, constituting the performances or scores made by the group on which the test was standardized. By design and definition, half the pupils in the nation will be below the median score, sometimes called the fiftieth percentile or average score.

Widely used standardized tests

Tests most frequently administered by teachers are educational achievement tests, general intellectual ability tests, often referred to as

---

[11] *Sequential Tests of Educational Progress, Handbook for Essay Tests, Level 1, College* (Princeton: Educational Testing Service, 1957).

scholastic or academic aptitude tests, and interest inventories. Teachers usually administer these tests to classroom groups, not to individual students. Other tests and inventories are used by school psychologists and counselors and are frequently administered to the student individually; also quite a number of instruments are used for research purposes.

Group tests of general intellectual ability

Group tests of general intellectual ability, sometimes called scholastic aptitude and mental ability, are used far more extensively in schools after the first grade than are individual tests of intelligence. The group tests do not require specially trained testers. For good results any group test requires that each student taking it understand the directions, want to do his best, and be physically and emotionally in good condition. A teacher in a class of 25 to 40 can observe each student fairly well to see that these conditions are met. When these tests are administered to large groups, it is more difficult to make certain that the three conditions are met.

Group tests of intellectual ability for use in school situations have been developed primarily to help make two types of decisions—what the student is ready to learn now and how well he will achieve in the future, in school, or in an occupation. In many cases, educational achievement tests give more direct answers to these questions, so that group intellectual ability tests are valuable supplements to achievement testing and provide good information in the absence of achievement testing. The achievement battery requires much more time to administer than the intellectual ability test.

Are IQs from different group tests comparable? Some tests yield higher IQs than others for all students, for the higher-IQ group only, or for the lower-IQ groups only. Differences among several commonly used group tests for small samples of subjects have been reported and can be studied by school people. A better way for a large school system to build its testing program is to set up carefully designed studies to ascertain testing needs. Caution must be exercised in judging how well a student will learn any subject matter when the judgment is based on only one IQ score.

Tests of educational achievement

Tests of educational achievement are designed to measure the extent to which students have acquired various outcomes of instruction. Early educational achievement tests measured knowledge and skills closely related to specific subject fields; they gave little attention to such outcomes as problem-solving abilities, understanding of principles, application of principles or knowledge, or evaluation of facts. More recent tests are attempting to measure the latter type of outcomes. Nevertheless, the best tests should not be treated as providing final or complete evidence about the quality of the educational program of a school or of a teacher's work in the school, or as an adequate basis for deciding what the objectives of instruction should be. Instead, they provide some evidence that fits into a balanced continuous evaluation program in which the objectives of education are stated clearly and a variety of teacher judgments and informal evaluation procedures also are used. In general, standardized achievement tests have been used too little to provide understanding of a pupil's present achievements and too much to categorize pupils and to grade.

Educational achievement tests are the most valuable of all standardized tests for use in a variety of school situations. They provide more direct information about each student's performances and abilities in relation to the school's central objectives than do any other currently available type of test. Further, one of the better sources of information to which a teacher can turn for finding models of well-constructed achievement test items is printed tests.

Interest inventories

During later adolescence, interests tend to become stable. Also, expressed interest in an immediate activity in the classroom provides a favorable motivational set toward the activity. Teachers seem to be able to ascertain the interests of students in immediate classroom activities. However, deciding which of many possible courses of study and occupations will be of interest after high school graduation is a more difficult task. Interest inventories have been developed mainly to facilitate this type of educational and vocational decision-making. Their efficacy with high school students, however, has not been fully established.

In an interest inventory, the respondent checks his preferences for a large number of activities. In this manner, the preferences of the respondent for many activities can be compared with those of other individuals in the standardization populations. The administration of interest inventories is fully as standardized as administration of educational achievement tests. However, the interpretation of interest inventories is not standardized, especially for junior and senior high school students who are not yet in adult occupations and whose interests are still in the formative stage. Much additional information beyond that from an interest inventory should be used in discussing with a student his occupational and other interests. At present, school people properly give much more weight to results from achievement and intellectual ability tests than to results from interest inventories in planning high school courses with the students.

Personality tests

Some theorists classify interest and intelligence as personality traits. Problems in personality testing were presented some time ago by Cronbach, including such matters as the respondent's faking the answers, the concealing of the purpose of the test from the respondent, and ethical issues in personality testing. This last is of the highest importance. Cronbach concludes,

> There remains the question of using personality tests when the tester has authority over the person tested. The psychologist diagnosing mental patients, the military psychologist, or the school teacher can enforce tests on his charges. The standards with regard to such practice probably should vary from institution to institution. In general, it seems that subtle tests may properly be used if they are valid and relevant in making decisions which would otherwise rest on less valid information. The tester should avoid misrepresentation in giving the tests. For example, it is quite improper to study an individual's beliefs under the guise of an opinion poll. Test records made for employee counseling should never be made available to the employee's superior.[12]

***

[12] Lee J. Cronbach, *Essentials of Psychological Testing*, 2nd ed. (New York: Harper & Row, 1960), p. 462. By permission.

Recently, increasing concern has been expressed about the use of personality testing in the schools. The publishers of personality tests intend them to be used primarily in understanding and guiding the student more effectively. In this respect, it should be noted that the meaning of these test results is not as clear as are the results from intelligence and achievement tests. We have not yet defined personality as clearly as we have intellectual abilities and educational achievements. The school system that uses personality tests would do well to carry out longitudinal research to ascertain the meaning of the scores and profiles.

VALIDITY AND RELIABILITY OF TESTS

Teacher-made and standardized instruments and procedures have been discussed in the preceding sections. For what purposes do teachers administer them? Perhaps the two most important purposes are to understand the student so that a better instructional program can be arranged for him and to evaluate his progress in learning or to ascertain how much he has learned. This information can subsequently be used for many purposes, one of which is to report to the student and parents as mentioned briefly at the outset of this chapter.

When using a published or teacher-made instrument, a teacher should be concerned with the validity of the test for achieving certain purposes. One of the main purposes, as indicated before, is to understand the student better in order to be able to organize effective instruction for him. Here we are concerned with the predictive validity of a test. We want to administer a test now—general intellectual ability, educational achievement, interest, or some other—that will be useful in predicting how the student will perform in the future. Predictive validity is concerned with the relation of current test scores to measures of performance at some time in the future. To plan a program of instruction for the second semester, based on performance this semester, we need scores or ratings now that will help us make the judgment about the future performance.

In order to write a test that does indicate how well the student has learned thus far, we need to sample from among all the things that he was supposed to learn. If he was to memorize information and also to improve in his abilities to apply, synthesize, and evaluate information, then we must be sure to sample from both (1) all the content or information that was to be learned and (2) all the abilities to be improved. Content validity is concerned with sampling a specified amount or universe of content, content being defined to include not only subject matter information but also skills or abilities.

Reliability refers to the extent to which a test or other instrument measures accurately or consistently. Although we cannot construct educational and psychological tests that are as accurate as linear and liquid measures—rulers and quart cans, for example—we may be able to construct better tests by considering some factors that produce low reliability.

Previously we have recommended general procedures for constructing tests. A test may be unreliable because of poorly constructed items that do not discriminate between students who possess the knowledge or skill being tested and those who do not. For example, if all students who do not know the material equally well get nearly all the items wrong or right, the items are not discriminating and low reliability will result.

The length of the test may also be related to reliability. A single spelling word or science concept is a poor and inadequate sample of a student's total performance. If only eight items are given, one student may guess three or four correctly. Chance would thus be an important determiner of the scores obtained. In a test of 50 items, we get more dependable scores because variations accounted for by guessing more likely cancel out. A test can, however, be made so long that students become tired or bored and respond unreliably.

Low reliability may result from inadequate scoring methods. This was pointed to as a principal weakness of essay tests. Tests in which unequal weights are given to items also are subject to low reliability, particularly if the students are unaware of the unequal weights. For example, if ten items of a 45-item test are scored ten points each and the other 35 are scored one point each, missing one or two of the former greatly lowers the score. It is good practice to inform students of the weights assigned to each item so that they can apportion their time accordingly.

Finally, reliability is lowered by insufficient time to complete the test in any test where time is not a criterion of performance. This is a difficult problem to overcome, for the rate at which students respond to a test varies markedly. If time is called when the first half of the group is finished, one cannot be certain how the other half would have scored had time been allotted for them to finish.

Undoubtedly you have taken tests that you judged to be low in content validity, or reliability, or both. Many students at all school levels complain that they are tested on material that was not emphasized in the course. Here low content validity is indicated. High-achieving students on some tests score in the lower half of a class, even though they have studied hard. Here low reliability is probably the cause. More attention by teachers to these matters could lead to significant improvement in student attitudes toward school and performance.

SUMMARY

For decades, high school teachers have been limiting themselves largely to the use of three types of measuring instruments: Objective tests to measure the students' memory and comprehension of information; essay tests to measure the students' ability to recall and organize information; and ratings of work completed by the students. In recent years, as the nature of abilities is becoming better understood, objective tests, essay tests, and other instruments and procedures are being developed to measure such abilities as to apply, to analyze, to synthesize, and to evaluate information in the various subject fields. This is a desirable direction in which to proceed, for what is tested tends also to be positively associated with what is learned. If a teacher wishes to develop the higher-level abilities of students, measurement and evaluation procedures should be developed to assess student progress toward this objective.

A comprehensive program of measurement and evaluation is required in the school in order to determine the extent to which significant objectives are achieved. Necessary are teacher-developed instruments and procedures: observations and ratings, work samples, objective tests, essay tests, and self-reporting devices. Also required are standardized tests, particularly tests of educational achievement and intellectual ability.

In constructing tests, the teacher is concerned with the reliability and validity of the tests. The goal is to devise tests and other procedures that measure reliably, as reliably or accurately, for example, as a yardstick or ruler. The instrument or procedure should always have high content validity; that is, it should sample from all the knowledge and abilities the students were supposed to have acquired as a result of instruction during the period included in the instrument.

QUESTIONS AND ACTIVITIES

1 Sanders defines seven mental processes related to content in any subject field that can serve as instructional objectives. Give two examples of each of them related to the content of this chapter; that is, indicate two things that might be memorized, translated, interpreted, or applied. Discuss these with two or three other students who have done the same thing.

2 Write two test items or activities for each of the objectives in Number 1 preceding. Review the sample objective and essay items presented in this chapter that have the same purposes.

3 Related to your major field of study and interest arrange the following types of tests from highest to lowest in terms of their possible use in classes that you teach: Teacher-made essay tests; teacher-made objective tests; teacher-made rating scales; student work samples; standardized tests of educational achievement; and standardized tests of intellectual ability. After putting them in rank order, discuss why you ordered them as you did.

4 Construct a rating scale of five or six items that require student self-rating and teacher rating. Have a few students who might use it provide suggestions for improvement.

5 List types of information that you think teachers might ethically secure from all their students by use of self-reporting devices, including interviews. Indicate which of these you would fully provide to your instructors.

6 Discuss the conditions that might lead to low content validity of a test. Indicate next the conditions that might lead to low reliability of a test.

7 Study each of the preceding questions and indicate whether it calls primarily on your part for memory, translation, application, synthesis, or evaluation, or some combination of these.

SUGGESTIONS FOR FURTHER READING

BLOOM, BENJAMIN, S., ED., *Taxonomy of Educational Objectives: Handbook I: Cognitive Domain*, New York: McKay, 1956.

CRONBACH, LEE J., *Essentials of Psychological Testing*, 2nd ed., New York: Harper & Row, 1960.

ENGELHART, MAT D., *Improving Classroom Testing; What Research Says to the Teacher*, No. 31, Washington, D.C.: National Education Association, 1964.

GOROW, FRANK F., *Better Classroom Testing*, San Francisco: Chandler, 1966.

LYMAN, HOWARD, *Test Scores and What They Mean*, Englewood Cliffs, N.J.: Prentice-Hall, 1963.

MICHAEL, WILLIAM B., ED., "Educational and Psychological Testing," *Review of Educational Research*, 35, No. 1, 1965.

SANDERS, NORRIS M., *Classroom Questions: What Kinds?* New York: Harper & Row, 1966.

STANLEY, JULIAN C., *Measurement in Today's Schools*, 4th ed., Englewood Cliffs, N.J.: Prentice-Hall, 1964.

13 *Reporting pupil progress*

*M*rs. Jones inspects the beef at the self-service counter of the grocery store. She examines it and thinks: Boneless roast beef, "Choice," 99¢ a pound. Can't afford to spend that much today. . . . There's another roast. Label says "Good," 81¢ a pound. Still too much. . . . Ah, here it is. "Commercial," 60¢ a pound. I'll take this three-pound package. . . . And here are some bones for the dog.

Mrs. Jones shops carefully. Sometimes she buys the choice grade, at other times the good or the commercial. Grading of meat is a real help to her. She examines the grades on canned foods and other products; this is helpful, too.

The Jones children, Mary and Bill, are in the eleventh and ninth grades of school, respectively. Mrs. Jones loves Mary and Bill. Her hopes for each are high. She wants them to behave well, to learn well, and to be good citizens. She feels that Mary and Bill are "choice" children, certainly not "good," "commercial," or even a lower grade.

Mrs. Jones, new to this community and school, has just received report cards which she examines more carefully than her meat purchases. But she is not sure how to interpret the grades on the report cards. She thinks: What do they mean? Mary had a C in United States history. Does that mean she is "good" or "commercial grade"?

And Bill had an F in English. I know he doesn't like English, but he did try. I helped him as best I could. I wonder, did Bill really fail? . . . No doubt about it, Bill thinks he did and wants to quit school. I wonder how Miss Blytt, the English teacher feels about him. . . .

Perhaps Mrs. Jones' predicament is more acute than that of many parents. Some schools help parents interpret grades and report cards more accurately. But grading on a comparative basis in subject achievement only is still widely used, and in some instances the letter grades in the various subjects are the main entries on the report card. The report card in turn is the principal informational link between the teacher and parent, the school and community.[1]

Much improvement remains to be made in reporting secondary school students' progress to their parents. Many high schools are years behind the elementary schools in the form of their reporting. In part, this shortcoming is attributable to the fact that high school teachers have many more students than elementary school teachers have. In part, it is attributable to the emphasis given in the present decade to preparing students for college. Or, again, it is sometimes occasioned by the parents' reluctance to relinquish a grading system that is familiar, if meaningless, to them. Nevertheless, in few areas of life outside the school is an attempt made to grade people on a five- or six-point scale. In most areas of adult life, emphasis is on a person's progress in his job and in helping him and others make reliable judgments as to how effective he is when compared with others.

In present-day use, the assigning of grades serves several purposes: (1) Grades have an administrative function. For example, grades serve as a permanent record for future employers to examine and are one criterion that college admission authorities consider. They are also the basis for promotion, graduation, or transfer to another school. (2) Grades have a guidance function. They serve as a basis for informing the student what skills, attitudes, and knowledge he needs to acquire at the moment. And they are a factor used by guidance personnel, teachers, and administrators in discussing with a student the probability of his success in a future vocation or profession, and in further education. (3) Grades have an information-giving function—to parents and to other teachers. (4) Grades have a motivational function in the classroom, as rewards or punishment. A certain type of student—middleclass, college-bound—will perform many learning tasks that he might not otherwise do to please his parents or to work toward a relatively far-distant goal. Both authors have observed classes in which the teacher motivated the writing of a paper, the answering of questions at the end

[1] Herbert J. Klausmeier, "Grading, Reporting, and Public Relations," *The High School Journal*, XL (January, 1957), 146–147. By permission.

of a chapter, or the committing to memory of a list of facts by threatening a zero, rather than motivating students through making the goal seem purposeful.

The opinion of these authors is that using grades for report cards and for permanent records, an arbitrary process at best, is only one step in reporting pupil progress. Other necessary and valid steps in a well-organized reporting system will emphasize progress in learning as of primary importance and will involve parent-teacher and student-teacher conferences. In the teacher's reporting, progress, not grades, should be emphasized. Grading should lead to student growth.

Progress in areas of learning other than subject-matter achievement should be reported, also. By observing pupils as they engage in various learning activities, the teacher gains important information about such things as the pupil's future plans; the pupil's conduct; the pupil's level of motivation and interest in school activities; the pupil's ability to work and learn independently; and the pupil's attitudes toward classmates, teachers, and self. These observations, too, must go into a well-organized reporting system.

In the next section of this chapter several marking systems presently used in the secondary school are presented, the rationale behind the use of the marking systems is discussed, and sample report cards are presented. Then, in the remainder of the chapter, a well-organized reporting system is described in terms of five characteristics:

1. Progress in learning is of primary importance
2. Comparative achievement is also important
3. Progress toward many important objectives must be considered
4. The reporting system is understood
5. Parent-teacher conferences are used

MARKING SYSTEMS

One system of grading fairly commonly employed in secondary schools is the percentage system, which is based on a 100-point scale. A score of 100 constitutes a perfect mark; 70–100 is passing or satisfactory. A score between 93–100 is translated as A and represents "excellent work"; 85–92 is termed B work and is often described by the words "above average." "Average" falls between 77–84 and is labeled C. A score between 70–76 is D work and characterizes the "below-average" student. Achievement below 70 represents "failure," an F. Report cards using the percent type of grade give little information and are difficult to interpret. Interpretation of the grade necessitates knowing the grading practices of the teacher assigning it in some detail. The percentage system also assumes a precision that is sometimes deceiving. Cutting-off points dictate that a student with 93 is an A student and that a student with 92 is a B student. If the teacher is an expert at constructing objective tests and if the goals are largely subject-matter goals, the percentage system is somewhat meaningful. But often, such marks quantify the trivial. And how does one indicate in terms of a 100-point scale complex attitudes and abilities?

Probably, the most widely used system consists of symbols on a five-point scale. These symbols are A, B, C, D, F, or 1, 2, 3, 4, 5. Each group has four categories of passing and satisfactory performance, and one category for failing or unsatisfactory performance. Some teachers add a + or − to these symbols in an attempt to achieve greater precision. Involving fewer categories than the 100-point scale, the letter grade can be defined with more precision than can the percent grade. The problem with any symbol is, of course, the matter of its denotation and connotation. Instructions need to indicate the referent of each symbol. J. N. Hook, in a book used for several decades in methods courses for English teachers, has defined items on the five-point symbol scale A, B, C, D, F as follows:

> The grade of A is distinctly a mark of superiority. It represents much more than mere competence in meeting assignments. There is a "plus factor" involved: The A student does not only what is expected of him but goes beyond it. He dares to be himself; he dares to use his initiative; he does not require prodding. Even his occasional failures are magnificent failures; like the late Babe Ruth, he strikes out with a mighty swing. He works well with the group and often assumes leadership in group undertakings.
>
> The grade of B indicates a high level of accomplishment, with the "plus factor" diminished. It represents less originality, less artistry, less depth of analysis than the A; yet all three qualities are sometimes present. A student may receive a B because he is in ability an A student who has not lived up to his potentialities, or because he is in ability a C student who has worked hard enough to pull himself up by his own bootstraps, or because he is an able student who does most things well

but does not possess a sufficient amount of ability, initiative, or aggressiveness to merit an A. The B student usually cooperates well with the group and sometimes assumes leadership.

The grade of C represents mediocrity of accomplishment (in the old sense of mediocris, meaning "in a middle state"). The student who is given a C has done what he was asked to do, but probably little more, possibly a little less. The quality of his accomplishment is neither high nor low. Sometimes a C is given a student poorer than average in ability who has worked hard enough to deserve it; sometimes it is given to a capable student who does not try to live up to his ability. Usually, though, the C goes to the student who is not very high or very low in native ability, energy, and productiveness. The C student cooperates fairly well with the group but rarely volunteers to lead.

The grade of D covers a multitude of sins, such as carelessness, indifference, sluggishness, or laziness. Or it may come as the result of virtually insurmountable handicaps such as low native ability, slowness in learning, or physical defects, over which neither teacher nor student has much control. Or the D may result from lack of reading skill, lack of ability to speak and write well, and inability to concentrate—all of which may be subject to correction. The D student is often pathetically eager to learn and hence may cooperate well; sometimes, though, he may be surly and resentful until the teacher gets his confidence. Only in the few areas where he believes himself skilful is he willing to accept leadership.

The grade of F indicates indifference and failure to try. It is not given to the student who plugs away, doing his pitiful best. In high school English (not necessarily in mathematics and kindred subjects) everyone who tries conscientiously to reach the objectives of the course deserves to pass. But the one who regularly loafs, who apparently does not care, who procrastinates, who fails to cooperate, who does not do the work that others do, deserves an F.[2]

Another system, designed in an attempt to avoid the arbitrary features of the percentage system and the five-point scale, indicates only "pass" or "fail," or "satisfactory" or "unsatisfactory." This system does tend to eliminate harmful competition. But, on the whole, teachers and parents have not been satisfied with this method of rating. It does not reflect a student's progress; it does not show how a student achieves in relation to his classmates.

Still another system is grading on a normal distribution curve. To use this technique, one predetermines the percentage of students to re-

---

[2] J. N. Hook, *The Teaching of High School English*, 3rd ed. (New York: Ronald, 1965), pp. 75–76. By permission.

ceive an A, B, C, D, or F. (Later in your course work in professional education, you will study the distribution of scores based on standard deviations and on the normal probability curve. At any rate, grading on the curve is undergirded by theory formulated by statisticians.) Four frequently used distributions of marks, presented in terms of the percent of students receiving a certain grade, are given in Figure 11. Marks given

Grade	Percentage of students per mark			
A	3	5	7	10
B	22	20	24	20
C	50	50	38	40
D	22	20	24	20
F	3	5	7	10

FIG. 11 *Several systems for assigning grades on a normal distribution curve.*

through the use of the normal distribution curve indicate neither progress nor the quality of work.

Finally, reports are sometimes made in descriptive systems. The report card is eliminated as the means of teacher-parent communication. The teacher writes to or talks to the parents of his own observations of a student's work habits, citizenship, performance compared with other students in the same grade, of progress in attaining subject-matter content and skills, and so on. The likelihood is that such a system results in effective communication.

REPORT CARDS

Figures 12a and 12b show a traditional but widely-used report card. On the front of this card (Figure 12a), each teacher gives the student a grade in each subject and makes a check in the effort column to indicate his concern with the student's progress. The reverse side (Figure 12b) contains an explanation of the grading system.

A majority of teachers continue to report comparative achievement in single letter grades. Few junior and senior high school teachers seriously attempt to appraise and report student progress toward the important objectives of the school. Many teachers have only a vague idea of any student's progress in reading, writing, speaking, listening, or study

FIG. 12b A traditional report card (reverse).

WEST SENIOR HIGH SCHOOL Home Room Number............

Report Card Giving Teachers' Estimate of the Accomplishment

of............ ....for the semester ending............, 19....

SUBJECTS	Grade Period 1	Effort	Grade Period 2	Effort	Grade Period 3	Final Exam. Grade	Final Sem. Grade	TEACHER
1.								
2.								
3.								
4.								
5.								
6.								

Absence

A check (/) in the Effort column indicates the teachers' concern relative to this area.

H. R. Teacher............

FIG. 12a A traditional report card (front).

habits, from the seventh to the twelfth grade. If teachers were required to estimate the amount of progress and to report it to parents, there could be a more consistent attempt by both teacher and parents to help each student make progress in school learning.

Figure 13a is the front side of the comprehensive report form used in the Monona Grove High School, Madison, Wisconsin. Each quarter, parents receive a report for each subject in which the student is enrolled. A letter grade of A to F is given in each of three areas: individual performance; knowledge and skills in subject; and school citizenship. These three areas receive equal weight in assigning a letter grade for total growth and performance. Three marks—minus, no, and plus—are recorded for 13 subareas: works up to ability; has a positive attitude; shows self-direction; and so on. On the back of the report form (Figure 13b) is space for parent or teacher comments.

Note that each teacher who has the student in class rates behavior according to the three main objectives of the school: To encourage desirable citizenship behavior, to encourage desirable individual growth in each pupil, and to encourage an optimum development of knowledge and skills in the subject.

At the Monona Grove High School, the individual's performance is considered a valuable indication of both his present and future success: His ability to plan, organize, and execute work; his skills in supervised study, in solving problems, in group research, in group discussion, and in individual research projects. The student is evaluated in these areas in relation to his own ability.

School citizenship represents performance and growth toward the qualities of a competent, cooperative, participating student. Such factors as care of personal and school property and effective cooperation in group projects are considered in this area. But school citizenship involves more than merely not causing trouble: It involves contributing to the welfare of other students and to the school.

Knowledge and skills in a subject include an evaluation of academic achievement through demonstrations, discussion, notebooks, projects, reports, and tests. Although less than the total growth and performance related to all educational objectives, knowledge and skills in the subject are more than an acquisition of skills and memorization of facts.

Figure 14 shows a progress form developed by Karl Gates for an

ACCUMULATED GRADE POINT INTERPRETATION

QUARTER	
FIRST	.7 to 0 = A+ to F
SECOND	.9 to 0 = A+ to F
THIRD	1.1 to 0 = A+ to F
FOURTH	1.3 to 0 = A+ to F

FINAL GRADE	
4.4 - 3.6	A
3.5 - 2.6	B
2.5 - 1.6	C
1.5 - .6	D
.5 - .0	F

TO PARENTS—

We share with you a mutual interest in helping your son or daughter become an academically and socially competent person. We encourage your understanding and ask for your cooperation.

THE FACULTY
Monona Grove High School

DATE	PARENT OR TEACHER COMMENTS

SIGNATURE OF PARENT OR GUARDIAN

FIRST QUARTER _____

SECOND QUARTER _____

THIRD QUARTER _____

If a conference with the teacher is desired, please check space above or telephone 222-1291

FIG. 13b Interpretation of student's grade point average.

REPORT TO STUDENTS AND PARENTS

MONONA GROVE HIGH SCHOOL — MADISON, WIS.

Fr. ☐ Jr. ☐
So. ☐ Sr. ☐

Name _____

Subject _____

Mr.
Teacher Mrs. _____
Miss

Home Room Teacher

Term beginning September 8, 1964 — ending June 15, 1965

GRADING SYSTEM

A=4.4 - 3.5 D=1.4 - 0.6   + Mark indicates superior achievement
B=3.4 - 2.6 F=0.4 - 0.0   No Mark indicates average achievement
C=2.4 - 1.5 Inc=Incomplete — Mark indicates need for improvement

	First Quarter	Second Quarter	Third Quarter	Fourth Quarter	
					FINAL EVALUATION
					KNOWLEDGE AND SKILLS AVERAGE

INDIVIDUAL PERFORMANCE
Works up to ability
Has a positive attitude
Shows self-direction
Plans work wisely

SCHOOL CITIZENSHIP
Is courteous and considerate of others
Is responsible
Contributes his share
Is a good leader or follower
Takes care of school, personal property

KNOWLEDGE & SKILLS IN SUBJECT
Develops skills
Indicates knowledge by assignments
Recites effectively
Scores satisfactorily on examinations

TOTAL GROWTH & PERFORMANCE
ACCUMULATED GRADE POINT

Days Absent
Times Tardy

(over)

FIG. 13a Report to students and parents. (Courtesy Mo-

individualized, student-centered English-history program for academically able students, grades 9 through 12, at Ridgewood High School, Norridge, Illinois. Utilizing the best features of new settings for learning (small student-centered seminars, as well as large-group instruction and a learning laboratory), the teachers serve as resource persons. Students are permitted to plan their own programs in English-history; they may deviate from the planned curriculum to pursue depth, or quest, work for as long as they like. Students determine the point at which they want to be tested over units. Papers are not graded, but are discussed in individual sessions with the teacher; when he is satisfied with his work, the student files his paper in a permanent record. To get students to accept responsibility for learning, to remove barriers to learning, to de-emphasize grading, the teachers in the program guarantee each student an A. The Individual Progress Report is issued to students whenever the instructors think it appropriate. The Individual Progress Report does not replace the standard report card, but is a step toward trying to report student progress more effectively than can be done by the standard report card. Of course, the standard report card for each of the students in the humanities program bears an A.

Note in Figure 14 the provision to estimate a student's performance in each of the program's major educational objectives in comparison with other students in the same phase of work. Note that mastery of the subject matter occupies only two of the items rated. Each student, and his parents, knows which goal requires greater effort, which goal he excels in.

PROGRESS IN LEARNING IS
OF PRIMARY IMPORTANCE

Suppose that in her English class, Miss Blytt accepts as her main task helping each student make progress in various phases of speaking, listening, reading, spelling, and writing. She evaluates Bill Jones' standing in these areas early in the semester and finds him especially poor in reading, spelling, and composition. Then Miss Blytt organizes activities to help Bill and the other students make progress. And Bill improves in spelling, punctuating, and capitalizing; in using the dictionary in read-

PROGRESS TOWARD INDEPENDENT LEARNING

Helping students learn to accept responsibility for their own learning is a major school objective. Comments below reflect each teacher's estimate of your progress to date.

ENGLISH	HISTORY

TEST PERFORMANCES—ENGLISH

American Lit.　　　English Lit.

_____ High Pass
_____ Pass
_____ Low Pass
_____ Inc.

INDIVIDUAL PROGRESS REPORT —HUMANITIES
Ridgewood High School
Norridge, Illinois

Student's Name: _____
Phase: _____
English Teacher: _____
History Teacher: _____
Date of Report: _____

SCHOOL PERFORMANCES

The following statements represent goals of the school's educational program. Ratings reflect each teacher's estimate of your position in your ability group.

RATING SCALE

W-top third. M-middle third. L-lower third: O-inadequate basis for judgment

ENGLISH READING COMPLETED TO DATE

	English	History
Expresses ideas clearly in writing	W M L O	W M L O
Utilizes speaking techniques effectively	W M L O	W M L O
Integrates knowledge learned	W M L O	W M L O
Demonstrates mastery of subject matter facts	W M L O	W M L O
Demonstrates theoretical understanding of subject	W M L O	W M L O
Performs on subject matter tests	W M L O	W M L O
Accepts responsibility for group's progress	W M L O	W M L O
Stimulates group with fresh ideas	W M L O	W M L O
Respects opinions of others	W M L O	W M L O
Evidences independent thought and originality	W M L O	W M L O
Seeks knowledge beyond basic requirements	W M L O	W M L O

FIG. 14　Individual progress report. (Courtesy of Karl Gates, Ridgewood High School, Norridge, Illinois.)

ing, writing, and spelling; and in speaking with greater ease and clarity. Toward the end of the reporting period, Miss Blytt's best estimate of Bill's progress is:

Speaking: Excellent progress with usual teacher help
Listening: Average progress with usual teacher help
Reading: Needs additional help
Spelling: Slow progress with much teacher help
Composition: Slow progress with much teacher help

From the papers Miss Blytt hands back to Bill, from the discussions that follow panel and individual reports, from the annotations on his themes, and from other evaluative devices such as those outlined in Chapter 12, Bill himself learns where he is making good progress and where he needs to improve. His knowledge of his progress, his feelings of success, and Miss Blytt's sincere interest encourage him to continue trying.

However, Bill Jones becomes discouraged when his parents and his friends see an F on his report card, a card that gives him no credit for his effort and progress. He believes that Miss Blytt thinks him a complete failure, although she has enabled him to see some progress from time to time. Miss Blytt assigned a single mark, F, in accordance with school or departmental policy. Had she been permitted to report Bill's progress in five areas in English, Bill might not have wanted to quit school; he would have continued to want to profit from Miss Blytt's helpful guidance. The teacher-student relationship would have remained pleasant, would not have become strained.

To live comfortably with themselves, most human beings need to receive approval from age-mates, teachers, and parents; to maintain self-respect and a feeling of well-being toward themselves; and to achieve success. Insofar as a student feels the need to learn subject content and skills and can set realistic goals, the teacher should do everything to help the student overcome fears of failure and should aid him in making progress toward his goal. Miss Blytt's making a positive statement on specific achievements, rather than a single arbitrary gross appraisal, might have avoided Bill Jones' becoming frustrated and wanting to give up his efforts.

COMPARATIVE ACHIEVEMENT IS ALSO IMPORTANT

By the time a student is in his last years in the secondary school, he and his parents should know his strengths and weaknesses quite clearly. A career cannot be planned wisely without this information. Therefore, the reporting system should inform parents how the student compares with other students in the various subject areas, as well as in all other important areas of school learning.

To illustrate how comparative achievements of high school students might be reported, let us assume that Miss Blytt knew that Bill had an IQ of approximately 90 and a grade placement of 7.0 in reading at the beginning of the ninth grade. At the end of the first reporting period, she estimated that he was in the lowest third of the class in reading, spelling, and composition; in the middle third in listening; and in the highest third in oral expression. This was her best estimate; but it was tentative, for she realized that by the end of the semester his position might change in one or more of the five areas. Instead of giving Bill an F because he was very low in comparison with other students, she might have indicated her estimates at the end of the first reporting period as follows:

Speaking: In the highest third of the class
Listening: In the middle third of the class
Reading: In the lowest third of the class
Spelling: In the lowest third of the class
Composition: In the lowest third of the class

Although Bill might find it difficult to accept being in the lowest third of the class in three areas, it would be better for him to know this than to receive an F in spite of his efforts.

Another teacher might estimate comparative achievement in terms of fourths. Still another teacher might make his comparisons, not in terms of a single class, but in relation to all the classes that he has taught in English or in relation to all of the classes taking ninth-grade English in the school, city, or state. This would necessitate each teacher's knowing how a particular class compares with the larger group.

In high schools with homogeneous grouping, where grouping is by achievement tests, students in the high sections would probably be reported as being in the top third; those in the low sections, in the lowest third; and those in the middle group, in the middle third. Students in the top section would not be given As and Bs, nor would students in the low section get Ds and Fs.

When it is desirable to continue to use single letter grades, either of the following systems would make such grades meaningful.

Based upon Thirds
A: The highest third
B: The middle third
C: The lowest third

Based upon Fourths
A: The highest fourth
B: The second highest fourth
C: The second lowest fourth
D: The lowest fourth

This rating in terms of thirds or fourths would be more meaningful to student, teacher, and parents than the present single-letter grade that supposedly can be used for subjects in which no tests are given as well as for subjects in which tests are given. In the system detailed here, F's would be given only to students who could achieve well but who do not, in spite of the teacher's best efforts. The seriously retarded, as proposed in Chapter 14, would take some of their work in special classes.

Finally, this system would be as valuable to employers and to institutions of higher learning as are single-letter grades based on the five-point scale. Numerical values could be assigned to the ratings to secure a composite cumulative record, including each student's comparative standing in his class at the end of his senior year.

PROGRESS TOWARD MANY IMPORTANT OBJECTIVES IS CONSIDERED

What does it mean to receive a C+ in shorthand? A 90 in Algebra I? And F in English 9? If the parents are to translate these symbols correctly, they must understand the school's goals. If the teacher is to assign symbols meaningfully, he must do more than merely give lip service to objectives. If the student is to grow in his learnings, he, also, must know the objectives, must be committed to them, and must know how to achieve them.

Often, there is a discrepancy between goals as stated in a curriculum guide and the teacher behavior that can be observed in a classroom. Thus, an English teacher conducting a unit in which Scott's *Ivanhoe* is taught says that he has such goals as establishing a life-long reading habit; teaching reading to comprehend form, or implied meaning, or clues to setting; or creating a desire to read further in Sir Walter Scott. Yet the tasks required in class, the pupil behavior that is graded and reported to parents, involve minute recall of details of the plot of the novel: "Where and how many times did Locksley hit the target with his arrows?" "How did Rowena react (externally) to Ivanhoe's being wounded?" And so on. Clearly, the student is being graded on remembering specific facts rather than on evaluating, problem-solving, divergent thinking, and so on. A grade of B+ in English may conceal the fact that a given student writes poorly, that he lacks ability to read critically and creatively, or that his best performance in cognitive learning is mere recall of specific bits of information and terminology.

If evaluation is to be in terms of the educational objectives of the school, marking and planning for meaningful reports of pupil progress is no facile job. The *Taxonomy of Educational Objectives*, mentioned in another chapter, grew in part out of an attempt to word objectives in terms that would facilitate the communication of educational goals. The taxonomy is also a tool that the classroom teacher can use to write test items or to plan questions for discusion in such a manner that the progress recorded is not exclusively from one class of objectives. Whether in terms of the work of Bloom, Guilford, or others, the teacher should consciously devise test and discussion items that call for differing cognitive or affective abilities. And he should be able to communicate his bases for evaluation to parents and students.

The progress report used in the Humanities program at Ridgewood High School (Figure 14) communicates well the goals of Ridgewood's system and includes the ratings of performances involving knowledge, comprehension, application, analysis, synthesis, and evaluation. The Humanities progress report gives the parents and students much more information on the student's potential for achievement and on his actual achievement—in terms of many objectives—than does C or 72. Such careful reporting of growth and final achievement arises as a consequence of careful planning of the curriculum, of well-constructed tests, and of sound observations and should lead to better relationships between teacher and pupil, pupil and home and school.

Resistance to a comprehensive progress report in each subject field is encountered when teachers feel that they cannot reliably estimate a student's progress in so many different areas. When a school abandons the single-letter report, the teachers would do well to discuss the main objectives to be rated and also to decide how many objectives they can appraise reliably. Some schools might have fewer objectives in each subject than in the all-school curriculum. It is better practice to group objectives so that there will be a smaller number of items so that the appraisals will be relatively reliable than it is to break them down into minute items and try to guess at the appraisal.

THE REPORTING SYSTEM IS UNDERSTOOD

The marks, ratings, and comments in a written report should convey the same meaning to all readers. It is unlikely that the teacher giving the grade, the student receiving the grade, and the parent reading the report attach the same meaning to the A, B, C, D, F ratings on the card shown in Figure 12b.

As proposed earlier, if single letters must be used, an A for the students in the top fourth of the class, a B for those in the next fourth, and a D for those in the lowest fourth will have the same meaning to everyone. Many misinterpretations and variations in meaning of the present single-letter grades can be eliminated by this system. But, if the single-letter system is used, progress toward objectives must be reported in a meaningful way. If only comparative achievements are reported, the credit that teachers should give for effort, cooperativeness, study habits, and other qualities will be lost.

Ratings of satisfactory, improving, and unsatisfactory in areas such as effort, courtesy, and care of materials can be understood by everyone. However, these ratings are preferable—excellent progress with usual teacher help, average progress with usual teacher help, slow progress with much teacher help, and needs additional help. When the teacher checks one of these on the report form, both parents and students understand exactly what is meant. The "needs additional help" is used only when the student is referred to someone else in the school, such as a counselor or a reading specialist. The inclusion of "with teacher help" in each rating conveys the idea that the student is not being allowed to drift, that the teacher is there helping him.

Many other reporting systems provide space for comments in addition to the academic marks and the progress ratings. In ceasing to rely completely on grades, many schools attempt to include more teacher comments in their reports. However, these comments are often as poorly understood and lead to as many misunderstandings as the single-letter grades. Frequently-used but ineffective comments include: "Can and should do much better"; "Poor work methods"; "Too talkative"; "Immature in conduct"; "Cheats"; "Lies." Such comments on a report give better clues as to how a teacher conducts his class and reacts to students than to student progress or to comparative achievement.

PARENT-TEACHER CONFERENCES ARE USED

Parents and teachers are partners in educating children. Each must assume a reasonable share of the responsibilities for the education of the adolescent. Although it is true that he spends 80 of the 168 hours each week in school, for about 40 weeks each year, the student is enormously influenced by the home environment. Before a child enters school, the parents have influenced conduct, beliefs, attitudes toward right and wrong, work methods, and interest in learning. The effect of family relationships on such development, especially on school adjustment, continues throughout one's entire education. Many parents want the teacher's help in influencing conduct, beliefs, work methods, and so on. They are willing to cooperate actively with the teacher so that the home and the school can complement each other. Parent-teacher conferences should be based on the idea of the complementing influences of the school and of the home on adolescents and young adults.

However, not all parents will be equally cooperative. Sometimes the student will have become so dissociated in behavior from the parents that they will show some form of "giving up"—indifference, hostility, and so on. Some parents from slum areas may place no high value on school learnings, and may, at least inadvertently, undermine any effort toward the continued education of their children. Sometimes, you will be able to work with parents from these groups. But, in other instances, only personnel highly trained in group differences—guidance workers, social workers, various administrators—will be able to have any impact.

Parents are individual representatives of various cultures and subcultures. The teacher should accept differences among parents in educational background, socioeconomic status, religious belief, race, and attitudes toward education. Many parents, including some who are in business and the professions, will not have the specialized education to enable them to understand readily current educational practices and problems. Many parents will not understand the terms that you use—core, homeroom, standardized tests, intelligence quotient, homogeneous groups, differential assignments, and the like. They will turn to you for help in understanding educational goals and terminology. In conferences, the teacher must accept parents without criticism and without posing as an expert in esoteric content. He must help parents understand his work with the student. Parent-teacher conferences must be based on mutual acceptance.

One plan that has been found practical in scheduling conferences is to have parents come to school before classes begin, or soon thereafter, for a group meeting with the teachers, guidance personnel, and principal. In the meeting, an agenda for the year specifying the number of individual conferences to be held, the time and place of conferences, and the over-all points for discussion is established. At the same time, procedures are established to facilitate the parents' requesting conferences.

Special arrangements are sometimes necessary for mothers who work, for parents with several children in school, for parents who have very young children, and for parents new to the community. In these cases, the teacher usually goes to the home for the conference. Special arrangements may also be required for disinterested and antagonistic parents. Here, social workers or attendance officers may have to be brought in.

For the most effective communication, the conference must be planned carefully. Make certain that the purposes of the conference are clear in your mind, especially if you requested the conference or if it is regularly scheduled. Set a definite time for the beginning and end of the conference. Such planning is important when a series of appointments run consecutively, and it helps the teacher end a conference easily. Before the conference, anticipate any pertinent information that you must have about the student or his parents. If you are to report progress, be certain that all of the records are at hand. When a home-room teacher or a member of a teaching team reports a student's progress and comparative achievement in several areas of school work, many records must be assembled.

Get to the purpose of the conference. If the parents have asked to see you, encourage them to state their reasons soon after they arrive. If you have asked them to come in, tell them why. It is usually advisable to get to this point within five minutes after beginning the conference.

If the parents have asked to see you, let them talk without interruption until they have said everything they want to say. Do not make them feel rushed. Nothing helps a person who is emotionally upset— be he parent, teacher, or student—to gain control of his emotions and to begin to think rationally about a problem more quickly than to have a sympathetic listener who does not interrupt. Getting rid of emotional tensions is better than suppressing them.

Some teachers have a tendency to dominate, to cross-examine, or to assume a patronizing manner. A conference is almost certain to have undesirable results unless the teacher listens graciously and can admit some of his own inadequacies and his possible errors. The parents should feel free to ask any questions or to make any suggestions that they care to make. In concluding a conference, outline the action that is to be taken as the result of it, or make plans for the next conference.

End the conference on an optimistic note. Although you feel sure that the parents' decision for their son to become an engineer is unwise, do not say so. Instead, mention some of their son's good qualities or some of the areas of the curriculum in which he is doing well.

If teachers are to be effective in conducting conferences with parents, it is important for a faculty to consider two matters: Making time available for holding conferences and securing cooperation from the entire school staff and from parents. Agreement must be reached as to whether all parent-teacher conferences should take place outside of regular class hours or whether the teacher should be allowed time for them during the regular school day. It is important that teachers, parents, and the administration approve the final decision and cooperate with it.

A variety of arrangements can be worked out so that the homeroom, team, or regular classroom teacher can have at least one conference a semester with the parents of 25 to 35 students. (1) On specified days, teachers can be in their classrooms for one half to three quarters of an hour before classes begin or end for the day. (2) While one member of a teaching team is conducting large-group classes, other team members can be conferring with parents. (3) Classes can be dismissed completely for half a day once a month for conferences. (4) Occasionally, cocurricular activities or whole-school assemblies can be scheduled at certain periods of the day and conducted by a few teachers, freeing most teachers for conferences. (5) Conferences can be scheduled in the evening. (6) An interested, capable parent can take over the teacher's class during conferences. (7) Substitute teachers can be hired for conference days. These procedures, alone or in combination, will work in any junior or senior high school without burdening anyone excessively if the administration, the teachers, and the parents want the procedures to work. Most parents will be generous with their time, will agree to the school's being dismissed for short periods of time, and will cooperate in many ways with the school in order to attend parent-teacher conferences and to learn about their children's progress.

Teachers must have the public and whole-hearted support of the entire school personnel—principal, administration, special teachers, and guidance people—if they are to carry through an effective conference program with parents. Honest disagreements about the reporting system and parent-teacher conferences are inevitable. However, although disagreements should be discussed freely in faculty meetings, they should not be argued in front of parents or other members of the community.

SUMMARY

Reporting pupil progress adequately has long been a perplexing problem for secondary school teachers. However, grades continue to serve administrative, guidance, information-giving, and motivational functions, among others; and there is small likelihood of their being abandoned. Among the marking systems in use today are the percentage system, symbols on a five-point scale, the normal distribution curve, and various descriptive systems.

In a good reporting system, progress in learning is of primary importance; comparative achievement is secondary. And progress toward several goals, rather than one, should be evaluated and reported. When a report covers subject-matter knowledge and skills only, many students are denied an opportunity to experience success, even though they are making progress toward important individual goals. Any reporting system must be understood by students, parents, and teachers.

The best-written reports are even more satisfactory when supplemented by parent-teacher conferences. In the conference, some of the student's work can be shown to parents, and any matters related to the student's school life, his parents' questions, or the teacher's viewpoints can be clarified.

QUESTIONS AND ACTIVITIES

1 Using *Education Index*, find recent discussions of one of the marking systems discussed in this chapter. Prepare a critical discussion of the major strengths and weaknesses of the marking system you choose.

2 What are the advantages in focusing reporting upon the student's progress in learning?

3 Why should progress toward several important objectives be reported rather than subject-matter knowledge and skills only?

4 Write a short critical evaluation of the report forms shown in Figures 11, 12a, 12b, 13a, 13b, and 14.

5 What advantages do parent-teacher conferences have over written reports?

6 Conduct a sociodrama in which a teacher informs parents that it is advisable to place their child in a special class.

7 For your subject-matter field, set up a combination written report system and parent-teacher conference schedule that you think would be practical and that you think would achieve the desired results.

8 Compare the Monona Grove report form with the one that was used in your own high school.

SUGGESTIONS FOR FURTHER READING

ASSOCIATION FOR SUPERVISION AND CURRICULUM DEVELOPMENT, *Reporting Is Communicating: An Approach to Evaluating and Marking*, Washington, D.C.: National Education Association, 1956.

KLAUSMEIER, HERBERT J., AND WILLIAM GOODWIN, *Learning and Human Abilities*, 2nd ed., New York: Harper & Row, 1966, Ch. 17.

ROTHNEY, JOHN W. M., *What Research Says to the Teacher: Evaluating and Reporting Pupil Progress*, Washington, D.C.: National Education Association, 1956.

STRANG, RUTH, *Reporting to Parents*, New York: Bureau of Publications, Teachers College, Columbia University, 1947.

part III

EXPANDING RESPONSIBILITIES AND CHALLENGES

14 *Providing for exceptional students*

A national concern for identifying and providing for gifted students was sparked by the race into outer space. The civil rights movement in the 1960s generated a national effort for better education of the culturally disadvantaged. Delinquency and technological unemployment have forced us to re-examine the role of the school in educating many students for useful citizenship through becoming economically independent workers. Concurrent with these recent concerns, we recognize the need to provide better education for normally developing youth. We realize more clearly with each passing decade that education cannot be identical mass education, the same prescription of 12 years of schooling for all, using the identical instructional materials and activities. Instead, the plea for individualization that psychologists and educators have been making for the past half century is assuming greater significance.

Earlier in this book, we outlined principles and methods of instruction. These are intended to be applicable to groups of students as well as to individuals. In this chapter, we are concerned with applications to gifted and talented children, slow learners, the culturally deprived, and the antisocial delinquents.

Two principal means of providing for differences among students are through individualization and various forms of grouping. Opportunities for individualization are much better now than in the past. Programed instructional materials make it possible for each student to study material suited to his rate of learning. These materials, used with electronic equipment, enable a student to speak a second language, to learn shorthand dictation, and to study other subject matter at a rate suitable for him. Instructional teams also lend opportunities for individual attention. New school buildings are being constructed in which individual study booths replace the old auditorium. Libraries make available not only books, but also recordings and television. Individualization is treated as essential to quality education and is receiving more attention.

We have been continuing our attempts at individualization primarily in comprehensive high schools rather than in specialized ones, such as vocational schools, science schools, or schools for delinquents. With adequate financial support, staff, and instructional materials, the comprehensive high school can meet the needs of students representing the entire range of abilities. However, it cannot work well when one English teacher is expected to provide effectively for 150 or more students representing the entire range of abilities, or when business education, home economics, industrial arts, and fine arts are treated as frills rather than as essential components of the total instructional program. If the comprehensive high school is to survive, it must accept all students as they come and provide guidance by which each student is placed in classes profitable for him. It is possible that more combined work-study arrangements are needed for many students. Special schools and other provisions are being arranged for delinquents and culturally disadvantaged youth through federally supported programs. Many innovations are needed to make high school education universally profitable for our youth. Within this context of the comprehensive high school and many innovations, we shall discuss provisions for the various groupings of students.

GIFTED AND TALENTED

Abilities can be identified in four areas: figural, semantic, social, and psychomotor, as was discussed in Chapter 2. A student might be superior in one or more of these. Much subject matter is comprised of semantic content. A student who is superior in most academic subjects, or who promises to be, is called a gifted student. One who is superior in only one field such as music, art, foreign language, or mathematics is called talented. The term *academically talented* is also being applied to the student who is a high achiever in one or more school subjects, such as English and math, with high semantic content. These designations have emerged historically and the terminology is not critical. Some designate an individual gifted who is superior only in social relations. As long as we clearly indicate the behavioral characteristics of those we refer to by name, we can communicate adequately. In this chapter we use the terms *gifted* and *talented* as defined in this paragraph and shall subsequently describe procedures for identifying each type. Students of junior and senior high school age who are superior in any area of human endeavor are included in the following discussion of objectives, identification procedures, and provisions.

Objectives

What should gifted and talented students learn while in secondary school? What abilities should they develop? These and similar questions are answered in a statement of objectives that has been agreed upon in a number of Wisconsin schools in which Mr. Klausmeier is conducting longitudinal experiments.[1]

In comparison with others, gifted and talented students are

1. To acquire the subject matter more efficiently; their more efficient acquisition of subject matter is to result in fuller knowledge and understanding of the physical and social world
2. To develop better work-study skills, including learning-to-learn procedures; in turn, this should lead to a higher degree of independence in learning efficiency in and out of school
3. To develop higher-level cognitive abilities, including *effective thinking, critical thinking,* or *reasoning*
4. To develop higher-level creative abilities in such areas as oral and written expression, art, music, dramatics, and physical activities
5. To acquire appreciations of beauty in more fields
6. To develop equally effective citizenship behavior

---

[1] Herbert J. Klausmeier and Dwight Teel, "A Research-Based Program for Gifted Children," reprinted from the November, 1964, issue of *Education.* Copyright, 1964, by The Bobbs-Merrill Company, Inc., Indianapolis, Indiana. In this article, the program of the Milwaukee Public Schools is outlined. Other reports are available from Klausmeier regarding programs in other Wisconsin cities.

7. To develop equally good personal-emotional adjustments as other children
8. To develop similar high-level ethical conduct and character; gifted high schol pupils also provide directions for their education.

At the end of the first year in an honors class in American history, the exceptionally able high school juniors enrolled in it said that they valued most from the course:

1. Learning how to study
2. Learning how to secure reliable information and to write research reports
3. Having long-range assignments rather than daily, short ones
4. Participating in panel discussions, whole-class discussions, and debates
5. Reading documentary and current material
6. Forming better reading habits
7. Learning to budget time
8. Gaining feelings of confidence when presenting information orally
9. Having freedom from routine assignments, including the learning of large amounts of factual information in chronological sequence

These bright students want considerable independence and respect as individuals; they want to feel secure with themselves and others; and they hope to contribute to the group. Undoubtedly, if asked why they valued these experiences, the students would reveal that their choices bore some relationship to their plans for later life—marriage and vocational success, for example.

Identification

Standardized intelligence tests, standardized achievement tests, tests of creativity, teacher observation, and other means of appraisal as outlined in Chapter 12 are used in identifying children of varying ability and achievement levels. When standardized test scores are used in identification, the tendency is to use a percentile score or some other deviation score so that, regardless of the test used, the lower limit is the same; for example, ninety-ninth, ninetieth, or seventy-fifth percentile. Some schools now set the lower limit of IQ at the eighty-fifth percentile and of achievement at the seventy-fifth percentile, intending to identify the top 10 percent or thereabouts. In some large city systems, the criteria are purposefully varied among schools within the city. In schools that draw pupils almost totally from lower socioeconomic status, it is assumed that an impoverished environment will depress IQ and achievement scores in relation to those of other children in favored environments; therefore, the criteria are at times lowered in these schools.

In order to identify high abilities and achievements, as well as deficiencies, in all students, the following procedures are recommended. Note that these start early in the school life of children. First, a group intelligence test, a battery of educational achievement tests, and creativity tests should be administered to all students every two years, starting in the second grade. Secondly, teacher observation and rating of each child's achievement, personal characteristics, and special abilities or deficiencies should be secured each year. Thirdly, additional group testing should be done as necessary to provide for children who transfer into the school system. Fourthly, a school psychologist should make an individual assessment of every student recommended for any special program. Fifthly, conferences with parents should be held. In certain cases, the school nurse, the social worker, and other specialists may also provide useful information. This type of comprehensive program is used to identify any special talents or any specific deficiency a child may possess. More specialized testing and other diagnostic procedures are often needed to identify disabilities.

Physical, social, and emotional maturity should be considered in identifying gifted students. However, if a special educational provision is to be made for gifted and talented students, no child should be eliminated simply because he is below the average of all children in physical development or because he is less well adjusted socially or emotionally than most children.[2] It is possible that poorer social and emotional adjustment in a bright child might result because the instruction is not suited to his needs; if special provision were made, his adjustment might improve markedly.

The use of creativity tests in identification is proposed, inasmuch as Gallagher reported several studies in which two phenomena were observed.[3] Some high IQ and high-achieving students did not score partic-

---

[2] Herbert J. Klausmeier, "Identifying Children through Measurements," *Education*, LXXX (November, 1959), 167–171.

[3] James J. Gallagher and William Rogge, "The Gifted," *Review of Educational Research*, XXXVI (February, 1966), 37–55.

ularly high on creativity tests. Furthermore, adding creativity tests to group ability tests markedly improved the prediction of achievement. One or two creativity tests that can be scored for productivity or fluency of ideas, quality of ideas, and cleverness of ideas might provide interesting results for planning instruction of the gifted. These could be used by the teacher to check against observation and rating.

Educational provisions

Individualization and grouping have been indicated as two possible organizational arrangements. Within these arrangements, provisions for gifted and talented students are usually classified as enrichment, acceleration, sectioning, and special classes. Special schools are applicable only to our largest school systems and will not be discussed further. Nongraded classes and instructional teams are promising, but will not be discussed in this chapter inasmuch as they are given attention elsewhere.

These provisions are means for bringing instructional content in line with the abilities of the student; they do nothing unless the instructional program for the gifted student is changed. For example, special sections or classes do nothing in themselves to improve instruction; but in them higher-level content can be arranged and discovery methods of teaching can be utilized more readily. A teacher with a group of bright individuals can do these things better than ten different teachers, each individualizing instruction for three bright children out of a heterogeneous class of 30 to 45. The special provisions now discussed are based on the assumption that instructional materials and activities should be different for gifted and talented students in some respects than for those not gifted.

Enrichment

Enrichment is the principal means of providing for the gifted in heterogeneous classes. The small school that has only 50 ninth-graders can enrich instruction for the brighter ones, as can the larger school with 1000 or more students. The main categories of enrichment applied generally to all subject fields are research activities; creative projects; experimentation and demonstration; leadership opportunities; club work; service to school and community; special talent activities—music, dramatics, dance, and athletics; independent work; and honors activities. Judgments favoring enrichment for gifted pupils in regular classes rather than grouping or accelerating include

1. Students of varying abilities and levels of abilities have an opportunity to work together and benefit from these contacts with one another
2. The less able students are encouraged by the presence of the more able
3. The heterogeneous class more closely parallels living outside of school
4. It is desirable for the more able students at times to help those of lower abilities

There are also drawbacks to enrichment:

1. It is difficult to provide competent teachers who have sufficient knowledge in several subject fields to do a good job of enrichment
2. There is insufficient time to work well with the gifted students, particularly if the teacher has as many as 150 students daily
3. It is exceedingly difficult, if not impossible, to do a good job of enriching instruction without drawing subject-matter content from the next higher grade level

This last drawback is critical in connection with enrichment in heterogeneous classes, for most schools have not found adequate means whereby the bright ninth-graders, for example, use regular tenth-grade textbooks, while the more average and the slower students use ninth- and eighth-grade texts, respectively.

Acceleration

By acceleration we mean that the students will finish 12 grades in less than 12 school years or, after finishing high school in 12 years, will receive college credit that permits completing the requirements for the baccalaureate in less than four years. Early admission to kindergarten or first grade, double promotion, and concentrating instruction in shorter time periods are the main methods of acceleration. Acceleration, like enrichment, can be applied from the smallest to the largest school system. Of particular interest in high school are concentrating instruction into shorter time periods, a lengthened school year, and admission to college with advanced standing.

Concentrating instruction into shorter time periods offers opportunities not provided by early entrance into kindergarten or double promotion. Bright students can finish three years of junior high school in two, four years of high school in three, or four years of college in three when arrangements are made to concentrate instruction into shorter periods of time, for example, six semesters of algebra and geometry in four. Condensing three years of junior high school mathematics into two years was found completely satisfactory for high-ability boys and for most girls; however, some girls experienced difficulty with geometry in the ninth grade. Condensing three years of science was advantageous for both sexes; the bright students achieved just as high when taking biology in the ninth grade as did equally bright tenth-graders who had not experienced the condensed program.[4] Condensing instruction works best in large schools when students can be put together in the same section for the condensed instruction.

The *lengthened school year* and the taking of additional courses during the regular school year enable gifted and talented students to complete 12 years of schooling in less than 12 years without skipping content. We are all familiar with these two procedures. At this point, recognize that concentrating instruction into shorter time periods or the lengthened school year does not require early graduation; it merely permits it.

Early admission to college can be accomplished in two desirable ways. One is to accelerate students by some means as indicated previously without their skipping any essential subject matter. Another is to enroll them in one or two classes in a local university or college during the last year or two of high school. Having students skip the senior year of high school, without any prior preparation for college, has met much resistance from high school principals. Only in poorly managed schools that do not have systematic provisions for the gifted would it appear advantageous to have exceptionally bright students skip the senior year and enter college.

Admission to college with advanced standing is being accomplished through high school seniors' taking advanced placement tests in various college subjects. Different from the student who enters college without

---

[4] Herbert J. Klausmeier and William Wiersma, "Effects of Condensing Content in Mathematics and Science in the Junior and Senior High School," *School Science and Mathematics*, LXIV (January, 1964), 4–11.

TABLE 14.1. *Methods for Accelerating Pupils without Skipping Subject Content.*

Method	Level	Investigator
Early admittance to kindergarten or first grade	Preschool	Hobson, Birch, Worcester[a]
Condensation of 6 semesters of non-graded primary school into 4 or 5 semesters	Primary	Klausmeier[b]
Summer-session attendance for entry into higher grade in the fall	Elementary	Klausmeier & Ripple, Klausmeier[c]
Condensation of content into less time; e.g., 3 years of English in 2 years	Junior high	Justman, Klausmeier, Klausmeier & Wiersma[d]
Taking advanced college-placement courses in the senior year of high school	Senior high	Meister, Barnette[e]
Taking additional courses; summer session attendance	College	Pressy & Flesher[f]

[a] James R. Hobson, "Mental Age As a Workable Criterion for School Admission," *Elementary School Journal*, XLVIII (February, 1948), 312–321. Jack W. Birch, "Early School Admission for Mentally Advanced Children," *Exceptional Children*, XXI (December, 1954), 84–87. Dean A. Worcester, *The Education of Children of Above Average Mentality* (Lincoln: University of Nebraska Press, 1956).

[b] Herbert J. Klausmeier, *Summary Report of Research Completed, 1958–1961, on Educational Provisions for Children and Youth of Superior Learning Abilities, Milwaukee Public Schools* (Milwaukee, Wisc.: Board of School Directors, 1962).

[c] Herbert J. Klausmeier and Richard E. Ripple, "Effects of Accelerating Bright Older Pupils from Second to Fourth Grade," *Journal of Educational Psychology*, LIII (April, 1962), 93–100. Herbert J. Klausmeier, "Effects of Accelerating Bright Older Elementary Pupils: A Follow-up," *Journal of Educational Psychology*, LIV (June, 1963), 165–171.

[d] Joseph Justman, "Academic Achievement of Intellectually Gifted Accelerants and Non-Accelerants in Junior High School," *School Review*, LXII (March, 1954), 142–150. Joseph Justman, "Academic Achievement of Intellectually Gifted Accelerants and Non-Accelerants in Senior High School," *School Review*, LXII (November, 1954), 469–473. Herbert J. Klausmeier, (see [a]). Herbert J. Klausmeier and William Wiersma, "Effects of Condensing Content in Mathematics and Science in the Junior and Senior High School," *School Science and Mathematics*, LXIV (January, 1964), 4–11.

[e] Morris Meister, "Cooperation of Secondary Schools and Colleges in Acceleration of Gifted Students," *Journal of Educational Sociology*, XXIX (January, 1956), 220–227. Warren L. Barnette, "Advanced Credit for the Superior High School Student," *Journal of Higher Education*, XXVIII (January, 1957), 15–20.

[f] Sidney L. Pressey and Marie A. Flesher, "Wartime Accelerates Ten Years After," *Journal of Educational Psychology*, XLVI (April, 1955), 228–238.

SOURCE: Herbert J. Klausmeier and William Goodwin, *Learning and Human Abilities*, 2nd ed. (New York: Harper & Row, 1966), p. 511. By permission.

having completed all high school work, the advanced-placement student is graduated with other students at the end of the senior year but receives credit for course work in college. Also, some school systems are working out arrangements directly with colleges in which certain courses in high school are automatically accepted as equivalent to the same course in the freshman or sophomore year of college.

Methods of acceleration that do not involve the skipping of content, the school level at which experimentation has been done, and the reference in which the results are reported are given in Table 14.1. Favorable results in terms of the educational achievements and the social, emotional, and physical adjustment of the accelerates were observed by all the researchers. Our research at the University of Wisconsin has clearly shown that acceleration does not result in lower educational achievements or in poorer social or emotional adjustment. With this type and amount of evidence mounting over the years, and with the present shortage of teachers and other educated talent, an appropriate national goal might be to have all bright students awarded the baccalaureate by their twenty-first birthday and the most able and rapidly maturing by age 20. Human resources are wasted by forcing bright students to spend 12 years completing their education through high school and 16 years in completing all requirements for the baccalaureate.

Sectioning and special classes

A school that has enough students for two sections can arrange them into a higher and a lower group. The school with as many as 150 or more students at each grade level can also section readily. A high section that contains only students of superior learning ability can be designated a special class for the gifted. The lowest section can be designated for slow-learning students. It is unfair to students, of course, to place them in these sections if they do not meet commonly accepted criteria of giftedness or slow learning. Unfortunately, some schools attempt to keep all sections equal in number, and this often determines the criteria used in placement in sections.

Sectioning and special classes are common in junior and senior high schools with enrollments of 150 or more pupils per grade. If special classes and sectioning are to work well in any school, differentiation of instructional materials and activities must be made in the various sections. Table 14.2 shows some features of the sectioning arrangements in the required English and history classes of Waukesha Senior High School. The total enrollment in English is 644; and in history, 666. The higher number in history results from more students failing the first time and repeating as seniors.

TABLE 14.2. *Features of Sections in Eleventh-Grade English and History (Waukesha High School, Wisconsin)*

| | Number of students enrolled | | Criteria of selection in both subjects | |
Section designation	English	History	Scholastic aptitude, local norms (percentile rank)	Achievement test, national norms (percentile rank)
Honors	24	25	90–higher	90–higher
One	262	264	60–99	75–99
Regular	264	279	18–59	25–74
Low regular	74	78	1–17	1–24
				Previous history of difficulty in the subject
Special	20	20	Individual appraisal	Individual appraisal
Total	644	666		

SOURCE: Herbert J. Klausmeier and William Goodwin, *Learning and Human Abilities*, 2nd ed. (New York: Harper & Row, 1966), p. 514. By permission.

Juniors in this school are invited to enroll in the honors sections, provided their scholastic-aptitude test score is at the ninetieth percentile or higher on local norms and their tested achievement in the particular subject is at the ninetieth percentile score or higher on national norms. Only four honors sections are available, one each in English, history, mathematics, and science. Although some students are eligible for all four, most enroll in only the two in which they are most interested and enroll in one section for the other subjects.

Although not directly pertaining to the gifted, students are given no choice in enrolling in the other sections for which they are eligible by the criteria. All students with scholastic aptitude at the sixtieth percentile or higher and with achievement in the particular subject at the seventy-fifth percentile or higher must enroll in the sections designated one. Teachers' grades and recommendations are given some consideration in admission to the honors sections and to the low regular sections. The special classes are for students identified as educable mentally retarded while still in the elementary grades. Class size is lowest in the special classes (20), about equal in the honors and low regular sections (about 25), and highest in the regular and one sections (about 30).

Noteworthy features of the program concern reading materials and instructional activities. The required textbook is different for every sectional level. In history, for example, a book normally used at the college level and supplementary readings of documentary materials are used in the honors section. The low regular sections use a junior high school history book with a low level of reading difficulty; the same type of reading material is used in the low regular sections in English. However, in the honors section in English, a regular high school text is used. The amount of writing activity goes up successively in all sections, regardless of subject, from low regular through honors. The amount of assigned reading goes up successively from low regular through one; in the honors sections the assigned reading drops off but is replaced with a heavier volume of voluntary reading. Objective tests are generally used from low regular through the one sections; in the honors sections, almost no objective tests are used.

The most heterogeneous sections are the regular, and the most difficult for which to find appropriate activities are the low regular. Publishers are now beginning to provide instructional materials for high school students whose reading achievements are at the junior high school level. Also, supplementary and general library books that have interesting content for students at about age 17 have quite advanced vocabulary. The teachers at Waukesha are earnestly attempting to provide differentiated instruction in line with the level of abilities and achievements of the students in the various sections.

Multiple provisions

A variety of provisions are necessary to meet the needs of the gifted and talented in medium-sized and large cities. What is done in high school must be related to the elementary school program, vice versa. After five years of intensive research, the following provisions were incorporated into the operating procedures of the Milwaukee Public Schools:

1. In the primary school, special attention is given to early identification and acceleration of children of superior ability. About 4 percent

of the children of above median CA and about 1 percent of the younger children who demonstrate exceptionally high abilities are accelerated one or two semesters at some point between kindergarten entrance and completion of fourth grade.

2. In the fourth grade, children of superior ability are placed in regular heterogeneous classes and appropriate enrichment opportunities are provided for them. Fourth-grade teachers are informed of identified children of superior ability in their classes. The fourth-grade program is intended to help the pupils acquire additional growth in independence, aid them in adjusting to the expanded curriculum of the intermediate grades before placement in special classes in the fifth grade, and help those accelerated in the primary school adjust to the higher grade before placing them in special classes.

3. In the fifth and sixth grades, children of superior ability are placed in special self-contained classes in certain elementary schools, or, in locations where special self-contained classes are not feasible, in a comparable alternative arrangement such as special classes that meet periodically with an itinerant teacher. In these special classes, there is some condensation of content in subject areas to permit progress in a designated subject at an accelerated rate, and there is enrichment of the entire curriculum to achieve higher-level competency than may be attained in the regular classroom.

Some pupils of superior ability are accelerated placement-wise during grades 4, 5, and 6, especially those who are in the older age group for their actual grade placement.

4. In the junior and senior high school, provisions for youth of superior abilities include courses in the regular program sequence for students talented in any one subject field or in several subject fields. In addition, specific opportunities for enrichment, acceleration, and condensed instruction are available. . . .

The superior-ability student at the junior and senior high school level typically pursues one or more courses one year in advance of the regular sequential program; for example, ninth-grade algebra, general science, and English may be taken in the eighth grade. High school credit toward graduation is given to eighth-grade pupils who satisfactorily complete these high school courses. . . .

Students of superior ability in the senior high school, having completed seven units by the end of grade 9, choose among three options: graduation one or two semesters early upon completing the 17 recommended units; remaining through grade 12 with some released time for enrollment at a college or university; or remaining through grade 12 with some released time for employment.[5]

5 Klausmeier and Teel, *op. cit.*, 4–5. By permission.

SLOW LEARNERS

Slow learners comprise about 12 percent of the total child population of school age, according to criteria of IQ based on the Revised Stanford-Binet Scale. Slow learners have IQs or scholastic aptitude scores ranging from the third to fifteenth percentile and have equally low achievements in the usual school subjects. Some students with IQs as low as 70 learn reasonably well and are properly classified as slow learners rather than as mentally retarded, and some with IQs as high as 75 who do not learn well are properly classified as mentally retarded. Refer back to Table 14.2. There it is seen that the "low regular" classes include students at the twenty-fourth percentile or lower on national norms in educational achievement and at or below the seventeenth percentile on local norms on a group test of general intellectual ability. About 12 percent of the total class is enrolled in "slow regular" sections. Most of these could be classified as slow learners on the basis of their test scores, although some quite able students might be included who performed poorly because of low motivation on the group tests.

Procedures for identifying slow learners, as noted in the preceding section, may be identical to those for identifying the gifted. Standardized tests, teacher-made tests, observations and ratings of the students, and cumulative records are used. When applied systematically, a school can quite readily identify a majority of the students who experience difficulty in learning, particularly in the courses required for graduation.

The administrative and curriculum arrangements for slow learners involve individualization and grouping, as was previously outlined for the gifted. Special classes or sections and enrichment are common. Unfortunately, failing students and not providing appropriate instructional materials or activities are also common. We have not yet developed appropriate programs in English, mathematics, the sciences, and social studies for slow learners as we have for learners of average and above average abilities. Furthermore, as indicated in Chapter 2 in the discussion of economic independence, work-study programs and vocational education are woefully inadequate. It is probably fair to conclude that most high schools do not have appropriate educational programs for slow learners. As will be noted subsequently, this situation may be improved with new programs for the culturally disadvantaged.

Excellent teaching of slow learners requires, first, a teacher who wants to teach them and who has developed some capabilities for doing so. There remains a dearth of instructional material that is pitched at a sufficiently easy reading level and yet has content of interest to students of this age. Therefore, the teacher must be aggressive in convincing school officials to try to secure more of this material.

In general, the slow learner in high school will be far behind most students in most of the required subject matter knowledge and skills. Remedial teaching is necessary, based on a careful diagnosis of the students' deficiencies. Many high school teachers have not prepared themselves for remedial teaching. They can, however, become self-educated. Excellent information can be found in a book by Otto and McMenemy.[6] They have outlined procedures to be used in reading, spelling, other language arts, and arithmetic. Although the ideas are perhaps more directly relevant to teachers of the elementary grades, high school teachers who have slow learners can use the ideas as a starting point. Otto and McMenemy write that a corrective and remedial teacher, in comparison with others, ". . . should be more aware of their pupils' needs, more skilled at diagnosing difficulties, more proficient in teaching, and more able to understand pupils' problems."[7]

Some teachers in junior and senior high school experience ethical conflicts when they must decide whether to maintain a minimum standard of achievement and fail the slow learner who has done his best or to pass him along even though he has not achieved a minimum standard. We should not require slow-learning children to attend high school if they do not learn as well as they might or if they continuously experience failure. Education must help most slow learners become independent economically and stable emotionally and socially. Although an exceedingly wealthy country, the United States cannot look forward to supporting slower learners throughout life through tax monies or charities. Depriving them of further education at around age 16 or not having them learn well in usual classes assures that a considerable number will never become economically self-sufficient.

---

[6] Wayne Otto and Richard A. McMenemy, *Corrective and Remedial Teaching* (Boston: Houghton Mifflin, 1966); provides a summary of cause and then outlines principles and procedures related to reading, vocabulary, study skills, spelling, arithmetic, handwriting, written and oral expression.

[7] *Ibid.*, pp. 341–342.

EDUCATIONALLY DEPRIVED STUDENTS

A new chapter in American education is embodied in the Elementary and Secondary Education Act of 1965 (ESEA). This act in its first year provided about $1,300,000,000 of federal funds to local schools for improving elementary and secondary programs for culturally disadvantaged children and youth—children of low educational attainments who come from low-income families and neighborhoods. Included also are children who are handicapped by physical, mental, and emotional impairment. Subsequently, a Teacher Corps was established in order to get a larger number of more able young people and experienced teachers in schools in low socio-economic neighborhoods.

The intent of Title I of the act, which provided most of the funds, may be inferred from a section of *Guidelines for the Elementary and Secondary Act of 1965* that deals with the evaluation of local projects and programs supported by the funds:

Evaluative criteria should be related to changes in educational status and opportunities, and indices of such change may include, but are not limited to, objective measures of:
1. Educational achievement in the basic educational skills
2. Levels of educational attainment, as may be indicated by dropout rates
3. Educational motivation as evidenced by attention, performance, and attendance
4. Behavioral deviations and other special handicaps to educational progress
5. Cultural and social conditions related to educational opportunity and progress
6. Educational opportunities provided in the school setting, including curriculums, special programs and services, staffing, facilities, and community support[8]

Higher educational achievement, fewer dropouts, higher motivation for schooling, better attention to behavioral deviations and special handicaps, improved cultural and social conditions, and better educational opportunities should be achieved.

---

[8] *Elementary and Secondary Education Act of 1965: Guidelines to Special Programs for Educationally Deprived Children* (Washington, D.C.: Office of Education, U.S. Department of Health, Education, and Welfare, 1965), p. 28.

These objectives are similarly implied in a series of recommendations by Bloom, Davis, and Hess, that are now summarized.[9] We have included recommendations not directly related to high schools in order to present more of the scope of this recent venture.

1. Breakfast and lunch, medical and dental care, and necessary clothing should be provided by the school or community.

2. Nursery schools and kindergarten should be organized for culturally deprived children. A national commission composed of teachers and other specialists should develop and coordinate this program. The teachers should be specially trained for this type of teaching. Parents must be sufficiently involved and committed to this type of schooling that they insure continuity in the child's experience. The main objectives of the preschool education are to improve the child's perceptual ability, language development, mastery over various aspects of the environment, enthusiasm for learning, thinking and reasoning abilities, and attention span for purposive-learning activities.

3. Special attention should be given to the education of the culturally disadvantaged child during the elementary school years. His perceptual development, language development, motivation, and ability to attend should be appraised at the beginning of the first grade. Appropriate instruction for each child should be arranged. The emphasis during the first three years should be on the development of each child's knowledge, abilities, and attitudes. A national commission of teachers and other specialists should develop and coordinate the instructional program. A variety of different educational approaches should be tried out and their effectiveness evaluated. The teaching staff must be carefully selected and educated in order to help each child master the fundamental skills in language, reading, and arithmetic and a general skill in learning itself. Home-school relations must be cooperative. Every available resource should be utilized with culturally deprived children who have not had preschool educational opportunity.

4. With special regard to Negro students, all children must learn under the most positive set of human interactions under teachers who are warm and supportive to all children. Children of all races should engage in common activities. With the rapid changes resulting from

---

[9] Benjamin S. Bloom, Allison Davis, and Robert Hess, *Compensatory Education for Cultural Deprivation* (New York: Holt, Rinehart and Winston, 1965), pp. 8–40.

the civil rights movement, Negro children will need more educational and vocational guidance than other children. Beginning with secondary school, Negro students should have periodic interviews with capable guidance workers.

5. A major effort should be made at the beginning of secondary education to identify culturally deprived students who will begin higher education upon completion of high school. Special instructional programs, tutorial help, counseling, and help with the basic skills must be provided. Modifications for those who are having difficulty with regular school subjects are needed whereby they specialize in an area of interest and continue to develop the basic skills in language and reading. Work-study plans are necessary, requiring effective cooperation between schools, industry, and public agencies. Especially for the culturally disadvantaged youth, there should be peer societies that have continuity over the age period 14 to 19. These societies should provide opportunities for social relations, service to others, and the development of meaningful value patterns.

One example of how these general statements are put into practice is provided in the proposal of the Marquette Junior High School of Madison, Wisconsin. Study it carefully to observe how the objectives, instructional program, and evaluation procedures are related.

MARQUETTE JUNIOR HIGH SCHOOL—ESEA PROJECT PROPOSAL

1. *Specific Objectives of the Project*
   The objective of this project is to get each culturally disadvantaged student to learn the usual subject matter as fast and as well as he can and to simultaneously improve his personality development through establishing a total instructional program designed for pupils of low educational attainment who come from low-income homes. The specific objectives of this project for the culturally disadvantaged are
   a. To upgrade their educational attainments in reading, English, mathematics, science, and social studies
   b. To increase their desire for participation in the fine arts
   c. To promote ethical values and citizenship behaviors
   d. To encourage improved health habits and attitudes
   e. To encourage more desirable attitudes toward work
   f. To develop more favorable attitudes and motives for learning and schooling
   g. To promote healthy personality development including adequate self-concepts

2. *Special Educational Activities and Services to Be Initiated and Maintained Under This Project*

   a. *Reading Program.* The main emphasis will be to provide special aids in the improvement of reading abilities—vocabulary development, reading comprehension, reading rate, and skills of listening. English courses will be modified so as to place heavy emphasis on reading skills. Additionally, all teachers will make special efforts in improving reading skills in the various subject areas. With an improvment in reading the expectation is that higher achievement will be experienced not only in English, but also in mathematics, science, and social studies. The reading program will require additional specialized personnel, modified instructional materials, new and additional instructional equipment.

   b. *Music and Art.* To provide reasonable educational advantages at Marquette for the culturally disadvantaged requires the recognition that many of our pupils are unable to purchase musical instruments. The band and instrumental music dropout is heavy after the seventh grade due to this inability to purchase instruments after rental instruments are no longer available. More musical instruments will be purchased and provided by the school so that these children can continue to participate rather than become dropouts due to economic factors.

   The program will be expanded so that all students from low-income and culturally deprived homes are exposed to a greater appreciation of the arts.

   c. *Ethical Values and Citizenship Behaviors.* Social studies courses will be modified to improve the awareness of the culturally disadvantaged regarding the importance of ethical values and the expectations of individuals in a normal society. Guidance services and the combined efforts of the entire instructional staff will make significant contributions toward achieving these goals.

   d. *Health Habits and Attitudes.* Improved health habits and attitudes are necessary for good learning. The total staff will participate in promoting this. Physical education, science and home economics courses will be modified to make a special effort in improvement in this phase of the instructional program.

   The nutrition of many students needs improvement through food supplements in the form of breakfasts or noon day school lunch program.

   Medical services and supplies are needed by many as school attendance is seriously affected through inadequate medical attention.

   e. *Desirable Attitudes Toward Work.* Desirable attitudes toward work are essential for successful participation in life as useful and productive citizens. Industrial arts and domestic science will provide special opportunities for appreciation of the values of improved work attitudes and habits. Cooperative work experience also will be provided at the ninth-grade level to help achieve this purpose.

f. *Favorable Attitudes and Motives for Learning.* All subject areas will be concerned with the improvement of favorable attitudes and motives for learning. Courses will be modified for the purpose of improving learning in reading and to increase achievements in English, social studies, math, and sciences. New techniques, additions of specialized personnel and the use of multimedia materials will be innovated to improve the motivational plane of underachievers to the levels of normal children.

g. *Healthy Personality Development and Self-Concept.* With improved learning abilities students should develop improved personality traits and self-images as an outcome and product of a quality education program that is designed around the specific needs of children in a depressed economic and cultural area. A modified pupil-teacher ratio will enable teachers to spend more time dealing with the personal problems of children. A school also has an image—when it can cope with the educational problems that are unique to its social setting and bring desired changes in the students that it deals with, the image of the school in the eyes of the public, is also improved.

3. *Name, Location, Personnel, and Types of Facilities to Be Used in Connection with Project. . . .*

4. *Proposed Procedures and Techniques Including Appropriate Measures of Educational Achievements for Evaluating.* In relation to the seven objectives previously stated, data will be secured annually to observe gains and improvements in the culturally disadvantaged students and to make comparisons with nondisadvantaged students in the same school. Specific techniques are as follows:

a. Educational attainments will be assessed through the use of the *Iowa Tests of Basic Skills.* Forms of this test battery will be administered to the entire student body of this school annually. This will provide information to assess the gains made by the culturally disadvantaged and will also permit comparisons to be made of the achievements of the culturally disadvantaged and other students. Teacher ratings of achievements will also be secured. The number of failures and dropouts will also be noted.

b. A record of participation in the fine arts and in the applied arts will be kept.

c. Behaviors indicative of ethical values and citizenship behaviors will be observed and recorded systematically; and incidence of participation in school and community activities, the incidence of referrals to school officials for disciplinary reasons, and the incidence of police and court cases will be noted.

d. Behaviors indicative of favorable attitudes and motivation for schooling and learning will be recorded systematically. Improved motivation and attitudes will also be inferred from interviews and observations by the counseling staff, from records of assignments and activities completed, and from the incidence of tardiness and absenteeism.

e. Behaviors indicative of normal personality development and adjustment will be recorded systematically by teachers and counselors.

f. Behaviors indicative of good health habits and attitudes will be observed systematically.

g. Behaviors indicative of work habits and attitudes will be observed and recorded. The counseling staff will estimate the appropriateness of the vocational plans and related educational programs of the culturally disadvantaged during the ninth grade.

In connection with (b) through (g), the behaviors will be incorporated in a combined checklist and rating scale to permit systematic observation, recording, and analysis throughout the school year.[10]

It is too early to decide how well the various programs for the culturally disadvantaged will achieve the objectives. There is yet no proven program for improving the educational attainments of the educationally disadvantaged. These authors believe, however, that a gradual improvement in educational attainment and motivation will occur and that dropouts will decrease. A minority, however, feel that compensatory education cannot achieve pronounced improvement of the lot of the poor. For example, Pearl states that educational reforms to provide job training and compensatory education to upgrade educational attainments are doomed to failure unless society can be restructured, a society in which new careers can be established for the poor and that brings dignity to the individual.[11]

Most persons do not share this pessimism about the possibilities for improving the lot of those low in educational attainments from families of low income. However, even before the ESEA of 1965, Kaplan did an excellent job of raising critical issues about the education of the culturally disadvantaged. Some of those, which were ignored as "crash" programs, got underway in 1966 following the passage of the act into law.[12] Reading the entire article will provide a better understanding of any of the issues that are not clear:

[10] This was one of the first proposals submitted by the Madison Public Schools, by Mr. George Maki, principal, and approved in Wisconsin under the provision of the ESEA of 1965. Only relevant parts of the proposal are reproduced here.

[11] Arthur Pearl, "Youth in Lower Class Settings," in Muzasfer Sherif and Carolyn W. Sherif, eds., Problems of Youth (Chicago: Aldine, 1965), pp. 89–109.

[12] Bernard A. Kaplan, "Issues in Educating the Culturally Disadvantaged," Phi Delta Kappan, XLV (November, 1963) 70–76.

1. Who are the disadvantaged and how are they identified?
2. Are programs to the disadvantaged "fair" to other school children?
3. Are programs for the disadvantaged just another method of maintaining de facto segregation?
4. Should progress for the disadvantaged concentrate on one specific grade level, e.g., the elementary grades?
5. Do programs for the disadvantaged require foundation funds or outside financial support?
6. Is additional money all that is needed to launch a successful program?
7. Is there a standard type of school program for the disadvantaged that a community can adopt?
8. Are programs for the disadvantaged unduly influenced by the "Hawthorne effect"?
9. Do programs for the disadvantaged overlook or minimize the attributes of the culture of these children and their families?

SOCIAL DEVIANTS

Recently, the stereotype of a delinquent as a law breaker of low IQ and educational achievement coming from a broken home in a poor neighborhood has been weakening. Delinquents and other less severely maladjusted students socially are found in all types of neighborhoods and manifest wide differences in IQ, educational attainments, and the like. Wattenberg puts delinquents into four broad categories:

1. Boys variously designated as explosive, ego-damaged, or unsocialized aggressive, who come out of homes usually described as rejecting, and whose offenses are often accompanied by outpouring of aggression. The tendency is to look to some form of residential treatment as most likely to be effective. This is generally regarded as a difficult group with which to deal.

2. Boys and girls whose delinquency seems to have a purposeless, compulsive quality that expresses, if anything, some type of inner conflict. There seems to be a tendency for them to come from homes in which parents are demanding, restrictive, or vacillating. Such young people often react well to probation, counseling, casework, or clinical treatment.

3. Boys and girls who have "weak consciences" but who form many apparently normal, good relationships with their peers. Most often, the families live in high-delinquency areas and, typically, do not supervise

the young people. Offenses are incubated in groups. The recommended treatment involves embedding the young person in a group that exemplifies socially acceptable norms.

4. Some writers also describe a "cool-cat" or "confidence-man" personality—boys and girls who are capable of self-control and who deliberately manipulate other people. Neither the description of the causes of the behavior nor the recommended handling of this group is as well documented as the three preceding categories.[13]

Havighurst differentiates deviances according to desirable, undesirable, and those about which people are ambivalent.[14] The desirable forms are highly intelligent behavior in school; creative behavior in the arts; highly developed skills in athletics, dancing, and the like; and physical beauty or attractiveness. These should be encouraged in school. The undesirable forms include hostile aggressive behavior; stealing; illegitimate motherhood; withdrawn apathetic behavior; psychotic behavior; neurotic behavior; gross physical handicap; and repulsive physical appearance. Those about which there is ambivalence are highly developed masculine skill among girls; highly developed feminine interests and skills among boys; skeptical and critical social attitudes; and privatist or beatnik behavior. Havighurst further stresses that education for desirable deviancy is as important as is education for conformity. Delinquency, however, is to be avoided.

Patterns of serious delinquency are represented in the following case histories by Havighurst, *et al.*

Rex. Rex was a boy of low mentality (IQ 77) who hated school and was frequently truant. His father was a steady worker but would frequently get angry with the boy and beat him. At the age of 13 the boy was picked up by the police and admitted stealing $20 from the pocketbook of a lady in a store. His mother repaid the money and no charges were pressed. At 14 he was arrested for an attempted break in at a filling station. He was later declared delinquent by the county court, placed in a detention home, and later transferred to a foster home for a short period. He

13 William W. Wattenberg, ed., *Social Deviancy Among Youth,* Sixty-fifth Yearbook, Part 1, National Society for the Study of Education (Chicago: University of Chicago Press, 1966), p. 13.

14 Robert J. Havighurst, "Social Deviancy Among Youth: Types and Significance," in William W. Wattenberg, ed., *Social Deviancy Among Youth,* Sixty-fifth Yearbook, Part 1, National Society for the Study of Education (University of Chicago Press, 1966), pp. 59–77.

was given a medical examination but no pathology was found. At 18 he was picked up several times for drunkenness, fined several times, and finally jailed. He is fast becoming an habitual drunkard. This is a case of emotional maladjustment abetted by a delinquent subculture.

Sue. Sue was first picked up at the age of 15 for hanging around downtown with a group of girls. A month later she was reported to the police by her father for being truant, not coming home nights, and being unmanageable. She was married at 16 but was reported to the police shortly afterward by her neighbors who complained of the filthiness of the apartment and the neglect of her small baby. The police found her at that time in a tavern. Two months later she was brought in for soliciting men in a tavern. She continues to live with her parents and to practice prostitution.[15]

The prevention of delinquency is a complex task, one of the most important problems faced by the United States, because the incidence of delinquency has risen in recent decades. The solution to the problem requires the active cooperation of many people and agencies: "The most effective preventive measures against juvenile delinquency seem to be (1) finding ways of improving the family life of socially and economically underprivileged boys and girls; (2) finding ways of making school a more successful and satisfying part of their lives; or (3) creating an alternative pathway to adulthood for boys through work experience and helping them to follow this pathway."[16]

To the problems of slow learners, the culturally and educationally disadvantaged, and delinquency there are no easy answers. Recent federal legislation has done much to make the public, and many high school teachers, aware for the first time that these are serious problems that have become progressively worse since 1945. Neither schools nor other community agencies, including the churches and civic organizations, have yet altered the trend in connection with delinquency. According to Wattenberg:

First of all it should be clearly apparent that, as yet, there is no proven program which by its application can reduce with certainty the amount of delinquency and other forms of social deviancy among youth. In fact, regardless of all the advances described in this chapter, over-all statistical indices agree in showing that there is an increase in known social de-

---

[15] Robert J. Havighurst, *et al.*, *Growing up in River City* (New York: Wiley, 1962), p. 70. By permission.

[16] *Ibid.*, p. 88.

viancies. Whether we accept crime statistics, records of children born out of wedlock to young girls, police contact reports, or juvenile court records, there appears to have been an upward trend in rates as well as in absolute numbers. The power of the forces producing deviancy seems to be gaining more rapidly than the power of the social, educational, or remedial technology that we can bring to bear.[17]

SUMMARY

The past decade has been characterized by many attempts to improve educational opportunities for exceptional students, particularly the gifted, the educationally disadvantaged, and the antisocial deviants. Less attention has been given to slow learners. With rapid advances in the means of individualizing instruction, such as programed instruction, team teaching, and independent study, our schools are equipped to move ahead rapidly. And much progress must be soon realized, for many people, including government officials at all levels, want quality education for all students now, not in 1980 or 2000.

Many programs for gifted students were started during the past decade. More reliable identification procedures were initiated, including greater use of teacher judgment and of creativity tests. Enrichment, special classes, and acceleration are common, all carried out through grouping or individualizing in one way or another. Provisions for slow learners are still generally poor. Until the Elementary and Secondary Education Act was passed in 1965, there was a continuous deterioration in the quality of high school education for students of low educational attainments from homes and neighborhoods of low socioeconomic status.

Although delinquency and emotional disturbance in young people are still increasing, many new school and school-community programs are being started to improve the situation. However, not enough attention has been given as yet directly to the improvement of curriculum content and classroom teaching for slow learners. Teachers must attempt to make school more relevant to more students. The usual motivational and curriculum approaches used with college-bound students have proven to be ineffective with most antisocial deviants.

---

[17] Wattenberg, *op. cit.*, p. 25.

QUESTIONS AND ACTIVITIES

1 Based on your recent experiences and knowledge, describe the two most promising innovations that should permit better individualization of instruction. Also, identify and discuss briefly the two main deterrents.

2 Evaluate the eight objectives for the education of gifted and talented students on the basis of their comprehensiveness and on the basis of their applicability.

3 Compare the nine values expressed by the high school juniors enrolled in honor classes with instructional practices in a high school with which you are most familiar.

4 Indicate how a comprehensive program of observation, rating, and testing could be used in appraising the characteristics and abilities of all students in a school and not merely of the academically talented.

5 Outline the possible strengths and weaknesses of each of the following procedures in providing well for gifted students: Enrichment in heterogeneous classes; acceleration through condensing instruction; early admission to college; sectioning and special classes.

6 Evaluate the multiple provisions of the Milwaukee Public Schools in terms of their providing the necessary flexibility for an excellent program for the gifted.

7 Outline what you consider to be the three most important deterrents to excellent education for slow-learning students in the junior or senior high school. Discuss possible means of overcoming each.

8 Discuss the extent to which the Marquette Junior High School program for the educationally disadvantaged meets the six areas of change set forth in the ESEA.

9 Which of any of the functions implied in the recommendations of Bloom, *et al.*, regarding the culturally disadvantaged should not be assumed by the school? Justify your answer on the basis of your value-system regarding the role of education in American democracy.

10 Wattenberg puts delinquents into four categories. On the basis of your acquaintance with delinquents, first-hand or through reading, evaluate the adequacy of the categories.

11 The last quotation from Wattenberg indicates that delinquency and crime by young people are still increasing. What remedies do you propose for this situation?

SUGGESTIONS FOR FURTHER READING

BLOOM, BENJAMIN S., ALLISON DAVIS, AND ROBERT HESS, *Compensatory Education for Cultural Deprivation*, New York: Holt, Rinehart and Winston, 1965.

"Education of Exceptional Children," *Review of Educational Research,* 36, No. 1, 1966.

GALLAGHER, JAMES J., *Teaching the Gifted Child,* Boston: Allyn and Bacon, 1964.

GETZELS, JACOB W., AND PHILIP W. JACKSON, *Creativity and Intelligence: Explorations with Gifted Students,* New York: Wiley, 1962.

KLAUSMEIER, HERBERT J., AND WILLIAM GOODWIN, *Learning and Human Abilities: Educational Psychology,* 2nd ed., New York: Harper & Row, 1966, Ch. 14.

OTTO, WAYNE, AND RICHARD A. MCMENEMY, *Corrective and Remedial Teaching,* Boston: Houghton Mifflin, 1966.

TORRENCE, E. PAUL, *Gifted Children in the Classroom,* Psychological Foundations of Education Series, New York: Macmillan, 1965.

WATTENBERG, WILLIAM W., ED., *Social Deviancy among Youth,* Sixty-fifth Yearbook, National Society for the Study of Education, Chicago: University of Chicago Press, 1966.

WHIPPLE, GERTRUDE, AND MILLARD H. BLACK, ED., *Reading for Children Without: Our Disadvantaged Youth,* Newark, Del.: International Reading Association, 1966.

WITTY, PAUL A., ED., *The Educationally Retarded and Disadvantaged,* Sixty-sixth Yearbook, National Society for the Study of Education, Chicago: University of Chicago Press, 1967.

15 *Promoting mental health and self-discipline*

One objective of the public schools is to produce individuals who possess a high degree of self-understanding, individuals who are high in self-acceptance and high in their acceptance of others. Such an objective involves the school in providing experiences that promote mental health and encourage personality integration. Some of the attributes of the individual characterized by good mental health have been identified by various authorities as:

1. *Objective judgment:* The ability to look at all kinds of facts squarely and accurately, neither overlooking some nor exaggerating others. This ability is also called rationality, good sense, and even common sense.

2. *Autonomy:* The ability to deal with daily events in a self-starting, self-directing manner. Such terms as initiative, self-direction, and emotional independence are often used to convey this idea.

3. *Emotional maturity:* The ability to react to events with emotions . . . appropriate in kind and in degree to the objective nature of the situation.

4. *Self-realizing drive:* The habit of working hard and purposefully to one's full capacity. People vary greatly in their physical, intellectual, and social potentialities, but it is possible to see in each case how far the given individual is putting his own particular potentialities to work to achieve personally worthwhile results. His powers, of course, are delimited by the stage of his development. They are shaped by the opportunities he has had as well as by his innate potentialities.

5. *Self-acceptance:* A positive, self-respecting attitude toward one's self. Conscious self-insight or self-understanding may not be absolutely essential to an attitude of self-acceptance, but either seems to enhance

considerably the objectivity and the wisdom of a person's self-regard.

6. *Respect for others:* A positive, acceptant attitude toward other people.[1]

Again, stated in still other terms, physical health, proficiency in various psychomotor skills, possession of knowledge and intellectual skills, satisfactory means of adjustment, a balance between personal needs and the

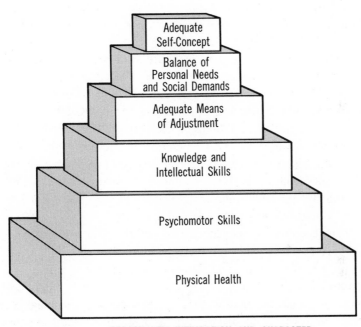

PERSONALITY INTEGRATION AND CHARACTER

FIG. 15 *The building blocks of personality integration and mental health.* (Herbert J. Klausmeier and William Goodwin, Learning and Human Abilities, *2nd ed., New York: Harper & Row, 1966, p. 381. By permission.*)

needs of others, and an adequate self-concept are also individual and environmental bases of personality integration and of mental health (Figure 15). Although heredity and conditions in the individual's out-

---

[1] Robert F. Peck and James V. Mitchell, Jr., *Mental Health*, a report prepared by the Department of Classroom Teachers and the American Educational Research Association (Washington, D.C.: NEA, 1962), pp. 3–4. By permission.

of-school environment may play a great role in shaping personality, the school, too, as it deals with abilities, attitudes, interests, knowledge, and values, is a strong force in promoting mental health.

Discipline and mental health are closely related. The goal of discipline is for the individual to possess self-control and self-discipline to help him overcome capricious or antisocial personal inclinations and whims. The goal of discipline is for the individual to acquire inner controls that permit him to reward himself for socially acceptable behavior and to punish himself for socially censured behavior—to acquire social conscience. The goal of discipline is achieved in the person who exercises self-control when coercion is removed.

Extreme forms of aggression, or withdrawal, and of anxiety can decrease learning efficiency and lead to antisocial conduct. The teacher, as he provides a model of good mental health and as he helps students gain emotional maturity and adequate self-concepts, affects each student's mental health and helps achieve the prerequisites to orderly conduct, mutual respect, and cooperation in the classroom.

Some principles through which the teacher can help each student grow in self-direction, in self-discipline, and in mental health are

1. Students are understood as individuals
2. An orderly work situation is maintained
3. The classroom climate focuses on self-discipline and group control
4. Correction and punishment are sometimes necessary
5. Some students and some classes require special treatment

Of course, discipline is also closely related to the worthwhileness of the content of the curriculum and the appropriateness of teaching methods for each individual. No teacher can have an inadequate organization of content and manifest an inept direction of learning activities, and, at the same time, maintain good discipline and promote the mental health of students.

STUDENTS ARE UNDERSTOOD AS INDIVIDUALS

If the teacher is to promote mental health and to minimize disruptive conduct and shy, withdrawing behavior, he must understand the developmental needs and problems of the individual student. Knowing any student involves, among other things, being familiar with his values, interests, aptitudes, home conditions, preferred companions, and achievements. Among the many ways in which a teacher can come to know a student are to visit the home, to allow each student to talk of problems and interests soon after the first class meeting, to study cumulative records, and to use informal evaluation procedures such as those described in Chapters 12 and 13.

Classroom disturbances are often related to the adolescent's failure to control the expression of his emotions, his inability to make satisfactory adjustments to his agemates, and his lack of methods for establishing new and satisfying relationships and effective communication with adults.

The adolescent frequently finds himself in situations in which disruptive emotions are involved. If he is to aid the student in controlling emotional expression, the teacher needs to be familiar with the situations that arouse disturbed emotions, to recognize symptoms of emotional stress, and to avoid crises in the classroom. The teacher who would help young people mature emotionally organizes constructive activities in which students learn about emotions, learn how to analyze situations objectively, recognize socially approved methods for relieving emotional tensions, develop skill in meeting problem situations, and learn to discard immature patterns of emotional response. Although these kinds of learnings might be largely incidental in many classrooms, every teacher may well give attention to the student who is highly immature or infantile emotionally. Such a student may be a constant source of irritation and disturbance for the group until he can become more mature.

Young people probably do not need approval and attention from their teacher so much as from their agemates. However, some will continue to relate dependently to the teacher throughout a large part of secondary schooling. Often, an adolescent's feelings toward adults are ambivalent: He would like to be independent of adult authority and control; but, at the same time, he feels insecure unless his parents and teachers approve of him. Thus, some young people need a great deal of approval and attention from their teachers, whereas others are relatively mature and independent. The teacher who uses constructive procedures for effective social responses will consider differences in development and ability, will give students increasing freedom to make decisions according to their maturity, and will utilize the students' need for adult approval to help him establish self-control. A teacher who makes all of the rules and who strives for uniform obedience is not helping students increase self-control. And a teacher who demonstrates inappropriate emotional responses to classroom situations, who is himself a model of high aggression or dependency, will not help students in social learning.

Classroom procedures designed to help students make satisfactory adjustments to their agemates utilize the adolescent's need for the attention and approval of his peers. Teachers should provide the opportunity for students to work together and to formulate rules for conduct for working together. They should see that each student has the opportunity to evaluate his own progress in living up to individual and group standards. The teacher serves as a leader, and a model, to insure that the need for attention and approval is satisfied in socially approved ways. He utilizes and capitalizes on the need for approval by peers as a positive method of creating a good learning situation.

Not to permit the adolescent to satisfy his need for approval by peers as he directs his efforts toward useful ends is to invite a variety of behaviors not favorable to learning. The antisocial behavior that is seen in its extreme form in gangs of delinquents may have had its origins in classrooms in which membership for some students did not entail approval or mutual support. Joining gangs enables the delinquent or predelinquent to obtain the approval of his agemates, but through means that are destructive and injurious both to society and to the adolescent.

AN ORDERLY WORK SITUATION IS MAINTAINED

Everyone tries to find meaning in his everyday activities. The student finds meaning in classroom learning activities as he can perceive order in instructional goals and in stable interpersonal relations in school groups. Disorderly learning groups, displaying socially censured patterns of behavior, are not conducive to efficient learning or to mental health. The teacher will establish an orderly work situation as he (1) manifests confident leadership, (2) establishes zest for learning, and (3) sets reasonable levels of achievement.

Manifest confident leadership

In his first meeting with the class, the teacher should establish an appropriate leadership role. Everyone—parents, students, employers—expects him to maintain the standards by which adolescents demonstrate self-control and self-discipline, standards by which order is maintained. The leadership qualities that the teacher uses to attain instructional objectives should foster in students inner controls that remain even when coercion is removed. Interpersonal relations in school groups improve when pupils participate in formulating behavioral standards so that their acts are governed by cooperation and by mutual respect rather than by unquestioning obedience to a leader.

Studying the behavior of 10-year-old boys in club settings, Lewin, Lippitt, and White examined group life under three types of leadership: authoritarian, democratic, and laissez-faire. In the authoritarian group, the leader determined all policy, dictating work tasks and assigning co-workers for each member of the group. The authoritarian leader, although friendly or impersonal, remained aloof from the work groups. In the democratic group, policy on work was determined by the entire group, guided and encouraged by a leader; each member chose the peer(s) with whom he would work. The democratic leader was a member of a work group, although he didn't do too much of the work. In the laissez-faire group, policy was determined by the group or by the individual with complete freedom from the leader. The laissez-faire leader provided materials and volunteered to give information when asked to do so, but he did not participate in activities or discussions.

Some of the findings of the study were (1) aggression was highest in the laissez-faire group; intermediate in the democratic; extremely high or low in the autocratic. (Aggression was low in the autocratic group when the leader was present; high when he was absent.) (2) The amount of time spent in group discussion was much greater under democratic than under authoritarian leadership. (3) Expressions of discontent were about ten times more frequent under authoritarian than under democratic leaders. (4) Loafing was three times greater in the authoritarian group than it was in the democratic. (5) The work output was somewhat greater under authoritarian than under democratic leaders when the leader was with the boys; it was two to three times greater under democratic leadership when the leader was absent; it fell off rapidly when the authoritarian leader was not present, but hardly at all if the democratic leader was not with the boys. (6) Under democratic leadership, the group was stimulated to self-direction six times more frequently than under the authoritarian.

In the Lippitt study, laissez-faire leadership ranked somewhere between the authoritarian and democratic in expressions of discontent, aggressiveness to members, and stimulation of group self-direction. Democratic leadership produced the highest group morale. Under the democratic leader, there were fewer disrupting incidents; the boys were happiest, learned to handle problems in group discussion, and wanted to continue club activities.[2]

However, to say that democratic leadership during an extended period of time leads to acceptable patterns of behavior in the classroom does not mean that the teacher will long tolerate socially censured acts in hope that students will unfailingly arrive at the correct pattern of behavior. Beginning teachers often find it advisable to be firm, rather than easy-going, in their early meetings with students. Teachers who lose classroom control early in the year find it difficult, if not impossible, to regain authority or leadership. Generally, the use of firmness during the first contacts does not frustrate the students who come to school to learn. And firmness pays with those students who are testing the teacher.

Students in many schools accept the teacher as a leader without question, as shown in the following:

> My classes are in United States history, eleventh grade, with classes of 30 to 36 students. The majority of these students assume much responsibility for mature conduct. The problem of discipline, with very few exceptions, does not occur. The students and I have a feeling of mutual acceptance; courteous behavior is neither difficult to develop nor hard to maintain.
>
> These students, as individuals, have every right to expect and receive treatment that I also desire to have afforded to me. When they come to me with reasons for failure to finish an assignment on time, I accept their reasons without questioning. Few take advantage of this, and instances are far between when students fail to have assignments in on time. In cases of disputed questions or wording in tests, I listen to their

---

[2] Ralph K. White and Ronald Lippitt, *Autocracy and Democracy* (New York: Harper & Row, 1960), pp. 129–310.

criticisms, and many times find them highly valuable and constructive. I believe that this acceptance of their ideas and views lends stature to the class and encourages growth in self-discipline.

This teacher displays a desirable attitude toward his students and enjoys a schoolwide reputation among the students as a good teacher. His students enjoy his classes, do well in them, and learn self-discipline and self-control.

Establish zest for learning

Everyone who has observed small children closely marvels at their exploratory behavior. Preschool children ask questions concerning all phases of their environment: What is the moon? What makes lightning? Where do babies come from? Where is the airplane going? Why does the baby cry? Most mothers spend a considerable amount of time trying to discover where curiosity has led young children in their outdoor play. And the nursery school and kindergarten build fences around playgrounds to keep this curiosity within supervisory bounds. With few exceptions, young children are curious, creative, exploratory, and eager to learn.

For many children, this zest is blunted during elementary and secondary school years by restrictions imposed in the home, the neighborhood, and the school. In the first grade, the urge for activity that leads to new discovery is thwarted by the need to conform to a confining situation—the classroom. The questions that the child wants most to answer now are deferred because a problem an adult wants solved takes precedence. Subjects in the high school are frequently taught as if every student needed the same dosage of an identical prescription. Eventually, the student no longer finds a challenge in the classroom and what was an eager search for solutions becomes a passive tolerance or even an open resistance.

The need to relate classroom experiences to out-of-school life and to help the student see practical applications of coursework has been mentioned earlier. However, this need for the practical should in no way mean that students should not be helped to experience the thrill of discovery for its own sake. Discovering how balance is achieved in a line drawing, how one solves a problem by using a symbol to represent an unknown quantity, how history seems to repeat itself—all of these may prove thrilling explorations. To what extent secondary school classrooms can be workshops in which students can feel the thrill of making important discoveries is not known. But the teacher's encouragement of a searching attitude, of creativity, of a host of new learnings and experiences is conducive to the acquisition of new concepts and to the broadening of partially developed concepts.

In classrooms where students are frustrated by having identical assignments, by conforming to overly restrictive rules of conduct, or by having to use monotonous work methods, many discipline problems arise. A teaching method that encourages passivity tends to destroy the zest for learning. Adapting learning experiences to student needs, using a variety of instructional materials, and encouraging students to find new solutions give zest to learning, promote mental health, and help avoid discipline problems.

Set reasonable levels of achievement

Some teachers set academic standards that are unreasonable. The student who is capable of performing slightly above average in geometry is encouraged to strive for perfection—to make a perfect score on timed tests. He is led to believe that he can and should achieve a perfect score, and he feels guilty when he fails to do so. Feelings of guilt that stem from failing to meet unrealistically high standards are common among better-than-average students. Teachers and parents who attempt to push adolescents beyond their present achievement by holding that perfection is the only goal create emotional barriers to normal development.

Perfectionism is often seen in the teacher's directions to entire class groups: "Do not be satisfied until your work is perfect"; "Work to get to the top"; "Solve these ten problems correctly in five minutes"; "Everyone should make 100 percent on this test." Generally, such demands are unrealistic because of the nature of the distribution of abilities among students.

If requirements are set too low—the opposite extreme—students become complacent; they have no need to work for higher achievement or to improve their work or study methods. When students are not challenged sufficiently, they become satisfied with doing just enough to get by or with being near the top with minimum effort. And, in a classroom in which standards are too low, boredom can lead to poor morale, to irritability, and to noisy, mischievous behavior.

To help a class set reasonable levels of achievement, the teacher must understand each student's abilities in relation to the work at hand, help him set realistic goals, and aid him in making progress toward instructional and institutional objectives. Every teacher should realize that students are relatively unequal in abilities, and that when equal time is used to develop concepts, understandings, and skills, differences in achievement become more rather than less evident. Each student needs to have standards commensurate with his ability. When the student is frustrated because he cannot reach a teacher-set standard, he may cheat, lie, become unruly, or give up. When the student is frustrated because standards are too low, he may spend his time idling, harassing the teacher and classmates, or engaging in other unproductive activities that tend to disrupt the classroom.

One phase of setting standards is the use made of teacher-made tests. Tests can facilitate learning if the students know that a test is being used to discover the extent to which correct concepts have been attained, to measure progress, and to overcome difficulties. Usually, a teacher-led discussion after the scoring of the test serves these purposes. Knowledge of his scores in relation to those of his classmates is also useful to the adolescent when interpreted properly. The student should realize that he may have done poorly because of poor work methods or because of insufficient preparation. The student who has worked hard and done poorly in relation to his classmates but well in relation to his abilities should not be ridiculed or made to feel insecure. As long as curricula cannot be sufficiently broad to fit the varying abilities of school-age youth, students who do their best should not experience failure repeatedly. They should not be "flunked out" of secondary school nor should they be encouraged to cheat to pass tests.

Any test can be used to arouse fear, jealousy, or antagonism among students. It is easy to construct a difficult test and to set such high standards for passing that few students will reach them. Students will surely become fearful of tests and antagonistic to them if the teacher uses tests in a punitive way, criticizes the class as a whole, or criticizes individual students in front of the class for having done poorly. Taking away privileges and assigning extra work for poor performance will also make students insecure and will not facilitate self-understanding.

Students frequently fear tests because they cannot do as well as their parents hope, because they want to excel a sibling or a classmate, or because they want to win recognition based on competitive test scores. Some adults fear all test situations largely because of the way teacher-made tests were handled formerly in schools.

Testing can be made constructive in the following ways:

1. Be certain that the purposes of tests are clearly understood
2. Give tests frequently so that any given test does not become overly important
3. Give tests only as scheduled
4. Use tests as a method by which students can measure their progress
5. Help students recognize the factors that produce differential test scores
6. Use test results as a means of understanding students better and of organizing more effective learning experiences

THE CLASSROOM CLIMATE FOCUSES ON SELF-DISCIPLINE AND GROUP CONTROL

Several forces operate simultaneously in producing the social climate of the classroom: (1) The feelings and behavior of students toward one another and toward the teacher; (2) the feelings and attitudes of the students toward learning and toward work procedures; and (3) the feelings of the teacher toward the individual student and toward the class as a whole. Because the social climate vitally affects conduct and work, it should reflect an emotionally secure environment: feelings of acceptance, self-discipline, group cooperation and group control.

The way in which a teacher organizes and conducts classroom activities can produce one of four categories of social climate in his classroom: (1) anarchic, (2) repressed, (3) competitive, and (4) cooperative.

Anarchic climates

An anarchic climate is one in which there is great confusion and disorder, in which standards for conduct and work have not been established. This climate can appear when a teacher overestimates the maturity of the class and puts the students completely on their own too suddenly. It may also appear when the teacher has a poor sense of educational values or does not know how to guide adolescents. In any event, because there are no accepted group standards of control and no feeling of unity among the members, the conduct of the group is erratic, undisciplined, and disruptive.

The teacher who is overly indulgent or who understands educational objectives poorly allows students to loaf rather than work, to ridicule one another, to express prejudices openly and maliciously, or to settle differences with physical aggression. Such student behavior, when condoned by a teacher, leads to great confusion in the class, to disunity, and to a poor learning situation.

The teacher who overestimates the maturity of adolescents and who suddenly makes them wholly responsible for deciding about work and about controlling their conduct fails to recognize that progressing from dependence to independence is a gradual process requiring careful direction. Complete laissez-faire leadership does not give students security, nor does it establish a feeling of unity and accord among them. Rather, laissez-faire leadership may lead to low work output, to a great deal of aimless activity, to aggressive conduct, and to withdrawal from classroom activities.

Repressed climates

A repressed climate is characterized by the absence of student initiative and participation in planning work or in setting goals. The students do not talk or work together, nor do they move about. They sit quietly and work individually in accordance with a leader's direction and rules. This climate occurs when the teacher remains aloof from his students and confines discussion to that between himself and a single student at any given time. Repressed climates range from apathetic to covertly rebellious.

Apathetic repressed

An apathetic repressed group has a social climate in which the members are thoroughly dominated by their leader. The students have lost their initiative and no longer assume any responsibility for discovering problems or for trying to solve them. This climate is exemplified outside the classroom in a caste system—a social organization in which individuals have yielded to an inferior status and do nothing about improving it. Another typical example of this climate is the home in which the father dominates and subjugates other members of the family so thoroughly that they become apathetic. Some prisons and schools for delinquents are also operated in this fashion. An apathetic repressed climate is possible in the classroom only when the home and community are also active in repression. Children who have learned at home that it is better to submit than to resist may be quite willing to yield to a repressive teacher.

Covertly rebellious

A covertly rebellious group is one in which the leader must constantly suppress surface aggression against himself. The members of the group are united in feeling resentment against him and, outside the situation that he controls, devise methods for resistance. When there is a unified feeling against the leader, class members use various methods for frustrating the teacher: They refuse to work to full capacity or to carry out his suggestions promptly; and they discover ways to irritate him. In the classroom, loud blowing of the nose, faked crying, loud coughing and clearing of the throat, "accidental" dropping of books, and similar devices are sometimes indicative of a repressed rebellious attitude.

Continued repression leads to widespread maladjustment because of the denial of the satisfaction of the students' needs for activity, attention, and approval. Any repressed group, whether in the home, the school, or the community, fails to achieve its potential production because initiative is either lost completely or it is directed against the leader. Even though a teacher may wish to establish a relatively repressed climate in his early meetings with a class in order to provide a good working situation, this climate should give way as quickly as possible to an atmosphere in which the focus is on the development of self-discipline and group control.

Competitive climates

A competitive climate is one in which group members direct their energy to attaining personal gain or prestige. Because our society is competitive to a great extent, many adolescents have learned to respond to competition as motivation. However, it is important to note that our society is also to some extent cooperative, and that, as a civilized society, we ought not sacrifice less effective adolescents or adults for the sake of achieving and maintaining superiority. It is false to assume that because our society is somewhat competitive, some adolescents should repeatedly experience failure because of competitive standards in school. On the contrary, it is a well-established fact that children need to be successful in school if they are to meet competitive situations outside school with a fair degree of emotional stability. Delinquents, criminals, and psychotics frequently have histories of many school failures, but few successes.

Competitive climates can be classified as friendly, hostile, and punitive.

Friendly competitive

Competition in which rules have been established and are followed may be friendly and conducive to excellent interpersonal relations. However, the occurrence or nonoccurrence of hostility and outward aggression does depend largely on the rules and on the goals of the activity. In high school wrestling, for example, definite rules are established, and equality in competition is provided for by having only wrestlers of fairly equal weight compete. The rule on weight helps eliminate the danger of serious physical injury, and a referee decides when violations of various rules have occurred. So also with basketball, state regulations hold that competing schools must have relatively equal enrollment. Frequently, the rules of competitive athletics provide that the losers take on other losers. These rules tend to insure friendly competition. When the goal is to be on the top and the desire to win becomes stronger than the willingness to abide by the rules, any friendly feeling is lost.

Competition in the classroom may be friendly and may stimulate work activity. The following factors contribute to an atmosphere of friendly competition: Students who are relatively equal are competing. Every student has an opportunity to win at some time. Each student understands and follows the rules. The goal is higher achievement or a better method of working, rather than a material or symbolic reward. The goal is not so desirable that students evade rules or take unfair advantage of one another. Losing does not result in continuing inferiority feelings or in eliminating the desire for further participation.

Hostile competitive

When members of a group compete with one another for material rewards such as prize money, symbolic rewards such as grades, or for special privileges and approval from the leader, hostility may develop. In reward-directed competition, where all members participate actively but relatively few members obtain the reward, intense rivalry is inevitable. And the work output of the entire group may decrease unless rewards are made progressively more desirable. The work output of the losers inevitably drops once they realize that they can never win the rewards.

Competitive hostility manifests itself in various ways: (1) Friendly relationships tend to break down. For example, it becomes increasingly difficult for Mary to be considerate of Esther and interested in Esther's problems, because Esther is doing her utmost to become class valedictorian, an honor that Mary also wants. (2) Aggressiveness increases. Jim wants to be first-violin in the orchestra. He verbally attacks his competitor, Bill, and encourages Sally to date Bill so that Bill will be late for practice or will miss practice entirely. (3) Withdrawal conduct increases. Frequently, the extremely hostile individual hides his feelings in a shell of isolation. He is not satisfied unless he wins, and so he withdraws from normal social relationships, devoting his time and energy to striving for his own superiority in various accomplishments. Because he feels that others are threatening his own superiority, he distrusts their motives and creates insurmountable barriers to normal interpersonal relationships.

Punitive competitive

In some competitive situations, the losers are punished. This is extremely undesirable when the individuals in a competitive situation are relatively unequal and when the losers are made scapegoats for the near winners. Sometimes the leader imposes the punishment in punitive competition; sometimes he arranges for the winners to punish the losers. Under such conditions, hostility is comparatively unrestrained, and open aggression is encouraged.

To some extent, the teacher who fails students who have done their best in a required class creates a punitive-competitive climate. When students are marked according to a predetermined system—for example, the top 10 percent As, the next 23 percent Bs, the next 34 percent Cs, the next 23 percent Ds, and the lowest 10 percent Fs—those students who do their best and still receive Fs are being punished. They must repeat the class or substitute some other class if they are to be graduated. Too, each student who hoped for a mark higher than the one he got may feel that he is being punished for not having done well enough. This may be true of the student who wants an A but gets a B, especially if he needs the A to win a scholarship or some other award he particularly desires.

Members of classroom groups may punish other members. For example, the French teacher organizes his 30 students into five teams for a vocabulary contest, with the first-place team getting an A, the second-place team a B, and so on. The team in last place receives an F and is given extra work or is deprived of some privilege. In organizing the groups, the teacher identifies the five best students and asks each to choose, in rotation, five other members for their teams. Then the teacher gives a French word for which each student writes the English equivalent. At the end of the contest, the team scores are computed on the basis of the total number of words that all the members of a team had correct. In such a situation, the better students on the losing teams will probably penalize the poorer ones for making them lose. The punishment will take the form of not choosing these students in the future, of finding fault with them, or snubbing them outside class, or of making them feel humiliated or inadequate.

Thus, the handling of achievement may produce a punitive-competitive climate. As the leader of the class, the teacher may consciously, or inadvertently, create this climate through the way in which he handles conduct, as when he encourages students to ostracize other students who have had little or no opportunity to learn the particular code of conduct he wants observed. Here again rewards for measuring up to codes of conduct are put on a competitive basis for students whose ability to achieve them is unequal. The teacher praises a particular kind of conduct, bestows favors on the students who conform, and either punishes or urges their classmates to punish those who do not conform. This is especially undesirable when students are punished for conditions they cannot control.

Cooperative climates

There is a basic difference in the motives underlying competition and cooperation. The motive for competitive action is twofold: to win and to achieve personal gain. The motive for cooperative action is also twofold: to improve oneself and to make a significant contribution to the group. Although the extent of personal achievement may not vary significantly between the types of action, personal feelings do vary. Although friendliness may be present in well-managed competitive groups, hostility and overt aggression are usually present in poorly managed competitive groups. But when members of a group are motivated to improve themselves for the group's advancement, in a cooperative climate, there is no hostility or aggression.

To establish a cooperative spirit among students already strongly conditioned by competition is difficult. The winners are often unwilling to give up personal objectives for the group's advantage; and, having become accustomed to receiving individual rewards, they do not accept group goals as incentives for effort. The "What's in it for me?" attitude may be difficult to overcome. Furthermore, students accustomed to occupying a middle or low place on the competitive ladder may not work toward a group goal because they feel inadequate in their relationships with high-achieving students.

Students usually work together best, as we saw in Chapter 8, when the groups are small, the members have similar interests and backgrounds, the goal they are working for is clearly understood, the leader's responsibility in the group is clearly established, and each member knows his responsibilities. If the teacher is planning to divide his class into groups, each group to contribute to a whole-class goal, he should consider these factors. If his students are relatively immature or are already strongly conditioned for competition, the teacher may need to specify the members of each group so that students who are friendly toward each other and who are interested in similar work activities will be in the same group. Moreover, it is often advisable to appoint the leader for each group, to outline the leaders' responsibilities to the class, to outline the work to be done within each group, and to help each group subdivide its responsibilities among its members. Even though the ultimate goal is to have students assume responsibility for self-discipline and for group control, the teacher must be careful to decrease his control gradually, rather than all at once.

The cooperative climate is an excellent climate for encouraging self-discipline and group control. The way in which to test whether students are becoming self-disciplined and responsive to reasonable group control is to arrange cooperative projects, gradually lessening teacher control. If the students are well disciplined and are responsive to group standards, they will proceed with committee assignments and various group projects with relatively little need for teacher control of their conduct. The teacher will serve mainly as a resource person, helping the students to obtain information, to develop better work methods and study habits, and to evaluate the outcome of their efforts.

CORRECTION AND PUNISHMENT ARE SOMETIMES NECESSARY

The disadvantages of using punishment as an incentive to learning and as a deterrent to undesirable conduct are several. The threat of punishment is less efficient than reward because punishment requires more policing, policing requiring teacher time that might be spent better in other tasks. Punishment has more unpredictable results than does reward. The threat of punishment produces more personality conflicts, such as aggression and withdrawal. And a constant threat of punishment may lead to complete aversion to the classwork.

Punishment to divert a student's attention from antisocial conduct or to prevent his interfering with the progress of the class may be the most constructive procedure a teacher can use under certain conditions. For instance, it may be necessary to punish a student in order to maintain group morale at a high level. However, the need for correction should decrease as the teacher becomes more familiar with his class and as he establishes good morale and an effective working situation in the classroom.

Problems concerning the use of punishment involve (1) criteria for deciding whether to punish, (2) time of punishment, (3) form of punishment, and (4) severity of punishment.

Criteria for punishment

In deciding whether to use punishment, two questions must be considered: "Will punishment help the individual student increase self-discipline and inner controls even after coercion is removed?" "Will punishment contribute to a more effective working situation for the learning group as a whole?" If the first of the questions cannot be answered positively, if the behavior is grossly deviant, if there is a danger of the teacher's losing leadership, the teacher may feel compelled to punish. Such punishment might not be necessary if he had time to investigate the causes of the student's misconduct. However, serious misbehavior sometimes arises suddenly; and action must be taken immediately to prevent the situation's getting out of control or to prevent the complete disruption of class activities.

Several other criteria may be useful in deciding whether to punish a student. First, how serious is the misconduct? Certain socially censured behavior such as use of profanity, destruction of school property, fighting, and sexual aggression must be stopped immediately. Secondly, how long has a given discipline problem persisted? Even though the misconduct may be less serious than the conduct mentioned here, punishment may be necessary for persistent disruptive conduct. Thirdly, how seriously does the student's conduct interfere with classroom activities? If there is no great interference with attaining class goals, it is better for the teacher not to punish but to investigate causes and to work out cooperative action and solutions with the student.

Time of punishment

According to present theory, punishment should not be delayed. It should be administered when misbehavior occurs. Cessation of punishment should be contingent upon the student's ceasing the misbehavior and demonstrating or manifesting the desired behavior.

Joe, an eighth-grade student, uses profane language in the classroom. He should be punished immediately so that he will associate punishment with the socially censured verbal behavior. To delay Joe's punishment will decrease the probability of his learning inner control of verbal aggression. The punishment—sending Joe to the principal, withholding privileges, reprimand, detention, isolation—should be continued until Joe shows self-control and socially approved behavior.

Form of punishment

The form of punishment should be related to the specific misbehavior. For instance, the student who deliberately damages school property or the personal property of another student should be required to make restitution unless the restitution would create extreme hardship for the offender and, thus, lead to more serious misconduct. For example, if a student deliberately breaks another student's glasses, he should replace them. If he mars the surface of a desk, he should refinish it.

Withholding privilege or assigning extra work is frequently used as punishment for cheating, for creating a disturbance in the classroom, for using profane language—offenses for which restitution or a punishment closely related to the act is not available. Not having a form of punishment closely related to the misconduct creates difficulties. It is possible that the punisher, not the punishment, will be associated with unpleasantness and that the individual, when coercion is removed, will lack inner controls and will continue to misbehave. Once punishment by withholding privilege or by assigning extra work is begun, it should be continued consistently until the student exhibits the desired behavior. As desired behavior occurs, it should be reinforced with rewards such as warmth, affection, or compliments.

Diverting attention from undesirable activity is another often-used form of classroom control. A student in a woodwork shop may deliberately create unpleasant sounds by using a saw on metal; or a student in a crafts class may wander from one student to another, interfering with the work of others. If the teacher assigns such a student a specific task to perform, such as helping straighten up the room, the student's attention may be diverted, creating a working situation for the other students that is free from disruptive incidents.

Forced public apology to the teacher or to classmates is sometimes employed as punishment, as is expulsion from the classroom or from school. These forms of punishment are severe, more severe perhaps than moderate corporal punishment, administered privately. Unless the student's conduct seriously interferes with class progress, these disciplinary techniques should not be used. Some authorities recommend that forced public apology or expulsion never be used.

Mass punishment is extremely dangerous, particularly when the entire class or several members of a group are punished for an offense that one student has committed. It is unwise to try to force adolescents to reveal the identity of an offender by punishing all of them. Extreme aggression toward a teacher is frequently generated in this way.

For minor offenses that incur punishment, it is best not to direct the attention of the entire class to the offense or to the punishment. The teacher should handle the problem firmly, quickly, and with the least possible disturbance to the class. Some classmates usually identify themselves with the student being punished; hence, advertising his punishment causes widespread resentment against the teacher. Also, the student who is punished loses prestige with his classmates and may become antagonistic toward the teacher. In all punishment, except for serious offenses, the effective procedure is to obtain the desired behavior quickly, to try to insure minimal resentment, and to see that productive work is resumed immediately.

Severity of punishment

When punishment is so severe that the student does not want to return to class, to alter his behavior, or to work with the teacher who administered the punishment, the teacher can no longer experience success with the student. The opportunity for helping the student increase his powers of self-discipline is lost, and the extreme punishment has only intensified the student's maladjustment. Except for extremely serious offenses that impede class progress markedly, punishment should never be this severe.

It is difficult for the teacher to predict accurately how severe a punishment is for an individual student unless he knows the student and his home environment. A sarcastic verbal attack may be more severe for the sensitive girl than a hard whipping for the boy who is whipped frequently at home. To decide how severe a punishment is, the teacher must consider the student's feelings about the form of the punishment.

Punishment versus substitution of desired behavior

Punishment is so fraught with unknowns that its use should be minimized. These generalizations may help: Realize that misbehavior is a symptom of maladjustment. Try to discover causes before giving punishment. Use punishment only if it seems the only way to divert attention from undesirable conduct or to prevent a student from interfering with the progress of his classmates or destroying group morale. Administer minor punishment yourself and complete it quickly. Whenever possible, relate the punishment to the offense. Consider the severity of the punishment carefully, and realize that severe punishment may deprive you of any further opportunity to help the student.

Punishment should be followed with correction. One effective technique for eliminating deviant patterns of behavior is to substitute and reinforce some other behavior that leads to the same goal in a more acceptable way. For example, securing attention is a socially acceptable goal. If achieving well in a given task, or cooperating in a class project, or maintaining a bulletin board—rather than bullying other students, using sarcasm with the teacher, and so on—can provide the student with the attention that he wants, these acts should be reinforced with teacher-peer approval. Finding socially approved substitutes for undesirable aggression is a constructive means of correcting behavior.

Reasoning, too, is a means of obtaining cooperation and mutual respect in the classroom. Noting that severe physical punishment serves as an aggressive model on which the child patterns his own behavior, Bandura and Walters discuss the use of reasoning as a disciplinary technique. Among the adult behaviors cited by them in discussing reasoning are (1) pointing out the consequences of undesirable behavior for other people; (2) explaining the reasons for putting restraints on the child's behavior; and (3) providing a model that the child can adopt.[3] Open communication and positive reasoning among adolescents, and between adolescent and teacher, can contribute to effective learning settings and to individual self-control.

Much misbehavior—talking, carelessness, inattention—would disap-

---

[3] Albert Bandura and Richard H. Walters, *Social Learning and Personality Development* (New York: Holt, Rinehart and Winston, 1963), p. 195.

pear if teachers sought to provide sufficiently interesting learning activities. High interest alone will contribute to the orderly attainment of instructional goals. And if the student lacks knowledge or skills to gain his objectives in socially approved ways, teaching him new knowledge and skills may help him correct his misbehavior.

SOME STUDENTS REQUIRE SPECIAL TREATMENT

Many students who misbehave and have to be punished need special treatment. Misbehavior is a symptom indicating that something is wrong with the learning environment or that the student has earlier acquired attitudes and behavior that manifest themselves in the classroom. Obviously, punishment itself does not help the teacher discover the cause of misbehavior.

While students characterized by extreme aggressive reactions will require study by the teacher, special treatment will also be necessary for the withdrawing student. The extremely shy adolescent, the daydreamer, or the isolate does not disrupt work and is frequently overlooked. However, the withdrawn student's mental health may be in danger if he has lost all interest in his work, if he has stopped trying to achieve, or if he is escaping into a world of fantasy.

What are the basic elements of a program for special treatment? What does the teacher do to help the personally maladjusted or antisocial student? The major steps in a remedial program involve analyzing the classroom situation to determine to what extent the causes are to be found in the classroom itself, analyzing the student to discover the causes of his behavior, and planning a program for special assistance and putting it into action.

Analysis of the classroom situation

We have already noted certain classroom procedures and group situations that sometimes lead to aggression or to withdrawal. Relatively few discipline problems occur in a well-managed classroom where learning activities are organized to meet the interests and needs of adolescents. Except in schools with low morale among both the student body and the faculty, and in classes containing many students who show antisocial conduct, it is probable that the causes of most discipline problems can be explained in terms of inappropriate curriculum, the teacher's failure to conduct learning activities properly, or poor management of interpersonal relationships in the classroom.

The classroom situation in which misconduct appears should be analyzed. Giving an unreasonable work assignment such as asking students to do 20 problems in ten minutes when few students can finish them in that time, arbitrarily demanding complete silence while the teacher reads poems in which the students are not interested, asking a girl who is unhappy about the clothes she must wear to give a five-minute oral report—any of these situations may produce undesirable conduct in the classroom.

In order to provide a different treatment for an individual student, the teacher may, in some instances, have to alter procedures that are generally effective for most of the students. Sometimes the classroom situation itself is not necessarily the direct cause of the maladjustment, but the student's reaction to the situation is not good.

Analysis of the student

The adolescent's learning environment includes his home, neighborhood, and the broader community as well as the school. His attitudes and behavior are shaped by his experiences and interactions with many people. His behavior in a certain situation is greatly influenced by his attitudes toward the situation and by his ideas of his future. Thus, a comprehensive analysis of the background out of which his behavior grows, together with his self-concept, is necessary. Ordinarily, the first step in this analysis is an interview with the student. Additional information can then be obtained through making an observational case study.

For the student who misbehaves grossly or repeatedly and for the student who withdraws, the most important fact to note in the interview is how the student feels toward himself in general and toward himself in the situation in which he has misbehaved. The adolescent's attitudes and feelings toward himself largely determine his behavior. If he feels happy and comfortable about himself, he has an adequate self-concept. If he feels unhappy or dissatisfied, he has an inadequate self-concept and may withdraw or engage in aggressive conduct as a means of bolstering his feelings as a worthwhile individual. A high congruence between the way a person actually sees himself and the way in which he views himself ideally indicates adjustment. A large discrepancy between concept of actual and ideal self indicates maladjustment.

To investigate the relationship between self-concept and behavior, Klausmeier conducted a study in which 17 experienced teachers identified one student in his class who was the most withdrawn or the most troublesome and one student who had the best feelings toward himself and who was a constructive influence on the behavior of other students. Various characteristics of the 17 students with the poorest self-concepts and the 17 with the best self-concepts are shown in Table 15.1. The columns headed Below, Average, and Above suggest how a particular student compared with the entire class on the various characteristics listed. The study also reported physical defects, occupation of father, and number of children in the family for each student.

TABLE 15.1. *Characteristics of Students with the Most Adequate and the Least Adequate Self-Concepts.*

Characteristic	Most adequate			Least adequate		
	Below	Average	Above	Below	Average	Above
Age	1	14	2	1	12	4
Height	2	14	1	2	11	4
Weight	3	11	3	3	9	5
Physical appearance	1	9	7	5	11	1
Clothing	0	8	9	5	10	2
Intelligence	0	2	15	8	8	1
Reading achievement	0	2	15	9	7	1
Arithmetic achievement	0	3	14	12	4	1
Speaking ability	0	6	11	5	11	1
Health	0	6	11	5	7	5
Attendance	0	3	14	2	8	7

A comparison of these two groups led to the following conclusions: (1) For the population studied, age, height, and weight were not closely related to the adequacy of the self-concept or to classroom conduct. (2) Physical appearance was related to the adequacy of the self-concept to some extent; clothing, to a more marked degree. (3) The students were sharply differentiated as far as intelligence and achievement were concerned: The students with adequate self-concepts were typically above the average of the class; and the students with the least adequate were average or below. (4) Speaking ability, health, and attendance were better in the students with the most adequate self-concepts. The study showed no difference between the two groups in the number of sensory defects or in the number of children in the family. Students with the most adequate self-concepts were more likely to have fathers in the professions or in business than were students with less adequate self-concepts.

Some of the conclusions drawn from the Klausmeier study were as follows:

> Because students with higher intelligence and achievement have better self-concepts, and consequently better self-control, teachers are faced with the problem of finding ways to help students of lower ability experience success that will bolster their self-concepts.
>
> Grouping students according to achievement level helps the students of lower ability experience success. Yet, at the same time, all students need to work together as a whole group on some activities so that the lower achievers will not associate the grouping with feelings of general inadequacy.
>
> The teacher should be on the alert to find areas in which students of lower ability can excel. Some of these areas may be sports, art, music, various manipulative tasks, and classroom routines. When an interest or ability is found, it should be incorporated into the total class activity, and the student should be rewarded for anything he does well.
>
> Parent-teacher conferences are important. These conferences often bring to the teacher's attention circumstances that cause the adolescent to have difficulty in school. Skillful advice from the teacher can help the parent accept the level of work which the student is able to achieve, and may relieve pressures on the student at home.
>
> When he accepts the student at his own ability level and helps him find satisfaction in the things he can do well, the teacher may be on the way to helping the adolescent improve his self-concept and classroom conduct.
>
> There does not seem to be much the school or teacher can do regarding poor self-concepts which arise from lower socioeconomic status of the parents if the larger community gives low prestige to members of lower socioeconomic status. However, the student of lower socioeconomic background can be accepted as a worthwhile person by the teacher. The teacher and other school people can help the student with personal appearance, clothing, and health. Certainly, the classroom must be a place where students are not discriminated against by the teacher or by other students on matters over which the student has no control.

Thus, understanding the student's attitudes and feelings toward himself in a situation is necessary if the teacher is to understand behavior. The teacher's understanding of the student's self-concept gives clues on the student's patterns of social interactions with other students. In some cases help in attaining an adequate self-concept and self-acceptance can be given by the teacher. In other cases, such help must come from highly specialized professionals such as counselors, physicians, psychiatrists, social workers, and so on.

A PROGRAM FOR SPECIAL ASSISTANCE

After examining classroom atmosphere and routines and the student's self-concept, the teacher may feel that a program of special assistance is needed if some of his students are to grow in mental health or in self-discipline. In some cases, the assistance can be provided by giving attention to tastes, attitudes, and values within the classroom setting. Or, assistance can be provided in special counseling interviews. Or, assistance can take the form of a change in the school program. In other cases, changes in the student's attitudes toward his home may be necessary. Generally, special assistance should begin in the areas over which the school has immediate control—the attitudes of the student toward the instructional setting and toward the instructional program.

The following students may need special assistance and may be helped by an open relationship with the teacher, by exemplary models, by consistent reinforcement of desirable attitudes, or by group activities in which he can better understand both himself and socially accepted attitudes: (1) The student who withdraws or overcompensates because of a physical defect such as poor vision that necessitates glasses; (2) the student who demands undue attention after prolonged illness; (3) the student who withdraws or becomes aggressive because of a developmental problem such as being fat or short or maturing unusually early or late; (4) the student who as a member of a minority group feels he is being treated unfairly when he is not; (5) the student who does not associate harmoniously with other students because he is of very high or low socioeconomic status; and (6) the student who sets unrealistic goals in terms of his own aptitudes and abilities. Special assistance will require the student's wanting to help himself and will involve the teacher's setting up situations that give the student appropriate emotional experiences.

Often, the teacher will need the cooperation of other teachers who also have the student in their classes. Cooperation from other teachers is required for the following students: (1) The student with low ability who is failing in several classes; (2) the student with high ability who creates a disturbance because he is not sufficiently challenged or who has already developed the idea of getting by with the least possible effort; (3) the student who for a reason not under his control is ostracized or ridiculed by his classmates; (4) the student who is far behind his classmates and who has lost hope of catching up in his work; (5) the student who has chosen an inappropriate curriculum or cocurricular program; (6) the student who cannot keep up in school because of work or other responsibilities outside school. In all cases in which the maladjusted behavior is related to the student's characteristics and to the requirements in various classes, the special program should include all teachers with whom the student has classes. Unless all of the teachers concerned are willing to cooperate, it is unlikely that a special program will be successful.

The teacher's skill in working with parents is probably the most important factor in deciding whether to try to effect some change in home conditions. When the home is involved, it is often easier to change the student's attitudes toward the home than to change the parents' attitudes toward the child. The following are students whose home life may lead to inadequate mental health or inadequate personality integration: (1) The student whose parents compare him unfavorably with siblings; (2) the student whose parents expect him to achieve beyond his abilities; (3) the student whose parents insist on an unwise choice of education or career; (4) the student who is overprotected; (5) the student who is neglected financially, emotionally, socially, or morally; and (6) the student who has rebelled against his parents because their attitudes or customs are different from those of the parents or his peers.

In working out a special program with parents, the teacher should enlist the support of trained counselors and of various community agencies whose specialty is working with the home. When the teacher takes the initiative in making contact with the parents, it should be assumed that any change that is made will result from the parents' knowing that the teacher is genuinely interested in the welfare of their child and from the parents' willingness to give his suggestions a fair trial.

If, after doing everything possible within the classroom setting, all efforts fail, the teacher should seek help for the student from counselors, school psychologists, social workers, and others. Clearly, many problems that arise in the student's mental health and in self-control are such that they require highly specialized knowledge and treatment that no teacher can possess or administer. But maximum help will be given only as counselors, psychiatrists, and teachers communicate and work together to help the student who has special problems.

SUMMARY

Mental health has as its bases physical health, proficiency in various psychomotor skills, possession of knowledge and intellectual skills, satisfactory means of adjustment, social sensitivity, and an adequate self-concept. Discipline has as its aim helping the student progress from dependence on adults for direction and control to self-direction and self-discipline, attributes of mental health and personality integration. If the teacher is to promote mental health and self-discipline, it is imperative that he understand his students as individuals and that he establish an orderly work situation from the first class meeting. Showing confident leadership early in meeting with students, increasing the students' zest for learning activities, and setting reasonable levels of achievement are essential to promoting mental health and to encouraging self-discipline and responsiveness to group control.

The social climate of the group is intimately connected with discipline and mental health. Generally, a cooperative climate is best for self-discipline and group control. A friendly competitive climate is also desirable in some cases. Anarchic and repressed climates do not lead to desirable results; however, there may be times when the teacher must be repressive in order to create a good working situation. In a cooperative climate, the teacher serves primarily as a resource person, aiding the students to secure information, to develop better study habits and work procedures, and to evaluate the outcomes of their efforts.

With some students, punishment, or at least a form of correction that the student interprets as punishment, may be necessary. Any punishment should take into consideration the seriousness of the misconduct, the effects of the punishment on other class members, the characteristics of the student being punished, and the probable effects of the punishment on future behavior. Whenever severe punishment rather than minor correction is necessary, special treatment should be considered so that the student will develop attitudes that will make future punishment unnecessary. By examining the situation preceding the misconduct and by studying the student in a given situation, the teacher can usually identify the causes of misconduct and devise special treatment that will lead to more acceptable behavior.

With some students, the teacher will need the cooperation of the parents and the help of specialists in order to formulate a good program of special assistance.

QUESTIONS AND ACTIVITIES

1 To what extent are mental health and self-discipline differing concepts? To what extent do they overlap?

2 From your memory of the emphases your high school teachers gave them, arrange in order the five principles given to help students grow in self-direction, in self-discipline, and in mental health; arrange the same principles in the order in which you think attention should be given to them in secondary schools today, and discuss briefly the reason for your own arrangement.

3 Arrange for a role-playing situation in which one person takes the role of a teacher strongly favoring a repressed climate; a second, a friendly competitive climate; a third, a hostile competitive climate; and a fourth, a cooperative climate. Have each teacher speak of the same group of students.

4 List several forms of punishment that you have recently seen parents or teachers use. What seem to be the controlling factors in whether or not a student is punished and how severely he is punished?

5 Give your reaction to the statement that a teacher is most likely to punish when a student's behavior seems to challenge his authority or his status.

6 Suggest additional ways of diverting an adolescent's attention from antisocial conduct.

7 Do you agree that much misbehavior would disappear if teachers provided sufficiently interesting learning activities? What evidence can you offer to support your position?

8 Read other studies reporting research on self-concept. Discuss how self-concept can be altered to achieve a higher congruence between a person's actual- and ideal-self concept.

9 Under what circumstances is it desirable for a teacher to secure assistance from others in working with a disturbed or misbehaving student?

10 In what ways might the school environment contribute to emotional problems? In what ways might the school environment help a student find security and satisfaction?

11 List some classroom situations that might be utilized in helping students attain objective judgment.

12 List and discuss some of the characteristics of a teacher who would provide a model of good mental health.

SUGGESTIONS FOR FURTHER READING

ASCD 1962 YEARBOOK COMMITTEE, *Perceiving, Behaving, Becoming: A New Focus for Education*, Arthur W. Combs, Chairman, Washington, D.C.: Association for Supervision and Curriculum Development, 1962.

ASCD 1966 YEARBOOK COMMITTEE, *Learning and Mental Health in the Schools*, Edited by Walter B. Waetjen and Robert R. Leeper, Washington, D.C.: Association for Supervision and Curriculum Development, 1966.

BANDURA, ALBERT, AND RICHARD H. WALTERS, *Social Learning and Personality Development*, New York: Holt, Rinehart and Winston, 1963.

BROWN, EDWIN J., AND ARTHUR T. PHELPS, *Managing the Classroom*, 2nd ed., New York: Ronald, 1961.

SHEVIAKOV, GEORGE V., AND FRITZ REDL, *Discipline for Today's Children and Youth*, rev. ed., Washington, D.C.: Association for Supervision and Curriculum Development, National Education Association, 1961.

16 Guidance and counseling

$\mathcal{T}$he National Defense Education Act of 1958 is a milestone in the guidance movement. Among other things, it provides for institutes to prepare guidance workers and to improve the capabilities of some personnel who are already in guidance. Subsequently, many states and localities have employed additional guidance workers, mainly in the senior and junior high schools. The number of guidance workers, usually referred to as guidance counselors, has increased greatly. Although these events have occurred, the high promise expected from the increased monies and personnel has not materially reduced the dropout rate from high school or the incidence of antisocial conduct and emotional disturbance among adolescents, as noted previously in Chapter 14. Furthermore, Rice points out that the articulation of guidance and instruction has tended to decrease as former teacher-counselors become specialists in guidance and cease teaching. Specialized counselors seldom enter into teacher-student interaction, although teachers engage in many group guidance activities.[1]

Not only have many who were part-time counselors and teachers become guidance counselors solely, but the latter are tending toward greater specialization within the schools' guidance program. Crary found

---

[1] Joseph P. Rice, "Cooperative Guidance and Instructional Programs for Leadership Preparation," *Personnel and Guidance Journal*, XLIV (May, 1966), 967–973.

a tendency, especially in the larger high schools employing more than one guidance counselor, for a considerable number of personnel to spend more than one half of their time on a single guidance area such as programs for talented students, personal-social problems of students, educational guidance and programing, vocational guidance, or college-bound students.[2] As knowledge increases, there is, of course, a tendency toward greater specialization. Specialization continues in teaching, too. For example, in the large high schools there are chemistry teachers, biology teachers, and physics teachers, not science teachers as there were a few decades ago.

Although specialization will and undoubtedly should continue in guidance, caution must be exercised concerning the amount of money to be paid to obtain specialists in comparison with that paid to secure more excellent teachers. A school may spend a considerable amount of money for specialists but be unable to secure good teachers, or it may give too many students to excellent teachers. Poor teaching continuously creates more problems than all the specialists can handle. Furthermore, teachers can be as helpful as or more helpful than professional counselors on some guidance matters. For example, Zuncker and Brown[3] had upperclassmen student counselors and professional counselors provide six and one-half hours of academic adjustment guidance to equal numbers of beginning college freshmen. The student counselors and professional counselors received an identical amount of guidance pretraining. The student counselors were as effective as the professional counselors on all the criteria used in the well-designed, controlled experiment. In addition, the freshmen counseled by the student counselors used information more effectively as determined by higher first semester grades.

The roles of the specialist and of the teacher in guidance are changing, especially in connection with the greatly increasing number of specialists. Precisely what the role of each should be is not clear. In part, how well each functions is related to what each does in addition to guidance and also to the type of guidance activity that he has the

---

[2] Robert W. Crary, "Specialized Counseling—A New Trend?" *Personnel and Guidance Journal*, XLIV (June, 1966), 1056–1061.

[3] Vernon Zuncker and William F. Brown, "Comparative Effectiveness of Student and Professional Counselors," *Personnel and Guidance Journal*, XLIV (March, 1966), 738–743.

time and capabilities to execute properly. The point of view in this chapter is clear. The teacher is still the central figure in guidance and counseling and should exercise a more prominent, rather than a less prominent, role. Also, individual counseling and some other guidance functions are becoming specialized. Thus, the intent of this chapter is not to offer guidelines for preparing counselors. The importance of the teacher will be more apparent in the next section dealing with group guidance by teachers, individual counseling by teachers, and other teacher guidance activities.

GROUP GUIDANCE BY TEACHERS

Teachers provide some information to students in groups, outline suggestions to groups of students for securing information, lead group discussions, and in other ways deal with groups rather than with students individually. Precisely what kind of guidance about academic matters, personal-social matters, vocational choices, home-school relationships, work-study habits, and the like can be handled well in groups of varying size has not yet been determined, according to Shaw and Wursten.[4] It would appear, however, that most student problems associated with the program of instruction and cocurricular activities, as well as some other problems, should be dealt with by the teachers in group situations or in individual counseling interviews, rather than by specialized guidance counselors. As you study the various opportunities for group guidance, think about your role as a classroom teacher in working with groups, your opportunity for individual counseling outside the group setting, and the role of a specialist who may not know either the subject matter or the student as well as you do.

The regular instructional program

The teacher's role as counselor and guide has been emphasized in earlier chapters. Using the techniques appropriate to the situation, the skillful teacher can fulfill the guidance needs of most students in the regular program of instruction, provided he accepts this as his responsibility and

[4] Merville C. Shaw and Rosemary Wursten, "Research on Group Procedures in Schools: A Review of the Literature," *Personnel and Guidance Journal*, XLIV (September, 1965), 27–32.

does not have too many students and classes. But if the majority of teachers in a school do not accept this responsibility or if the instructional program does not consider variations in student interests and abilities, more problems are created than can be handled by even a large number of specialists in guidance.

We will now review briefly some features of classroom instruction, already discussed, that emphasize the teacher's guidance role. The teacher plans unit and daily activities as required for the varying interests and abilities of his students. In initiating these activities, he works with the students in clarifying individual and group goals, he studies the characteristics of the students, and he creates a favorable emotional atmosphere for learning, including individual and group control of conduct. While activities are being completed, the teacher provides for goal-reorientation and modifies objectives, content, and activities as required by the varying interests and abilities of his students and the class as a whole. He assists the students in self-appraisal, the focus being on the individual student's progress. These are all guidance functions.

Specific examples were provided in previous chapters showing why and how the teacher works with the individual student, with the class as a group, and with smaller groups within the class to assist them in gaining skill in securing information, planning, and carrying out plans —some of the most important objectives in guidance work.

The more specific teaching-learning activities discussed in Part II— including individual and group work, the use of audio-visual materials, and the development of effective study and work methods—also brought out the need for guidance. Some guidance specialists treat instruction in study and work habits and improvement in communication skills as group guidance activities. These authors feel that such responsibilities belong to classroom teachers and that only in a very large school might a guidance specialist be needed to assist with this form of instruction.

Why must the teacher accept guidance as one of his responsibilities? The principal points have been made previously: Students will not learn subject matter efficiently unless they are understood as individuals and as a group; self-discipline and responsiveness to group control are as important in the regular program of instruction as are other understandings and skills; instruction that is not oriented in terms of guidance contributes to severe, deepening emotional disturbances among students and to antisocial conduct, including delinquency, outside of school.

The multiple-period class

Many multiple-period classes are in operation, principally in grades 7, 8, and 9. The most common combination of subject fields is English and social studies. In some junior and senior high schools that have class periods of 70 minutes or more, a certain class required of all students in a grade—for example, eleventh-grade social studies—incorporates the guidance functions performed by the homeroom or the multiple-period class in other schools.

The longer class period has advantages over the shorter period for guidance in that the teacher has fewer students each day, a longer period of time to know these students well as individuals, and a better opportunity to allot time for individual conferences, group activities, and pupil-teacher planning. Furthermore, if the multiple-period class is organized on a unit plan of instruction, guidance emphases such as study habits, work methods, regular classroom and cocurricular programs, occupational information, and career-planning can be taken care of well. The longer period also allows the student to develop closer identity with the school. Completely departmentalized instruction, especially when class periods are short, gives little opportunity for the teacher to know the students well or for the students to feel that any one classroom or activity is intended particularly for him. Group interaction and friendships are promoted in the longer class period better than in the short period. The multiple-period classroom becomes home to the student. As we move into more team teaching and modular scheduling, there are also extended opportunities for guidance by teachers.

The homeroom

Homerooms vary widely in their guidance functions. Some schools give administrative matters more attention than they give to guidance. The homeroom program of Broad Ripple High School in Indianapolis, Indiana, indicates the variety of responsibilities assumed by the homeroom teacher.[5] In addition to the homeroom program, there is a 40-minute period for conferences every day. The dean of girls, the dean of boys,

---

[5] The information concerning this program came from booklets issued by the school and from personal conferences with the principal. The program is continuously being revised and improved.

the director of counseling, a coordinator who handles the part-time work and distributive education arrangements, a nurse, and a social worker participate in guidance activities, along with other school administrators. In this school, however, guidance and counseling are mainly the responsibility of the homeroom teachers, with the specialists already named assuming major responsibility for coordination and for work with exceptional students.

In the Broad Ripple High School, the homeroom period lasts from 9:45 to 10:00 A.M. every day. There is also a 40-minute conference period from 3:20 to 4:00 P.M. *The Handbook for Broad Ripple High School Students,* a 92-page booklet, gives students the following information about the homeroom:

> All pupils assemble in the homeroom each day at the close of the second period. During this period announcements are made over the public address system and the all-day attendance record is made. The remainder of the period is used for counseling, special activities, and the making of school records.
>
> Educational plans of pupils are developed through the homeroom counseling program. The homeroom teacher is the pupil's first counselor. Pupils are encouraged to ask questions and to consult or discuss with him or her any problems that may arise. When a pupil returns to school following an absence that included the homeroom period, he should obtain an admission blank from his homeroom teacher.

The homeroom teacher, who also teaches regular classes, uses the 40-minute conference period from 3:20 to 4:00 P.M. to counsel with individual students or to confer with groups, including students in his homeroom. Instructions to the teachers about this period state that any teacher may assign a conference period for any pupil to (1) help him with his work, (2) take care of a classroom problem, or (3) discuss a school or personal problem. A pupil may request a conference period with any teacher.

The following brief edited excerpts from the *Manual for Broad Ripple High School Teachers* describe the functions of the homeroom teachers:

1. Homeroom organization: Homerooms are organized so that all the pupils are at the same grade level. They are grouped as freshman, sophomore, junior, or senior homerooms. The organization of individual homerooms is left to the discretion of the respective homeroom teachers. The teacher is free to have officers, monitors, or other special representatives in the homeroom. Homeroom teachers at each grade level form a committee that is re-

sponsible for group or class activities; a teacher-chairman appointed for each committee assumes the responsibility for directing the activities.

2. Attendance: The homeroom teacher is responsible for checking and reporting attendance, taking care of excuse forms, and discussing with parents, whenever possible, all cases of irregular attendance, tardiness, and part-time absence.

3. Making out pupil program and nativity cards: The teacher sees that the pupil program card and nativity card (identifying information) are properly made out and that the information is recorded accurately.

4. Report cards: Homeroom teachers take care of distributing report cards to their students and collecting them.

5. Homeroom teacher's record: A four-page cumulative record is issued to the freshman homeroom teacher, who passes it on from year to year to the student's next homeroom teacher.

6. Study slips: Study slips (schedule of classes) are filled out for the next semester about six weeks before the end of each semester. Before the study slips are due in the office, the teachers talk with the pupils about their plans during the homeroom periods. The four-year plan of the homeroom teacher's record is the basis for this counseling.

7. Requests for change in pupil program: Changes in students' programs at the beginning of each semester may be necessary for many reasons, including failure and changes in educational or vocational plans. The homeroom teacher considers each such request, except in case of failure, and approves or disapproves it as the evidence indicates.

8. Requests for short hours because of outside employment: Handling requests for shorter hours in school is one of the guidance coordinator's several responsibilities. A student may be employed, but only with his parents' approval. The homeroom teacher is notified that he has permision to work, and he is accordingly excused for one or more periods of the school day.

9. Testing and personality evaluation program: The *Otis Group Mental Ability Test* is given each freshman and also to pupils who transfer to the school. The *Kuder Preference Inventory* is given to all sophomores. Juniors are evaluated by teachers on certain personal traits, and a senior English test and psychological tests are given to all seniors. In addition, other tests are made available by the coordinator and/or director of counseling at the request of parents, teachers, or pupils. Test results are entered in the homeroom teacher's record, and are also filed in the central office. The teacher may consult with the director of counseling about their interpretation.

10. State requirements and information about high school graduation: The homeroom teacher should know Indiana's requirements for graduation and the entrance requirements for many colleges in that state. He should also have general information about graduation requirements of the particular high school. This information is available to every homeroom teacher in the *Manual*.

11. Honor point system, honor roll and point average, and class standing:

Each semester the homeroom teacher computes the number of credits earned by each student, the number of credits undertaken, and the number of honor points earned. The director of counseling computes the student's standing in the class from highest to lowest.

12. Subject order for all school records: In recording subjects taken by the student for permanent school records, the teacher follows a schoolwide form.

13. Class elections: Nominations and elections of class officers are carried on during homeroom periods by the homeroom organization.

14. Student council elections: The student council consists of pupils elected from the four classes. Officers are elected by the members of the council. The homeroom teacher's responsibilities are primarily to announce and publicize elections.

15. Services of the director of counseling: The homeroom teacher may confer with the director of counseling in matters concerning tests and their interpretation, and educational and vocational planning with students.

16. Career talks and conferences: During the junior year the homerooms sponsor an extended series of short talks by pupils who are interested in various careers. The school also cooperates with various agencies in arranging career conferences.

17. Conferences with college representatives: Visits by representatives of various colleges are announced during the homeroom period and pupils interested in conferences are notified. One evening each year is set aside for conferences with these representatives, parents, and pupils.

18. Class-sponsored activities: The principal activities sponsored by the four classes are: freshman—mothers' tea and conference; sophomore—career conferences; junior—junior-senior reception, career and vocational talks, junior-senior assembly; senior—class day, senior mothers' tea, baccalaureate, and commencement.

19. Subscription and ticket sales: Subscriptions to the school newspaper and yearbook are solicited during the homeroom period.

20. Scholarships: Beginning in the freshman year, the homeroom teacher provides students with scholarship information; he refers special questions to the director of counseling.

21. Homeroom transfers: Pupils are transferred from one homeroom to another primarily on the basis of credits completed.

This outline indicates some administrative uses of the homeroom and also the clerical duties performed by the teacher. However, the most important decisions that the student makes about his courses, his co-curricular activities, and eventually his career are based on discussions with the homeroom teacher. Furthermore, although this is not too clearly brought out, personal problems, difficulties with school work, and the like are taken care of in the conference period held by the homeroom teacher. This teacher is the key person in uncovering any problem a student may have. The dean of girls and the dean of boys have as their primary responsiblities conferring with and helping students who have financial problems, counseling with deeply disturbed students, and conferring with parents. The director of counseling provides over-all coordination of the guidance program; he serves mainly as an administrator and assistant to the teachers in interperting test results and other information. The coordinator administers the individual and group testing programs, handles employment services, and takes care of the distributive education work. The nurse keeps health records for each student and works with individual students and their parents on many health problems. The social worker works directly with the student, with the school personnel in connection with him, and with the student's home. The social worker deals chiefly with situations involving lack of cooperation at home, homes of low economic status, and broken homes. An assistant principal supervises all the work and problems connected with attendance. These specialists are thus available to the homeroom teacher for referral.

In other schools, the homeroom serves some of the same functions that the homeroom in Broad Ripple serves, but there is a more definite program for group guidance activities. Topics such as becoming acquainted with the school, using the library, forming good study habits, planning study schedules, finding hobbies, and planning careers are given systematic attention.

Cocurricular activities

As will be shown in Chapter 17, the cocurricular program is of greater help than the regular classroom program to some high-school students in developing a well-rounded personality and in acquiring interest and skill in leisure-time pursuits. Furthermore, the teacher incorporates student planning of projects and activities in some cocurricular activities, thus making learning more meaningful than it is in some regular classes. To achieve desirable results such as these, the teacher in charge, or sponsor, must confer with individual students, particularly class officers; with small groups such as committees who are planning and carrying out parts of the program; and with the whole class on such matters as social-emotional control, wise use of time, relationships with the opposite sex, social amenities, student government, and relations with adults in the community. All these are guidance activities.

How does guidance function in connection with the student's selecting cocurricular activities? Students are helped to select appropriate cocurricular activities just as if they were planning a regular classroom program. Furthermore, student participation may be encouraged or restricted. Thus, the shy, withdrawing student is encouraged to enter at least one cocurricular activity, but a more outgoing student is definitely limited as to the number of activities and the amount of school time he may spend in cocurricular activities. To accomplish this effectively, the teacher must confer individually with some students and with small groups of others.

How actually sponsoring and leading cocurricular activities involve guidance will be treated more fully in Chapter 17. Suffice it to say here that the cost of such activities to the student is kept down and that they are carried on mostly during school hours so that all eligible students can participate. Furthermore, the sponsor's methods focus upon student self-direction and group control. This focus means that a primary purpose of guidance is achieved; namely, assisting the student to cope with his developmental needs with a minimum of adult control and with a maximum response to individual and group controls. High student interest and a permissive attitude on the part of the teacher are found in many cocurricular activities; hence, students have many opportunities to practice an adult type of self-direction and to enjoy an informal association with both agemates and the teacher.

INDIVIDUAL COUNSELING BY THE TEACHER

Counseling involves a face-to-face conference between the counselor and the student, the purpose of which is to help the student clarify his feelings and problems, make better adjustments to himself and others, and learn to plan wisely. The number of counseling conferences needed for individual students varies. One student may have a good self-concept, may make decisions easily and wisely, and may have few adjustment problems involving emotions; a student with a poor self-concept may have many problems and therefore may need counseling at frequent intervals over long periods of time. If the teacher is skilled in counseling and if the time and a place appropriate for it are available, he can effectively counsel students who are not severely disturbed. But, to be effective in counseling, certain attitudes, understandings, and skills are requisite.

Basic to counseling are certain attitudes toward the student and toward the nature of the information to be obtained: (1) Each student is worthy of respect and is therefore accepted and not rejected. (2) The student can be helped in solving problems and in making plans. (3) Personal problems that students discuss with the counselor must be held in strict confidence. One anecdote illustrative of each principle makes clear the crucial importance of attitudes in counseling.

Mary, a junior, says that she left home two nights ago because her parents do not buy her nice clothes. Early in the interview, the teacher discovered that the real reason was her parents' refusal to allow her to continue dating a man of 22. When her parents found that Mary had repeatedly lied about this, they refused to let her go out, so she left home and was then living with a girl friend. Mary says that she never wants to see her parents again because they are too strict. Is Mary still worthy of respect as an individual? Can the teacher who answers negatively help her solve her problem?

Jim, a senior, has been picked up by the police for stealing on three occasions during the past year. Currently, he reports to a judge once each month in accordance with a suspended jail sentence. Jim is above average physically and mentally and likes physical activities in school, but he shows disrespect to teachers and has no interest in academic classes. To graduate, he will have to remain in school for one semester beyond the senior year unless special arrangements are made. Can Jim be helped?

While scuffling with another boy in the laboratory during a science class, Bill accidentally knocked a microscope off a table. The teacher was out of the room at the time, and no one reported the breakage to him. Later, he found the broken microscope and withdrew laboratory privileges until the culprit was identified. The principal called the whole school into assembly in an effort to discover the guilty student. Bill does not admit his guilt to the principal because he is afraid that he will be expelled from school; instead, he goes back to the teacher. He is dejected and conscience-stricken. He tells the teacher what he has done. Should the teacher report him at once to the principal? Should the teacher work with Bill until he himself wants to talk to the principal? Should the teacher help Bill in presenting his case? The teacher who reports Bill to the principal without the boy's knowledge will probably have few students coming to him voluntarily in the future.

To organize and conduct a counseling interview successfully the teacher must be able to (1) outline general plans for the interview; (2) establish rapport with the student quickly and effortlessly; (3) help the student identify and state his problem; (4) help him understand information about his problem and to outline procedures for obtaining other information; (5) help him make plans for solving his problem; (6) know when to refer a student to another person for counseling, and (7) end the interview or series of interviews.

The ideas that follow should be studied carefully in order to determine how well you can execute each when counseling with an individual.

1. Be courteous and friendly, regardless of the student's emotional state. For example, if the student is angry because he received a much lower grade than he expected, be calm and friendly as you ask him to tell you how he feels about the situation and what he thinks should be done about it.

2. Reflect the student's feelings in your comments and questions until the student gets his grievance "off his chest." Ask questions of the withdrawing or defensive student to keep him talking about his problem, but do not cross-examine. Unless severely upset, the student will give you all the information you need without much questioning.

3. Accept what the student says without contradicting him. If emotional, he will not accept contradiction from another person. If he is allowed to express his feelings, he will recognize when what he says is not factual.

4. Use words the student understands, for a counseling conference is basically a learning situation for him.

5. Reassure the student whose main problem is lack of assurance. A pat on the back and praise for what he has done well is all that is needed in some cases. But never deceive a student by telling him that everything is all right when it is not.

6. Provide the student with the necessary information about any area in which he is in the process of making a decision—choice of courses, cocurricular activities, friends, dating, and the like. Only give him enough information, however, to get him started securing information for himself if he can readily do so. In many places throughout his school life, the student needs information that is based upon adult experiences and he cannot readily get it except from adults. This is especially true in all situations involving conflicting values.

7. During the conference, summarize what has happened; do this yourself or ask the student to do it. For example, asking an emotionally upset student to summarize what has been said may help him to think more rationally about his problem. In discussing career choices, such a summary aids the student in clarifying his choice.

8. Encourage the student to propose a plan of action or to give a reasonable explanation of his problem. You may need to make suggestions to the student who apparently cannot bring himself to do this. You may find that such a student is severely disturbed emotionally or is faced with unfavorable conditions at home or in school that he cannot control.

9. Close the conference by summarizing what has happened, stating what apparently has been agreed upon concerning plans, or arranging for another conference.

After the conference, a written note might be made for the student's folder. If action by you is required, start it as soon as possible. For example, if some condition in the student's home or school life should be changed, initiate such changes yourself or go to the person who can. If the student is so severely disturbed that you cannot help him, begin referral procedures. After a series of conferences, further observation of the student is required to note any improvement; this follow-up helps in deciding whether future conferences may be helpful.

Each teacher, whether he wants to or not, must counsel students at some time. It is rare to find a student who can solve his problems without individual guidance from adults. The student's success or failure in solving his problems and the help he receives from teachers and other adults are important in determining his success or failure as an adult. A little time spent with a student in individual counseling can save years of therapy later in his life or even years in a penal institution.

OTHER TEACHER GUIDANCE ACTIVITIES

Although the guidance activities of the teacher involving students are conducted individually with students or with students in groups, there are certain types of problems and other activities not directly involving students that merit special attention. These are now considered in a framework of working with specialists and the formulation of guidance policies in the school.

Working with specialists

The number of specialists working with the student and the classroom teacher may exceed 15. The number of students needing specialized assistance after the teacher has done his best varies markedly. However, nearly every teacher identifies students with difficulties who could profit from specialized assistance. A guidance counselor normally coordinates the entire program of specialized assistance, although an assistant principal or the principal might do this in some schools. An overview is presented next concerning groups of students and types of information with which specialists might be particularly helpful to the student and teacher.

Student appraisal

The school counselor, psychometrist, and psychologist are specialists in appraising and diagnosing individual students. Having been educated for this type of work, these specialists can give the teacher valuable assistance in selecting, administering, and interpreting group achievement and other tests. In addition, as was brought out in Chapter 12, inventories, individual intelligence tests, group and individual aptitude tests, personality inventories, and other instruments are being widely used. Many teachers do not have the education needed to administer and interpret some of these tests and inventories. Consequently, when a student is identified who appears to learn very easily, to be especially good in some expressive area such as voice or dramatics, to have a serious emotional problem, or to be especially slow in learning, the teacher can refer him to the appropriate specialist for appraisal and for suggestions regarding a plan of action.

Occupational information and career-planning

If a teacher does not have information about various careers or cannot advise a student well about plans for a career, he refers the student to a counselor or teacher who is responsible for this type of counseling. This holds true for any teacher who is new in the school system or is unable to keep up with occupational information but who is responsible for helping students plan in relation to a career.

Students need to learn about various occupations, including qualifications, duties, working conditions, permanence of employment, and opportunities for advancement. Many pamphlets, books, and catalogues containing pertinent information are available for most occupations; the specialist in this field may have arranged for them to be placed in the library. Also important in this connection is occupational information obtained in field trips, in talks given by members of the community, and sound films. Information about occupations should be presented differently at different levels of student development. Appropriate information presented during the intermediate grades and junior high school years may increase understanding and awareness of occupations, develop other attitudes and values, and thereby reduce dropouts, according to Sinick, Gorman, and Hoppock.[6]

Part-time work and financial assistance

Some students need jobs in order to secure a high school education. Questions such as the following arise in connection with securing and supervising student employment: (1) What are the state laws regarding age, hours per week, and minimum wages for minors? (2) What are the local policies of both government and school? (3) What are the union regulations concerning jobs? (4) How can the school make certain that students are not being exploited?

Some students who are too young or who cannot be employed for other reasons need financial assistance if they are to continue school. The teacher may be the first to notice these students because of their

---

[6] Daniel Sinick, William E. Gorman, and Robert Hoppock, "Research on the Teaching of Occupations, 1963–1964," *Personnel and Guidance Journal*, XLIV (February, 1966), 591–595.

clothing and their lack of money for lunch or books or for the very low club dues. Although no teacher can be expected to make the necessary arrangements for providing work or financial assistance for every such student, teachers in most schools are expected to know the students sufficiently well to identify any for whom lack of funds may be a severe problem and to refer them to the proper person. In the small school, the person to assist may be the principal; in medium-sized and larger schools it may be someone on the counseling or administrative staff.

Severely disturbed and antisocial students

In spite of years of education beyond the baccalaureate degree and long experience, psychiatrists have not yet discovered a therapy that in a short time will bring the severely disturbed student back to normal emotional expression and behavior. It is not yet possible to keep every student who has committed one minor offense from continuing to commit such offenses or from getting into more serious difficulties. Obviously the teacher cannot be expected to have the skill required for counseling effectively with all his students. However, every teacher should know when emotional behavior and antisocial acts in the classroom call for referral to the school counselor rather than for punishment. Even though a student exhibits less serious symptoms of emotional disturbance or antisocial conduct, unless the teacher refers him the situation may become progressively worse until eventually drastic action is necessary. In most cases, it is much easier to deal with the younger and less severely disturbed student than with the older and more disturbed one.

Some teachers hesitate to send an extremely withdrawn or poorly behaved student to a counselor because they feel that this reflects unfavorably upon their own prestige and status. This attitude should be avoided. Recognizing that behavior results from a cause and that many causes of disorderly conduct are to be found outside the classroom, the teacher should try to discover why a student is disorderly and then work out a solution. Where no solution can be found and the behavior becomes worse, he should refer the student to the proper person. When no counselor is available, as in a small school, the teacher must assume more responsibility for locating community agencies and for working with them in setting up remedial programs.

Difficult home situations

Many students are still neglected morally, financially, and emotionally at home. Many homes present closed doors to the teacher and counselor. For students from such homes, the school is the last hope; if the school does nothing, no one will.

In connection with a longitudinal research project, these authors experienced considerable difficulty in arranging to see some parents. The parents simply refused to respond to a knock on the door or to answer the doorbell, probably because they wanted to avoid bill collectors and salesmen. Even when the interviewer was admitted, it was sometimes impossible to ascertain the student's true father; the mother herself sometimes did not know. Yet, once whoever had charge of the student was convinced that the visitor was truly interested in helping the youngster, cooperation was usually wholehearted.

Social workers, more than any other specialists, are skilled in working with parents and with parent substitutes who represent the entire range of cooperativeness—from those who try to keep the student out of school to those who are vitally interested in the student's education. When a student's statements or behavior indicates difficulties at home and the teacher or other school person cannot set up an effective relation with the parents, it is best to refer the case to a skilled social worker. When no social worker is available, an interested physician or nurse, or a representative of a community agency, such as the Red Cross or the church, can be appealed to. Attendance officials in some schools also function as social workers.

Medical assistance

The school nurse has become an invaluable member of the school staff. She can appraise the students' health, care for the student who is injured or ill, handle home and school relations involving health, and advise girls about personal hygiene and sex as necessary. In most schools with a full-time nurse, she keeps all the health records and also tests vision and hearing and gives other tests of physical fitness. Although not trained to make accurate diagnoses, she can handle many health problems that arise in the daily life of adolescents and is much better qualified than most teachers to decide about referring a student to a physician or other specialist for medical attention.

Unless the school gives systematic physical examinations, teachers are usually the first of the school personnel to note possible poor health and hearing and vision defects. Even when good medical examinations are given annually—not the routine ten-minute variety that are so common—the teacher is still usually the first to note acute illness, disease symptoms, sensory defects that appear suddenly, and poor general health. Educators are gradually accepting the idea that perfect attendance is not so desirable as caring for one's health by staying home when ill and obtaining needed medical attention from a physician or dentist, even during school hours. The teacher who accepts this point of view will be especially alert to symptoms of illness and to physical defects and will refer such students immediately to the nurse or other appropriate school person. In the small school, the appropriate person is often the principal, who may take an ill child home and refer other health matters to the parents for action.

Special student groups

With each succeeding decade, a larger percentage of all students of high school age continues school until the age of 18. As a result, an increasing number of students in secondary schools have very low intelligence and show severe deficiencies in language arts and mathematics, serious emotional disturbances, antisocial attitudes, or physical handicaps. The total percentage of students age 12 to 18 with one or more of these conditions varies from community to community but is generally not less than 5 percent and may be as high as 15 or 20 percent.

Society requires these students to remain in school until age 18 on the assumption that attending school and living at home are better than being institutionalized. However, unlike elementary schools, many secondary schools have failed to make adequate provisions for such students. They prefer to retard the student, give him failing marks, or let him sit in class doing nothing or misbehaving, rather than provide the essential special classes taught by specially prepared teachers. In Chapter 14 large special groups are treated in detail. At this point, the mentally retarded, those deficient in reading, and the physically handicapped are mentioned for illustrative purposes.

Many students with IQs ranging from 55 to 80 and with other characteristics that identify them as extremely slow learners can profit from attending secondary school only if programs suited to their abilities are available. Having one or two extremely slow learners in each of his five English classes makes providing for the more average and gifted students unnecessarily difficult for the teacher. Requiring these retarded students to take three or four of the classes to be eligible for graduation is a poor way of helping them and prevents the teachers of those classes from doing their best with the students who can learn more efficiently.

A junior high school with 800 students is likely to have from ten to 20 or more extremely slow learners in the various regular classes unless such students have been identified. These students should be assigned to a special class taught by a specially prepared teacher. Because they may be good in physical activities, these students might take regular classes in physical education, art, shop, home economics, and the like.

Many high school students are deficient in reading. They are retarded in reading by two or more years when they enter the seventh grade and they fall further behind as they go through successive secondary school grades. This situation is widespread in our schools today and it will continue unless more adequate provisions are made. Some junior and senior high schools are now setting up developmental reading programs for such students. Typically, the students whose IQs range from average to higher but who are seriously retarded in reading are placed in a class for remedial reading; they attend the other regular classes. In some smaller schools, students with reading deficiencies are given reading instruction with students with low IQ's. Although this is not the most desirable arrangement, it is better than putting them in regular English classes where they make no progress in reading. In schools with no provisions for those deficient in reading, the teacher who has five sections of tenth-grade English, for example, identifies these students, forms a special small section for them, and has four somewhat larger sections of regular English. He finds this arrangement better for meeting the needs of all the students, even though he may not be particularly competent in teaching basic reading and other language skills that the retarded need.

Many school systems have special classes for younger children who have severe vision, hearing, or other physical handicaps. But at age 14 to 16 these students are sent to the regular secondary schools in many communities, where no special provisions are available except as can be made by the classroom teachers. Their being assigned to the regular instructional program is often the result of failing to meet their special needs, rather than of sound judgment that this is best for such students. The special instruction that many communities provide at the elementary school level is expensive; it costs four times as much as instruction in the regular classes costs. Handicapped students can participate in many regular classroom and cocurricular activities, but they definitely need special instruction in certain areas. When these students are reasonably well provided for, there is less need for sectioning in the regular classes and teachers can devote more time to the average and gifted students.

Participation in case conferences

A tenth-grader who has an IQ of 150 and who has made mostly As in the ninth grade is not doing well in any of his classes. Each of his teachers is aware of this but cannot find a way of overcoming it. In a conference with this student, a school counselor finds that he was given many long assignments as a freshman and that at the beginning of the school year he decided not to work. The counselor is uncertain that this student's attitudes will improve markedly with counseling. Furthermore, he feels that the teachers can make suggestions to improve the situation. Accordingly, he calls them into a case conference to describe the situation, ask for suggestions from them, and work out with them a plan for helping the student.

In the conference, each teacher offers ideas and suggestions freely. Eventually, a plan is made under which each teacher will confer briefly with the student and suggest that the boy decide how much he will do in addition to the usual class work. He may do nothing beyond the usual work if he so desires. This plan works; the student is soon seeking his various teachers' help in outlining additional projects, rather than doing the routine drill-type extra assignments he was given so often in his freshman year.

Had the plan not worked, the counselor would have had a case conference with the student, his parents, and one or two teachers. Many other problems can be handled well by counseling with the student and by then having a case conference with people who work with him.

In summary, the case conference is useful when one teacher or counselor cannot work out the problem in counseling interviews with the student; when changes are necessary, as in classroom or cocurricular activities; and when any plan of improvement calls for action by several individuals.

Formulation of guidance policies

If a school has a guidance committee to determine policies for the over-all guidance program, why should teachers serve on this committee? There are four good reasons:

1. The budget for the school year is fixed. Employing a special teacher for the slow learners will mean larger classes for the regular teachers because funds are not available to pay a new special teacher. Teachers on the committee may decide in favor of the special teacher, accept the increase in the size of their classes, and work with enthusiasm in the community to gain more support for this program. If teachers have no voice in this policy, they may resent the hiring of the special teacher.

2. A counselor may have only one regularly scheduled conference with each student every semester. The counseling conferences are scheduled to fit the counselor's rigid time schedule. This means that students may have to miss a class for this conference—or several classes if they need several conferences. If teachers serve on the counseling committee, it may be possible to prevent this; if not, the teachers will know that such conflicts in time are unavoidable.

3. A principal who has just become interested in the homeroom's potential guidance function assigns 30 to 40 students to each homeroom teacher. The teacher learns that he is to be responsible for all guidance activities, including counseling. But the principal fails to make any provisions for reducing this teacher's five regular classes and his sponsorship of a cocurricular activity. Teachers need to serve on the guidance committee to prevent the formulation of such policies.

4. Many teachers refuse to accept any guidance or counseling responsibilties. Such teachers are likely to have many maladjusted and unhappy students and many who fail; generally, these teachers violate many mental health and guidance principles in their instruction. Some teachers are not interested in the students; others are not happy teaching. Because this is a profesional problem, teachers on the guidance committee need to assume a reasonable share of responsibility for dealing with their maladjusted, indifferent, or antisocial colleagues.

An approach to guidance such as the one presented in this chapter—that guidance is part of regular instruction and of cocurricular activities, that special help should be available whenever necessary, and that students with special needs should be provided for—makes teachers responsible for the effectiveness of the program. Specialists in guidance and special teachers are available for help with problems that most teachers are unprepared to deal with. However, over-all policies should be formulated by a committee, and this committee should include teachers.

SUMMARY

Secondary education today requires that the teacher act as a counselor to young people. Accordingly, in the regular instructional program, in cocurricular activities, and in the homeroom and multiple-period class, the teacher's activities are directed toward understanding the student, working with him individually, working with the class or with smaller groups of students, working with parents, and cooperating with others when a student is not understood well or needs special assistance. The goal is to help students satisfy their developmental needs on a day-to-day basis and to supply special help when necessary—for example, in the area of emotional problems, selection of courses or cocurricular activities, financial problems, and the like. Regular classroom teachers can carry out these guidance responsibilities with most students.

Some students, however, have special problems both as individuals and as members in groups. The school counselor, social worker, nurse, and those in charge of part-time employment can help students with their individual special problems. Students with very low learning abilities, severe deficiencies in reading or in subject areas, emotional problems, or serious physical handicaps are usually best provided for in special classes taught by special teachers, at least for part of the school day.

A guidance program needs direction, just as the regular program of instruction and cocurricular activities does. Increasingly it is becoming the practice for someone who has specialized in guidance or school psychology to assume over-all coordination of the guidance program, and for a committee, representing teachers and administrators and sometimes parents and students, to meet with the director to formulate the over-all policies.

QUESTIONS AND ACTIVITIES

1 Discuss the relationship of the teacher's attitudes toward guidance and counseling to the number and severity of problems that students have in the regular classroom.

2 Give your opinion of the advantages and disadvantages of guidance and counseling in the multiple-period class.

3 List some of the chief guidance emphases in cocurricular activities.

4 Under what circumstances might a case conference be helpful for a student?

5 When should the classroom teacher refer a student to a specialist?

6 Why should teachers participate in the formulation of guidance policies?

7 Read several recent articles on the effect of the National Defense Education Act of 1958 on the guidance movement. Compare and contrast the opinions on the effects of the federal aid.

8 In this chapter, it is pointed out that, increasingly, guidance counselors are specializing. What are the advantages of this specialization? What are the disadvantages?

9 What kinds of guidance and counseling functions might be performed by a student counselor?

10 Describe briefly some of the major attitudes, understandings, and skills essential to counseling.

SUGGESTIONS FOR FURTHER READING

BYRNE, RICHARD H., *The School Counselor*, Boston: Houghton Mifflin, 1963.

FARWELL, GAIL F., AND HERMAN J. PETERS. *Guidance Readings for Counselors*, Chicago: Rand McNally, 1960.

JOHNSON, MAURITZ, JR., WILLIAM E. BUSACKER, AND FRED Q. BOWMAN, JR., *Junior High School Guidance*, New York: Harper & Row, 1961.

MILLER, CARROLL H., *Guidance Services: An Introduction*, New York: Harper & Row, 1965.

17 Cocurricular activities

$\mathcal{T}$he value of cocurricular activities, sometimes called extraclass or extracurricular activities, is suggested by the following quotations:

> Extracurricular activities can be defended adequately on the same traditional grounds as curricular ones. . . . But when education is conceived as personality development, school activities find their best support, for they, more than formal classes, are conducive to leading pupils out in ways which make their personality attractive.[1]

> The program (of extracurricular activities) is no longer regarded as *extra*. It probably provides the best experiences in the entire curriculum from the viewpoint of training boys and girls in the techniques of getting along with one another. Many important, interesting lessons of lasting value are learned in the activities.[2]

> Activities are designed to develop leadership, responsibility, and respect for others that cannot always be gained from the academic program. Participation in sound activity programs also contributes to the health and happiness, physical skill and emotional maturity, social competence and moral values of the student. Cooperation and competition are both important components of American life. Participation in activities can help teach the value of cooperation as well as the

---

[1] John R. Shannon, "School Activities and Personality Development," *School Activities*, X (May, 1949), 275.

[2] Adolph Unruh, "Some Criteria for Evaluating a Program of Activities," *School Activities*, XI (September, 1949), 3.

spirit of competition. Working hard in activities and playing to win as in athletics can and will build character in the individual.[3]

As we shall see in the next sections of this chapter, the value of co-curricular activities in a school is related to how well they satisfy adolescent needs and promote meaningful learning. In turn, leadership of the activities is critical in order for activities to be instrumental in achieving significant values.

NEEDS OF ADOLESCENTS

The regular program of classwork and the student's home and neighborhood activities do not satisfy his needs adequately. If students are to learn efficiently in the regular classroom program, needs such as those listed in Chapter 2 must be met: Achieving satisfactory relationships with agemates and more mature relationships with adults; attaining emotional maturity; securing a measure of economic independence; and formulating a relatively stable philosophy of life. The class program is adequate for some students, but not for others. Furthermore, many regular classroom teachers give students little assistance with the first two needs listed.

TYPES OF ACTIVITIES

The variety of cocurricular activities offered in one high school is shown in Table 17.1. Some of these, such as intramural sports, have many subgroups. Most of these activities are included in the subsequent discussion.

Subject-affiliated, hobby, service, and honor clubs

Some high schools have a club related to every main subject field: algebra, art, business, chemistry, debate, foreign language, history, industrial arts, music, science, and so on. These clubs reflect the interests of stu-

---

[3] Kenneth Wilcox, "Testimony," *School Activities*, XXXVII (April, 1966), 2.

dents and teachers in a certain area of knowledge. They provide a more permissive environment than the regular classroom does. Besides learning subject matter and widening their interests, the students have an

TABLE 17.1. *Cocurricular Activities in West Senior High School, Madison, Wisconsin, June, 1966.*

A. Publications

1. *High-Times*	3. *Spanish Newspaper*
2. *Patterns in Print*	4. *Westward Ho*

B. Government and service clubs

1. Student Senate	7. American Field Service
2. Student Forum	8. Friends of Foreign Students
3. Student Library Staff	9. Office Staff
4. West Service Club	10. Red Cross
5. Stage Crew	11. Regent Roster
6. Ushers' Club	12. Movie Crew

C. Vocations and hobby clubs

1. Future Homemakers	4. Coin Club
2. Future Teachers	5. Radio Club
3. Chess Club	

D. Clubs for the arts and sciences

1. Art Angle	6. Science Club
2. Creative Writing	7. Math Club
3. Debate and Forensics	8. Modern Language Clubs
4. National Thespians	9. International Club
5. Biology Club	10. Philosophy Club

E. Vocal music organizations

1. Mixed Chorus	4. Girls' Ensemble
2. A Capella Choir	5. Girls' Chorus
3. Boys' Double Quartet	6. Operetta or Musical Comedy

F. Instrumental music organizations

1. Band and Marching Band	3. Instrumental Ensembles
2. Orchestra	

G. Sports and athletic activities

1. Pep Club	6. Athletics for Boys
2. Cheerleaders	7. W Club
3. GAA	8. Ski Club
4. Girls Rifle Club	9. Scuba Club
5. Catalina Club	

SOURCE: Information concerning this program came from booklets issued by the school and from a conference with the principal, Mr. Douglas S. Ritchie.

opportunity to develop social skills and to establish more mature relationships with adults if the club's activities extend beyond the school environment.

Although many of the students now in high school will work less than forty hours per week as adults, the program of regular instruction, particularly in the smaller schools, gives little or no attention to leisure-time hobbies. In the larger schools hobby clubs are often more popular than the subject-affiliated clubs. Archery, aviation, chess, folk-dancing, garden, knitting, music appreciation, photography, creative writing, and swimming are some of the many hobby clubs. Under the leadership of interested teachers, some hobby clubs are making good provision for leisure-time pursuits.

Service clubs, known by a variety of names and having a wide range of objectives, attempt to do somewhat the same thing at the adolescent level as community service clubs do at the adult level. One such club found in many junior and senior high schools is the Junior Red Cross. Collecting money, clothing, books, and Christmas gifts for needy children, and other humanitarian activities of a similar nature, are the immediate goals of school service clubs. Entertaining hospital patients and parents and directing school traffic are also included in their programs.

Honor clubs may be affiliated with subject fields, as in the case of the National Thespian Society, or with high achievement in general as in the National Honor Society. The Future Teachers of America and other organizations based on career interests bring together students with common interests and usually with above-average achievement in one or more subject fields. These honor clubs are open only to students whose achievements and conduct attain specified levels; no student, however, may be denied admission for other reasons.

Fraternities, sororities, and secret societies

Most states ban high school secret societies.[4] Also, high schools have explicit statements, such as the following, regarding secret societies:

> The board of education disapproves of sororities and fraternities under Greek letter or any other designation which admit or include high

[4] See Robert W. Frederick, *Student Activities in American Education* (New York: Center for Applied Research in Education, 1965), for an appraisal of many activities, including sororities and fraternities.

school pupils in their membership. Any recognition of such organizations in any manner in school is prohibited. Any activity by such organizations on school property or at school functions—such as conducting membership drives, passing out invitations to teas, selling of tickets, or carrying out initiations—shall be considered just cause for disciplinary action.[5]

The fact that secret societies are banned suggests their undesirability to school authorities and also their attractiveness to a segment of the student population and parents. Are fraternities and sororities secret societies? They are when admission is determined by vote of the present members, as is true of most social fraternities and sororities. No one who teaches in a state where high school secret societies are banned by law can be legally required to sponsor or to have any connection with such a group.

Regardless of whether the state bans or permits secret societies, the high school teacher should consider the following factors before he consents to act as an adviser or sponsor for such a group:

1. Any high school organization that admits new members by vote of its present membership, rather than open its ranks to any student who is qualified by the school, is inimical to the public good in that it is exclusive, undemocratic, and secretive, and circumvents school control. Furthermore, it is a disruptive, divisive force in the student body.

2. No high school fraternity or sorority can provide any democratic value better than can school-sponsored, open organizations.

3. To eliminate already existing secret societies, the school should sponsor nonsecret organizations and seek the cooperation of both students and parents in making them successful. Legal means should be the last resort for ridding the school campus of the secret societies.

It may be difficult for beginning teachers who had pleasant experiences in college secret fraternities or sororities to accept this point of view. It is accepted much more easily by teachers who either chose not to join such a society or who were prevented from joining because of socioeconomic status, social qualifications, religion, race, appearance, or other grounds. Also pertinent here is the fact that college sororities and fraternities are for young adults, not adolescents. Moreover, a col-

---

[5] *Handbook for Teachers* (Madison, Wisc.: Board of Education, 1963), 66.

lege education is elective, not compulsory as is a high school education. College officials can and do remove undesirable students and groups. The high school cannot so readily remove students who do poorly academically or who might organize a secret society. Furthermore, high school students who might wish to transfer to another school to get away from a discriminating group usually cannot do so, whereas college students can transfer from one college to another.

School government and assemblies

Desirable citizenship skills and a "we" feeling can be developed in any classroom, but many classrooms give little attention to these matters. When managed intelligently, school government and assemblies, together with athletic, musical, and other events, achieve these goals for most students.

The term student council is generally used for the organization of students that represent various classes, various grade levels, and various major activities. If the student council is to be effective, representatives of the school's administrative, teaching, and guidance staff are also needed. Many needs of youth can be satisfied through a well-organized school government.

Sometimes the student council or school government fails to satisfy student needs. Especially to be avoided are having the council members serve as a police force, giving them custodian functions, and having the council or its representatives serve as attorney, judge, and jury in cases of student misbehavior. Although the school council can assist in these fields, its main function is to handle the needs of its constituents, the student body. Law enforcement and punishment should be minor functions.

Athletics, music, dramatics, art, and school publications

Many college students who are preparing to teach in high schools and many inservice teachers have participated during high school or college in one or more athletic, music, or artistic activities. Their own experiences enable them to recognize the values and some of the limitations of such activities. Two main issues are related to this area of cocurricular activities.

Should these activities be engaged in primarily to promote school-community relations and for audience recreation or to benefit the students? If the latter purpose is foremost, primary attention is given the students, with secondary consideration going to the degree of perfection achieved in interscholastic athletics, music festivals, plays, art exhibits, and school annuals or yearbooks. As finished performances, they may be the culminating activities of fruitful learning experiences, particularly in the senior high school; and they should be scheduled for the most part during regular school hours to encourage widespread student participation rather than audience entertainment. Many of these culminating activities are necessary to promote "we" feelings in the student body and to foster good school-community and parent-teacher relations.

Should these activities be open to most students or only to the high achievers? Many students participate in small junior and senior high schools. But in the larger senior high school, the athletic teams, music organizations, and participants in plays, art exhibits, television productions, and school publications represent a small percentage of the total enrollment. It is not uncommon to find only 5 percent of 3000 students enrolled in grades 7 through 12 in the combined activities. From the elementary grades through the senior high school in some school systems at present, an attempt is made to identify talented children and continuously, at successive grade levels, to eliminate increasing numbers of the less talented and poorly motivated. Undoubtedly, this competitiveness, and the resulting waste of talent derives in part from real or imaginary pressure from colleges and universities, which supposedly want to admit as freshmen only a few of the "stars" from each of many high schools. Much of this pressure is imagined, however, for our colleges and universities provide intramural athletics, clubs, and other activities in which any student with any degree of talent can participate if he desires.

The junior or senior high school that wants its students to win—athletic events, music and dramatic contests, or whatever—and that uses cocurricular activities for this purpose should study its regular class and cocurricular program seriously to make certain that it has done reasonably well in identifying and developing the expressive abilities of all its students. Unequal opportunities for learning at earlier school levels and unequal rates of development in boys and girls suggest, for example, that dropping ninth-graders because they rank average to lower in music performance at present eliminates many with exceedingly good potentialities in the field of music.

Social activities

Parties, dances, dinners, and the like are important in the life of most adolescents. Such activities, when under good leadership and when their cost is kept low, give many students an opporunity to practice the social amenities that make living more gracious. Because of differences in family customs and environment, many students do not know how to act with each other in social situations, such as dances and parties.

Adolescents need recreation in groups that include both sexes. Many go to dances or parties outside school without any adult supervision. In smaller and medium-sized schools, class parties and dances fill the need for this form of recreation more adequately than do private or commercial parties and dances. A party or dance in the larger school may be given for a club or other organization rather than for a class or the entire student body.

School social events need supervision to about the same extent as a musical festival, athletic field day, or art exhibit. The school person in charge makes certain that all the students can attend if they want to, and that their conduct is reasonably good.

Senior night in one high school in Madison, Wisconsin, is noteworthy as an example of adequate supervision and good attendance. For years, the seniors had had parties that lasted all night, with no supervision after the senior dance ended at about midnight. Both parents and the school people found this undesirable, so, working together, they planned an all-night party with supervision. Some of the parents and teachers chaperone during the dance; others prepare refreshments and entertainment following the dance. The parents serve breakfast to the seniors at the end of the festivities. The dance and the following entertainment are given in a large auditorium. The adults stay as long as the seniors want to stay, but no senior may leave except to go home. Thus, the parents avoid worrying about where their young people are. Furthermore, the party costs the seniors relatively little, for the parents and other sources contribute for the dance and refreshments, and the only expense the students bear is the cost of clothing.

School camping

Camping over the weekend, during the regular school year, and in summer is rapidly increasing. Often camping arrangements are handled cooperatively by a school district and the unit of local government.

Several needs of adolescents can be provided for in camping, the most important of which are the assumption of greater responsibility for self-direction and the ability to live closely for extended periods with agemates of the same sex in the absence of parental supervision.

Camping is handled under a variety of plans, depending on the sites available and the attitude of the school and community toward its values. Under one plan, each student goes camping for a day or two each month of the school term. Under another plan, groups of students go for a longer period once each year. Under still another, with the camp site near the school, the students go only overnight. Some school camps operate primarily during vacations and the summer months.

The teacher's responsibility in respect to camping varies. In some programs, several teachers assume almost complete responsibility, just as a group of teachers do for an instructional area such as science. In other programs, one person who has taken special training in camp leadership and teaching assumes the major responsibility. Under the 12-month contract for teachers, which is becoming more prevalent, it is possible that the contract will call for ten months of classroom instruction, one month of camping or other school-connected activity, and one month of vacation, with provision for further education or travel during a portion of certain years.

Because of the variety of other activities that is possible on a good site with adequate equipment, camping is another "frill" of education that has persisted, is gaining acceptance, and will eventually attain great respectability and prestige. Home economics, business education, and physical education were largely "frills" until 1920; so was science until about 1860. People are increasingly seeking the outdoors, and the idea that people in sedentary occupations, including executives, work more efficiently if they take an occasional break for golf, swimming, tennis, fishing, and similar activities is becoming generally accepted. High school students, too, probably learn more efficiently in the classroom with an occasional short period at camp.

MEANINGFUL LEARNING

The first step in making an activity meaningful is to discover the interests and needs of the group. The interested student tries to get meaning from what he does. Being interested, he sets a goal. As he makes daily and longer-range plans and feels he is progressing toward the goal, he reads, listens, explores, practices, studies; in other words, he seeks and finds meaning in his activities.

When cocurricular activities are meaningful, four factors are probably responsible: (1) Only students who are interested participate in a given activity. In some schools, all students in a grade submit their preference for clubs and other school-sponsored activities and, except for the limits set by the size of the groups, each student is given his first choice. (2) From the adolescent's point of view, cocurricular activities satisfy his immediate needs. Students feel a strong need to make a dance a success, to give a good performance at the music festival, to finish building the radio set. (3) The leadership is in terms of the students' interests and needs. The teacher or other leader maintains a good balance between being direct—to get things started—and permissive—to allow the students considerable initiative. (4) Individual differences are recognized. There is no reason to grade students and no need for them to reach a certain achievement level. As long as they behave decently and work cooperatively, they will not fail and hence can continue to experience success. Further, the student gifted in art, music, dramatics, social leadership, or other areas is not held back lest he get too far ahead of classmates; on the contrary, he is encouraged to go ahead as rapidly as he can.

RESPONSIBLE LEADERSHIP

The school people in junior and senior high schools should organize only those cocurricular activities that meet the important needs of young people, promote meaningful learning, and encourage democratic practices. Consequently, responsible leadership of cocurricular activities might well include the following factors:

1. Participation is both encouraged and controlled
2. Participation is inexpensive and takes place mostly during school hours

3. Self-direction and group control are encouraged
4. School-community relations are improved
5. Sponsorship should be counted as part of the teaching load

Widespread participation

The shy, withdrawing child is encouraged to participate in a cocurricular activity, whereas a definite limit on the number of activities and the amount of time spent in them is necessary for many students. Also, for activities for which certain minimum school-adopted standards are set, only students meeting these standards are eligible; but no student who meets the standards should be excluded.

When such activities as athletics, music organizations, and clubs were considered extracurricular activities, only students who did well in the regular class program were permitted to participate in them; but when they are accepted as cocurricular activities, nearly every student participates. If the shy student who wants to belong to a group, as most adolescents do, cannot find an opportunity in his regular class work, every attempt should be made to find some activity in which he is interested and shows promise. Among other students with similar interests, he may make friends and learn to interact freely. Moreover, there must be enough cocurricular activities so that every student can participate in at least one. Only the students who are so severely disturbed emotionally or whose conduct is so antisocial as to interfere with the group should be excluded. As was said earlier, these students need special assistance.

How many cocurricular activities should any one student be allowed to enter? It is not at all uncommon in a small high school to find a senior participating in athletics, music, student government, and a hobby club. This is too much. No student can spend 15 hours a week on athletics, six to ten hours a week in a music organization, several hours in student government meetings, an hour or two for a hobby club, and still have enough time for his class work. The number of activities a student undertakes must be decided on the basis of the time required for each activity, his program of class work, and his interests and abilities. These authors are strongly opposed to a program of cocurricular activity, including athletics and music, that requires more than ten hours of a student's time per week.

Expense and timing

Club dues, initiation fees, banquets and dinners, cost of musical instruments, fees for the yearbook or annual, admissions to athletic events, new outfits for dances—such expenses prevent many students from taking part in cocurricular activities. Although the cost of books, clothing, food, and the like in many of our high schools is sharply increasing, students should not be expected to carry the entire cost of cocurricular activities, nor should the school provide more funds for them than for regular class work. If a school finds that expense is preventing general participation, it should examine its cocurricular program to make certain that it is not too elaborate in terms of student needs and the resources of the parents. Formal and semiformal dances can be replaced by informal dances and parties. Interscholastic athletics can give way to intramural sports that do not require admission fees or expensive equipment. Clubs can have no dues, or a nominal due each month.

The more expensive events often take place after school hours and away from school. As will be pointed out later in discussing school-community relations, some activities outside school hours are needed to provide opportunities for parents to act as spectators and to participate. However, to make certain that most students can take part, most cocurricular activities should be scheduled to occur during regular school hours.

Student self-direction and group control

The age at which people become economically independent increases for those preparing for careers via higher education. Medicine, law, teaching, nursing, engineering, and the other professions require lengthy preparation. But jobs in unskilled and semiskilled occupations are available to 18-year-olds. In other words, high school graduates can start working immediately and make a fairly comfortable living. Those students who start to work and those who go on to college need practice in self-direction as early as 12 or 13, and by their senior year in high school they should be able to assume fairly complete control of themselves and their lives. A variety of techniques are necessary here, the chief consideration being a careful balance between teacher direction and student initiative. At times the teacher gives the adolescent positive directions and assurance; at other times, he allows the youngster to go ahead on his own, even when it means making mistakes and later correcting them.

Group control should also be encouraged in cocurricular activities. As the teacher works with a group, the amount of control he exerts gradually decreases as the group members assume increasing responsibility for planning, initiating, and executing activities. Noncredit cocurricular activities usually give the teacher a better chance to encourage the development of group control than credit classes do. However, a good program of class instruction should also lead to the development of many social skills, for the cocurricular program cannot be expected to do the entire task.

School-community relations

Student participation comes first in cocurricular activities, and adult recreation and participation second, as in the regular program of instruction. At present, interscholastic athletics, with band and cheerleaders, violate this principle more directly than any other cocurricular activity. In the larger schools, few students participate in athletics and band, as against large crowds of adult rooters. Furthermore, both losing teams and championship teams disrupt school-community relations. The community's attention given to athletics de-emphasizes the rest of the cocurricular progam as well as the regular class work. Basketball games, in particular, grip the student body and community from the first small-district play-offs to the state championship game four or six weeks later. Interscholastic competition in senior high school athletics will probably remain keen, but it should not be allowed to increase in the junior high school. If good school-community relations and equally important feelings of unity among the student body are to be maintained, school administrators and the teaching staff must continually guard against overemphasis on athletics in the cocurricular program.

In secondary schools in general, closer relations are needed between parents and the school personnel. The PTA groups in the high schools are seldom as strong as in the elementary schools, even in the same city. Cocurricular activities, perhaps better than the regular class program, can lead to cooperative enterprises among the teachers, the parents, and the students.

How can parents participate in these activities? Subject-affiliated, hobby, and service clubs can call on parents as resource persons and as assistants to the sponsors and student officers. Members of honor clubs can prepare presentations for their parents. Interested parents should be asked for their opinions in school government. The lawyer, union leader, business executive, and homemaker can present specialized viewpoints. Instead of having just a few students participating in athletics, music, or dramatics, the teacher should prepare less elaborate but more carefully planned and more frequent presentations, in which many students take part, for the parents.

Teaching load

Although cocurricular activities are no longer regarded as extracurricular for the students, they often mean extra work for the sponsor. Only the regular course offerings are usually mentioned when interviewing a perspective teacher. After the school term begins, the new teacher is told which club or other activity he will sponsor. Cocurricular activity sponsorship, however, requires time and effort.

What does the sponsor do? Suppose that a hobby club is to meet for one class period each week and that the members are to meet informally for another two hours during or after school. The club sponsor brings the members together for a first meeting and, with his help if needed, they elect temporary officers. If they need information, he outlines some possible objectives and helps the officers and members conduct meetings. With this accomplished, a tentative program of activities for a specified period is planned. Usually the officers need the sponsor's help outside regular hours for discussing various problems. The sponsor attends each meeting of the club; he stays in the background unless he is needed to maintain order, to help in planning activities, or to answer questions about the proposed activities. If money is collected at the meetings and no school person is responsible for the amount collected, the sponsor helps the treasurer to keep accurate records. The sponsor of a club that meets regularly one period per week will spend at least two to four hours each week meeting with individual students, small groups, and parents, and making plans or gathering information for the regular meetings. Students, especially in junior high school, must be taught many activities because their skills are often inadequate.

How much sponsoring a club should count in the teacher's work load or whether sponsoring a club for a full year should be equivalent to offering a regular class for a semester cannot be answered definitely. Many schools cannot decide whether teaching three groups of 25 students for two multiple periods (a total of six periods) is equivalent to teaching five groups of 30 students for five periods. However, in spite of the existing disagreement about the teaching load, a school that has so many clubs and other cocurricular activities that adequate sponsorship is impossible should seriously consider incorporating some of them in the appropriate regular classes. Any school that wants a well-organized, well-directed cocurricular program must give the sponsors appropriate recognition.

SUMMARY

Cocurricular activities satisfy some students' needs more adequately than the regular program of instruction. Subject-affiliated, hobby, and service clubs often give students more opportunity for self-direction and group planning than regular classes do. Similarly, school government and assemblies, and the various athletic, music, dramatic, and art activities, typically permit more creative expression than classes do. In addition, cocurricular activities provide well for the students' need to achieve emotional maturity, a system of values, and satisfying relations with agemates and adults. High school secret societies have repeatedly been found undesirable; but camping, social activities, and other similar activities are proving of real value to students in connection with wholesome recreation.

For cocurricular activities to be worthwhile, the learning thus acquired by the student must be meaningful, and the teacher must accept his full responsibility both as a director of learning and as a counselor and guide. The responsible leadership required rests on these principles: Student participation is encouraged and controlled; activities are inexpensive and occur mostly during school hours; student self-direction and group control are encouraged; school-community relations are improved; and sponsorship counts as part of the teaching load.

QUESTIONS AND ACTIVITIES

1 Current criticisms of the secondary school include the statement that cocurricular activities are more important to students than the regular classroom program. To some extent this criticism is justified. What

has happened to the regular program that has led students to regard the cocurricular program as more important?

2 Under what circumstances might cocurricular activities contribute more to the personality development of students than the regular instructional program?

3 Discuss circumstances in which it might be more effective to incorporate subject-affiliated and hobby clubs in the regular program of classes rather than consider them as cocurricular activities. Under what circumstances might it be better to continue them as cocurricular activities?

4 "No democratic value can be achieved through secret societies or social fraternities and sororities that cannot be achieved more effectively through nonsecret, school-sponsored organizations in the high school." Discuss briefly.

5 List values to be derived through school government, including the student council, and also list some practices in student government that should be avoided.

6 Which student needs can be met well by means of athletics, music, art, dramatics, and school publications? How should these cocurricular activities be handled if they are to meet student needs effectively?

7 What values might accrue if each student went to a school camp for about one month every year? Should camping be available to each student in one longer period or in several shorter periods?

8 List and discuss briefly the major conditions that must be present if cocurricular activities are to promote meaningful learning.

9 On the basis of your experiences, cite good and poor examples of leadership in cocurricular activities.

10 Attend a school club for several consecutive meetings. On the basis of your observations, describe briefly the sponsor's major responsibilities in making the club successful for the students.

SUGGESTIONS FOR FURTHER READING

FREDERICK, ROBERT W., *The Third Curriculum*, New York: Appleton-Century-Crofts, 1959.

FREDERICK, ROBERT W., *Student Activities in American Education*, New York: The Center for Applied Research in Education, 1965.

SAPORA, ALLEN V., AND ELMER D. MITCHELL, *The Theory of Play and Recreation*, 3rd ed., New York: Ronald, 1961.

SMITH, JULIAN W., ET AL., *Outdoor Education*, Englewood Cliffs, N.J.: Prentice-Hall, 1963.

18 *Professional ethics and responsibilities*

*B*ecause the classroom teacher has face-to-face relationships with adolescents, he is the key person in rendering educational services both to youth and to society. Teachers have always found great satisfaction in developing the attitudes, understandings, and skills that contribute to the personality-integration and mental health of students. Teachers have always experienced gratification in helping young people acquire the understandings, skills, and attitudes that help each student attain a reasonable measure of success and achievement commensurate with his abilities and aspirations. Teachers have long found it gladdening to help young people assume positions in the adult world as efficient producers in and as socially conscious members of a democratic society. Teachers and teaching are important not only to high school boys and girls, and to their parents, and to communities throughout the United States, but also to the survival and advancement of civilization.

To prepare youth as well as America's citizens want them to be prepared, the teacher must be broadly educated, with skills and understandings in a number of subject-matter fields. He must be specialized in at least one broad subject field. He must be emotionally stable and secure in the face of many, and often conflicting, demands on his daily professional life.

To prepare youth, the modern teacher must play several roles. These roles or areas of activity can be described as:

1. Director of learning
2. Guidance worker or counselor
3. Member of the school community
4. Mediator of the culture
5. Link between school and community
6. Member of the profession[1]

This chapter discusses the teacher as a member of the teaching profession and his professional ethics and responsibilities. Among the characteristics of a profession are

1. A unique, definite, and essential social service
2. An emphasis upon intellectual techniques in performing its service
3. A long period of specialized training
4. A broad range of autonomy for both the individual practitioners and for the occupational group as a whole
5. An acceptance by the practitioners of broad personal responsibilities for judgments made and acts performed within the scope of professional autonomy
6. An emphasis upon the service to be rendered, rather than the economic gain to practitioners, as the basis for the organization and performance of the social service delegated to the occupational group
7. A comprehensive self-governing organization of practitioners
8. A code of ethics which has been clarified and interpreted at ambiguous and doubtful points by concrete cases[2]

Like most teachers, you will probably fulfill one of the roles of the teacher more adequately than you will others. Absolute perfection is not expected of the teacher in all areas of his professional work any more than it is expected of members of the medical and legal professions, or of adolescents in the various classes in school. Professional people are expected to give generously of their time and specialized abilities in service to society; this holds true for teachers in improving education for children and youth.

To help clarify the challenges of being a member of the teaching profession, we will examine two axioms concerning professional ethics

---

[1] National Commission on Teacher Education and Professional Standards, *Factors in Teaching Competence* (Washington, D.C.: NEA, 1954), p. 4.
[2] Myron Lieberman, *Education as a Profession*, © 1956, pp. 2–6. Reprinted by permission of Prentice-Hall, Inc., Englewood Cliffs, New Jersey.

and responsibilities. The professional teacher should (1) maintain continuous educational growth and utilize all resources for improving teaching; and (2) translate the NEA Code of Ethics into action.

MAINTAIN CONTINUOUS EDUCATIONAL GROWTH AND UTILIZE RESOURCES FOR IMPROVING TEACHING

The best teachers find it necessary to fill in gaps in background and training. The most experienced teachers often find it dull and unrewarding to teach the same old units in the same way year after year. To continue to learn and to grow, the professional should

1. Become actively involved in professional organizations at local, state, regional, or national levels
2. Experiment with recent innovations
3. Study professional books and periodicals and build a professional library
4. Write reports of successful teaching-learning practices and participate in research
5. Utilize supervisory and consultant help and instructional leadership
6. Participate in other inservice education
7. Resist censorship pressures

Become actively involved in professional organizations at local, state, regional, or national levels

If he is to grow, the teacher will find that membership in various professional organizations brings an exchange of new ideas and helps him learn of recent innovations. Such organizations also help in obtaining better teaching conditions, in setting high standards of preparation for teaching, in supporting research, in obtaining higher salaries, and so on.

Your largest professional organization is the National Education Association (NEA). Its annual meetings provide a forum for discussing ends and issues. It has departments in most fields of study, including: the National Science Teacher Association, the National Council of

Social Studies, and the National Council of Teachers of Mathematics. The departments conduct many types of programs, research, and studies. At any given time, NEA conducts a number of special projects. Currently, some of these are the Project on Language for the Deaf; Time to Teach; the Project for the Academically Talented; the Project on the Educational Implications of Automation; the Project on School Dropouts; and the Urban Project. These special projects are instrumental in change and innovation: For example, the Project on Instruction has published such valuable books as *Schools for the Sixties, Deciding What to Teach, Education in a Changing Society,* and *Planning and Organizing for Teaching.* NEA's several committees and departments suggest policy for credit union and finance, international relations, professional ethics, and so on. It publishes many valuable materials. It defends teachers against unjust attacks, investigates controversies, and so on.

To learn more of the structure and resources of the association, you might consult the most recent annual *NEA Handbook.* You might also be aware that there is a student NEA that is the national professional organization for college students entering the teaching profession.

Membership in a professional organization in your teaching field is extremely valuable. The National Council of Teachers of English (NCTE), to name but one example, has a long record of leadership and of assistance to the profession of teaching English. With its more than 100,000 members and subscribers, it is the largest subject-matter organization in the world for elementary, secondary, and college teachers. NCTE supports the work of 80 committees and commissions. Each year it has a national convention, and sponsors the Conference on College Composition and Commuication, the Conference on English Education, study tours abroad, study groups, and institutes and conferences. It publishes *Elementary English, English Journal, College English, Abstracts of English Studies,* and *Research in the Teaching of English.* It has some 140 local, regional, and state affiliates. It prepares and publishes, or distributes, many pamphlets, books, recordings, filmstrips, and maps. It exerts an enormous impact on content, emphasis, and methodology in the English classroom. Membership in the organization that corresponds to NCTE in your field will afford you balanced perspective and practical resources for improving instruction in your field.

Experiment with recent innovations

The professional will examine critically and implement recent innovations in education such as autoinstruction, flexible scheduling, new media, new teaching materials, nongrading practices, and team teaching. Too often, innovations are treated lightly as a result of reading secondary sources or of hearing a few personal opinions.

Implementing new designs for teaching is no easy task: Often new materials, new teaching methods, and new strategies are necessary. To choose but one example, team teaching, with its flexibility in the grouping of students, and with its provisions for teaching to the instructor's individual strengths, is an exciting new instructional arrangement. But building a teaching team is arduous. It requires new patterns of organization; it entails large amounts of time devoted to detailed planning and to curriculum-revision. It involves good team spirit and close, warm, accepting interpersonal relationships. These things are seldom accomplished in a single semester or in a single year. To condemn team teaching on the basis of a semester's experience, using hastily constructed materials and inept and ill-conceived means of organizing instruction by teams, is a real disservice to the profession of teaching. The implementation of teaching teams requires a great deal of patience, work, and commitment to improving learning.

The most recent generation of teachers has acquired overhead projectors, language laboratories, programed texts, extensive classroom libraries of paperbacks, and so on. It has been shown new ways of utilizing teaching competencies and of providing for individual differences. It is the teacher's responsibility to see that these innovations receive a fair trial.

Study professional journals and books and build a professional library

The fully qualified teacher will, of necessity, have kept reading avidly since being graduated from college. Although curriculum-building, unit and daily planning, selecting textbooks, teaching, guiding and counseling, advising cocurricular activities, and so on, seem to leave little time, the professional will find opportunities to read during evenings, weekends, and summers in order to fill in gaps in his background and to keep up to date in content and methodology. The professional's library will contain not only standard books and magazines in his teaching field but also works in adolescent development, in learning and human abilities, in philosophy of education, in social bases of education, in history of education, in curriculum-planning, in the teaching of reading, in testing and measuring, and so on. He may also want to own a few standard reference works such as the *Encyclopedia of Educational Research* or the *Handbook of Research on Teaching.* In addition to his regular subscriptions, he may wish to subscribe to issues of journals such as the *Review of Educational Research,* the *American Educational Research Journal,* or the *Journal of Experimental Education.* If it is beyond his means to purchase so many books and journals, the teacher can encourage the faculty to maintain an up-to-date library of professional books and can promote its effective use.

Write reports of successful teaching-learning practices and participate in research

Hopefully, a teacher will widely disseminate successful methods of accomplishing such objectives as introducing students to a study of solids—the cone, cylinder, pyramid, and sphere; as organizing a science club; as using tapes to develop aural facility in modern languages; as presenting concepts underlying propaganda; and so on. An organized exchange of such ideas is of inestimable value in helping other teachers learn new practices.

Hopefully, the teacher will also participate in research. Too often, the scientific movement in education has had little effect on the schools; the findings of research scholars have often lain unread and forgotten. Among the reasons given for the practitioner's failure to use findings are these:

1. Teachers do not always have training in statistics and research design
2. Supervisors and administrators are not effective in presenting the results of educational research to teachers
3. Reports of research are often very dull and very abstruse; the language of such reports is not readily understood by many teachers
4. Research deals with such molecular aspects of a total school program that many classroom teachers cannot see any use for the research in their daily programs

5. Teachers lack time for the thought and effort requisite to research-based changes
6. Deficiencies in the conception or in execution of research sometimes make the conclusions misleading

All of these things are true to some extent. However, professional researchers are learning to communicate their findings better. Classroom teachers are learning to communicate their problems better. Colleges and universities are giving future teachers more work in research design and in statistics. And machinery has now been created within and among many school systems and institutions to identify significant educational problems and promising innovations in order to focus research efforts.

The teacher himself should participate in attempts to solve professional problems through research. According to what we know of learning theory, it would seem that the teacher is more likely to change if he wants to teach more effectively. According to what we know of motivation, it would seem that changes in practice are more likely to occur if they are based on evidence that the teacher has helped gather and interpret in an effort to solve some of his own professional problems. The results of research will be absorbed or internalized more if the teacher plays a role in testing out promising procedures.

As you read in Chapter 1, *Schools for the Sixties* recommends that local school systems allocate not less than 1 percent of their annual operating budgets for experimentation, innovation, and research, involving each staff member in activities to improve teaching and learning. In addition to local funding, the U.S. Office of Education, through Research and Development Centers, Regional Educational Laboratories, grants to school systems, state departments of public instruction, and other agencies, provides opportunity to improve education through research. At the time of the writing of this book, there are eight Research and Development Centers operating at eight universities. Each Center is establishing national leadership in connection with a broad problem area of high concern to education. One excellent relationship of a Research and Development Center with school systems can be seen in the Research and Instructional Units working with the Research and Development Center for Learning and Re-Education at The University of Wisconsin, Madison, Wisconsin. In the fall of 1966, there were over 40 Research and Instructional Units in Wisconsin schools.

These Research and Instructional Units are small research and development centers in local school buildings. They have been designed to develop exemplary instructional programs in the local schools through research, development, and dissemination. The Research and Instructional Units effectively bring together staff from the Center, the State Department of Public Instruction, and the local school systems in the solution of significant educational problems. The Regional Educational Laboratories provide institutional linkage for research and development, innovation, field-testing and evaluation of materials, preparing personnel, and so on. The Laboratories and Centers represent the vigorous partnership of a number of institutions and people in finding a better way of life through improved education.

Decisions made by statistical evidence are probably better than those made by resorting to custom and tradition, to authority, to personal experience, or to syllogistic reasoning. It seems that the most effective use of statistical evidence is obtained when the group to be affected is involved in the entire study and identifies with and involves itself in the research. There seems to be little question that each of us can make better decisions and initiate more effective practices if we use existing research as a basis for teaching and if each of us participates in research in his own environment. Many curriculum problems can be solved only through the involvement of the classroom teacher in research, development, and dissemination.

Utilize supervisory and consultant help, and instructional leadership

Increasingly, assistance in improving instruction in the classroom is being provided through the appointment of supervisors at the state and the local level. One study has shown some of the responsibilities of supervisors to be

1. Classroom observation
2. Curriculum development
3. Organization of the instructional program
4. Development, recommendation, and distribution of new materials and equipment
5. Textbook evaluation
6. Direction of experimental or pilot programs
7. Research

8. Articulation of program with colleges and universities
9. Inservice training
10. Organization of and participation in local and regional meetings
11. Participation in general curriculum program-planning with other supervisors and administrators
12. Citywide or regional or state meetings of department heads or other liaison persons
13. Interpretation of program to parents and general public[3]

The supervisor, as well as the college or university consultant, is a co-worker who brings a knowledge of curriculum and instruction that can improve the teaching-learning situation. But he can assist you only as you participate in decision-making and in curriculum improvement and in innovation.

Participate in other inservice education

Because content changes rapidly, because of the development of new technology for use in education, and because of new knowledge about learning, the professional will want to participate in many inservice education activities other than those listed here: workshops and institutes at local, regional, and national levels; local extension courses; work in the colleges and universities in the evenings, summers, or during sabbatical leaves. To the extent that he engages in inservice education will the teacher increase his professional competence.

Resist censorship pressures

The student's right to consider all sides of an issue, controversial though the issue may be, is basic to democratic society. One basic assumption in a democracy is that the individual possesses powers of discrimination and can be trusted to determine his own actions. Although the right to examine controversial issues may be used wisely or foolishly by a teacher or student, the denial of the opportunity of choice through fear that such freedom might be used unwisely is to destroy the freedom. We should respect the individual's right to examine controversial

---

[3] Committee on National Interest, *The National Interest and the Continuing Education of Teachers of English* (Champaign, Ill.: NCTE, 1964), pp. 160–161.

issues and materials and to express his views for the guidance of others. We should oppose efforts by individuals or groups to impose their own ideas, standards, or tastes upon the schools.

Increasingly, the social studies teacher is challenged by highly organized, well-financed censorship groups that oppose many of the social changes brought about during the last 30 years. In a desire to return to better days, these groups oppose such things as the United Nations, UNESCO, income tax, savings bonds, or fluoridation. In an effort to undermine public confidence in the schools, censorship groups often attack textbooks as un-American, socialistic, materialistic, or atheistic. They are often particularly vehement about what they term the damage done by progressives during the past 25 years. The social studies teacher should see that parents have information on censorship groups and are aware of the bases on which the groups are arguing against instructional materials and objectives.

The English teacher, too, is under increasing pressures to restrict the access of students to certain ideas and books. In communities across the nation, censors have requested the removal of literary works from classrooms and from school libraries. Certain writers praised by critics and well established in the English classroom, are attacked. Overt pornography is discovered in familiar classics, as well as in literature of the twentieth century. A partial list of authors whose works have been considered unsuitable for school use is Geoffrey Chaucer, William Faulkner, Nathaniel Hawthorne, Aldous Huxley, Thomas Mann, Plato, J. D. Salinger, William Shakespeare, John Steinbeck, Henry David Thoreau, Mark Twain, Walt Whitman, and Thomas Wolfe.

Objections have been raised to the use of the *Atlantic Monthly*, *Ebony, Holiday, Life,* the *Saturday Review,* and *Theatre Arts.*

To preserve freedom to teach and freedom to learn, various professional organizations have adopted policies for handling controversial matters. A detailed discussion of plans and committees to oppose censorship is not feasible here. But, to choose one example, such an organization as the NCTE has made a continuing effort to outline detailed ways to defend the right to read. In a recent pamphlet entitled *The Students' Right to Read,* NCTE's Committee on the Right to Read advocates a two-step program consisting of (1) establishing a group of teachers to consider book selection and to screen complaints and (2) maintaining a vigorous campaign to establish a community climate in which well-informed citizens will support the freedom to read. Figure 16 reproduces an NCTE form used to respond to complaints coming by letter or telephone. Such a form helps identify the complainant and requires him to evaluate the book and to demonstrate his familiarity with it.

Responsibility for selecting teaching materials lies with the groups of teachers concerned. To transmit our cultural heritage intact, teachers must be active in resisting censorship attempts and in keeping the public informed on matters of intellectual freedom.

TRANSLATE YOUR CODE OF ETHICS INTO ACTION

One of the attributes of a profession indicated at the opening of this chapter is that it has a code of ethics. The teaching profession has had a code of ethics since 1929. The most recent version of the NEA Code of Ethics is reproduced here. It was proposed by the association's Committee on Ethics for the Profession and adopted by the NEA Representative Assembly in 1966. After a preamble, the code sets forth four principles. The four principles deal with the classroom teacher's commitment to the learner, to the community, to the profession, and to professional employment practices. Listed beneath each separate principle are axioms that suggest ways and means of fulfilling professional obligations.

THE CODE OF ETHICS OF THE EDUCATION PROFESSION

Preamble

We, professional educators of the United States of America, affirm our belief in the worth and dignity of man. We recognize the supreme importance of the pursuit of truth, the encouragement of scholarship, and the promotion of democratic citizenship. We regard as essential to these goals the protection of freedom to learn and to teach and the guarantee of equal educational opportunity for all. We affirm and accept our responsibility to practice our profession according to the highest ethical standards.

We acknowledge the magnitude of the profession we have chosen,

CITIZEN'S REQUEST FOR RECONSIDERATION OF A BOOK

Author   Hardcover   Paperback

Title

Publisher (if known)

Request initiated by ——————————————————————

Telephone —————————— Address ——————————————

City —————————————————————— Zone ——————

Complainant represents

—————— himself

—————— (name organization) ——————————————————

——————(identify other group) ——————————————————

1. To what in the book do you object? (Please be specific; cite pages.)
   ——————————————————————————————————————

2. What do you feel might be the result of reading this book? ——————
   ——————————————————————————————————————

3. For what age group would you recommend this book? ——————————
   ——————————————————————————————————————

4. Is there anything good about this book? ————————————————
   ——————————————————————————————————————

5. Did you read the entire book? —————————— What parts? ——————

6. Are you aware of the judgment of this book by literary critics? ——————
   ——————————————————————————————————————

7. What do you believe is the theme of this book? ——————————————
   ——————————————————————————————————————

8. What would you like your school to do about this book? ————————
   ——————————————————————————————————————

   —————— do not assign it to my child
   —————— withdraw it from all students as well as from my child
   —————— send it back to the English department office for reevaluation

9. In its place, what book of equal literary quality would you recommend that would convey as valuable a picture and perspective of our civilization? ————————————————————————————————
   ——————————————————————————————————————

——
Signature of Complainant

FIG. 16   *Form for request for reconsideration.* **(Committee on the Right to Read, The Student's Right to Read,** *Champaign, Ill.:* **National Council of Teachers of English, 1962,** *p.* **17. By permission.)**

and engage ourselves, individually and collectively, to judge our colleagues and to be judged by them in accordance with the applicable provisions of this code.

Principle I

Commitment to the student

We measure success by the progress of each student toward achievement of his maximum potential. We therefore work to stimulate the spirit of inquiry, the acquisition of knowledge and understanding, and the thoughtful formulation of worthy goals. We recognize the importance of cooperative relationships with other community institutions, especially the home.

In fulfilling our obligations to the students, we—
1. Deal justly and considerately with each student
2. Encourage the student to study varying points of view and respect his right to form his own judgment
3. Withhold confidential information about a student or his home unless we deem that its release serves professional purposes, benefits the student, or is required by law
4. Make discreet use of available information about the student
5. Conduct conferences with or concerning students in an appropriate place and manner
6. Refrain from commenting unprofessionally about a student or his home
7. Avoid exploiting our professional relationship with any student
8. Tutor only in accordance with officially approved policies
9. Inform appropriate individuals and agencies of the student's educational needs and assist in providing an understanding of his educational experiences
10. Seek constantly to improve learning facilities and opportunities

Principle II

Commitment to the community

We believe that patriotism in its highest form requires dedication to the principles of our democratic heritage. We share with all other citizens the responsibility for the development of sound public policy. As educators, we are particularly accountable for participating in the development of educational programs and policies and for interpreting them to the public.

In fulfilling our obligations to the community, we—

1. Share the responsibility for improving the educational opportunities for all
2. Recognize that each educational institution may have a person authorized to interpret its official policies
3. Acknowledge the right and responsibility of the public to participate in the formulation of educational policy
4. Evaluate through appropriate professional procedures conditions within a district or institution of learning, make known serious deficiencies, and take any action deemed necessary and proper
5. Use educational facilities for intended purposes consistent with applicable policy, law, and regulation
6. Assume full political and citizenship responsibilities, but refrain from exploiting the institutional privileges of our professional positions to promote political candidates or partisan activities
7. Protect the educational program against undesirable infringement

Principle III

Commitment to the profession

We believe that the quality of the services of the education profession directly influences the future of the nation and its citizens. We therefore exert every effort to raise educational standards, to improve our service, to promote a climate in which the exercise of professional judgment is encouraged, and to achieve conditions which attract persons worthy of the trust to careers in education. Aware of the value of united effort, we contribute actively to the support, planning, and programs of our professional organizations.

In fulfilling our obligations to the profession, we—

1. Recognize that a profession must accept responsibility for the conduct of its members and understand that our own conduct may be regarded as representative
2. Participate and conduct ourselves in a responsible manner in the development and implementation of policies affecting education

3. Cooperate in the selective recruitment of prospective teachers and in the orientation of student teachers, interns, and those colleagues new to their positions

4. Accord just and equitable treatment to all members of the profession in the exercise of their professional rights and responsibilities, and support them when unjustly accused or mistreated

5. Refrain from assigning professional duties to non-professional personnel when such assignment is not in the best interest of the student

6. Provide, upon request, a statement of specific reason for administrative recommendations that lead to the denial of increments, significant changes in employment, or termination of employment

7. Refrain from exerting undue influence based on the authority of our positions in the determination of professional decisions by colleagues

8. Keep the trust under which confidential information is exchanged

9. Make appropriate use of time granted for professional purposes.

10. Interpret and use the writings of others and the findings of educational research with intellectual honesty

11. Maintain our integrity when dissenting by basing our public criticism of education on valid assumptions as established by careful evaluation of facts or hypotheses

12. Represent honestly our professional qualifications and identify ourselves only with reputable educational institutions

13. Respond accurately to requests for evaluations of colleagues seeking professional positions

14. Provide applicants seeking information about a position with an honest description of the assignment, the conditions of work, and related matters

Principle IV

Commitment to professional employment practices

We regard the employment agreement as a solemn pledge to be executed both in spirit and in fact in a manner consistent with the highest ideals of professional service. Sound professional personnel relationships with governing boards are built upon personal integrity, dignity, and mutual respect.

In fulfilling our obligations to professional employment practices, we—

1. Apply for or offer a position on the basis of professional and legal qualifications

2. Apply for a specific position only when it is known to be vacant and refrain from such practices as underbidding or commenting adversely about other candidates

3. Fill no vacancy except where the terms, conditions, policies, and practices permit the exercise of our professional judgment and skill, and where a climate conducive to professional service exists

4. Adhere to the conditions of a contract or to the terms of an appointment until either has been terminated legally or by mutual consent

5. Give prompt notice of any change in availability of service, in status of applications, or in change in position

6. Conduct professional business through the recognized educational and professional channels

7. Accept no gratuities or gifts of significance that might influence our judgment in the exercise of our professional duties

8. Engage in no outside employment that will impair the effectiveness of our professional service and permit no commercial exploitation of our professional position [4]

The code can serve as a fitting reaffirmation of many of the tenets in this book. Indeed, Principle I requires little elaboration here. Although the issue of remuneration for tutoring has not been discussed, it stands to reason that a teacher might well avoid tutoring one of his own students lest he be charged with pursuing his own gain. And it also seems obvious that the teacher, having access to the past histories of students, would be loath to release confidential information except to the proper authorities. Physicians, attorneys, and other professionals keep their own counsel on clients' affairs.

Principle IV sets forth preferred practices for employer-employee relations. The teacher should use proper channels in complaints. For instance, if a teacher were distressed at the dearth of teaching materials

---

[4] Committee on Professional Ethics, *Opinions of the Committee on Professional Ethics*, 5th ed. (Washington, D.C.: NEA, 1966), pp. 11–22. By permission.

in his classroom, he might well consult his department chairman, the director of the instructional materials center, the curriculum coordinator or supervisor, or the principal before complaining to the general public, the superintendent, or the board of education. The teacher should gain employment through his own excellent credentials rather than through using his influence with the affluent or with the politically powerful. The teacher should refuse to fill a position that has been vacated because of unfair practices—violations of tenure rules, purging by censorship groups, and so on. Before vacating a teaching position for any reason whatsoever, the professional will give as much advance notice of his intent as is possible— certainly no less than four, six, or eight weeks' notice. Knowing that different teaching methods, styles, and personalities are sometimes successful with young people, the teacher should be fair in his recommendations of other teachers. He should discourage students' gossiping about other teachers and should suspend his own opinion if he inadvertently hears students complaining of another teacher's behavior. The teacher should refuse gifts from businessmen promoting their products. For example, the yearbook advisor or the textbook adoption committee should refuse entertainment from publishers' representatives lest, unjustifiably, someone might think a purchase was dictated by personal matters. Although some teachers, especially the heads of families, may feel the need to supplement their income, they should not work such long hours on a second job that their work with students suffers; nor should they work at tasks not approved by the community in which they live.

At various times, through the efforts of the NEA and its affiliates and other professional organizations, this code of ethics is made increasingly meaningful through the compilation of opinions that help interpret ambiguous points.

Next to parents, the teacher exerts the most important influence on what kind of person the adolescent is now and what he will become later in life. To the extent that the teacher adopts and implements his code of ethics, the influence he exerts on the adolescent's world and life view will be exemplary.

SUMMARY

For the teacher to continue to grow in knowledge, to serve as an exemplary model of conduct, to assist students in obtaining long-range and short-term goals, to be a professional, he will want to do a number of things: He will participate in professional organizations. He will consider recent innovations for use with his students. He will read widely. He will disseminate his own successful practices and, possibly, conduct research. He will welcome working with supervisors and other consultants. He will participate in inservice education other than that listed here. He will resist efforts of outside pressure groups to influence curriculum and instruction if such groups act from motives that are suspect.

To be a true professional, the teacher will help translate the NEA Code of Ethics into action. He will exemplify the ideals of the democratic way of life in working with his students. He will strive to obtain good relationships between school and home, school and community. He will work in good faith and respect with his employer. He will respect and support colleagues. He will make the teaching profession attractive to young people.

QUESTIONS AND ACTIVITIES

1 Teacher unions have been said to be controversial because members use strikes to gain their ends, and participation in strikes is said to be unprofessional. Discuss.

2 Go to one of the standard journals reporting educational research (for example, *Journal of Educational Research* or *Journal of Experimental Education*) and read several articles related to your field of interest. On the basis of your reading, discuss how the reporting of research might be improved.

3 Write your suggestions for a minimal professional library in the teaching of your area of curriculum.

4 Discuss points at which censors or pressure groups try to influence curriculum and instruction in your subject-matter field.

5 Recalling the generalizations and principles that you studied in the chapter "Conditions of Learning," formulate some hypotheses that you would like to see tested.

6 Learn if the professional organization in your field offers membership to college students. Investigate what benefits are to be gained from membership.

7 Do teachers have the broad range of autonomy said by Lieberman to characterize professionals? Why or why not?

8 Is there danger in trying to meet too many of the responsibilities listed in this chapter?

9 Do you think that the NEA Code of Ethics stresses the students' personal and social growth toward citizenship at the expense of academic knowledge and vocational skill?
10 Do you find any principle or axiom in the Code of Ethics that is ambiguous? How might it be stated better or how could it be clarified?
11 Try to list some of the activities of a teacher with whom you have studied who maintained continuous educational growth and who utilized many resources for improving teaching.
12 Discuss the image of the secondary school teacher as you have seen it portrayed in recent movies and television shows. Is the image such that the teaching profession is attractive to young people?

SUGGESTIONS FOR FURTHER READING

ASCD 1965 YEARBOOK COMMITTEE, Role of Supervisor and Curriculum Director in a Climate of Change, Edited by Robert R. Leeper, Washington, D.C.: Association for Supervision and Curriculum Development, 1965.

CARLSON, RICHARD O., ET AL., Change Processes in the Public Schools, Eugene, Ore.: The Center for the Advanced Study of Educational Administration, University of Oregon, 1965.

COURTNEY, E. WAYNE, ED., Applied Research in Education, Totowa, N.J.: Littlefield, Adams, 1965.

HENRY, NELSON B., ED., Education for the Professions, Sixty-first Yearbook of the National Society for the Study of Education, Part II, Chicago: University of Chicago Press, 1962.

Leadership for Improving Instruction, Washington, D.C.: Association for Supervision and Curriculum Development, 1960.

LIEBERMAN, MYRON, Education As a Profession, Englewood Cliffs, N.J.: Prentice-Hall, 1956.

The Way Teaching Is, Washington, D.C.: Association for Supervision and Curriculum Development and the Center for the Study of Education, 1966.

INDEX

Acceleration of gifted students, 450-453
Achievement, comparative, reporting of, 431-432
previous, 356
reasonable levels of, 482-484
Achievement tests, 408
Activities, cocurricular, see Cocurricular activities
individualized, see Individualized activities
Adams, Sam, 122
Adjustment problems, see Maladjustment
Administration, personnel, 156
Adolescent development, 38-72
See also Students
Advance organizers, 90-91, 301-303
Aggression, 479, 491, 500
Aikin, Wilford M., 162, 163
Alberty, Harold B., 166
Alexander, William M., 187
Allen, William H., 344-345
Alternate-choice tests, 395-396
American Council on Education, 16
American Educational Research Association (AERA), 114
American Educational Research Journal, 557
American High School Today, The, 14, 17-20

American Institute of Biological Sciences, 178
American Youth Commission, 14, 16-17
Anarchic climate, see Classroom climate
Anderson, Robert H., 170
Antisocial students, counseling for, 523
Application, of knowledge and skills, 81
Arithmetic, see Mathematics
Assemblies, 539
Assignments, achievement-level, 280-281
common, 280
individual, 281
Athletics, 539-541
Atmosphere, for achievement, 86-87
Attitudes, learning of, 101-106
Audio-Lingual Materials Project, 149
Audio materials, language laboratories, 335-336
radio, 333-335
records and transcriptions, 336-337
tape recordings, 337-338
See also Audio-visual materials
Audio-visual materials, 324-348
evaluation of, 345-346
instructional functions of, 346-347
intelligent use of, 342-346
preparation for, 343-344
sound motion pictures, 339-340
television, 340-342

Remedial reading, 526
Reporting system, comparative achievement, 431-432
parent-teacher cooperation, 435-438
report cards, 425-429
understanding of, 434-435
See also Grading
Research, 22-23
literature of, 556-557
and the teacher, 557-559
Research and Development Centers, 558-559
Resource unit, 186, 189-199
example of, 190-199
Retention, 81, 106-109
Review of Educational Research, 557
Rewards, as motivational devices, 87-88
concrete, 87
symbolic, 87
See also Punishment
Rice, Joseph P., 508
Ridgewood High School, 433
Role playing, 276-278
Russell, David H., 369-370

Sanders, Norris M., 388-390
Saylor, J. Galen, 187
Scholastic aptitude tests, 407
School health education study, 116
School Mathematics Study Group (SMSG), 92, 129, 130
School nurse, 524
Schools for the Sixties, 6, 14, 17, 21-32, 33, 558
Science, curriculum, 140-143
unit in, 243-247
Science Manpower Project, 143
Science Research Associates (SRA), 298
Sears, Pauline S., 82, 87
Secondary school, creation of, 159
Secondary School Curriculum Committee, 121, 122
Secret societies, 537-539
Sectioning, 453-455
See also Grouping
Self-concept, 497-500
Self-discipline, 474-503
special assistance in, 500-502
Senior high school, 11-13

Senior night, 541
Service clubs, 537
Sex characteristics, secondary, 39
Shaw, Merville C., 510
Shipp, Donald E., 122
Sinick, Daniel, 522
Skinner, B. F., 304-305
Slides, 331-332
Slow learners, 380, 457-458, 525-526
Slums and Suburbs, 14, 20
Small-group activities, 270-278
debate, British style, 274
formation of, 271-272
panel discussion, 274-276
panel reporting, 274-276
role playing, 276-278
sociodrama, 276-278
study of text and reference materials, 272-274
Smith, Dora V., 371-372
Smith, Karl, 49
Smith, Louis M., 38
Social activities, 541
Social deviants, 465-468
Social studies, curriculum revision in, 143-147
Social workers, 524
Sociodrama, 276-278
Sororities, 537-539
Special classes, for gifted students, 453-455
for the handicapped, 526-527
for poor readers, 526
for slow learners, 525-526
Specialized personnel, 30
Standardized tests, 404-410
characteristics of, 404-406
educational achievement, 408
general intellectual ability, 407
interest inventories, 408-409
personality, 409-410
Stanley, Julian C., 400-401
Stark, Robert E., 317
Stolz, Herbert R., 41
Stolz, Lois M., 41
Structure of knowledge, 116-118
Student council, 539
Students, characteristics of, 237-240
as individuals, 476-478

Designed by Gayle Jaeger
Set in Linotype Electra
Composed by The Haddon Craftsmen, Inc.
Printed by The Murray Printing Co.
Bound by The Haddon Craftsmen, Inc.
Harper & Row, Publishers, Inc.